The International Society for Science & Religion was established in 2002 to promote education through the support of inter-disciplinary learning and research in the fields of science and religion. Our current membership of 140 comes from all major faith traditions and includes non-religious scholars. Inducted by nomination only, they are drawn from leading research institutions and academies worldwide. The Society embraces all perspectives that are supported by excellent scholarship.

In 2007, the Society began the process of creating a unique resource, *The ISSR Library*, a comprehensive reference and teaching tool for scholars, students, and interested lay readers. This collection spans the essential ideas and arguments that frame studies in science, religion, and the human spirit.

The Library has been selected through a rigorous process of peer review. Each constituent volume makes a substantial contribution to the field or stands as an important referent. These books exhibit the highest quality of scholarship and present distinct, influential viewpoints, some of which are controversial. While the many perspectives in these volumes are not individually endorsed by the ISSR, each reflects a facet of the field that is worthy of attention.

Accompanying the Library is *The ISSR Companion to Science and Religion*, a volume containing brief introductory essays on each of the Library's constituents. Users are encouraged to refer to the *Companion* or our website for an overview of the Library.

Preaching Eugenics

*Religious Leaders and the American
Eugenics Movement*

CHRISTINE ROSEN

OXFORD
UNIVERSITY PRESS

2004

OXFORD
UNIVERSITY PRESS

Oxford   New York
Auckland   Bangkok   Buenos Aires   Cape Town   Chennai
Dar es Salaam   Delhi   Hong Kong   Istanbul   Karachi   Kolkata
Kuala Lumpur   Madrid   Melbourne   Mexico City   Mumbai
Nairobi   São Paulo   Shanghai   Taipei   Tokyo   Toronto

Copyright © 2004 by Oxford University Press, Inc.

Published by Oxford University Press, Inc.
198 Madison Avenue, New York, New York 10016

www.oup.com

Oxford is a registered trademark of Oxford University Press

Library of Congress Cataloging-in-Publication Data
Rosen, Christine.
Preaching eugenics: religious leaders and the American eugenics
movement / Christine Rosen.
p. cm.
Includes bibliographical references and index.
ISBN 978-0-19-515679-9
1. Eugenics—United States—History—20th century.
2. Eugenics—Religious aspects. I. Title.
HQ755.5.U5 R67 2003
363.9' 2' 0973' 0904—dc21   2003010981

Printed in the United States of America
on acid-free paper

For my beloved parents,
Louis and Pamela Stolba

Preaching Eugenics

Acknowledgments

The completion of this book would not have been possible without the generous support of the Ethics and Public Policy Center in Washington, D.C., which has provided me with an intellectual home and access to colleagues whose insights I benefit from on a daily basis. I owe special thanks to Hillel Fradkin, the president of the Center, for his enthusiasm and encouragement of this project.

A grant from the Earhart Foundation and its president, David Kennedy, gave me the opportunity to see this project through to completion. The American Philosophical Society provided research support in the earliest stages through a resident fellowship at the Society's Library in Philadelphia. The History Department at Emory University provided years of support and an ideal graduate learning environment. When I first came to Washington, D.C., Chris DeMuth and the American Enterprise Institute provided a first-rate introduction to the world of public policy. Appreciation and thanks are due to the outstanding archivists I had the pleasure of meeting during the research and writing of this book, including those at the American Philosophical Society Library, the Mullen Library at Catholic University, the Manuscript Division of the Library of Congress, Sterling Library at Yale University, Burke Library at Union Theological Seminary, the Rare Books and Special Collections division of the New York Public Library, and the Southern Historical Collection at the University of North Carolina, Chapel Hill.

Thanks are also due to Cynthia Read at Oxford University Press, who has been an enthusiastic editor and supporter of this book from the beginning.

The deep gratitude I feel for Georg Kleine, who first encouraged me to study history, can hardly be conveyed here. His influence has been immeasurable, both as a teacher and a friend, and I never would have embarked on this path without his support and fine example. To have someone of his acuity, humor, and intellectual generosity as a mentor is a rare privilege.

I was extremely fortunate to have had the opportunity to learn how to research and write about history from a scholar and teacher as exemplary as Patrick Allitt. It was in one of his provocative graduate seminars that I first learned about the eugenics movement, and he has encouraged that interest ever since. The great insight and joy he brings to his work as a historian and the friendship and excellent guidance he has offered me over the years have been a constant source of inspiration.

As a student at Emory, I also had the opportunity to study with several historians who are model teachers and scholars, including Elizabeth Fox-Genovese, Eugene Genovese, Mary Odem, and Jonathan Prude.

Many friends and family offered moral and intellectual support during the writing of this book: Kirsten Orr, Christina Manning, John Hynes, Marnie Kenney, Marci Sliman, Sally Satel, Christina Sommers, Charlotte Hays, Karlyn Bowman, and Alexander Rose; Sidney and Estelle Rosen, Joanna Rosen, and Neal Katyal were especially supportive. My sisters, Catherine Remick and Cynthia Stolba, offered boundless encouragement throughout; our frequent conversations about our own family's odder traits served as useful reminders of the dangers of too much hereditarian thinking.

The gratitude and appreciation I feel for my husband, Jeffrey, are without limits.

Contents

Preaching Eugenics

Introduction

Sermonizing is a science of sorts, at least to its more avid practitioners. On 8 May 1926, the Reverend Phillips Endecott Osgood, rector
of St. Mark's Church in Minneapolis, ascended the pulpit to deliver
his 11:00 A.M. Sunday sermon. It was a balmy spring day in the city,
and Osgood's congregation of Protestant Episcopal believers was
large; over the years St. Mark's had grown from a small, frontier
parish to a major force in the community, with more than a thousand members. The airy limestone expanse of the neo-Gothic sanctuary, perched above Loring Park near downtown Minneapolis, attested to the success of the church, whose first home had been a
small mission, trundled to parish property on sled runners by thirty-
three yoke of oxen, in 1863.

That Sunday was Mother's Day, and from his pulpit, designed
in the form of a chalice and encircled by intricately carved wooden
figures of famous predicants, Rev. Osgood eschewed the usual
praise of womanly virtues in favor of the exotica of an Oriental ba-
zaar. Amid the haggling shopkeepers and motley crowds of such a
bustling marketplace, Rev. Osgood told his congregation, you will
come across a man quietly toiling over a charcoal brazier. He is a
refiner, bent on his task of purging dross and alloy from his bubbling concoction of metals to reveal pure silver or gold. So, too, are
we refiners, Osgood said, but with a very different task: improving
the human race. "We see that the less fit members of society seem
to breed fastest and the right types are less prolific," Osgood
preached, but he emphasized that a practical solution to this
alarming problem was at hand. "Taking human nature as it is and

not ignoring any legitimate emotion or tendency, eugenics aspires to the refiner's work." Decrying the "insane and criminal specimens of humanity"
whose "slatternly daughters" and "idle, ignorant" sons strained social institutions, Osgood warned his flock, "Until the impurities of dross and alloy are
purified out of our silver it cannot be taken into the hands of the craftsman
for whom the refining was done." The Kingdom of God required eugenically
fit believers, Osgood said: "Grapes cannot be gathered from thorns nor figs
from thistles."[1]

Science can also contain hints of the sermon. That same year, as Osgood
invoked the power of the refiner's fire for ushering in a eugenic Kingdom of
God, Sinclair Lewis, that wayward son of nearby Sauk Centre, Minnesota, won
the Pulitzer Prize for fiction for *Arrowsmith*, his satire of the evangelical fervor
of devotees of science. "Boil the milk bottles or, by gum, you better buy your
ticket to Kingdom Come," warned Dr. Almus Pickerbaugh, the perennially self-
promoting public health officer under whose wing the bumbling physician
Martin Arrowsmith uncomfortably rested. Lewis's satiric eye had not yet
reached the clergy (*Elmer Gantry* would appear the following year), but his
description of the twin passions of science and faith retains its withering ac-
curacy. Like so many pulpit Arrowsmiths, preachers had become enamored of
the possibilities science presented; in eugenics they found a science whose
message moved effortlessly from laboratory to church.

In 1926, hundreds of Osgood's fellow clerics, representing nearly every
major Protestant denomination, as well as several Reform rabbis, preached
eugenics across the country, in venues demographically diverse: San Francisco,
New Orleans, Brooklyn, Austin, and Nashville, and lesser city lights like Topeka, Kansas and Sparks, Nevada. The preachers spoke vividly of the powerful
force of heredity and urged their congregations to put the tenets of this new
science to the test in their own communities. Their efforts were part of a
"eugenics sermon contest" sponsored by the country's preeminent eugenics
organization, the American Eugenics Society, but the impulse to link organized
religion with eugenics was much broader than a single contest could capture.
During the first few decades of the twentieth century, eugenics flourished in
the liberal Protestant, Catholic, and Jewish mainstream; clerics, rabbis, and lay
leaders wrote books and articles about eugenics, joined eugenics organizations,
and lobbied for eugenics legislation. They grafted elements of the eugenics
message onto their own efforts to pursue religious-based charity in their
churches and adopted eugenic solutions to the social problems that beset their
communities. They explored the eugenic implications of the biblical Ten Commandments and investigated the hereditary lessons embedded in the parables
of Jesus.

Why was eugenics so appealing to these religious leaders? The image of
the minister in U.S. history has sustained colorful interpretation: sturdy revi-
alists like Methodist John Wesley; crusading, if slightly scandalized, orators

like Congregationalist Henry Ward Beecher; and Sinclair Lewis's fictional, hustling man of the cloth, Elmer Gantry. But few U.S. ministers have gained a place in history for their championing of science, despite the fact that many religious leaders have been its staunch defender. It is the colorful religious opponents of science whom we remember: Charles Hodge, Billy Sunday, and other excoriators of Darwinian evolutionary theory, for example.

Certain kinds of religious leader gravitated toward eugenics in the early twentieth century, ministers anxious about the changing culture but also eager to find solutions to its diagnosable ills. Theirs was a practical spirituality better understood in terms of worldviews than theologies. Many of the religious leaders who joined the eugenics movement were well-known, even notorious, for their lack of coherent doctrinal vision; of one Congregationalist advocate for eugenics it was said, "He is not a theologian in the ordinary sense, for he loves flowers more than botany." Of another, a well-known Baptist minister, one critic noted the impossibility of constructing even a preliminary image of his beliefs: "No painter who ever lived could make a picture which expressed the religion of the Rev. Harry Emerson Fosdick."[2] These were preachers who embraced modern ideas first and adjusted their theologies later. Theirs were the churches that had naves and transepts modeled after gothic European cathedrals—as well as bowling alleys. And it was when these self-identified liberal and modernist religious men abandoned bedrock principles to seek relevance in modern debates that they were most likely to find themselves endorsing eugenics. Those who clung stubbornly to tradition, to doctrine, and to biblical infallibility opposed eugenics and became, for a time, the objects of derision for their rejection of this most modern science.

At first glance, religion and eugenics seem an odd mix. In 1883, Francis Galton, a British scientist and cousin to Charles Darwin, coined the term "eugenics" (from the Greek meaning "good in birth") to describe his plan to improve the human race through better breeding. Evolution was a "grand phantasmagoria," Galton said, a purposeless, tumultuous performance, spurred on by natural selection. Eugenics promised to give human beings control over this heretofore untamable process by encouraging the reproduction of the fittest specimens of humanity (a process Galton called positive eugenics) and preventing that of the unfit (negative eugenics). "What nature does blindly, slowly, ruthlessly, man may do providently, quickly, and kindly," Galton assured.[3]

Galton's goals were no less lofty than the soul saving pursued by the most spirited Christian minister; his descriptions of eugenics resembled an evangelical vision as much as a science.[4] Eugenics "must be introduced into the national conscience, like a new religion," he argued. It has "strong claims to become an orthodox religious tenet of the future."[5]Delivering the Huxley Lecture at London's Anthropological Institute in 1901, Galton invoked Jesus' New Testament Parable of the Talents to explain why the human race needed eugenics. "We each receive at our birth a definite endowment," he said, "some receiving many talents, others few, but each person responsible for the profitable use of that which has been entrusted to him." The eugenicist was like the "good and faithful servant" of the parable, who turned his five talents into ten through wise investment; like this servant, the eugenicist would improve upon man's endowment by applying the wisdom of heredity to the task of reproduction.[6]Admiring the disciplined devotion that organized religions demanded of their adherents, Galton hoped that eugenics would inspire an equal level of reverence and faithful effort in its followers.

Galton's eugenic evangel took firm root in U.S. soil. Beginning in the early years of the twentieth century and spanning the decades of the 1910s, 1920s, and 1930s, eugenicists in the United States called for programs to control human reproduction. They urged legislatures to pass laws to segregate the so-called feebleminded into state colonies, where they would live out their lives in celibacy; they supported compulsory state sterilization laws aimed at men and women whose "germplasm" threatened the eugenic vitality of the nation; they led the drive to restrict immigration from countries whose citizens might pollute the American melting pot. Their science filtered into popular culture through eugenics advice books and child-rearing manuals, eugenics novels, plays, and films, and scores of magazine and newspaper articles.

Americans avidly embraced arguments about hereditary determinism; at its zenith, eugenics enjoyed the support of a broad range of intellectuals, reformers, and political leaders. Galton's science was only the latest effort to realize the latent human impulse to improve the race. Plato argued in *The Republic* for the merits of a guardian class of superior hereditary endowments, and the Spartan *apothetae*, the chasm where feeble infants were left to die of exposure rather than weaken the community's martial spirit, was a crude, early expression of the same principle. The dictum "like begets like" and biblical warnings of the iniquities of the fathers being visited upon future generations had informed philosophers for centuries. By 1833, a Protestant missionary to the Indiana frontier was writing home of the "croaking jealousy, bloated bigotry, coiling suspicion, wormish blindness, crocodile malice" of the locals, whom he deemed "Ignorance and her squalid brood." "Need I stoop to remind you," he shuddered, "of the host of loathsome reptiles such a stagnant pool is fitted to breed!"[7] In the mid-nineteenth-century utopian community of Oneida in upstate New York, religious fervor prompted followers of John Humphrey Noyes to experiment with breeding better children, a practice Noyes likened to plant breeding and called "human stirpiculture." "We are opposed to random procreation, which is unavoidable in the marriage system," Noyes explained of his proto-eugenic adventure, "but we are in favor of intelligent, well-ordered procreation."[8] The Oneidans' breeding arts earned them less notoriety than their system of "complex marriage," which, unlike their views on heredity, challenged prevailing norms by upsetting the convention of monogamous unions.[9]

Devotees of phrenology in the early nineteenth century, who believed that the shape of one's skull offered useful portents of one's character and mental faculties, shared with later eugenicists a concern for the degeneration of the race and a belief in the idea that the progress of mankind would come only with the improvement of man's biological capacities.[10]Italian criminologist Cesare Lombroso's studies of criminal anthropology in the 1880s suggested hereditary origins for criminal behavior and concluded that all criminals demonstrated certain physical characteristics (namely, facial features and head shapes). By 1891, as Robert Fletcher's presidential address to the Anthropological Society of Washington, D.C., attested, U.S. social scientists had incorporated Lombroso's theories into their work and could state reasonably, "The influence of heredity in the formation of criminal character has been long since admitted."[11] While the U.S. eugenics movement was still in its infancy, theories of hereditary criminal degeneracy had already provided justification for the passage in four states of laws mandating the sterilization of criminals.[12]

Eugenicists added to this alluvial mix of conventional wisdom, experimental religiosity, and hereditarian criminology the veneer of respectable, modern science and a sense of urgency. So dire was the deteriorating state of human heredity, they said, that its correction could no longer be left to the ad hoc efforts of amateurs, among whom eugenicists included those traditional arbiters of marriage and reproduction, the churches. Eugenicists viewed the scourges of their age—pauperism, crime, disease, prostitution, alcoholism— not as evidence of individual moral failing, but as problems to be solved scientifically. Preachers' pulpit admonitions to parishioners to morally fortify themselves against sinful behavior were picayune by comparison.[13] Ministers fought their battles for race improvement in a small theater, literally soul by soul. Eugenicists, by contrast, embraced a much broader field and newer tactics.

The eugenics movement straddled several cultural epochs in the twentieth-century United States, from the Progressive Era through the 1920s and 1930s, but the roots of eugenic science rested firmly in the nineteenth century.[14] It grew out of the inquiries of the natural sciences, which had a concrete impact on people's understanding of their world, particularly their experience of religious faith. New ideas about the natural world, particularly geologists' evaluations of the earth's age, challenged a literal interpretation of the Bible and seemed to strengthen the materialistic elements of life while undermining the miraculous elements of the Judeo-Christian tradition. A proliferation of pseudosciences such as phrenology, anthropometry, and a panoply of race theories, all popular in the 1820s and 1830s, further challenged the faithful by placing increasing emphasis on the need for empirical, rather than theological, assessments of the natural world.[15]

Still, the clergy exercised widespread intellectual influence in the nineteenth century, a fact reflected in the work of scientists of the period, whose essays and books often included hymns to the mysterious power of Nature's God. Theology itself was considered a science—the "queen of the sciences," by some reckonings—well into the early twentieth century, even though evidence of its gradual, involuntary cession to science was beginning to emerge. Theologians' thoughts on the technical practice of science were less welcome among scientists themselves, and the public sought its scientific information from experts in the field, not local preachers. *Popular Science Monthly* began publication in 1872, and by century's end the label "unscientific" was becoming a term of opprobrium.[16]

Most ministers responded to the growing influence of science not with denunciations, but with well-intentioned efforts to incorporate scientific methods into their own belief systems. For hundreds of years religious leaders had promoted varying forms of natural theology, holding forth the claim that one could know God through His works, particularly Nature.[17] When a severe earthquake struck New England in the fall of 1755, for example, Rev. Charles Chauncy of Boston interpreted the event as both an act of Nature and a warning from Nature's God—an occurrence of both spiritual and earthly significance.[18] In crafting such a persuasive reconciliation, religious leaders lent credibility to the scientific enterprise at the same time that they unwittingly prepared the ground to receive a science with far more radical implications for their faiths: Darwinian evolution.

Faced with the challenge to faith posed by Charles Darwin's *The Origin of Species* (1859), many Protestants again searched for compromise. They found it in Lamarckianism. The Lamarckian view of evolution comported better with their Christian theology than the rigorous weeding of Darwin's natural selection. Lamarckianism offered a world kinder in its modifications than "nature red in tooth and claw." During the late nineteenth century, many scientists still subscribed to the theory of the inheritance of acquired characteristics. The most notable proponent of this theory, French naturalist Jean Baptiste de Lamarck (1744–1829), had claimed that, over time, as living things adapt to their environments, these adaptations became permanent characteristics of newly evolved species. The classic example of this process was the giraffe, whose long neck supposedly developed after many generations of stretching to eat leaves growing higher in the trees. In the late decades of the nineteenth century, ethnologists such as John Wesley Powell (1834–1902) crafted a "sociology of progress" that merged accepted notions of Christian progress toward the millennium with Lamarckian science, and that viewed evolutionary progress as the result of the constant, often minute, interactions of nature and environment. Similarly, geologist Joseph LeConte (1823–1901) reconciled Christianity and science by crafting a neo-Lamarckian version of evolution that allowed for one overarching master plan, with limitless individual variations: "There is still design in every object," LeConte claimed, "but no longer separate design, only a separate manifestation of one infinite design."[19] The late-nineteenth-century debate over Darwinian evolution, particularly its usefulness for Christian theology, yielded many Protestants unable to craft such a reconciliation, however. Competing camps were forming, one holding doggedly to the belief that the Bible remained the infallible source of truth about the natural world, the other more willing to cede control of the debate to professional scientists.

This intellectual milieu produced two books whose shared thesis was that the history of the relationship between science and religion had been a centuries-long story of acrimonious attacks, retreats, and counterattacks. The first, John William Draper's *History of the Conflict between Science and Religion* (1874), framed the story in terms of light versus darkness, reason versus superstition, with religion as the intractable foe of enlightened scientific progress—particularly the religion of Roman Catholicism. A slightly less polemical though no more nuanced exposition of the relationship came in 1896 from Andrew Dickson White, president of Cornell University, in *A History of the Warfare of Science with Theology in Christendom*. White was more ecumenical in his indictments, blaming Catholics *and* Protestants for thwarting science.[20]

The books, with their metaphors of warfare and their emphasis on conflict rather than consensus, obscured for contemporaries and later historiography the ambiguities of the relationship between purveyors of science and those of religion. Had the authors had something other than polemic on their minds, their books would have chronicled the long and difficult adjustments religious leaders had been making to science, and perhaps even the enthusiasm of those for whom the weight of cassock or vestment could not stifle genuine curiosity about the workings of the natural world. Even in 1925, the year the Scopes "Monkey" Trial captivated the American public with its sensational story of the "war" between Creationism and Darwinian evolution, one of the largest standing committees of the American Eugenics Society was the Committee on Cooperation with Clergymen.[21] Far from warring, scientific and religious leaders often cultivated cooperative relationships and felt they shared a common purpose. Regarding eugenics, they shared a respect for the *quality* of human life as well as a belief in its perfectibility, though they often approached these issues from different perspectives.[22] Just as ministers had accepted a version of evolution that best suited their worldview, so, too, would they endorse a version of eugenics that did not, on the surface, undermine their theologies—theologies that were, for many of them, pliable compendiums of belief to begin with.

Of course, reconciling faith with Darwinism required no more than adjusting one's personal views; embracing eugenics meant taking a stance on concrete policy actions such as state sterilization laws and immigration restriction. Eugenics posed an intellectual and practical challenge to religious leaders'

worldviews, but it did so at a time when churchmen welcomed practical challenges, sometimes too eagerly, as opportunities to test new, reform-minded
solutions. Eventually, Protestant intellectuals and churchmen would find that,
in embracing the solutions offered by professional science, they were left with
no compelling language of their own to combat scientists who then attempted
to lay claim to the strongholds of religion.

The late nineteenth century witnessed the birth and growth of social problems that sparked the reforms of the Progressive movement. The arrival of
staggering numbers of new immigrants from southern and eastern Europe,
increased industrialization, urbanization, economic depressions, and labor upheavals all generated a feeling of social dislocation among many Americans;
one social worker aptly titled his study of the country's urban conditions *The
City Wilderness*.[23] Declining birthrates, rising divorce rates, and the widening
scourge of syphilis prompted many observers to fear for the fate of the American family and, by implication, for the nation as a whole. Theodore Roosevelt's
plea to married couples of the white, middle class to have more children to
combat "race suicide" was not fueled by paranoid fears for the nation's fecundity, but by fact. In 1840, the average American family had 6.14 children;
by 1900 that number had dropped to 3.56. A growing population of "feebleminded" men and women was also seen as a potential menace to social order.[24]

This bewildering array of social problems produced vivid tracts for the
times, as observers struggled to make sense of new social conditions and offer
their remedies for social ills. A host of "visiting Jesus" books such as William
T. Stead's *If Christ Came to Chicago* (1894) and Edward Everett Hale's *If Jesus
Came to Boston* (1894) emerged. These hypothetical stories of the Savior's return to urban America implied that He would not be pleased with the way
people were living. Anxieties about modernity and the advance of technology
produced a related crop of utopian and dystopian fiction in the 1880s and
1890s: Edward Bellamy's *Looking Backward* (1888), Mark Twain's *Connecticut
Yankee in King Arthur's Court* (1889), Ignatius Donnelly's *Caesar's Column*
(1890), and William Dean Howells's *A Traveler from Alturia* (1894), many of
which made pessimistic predictions for the fate of the populace. "It is conceded
that life is a dark and wretched failure for the great mass of mankind," Donnelly
wrote in the introduction to his book.[25]

As Darwin's theory of evolution gained a more secure foothold in U. S.
culture, older depictions of nature as a single, great chain of being gave way
to new metaphors better suited to Darwin's claims. Students of the natural
world now invoked the "tree of life," with its extensive system of branches,
representing the ever-increasing complexity of earth's many species.[26] Eugenicists adopted the metaphor as their own at the Third International Eugenics
Congress held in New York City in 1932. Visitors entering the exhibit hall
confronted a large mural depicting an enormous tree heavy with foliage and

with a banner unfurled across the top that read, simply, "Eugenics." Feeding into the formidable timber were dozens of thick roots that criss-crossed the bottom half of the panel, each representing a different element of the eugenics movement's intellectual origins, including the disciplines of statistics, anatomy, biology, psychology, genetics, anthropometry, and geography, as well as population studies, law, politics, education, biography, and religion. The imposing panel included a single descriptive caption: "Like a tree, eugenics draws its materials from many sources and organizes them into an harmonious entity."[27]

This wall panel reveals how eugenicists were inclined to describe their science's historical pedigree broadly. While this vision accounts for the diversity of the movement's converts, it also demonstrates the difficulties inherent in defining eugenics with precision. From its inception, eugenics claimed for itself a vast field of interest and, as the image describes, an expansive system of roots. Eugenics became a fluid term that had a wide application even during the earliest years of the movement. By 1914, one physician noted that eugenics had become "a mere catch phrase which covers any rubbish which any crank chooses to inflict upon the world."[28]

Ambiguity had its advantages, at least from the perspective of those who were eager to have eugenics lend itself to their plans. If the trunk of the eugenics tree was the work of Galton and other "official" eugenicists, then its branches grew to include purity reform, health reform, sex hygiene, radical sex reform, marriage counseling, antivice campaigns, "fitter family" contests, the child-rearing advice industry, and, eventually, the birth control movement. Many enthusiasts grafted elements of the eugenic program onto their own, often peculiar, reform movements. Each of these new offshoots brought to the public's attention new spokesmen for the eugenics cause, not all of whom eugenicists welcomed as allies. As well, amateur interpreters of eugenic theories frequently marshaled evidence from Scripture to buttress their claims. The Bible became the most popular cultural reference point for amateur enthusiasts of Galton's science, and although few of these popularizers were themselves trained clergymen, their success in linking eugenic and religious sentiments laid the groundwork for a more explicit partnership between religious leaders and eugenicists in the 1920s.

The biologists, embryologists, zoologists, and other scientifically trained proponents of eugenics often expressed alarm over the eugenic claims made by nonscientists. From the scientists' perspective, amateurs popularized eugenics at the expense of the very science that fueled it. The disapproval of eugenicists notwithstanding, the eugenics movement benefited from the participation of amateur enthusiasts. Their voluntary efforts made eugenics a shibboleth of the Progressive Era.[29] The institutional eugenics movement, which incorporated the work of the scientists and social scientists who were the majority of the members of "official" eugenics organizations, is only one element of the story of eugenics, though one ably told by a number of historians.[30] Assessing the impact of the eugenics movement on U.S. scientific, social, and intellectual life requires tracing the noninstitutional roots eugenics planted in U.S. culture. In doing so, the motivations of ministers who embraced eugenics become clearer. The man who must ascend a pulpit every week to inspire or cajole a congregation looks to culture for expository guidance. In the early twentieth century, that culture was suffused by the science of heredity.

It was also a culture of self-styled progressives, and eugenics is best understood within the context of progressive reform ideas. If Darwinian evolutionary theory made the science of eugenics conceivable, it also made the ethos of progressivism viable. The gradual improvement of the human race, aided by new contributions from machinery and science, required stewards, and progressives were eager for the challenge.[31]

Many religious leaders arrived at eugenics through their own experiences with progressive-style reform. With secular progressives, they shared a fear of social unrest as well as optimism about people's ability to improve their circumstances. And although they came to reform with different traditions of social service, Protestants, Catholics, and Jews nonetheless confronted similar questions about society. They understood with progressives the challenge of assimilating thousands of immigrants and embraced many of the era's prejudices about these new arrivals to the United States. At an 1888 meeting of the National Conference of Charities and Correction, Rev. Myron W. Reed of Denver recounted the horror he had experienced during a recent visit to the East Coast, as he watched thousands of immigrants disembarking to begin their new lives. "It is difficult to find in a shipload of Poles or Huns ten men that will make Americans," he said. "Like the insects under the rotten log, they like darkness and confinement."[32]

Religious leaders' fears about the character of new immigrants were linked as well to the explosive growth of the nation's cities; by 1920, the United States was an urban nation, one invested in manufacturing more than agriculture, with significant population increases in cities such as Chicago, Boston, and New York.[33] Although organized religion continued to enjoy considerable cultural visibility, these developments created institutional and financial challenges for urban churches and synagogues. Competition in the spiritual marketplace was growing fierce.

The new industrial order enhanced the prestige of scientists, professional reformers, and a range of social "experts," at the expense, some feared, of traditional guides such as the clergy. After conducting his own informal survey of the cultural landscape in 1882, Noah Porter, the president of Yale University, observed that "the multitudes are drifting into the half-formed conviction that the reasons for faith seem one after another to be dissipated by the advance of science and culture."[34] Writing in the *Chautauquan* a few years later, one observer asked, "Is the preacher's influence really decreasing?" His answer was "No—emphatically no!" The preacher "still remains . . . a social influence for good that no observing unbeliever dares belittle and which no Christian can overestimate."[35] Others weren't so sure of the clergy's continued importance— or of the need to flatter their pretensions. By 1926, H. L. Mencken, the curmudgeonly *American Mercury* critic, was declaring, "That Protestantism in this great Christian realm is down with a wasting disease must be obvious to every amateur of ghostly pathology." As for Protestantism's purveyor, the minister, Mencken dismissed "his body of knowledge" as "that of a busdriver or a vaudeville actor."[36]

Many religious leaders voiced an awareness of their own declining prestige—an expression of "status anxiety" that led them to search for relevance and, as a result, cast off the more cumbersome elements of their theologies.[37] But they did not, for the most part, join reform movements merely to regain cultural power. In their confrontation with the growing power of science, status anxiety was a palpable force, but it does not capture fully the genuine enthusiasm many clergymen felt for their challenger. Liberal religious leaders saw great possibility in science, particularly its promise to alleviate human suffering. In their response to new cultural strains, particularly scientific reforms such as eugenics, religious leaders did not wholly relinquish their responsibilities as social leaders to scientists or social scientists.[38] On the contrary, they viewed their efforts as an intrinsic part of a broader campaign to cure social ills.

In this, progressive-minded ministers were genuine reformers, though few fit the stereotype, a "truculent, humorless" character who "makes virtue repulsive." They were, however, often uncritical in their embrace of certain reforms and shared with their secular counterparts an eagerness to control the behavior of their fellow citizens in ways that appear, in retrospect, heavy-handed. In confronting contemporary challenges, they many times availed themselves of old-fashioned forms of social control, placing them in the paradoxical position of "reactionary modernists."[39] Still, many religious leaders viewed the social upheavals of the early twentieth century as an opportunity to turn their churches and synagogues into miniature laboratories, places to test the reform ideas of the social sciences.[40] Their efforts to incorporate new ideas were in some sense a tug-of-war with secularism; preachers had to convince their flocks that they could still offer effective solutions to social problems while also continuing their more traditional spiritual ministries. Many succeeded in refashioning their churches to allow the two impulses to coexist peacefully, at least for a time.[41]

Organized charity offered a unique proving ground for these impulses. Beginning in the late nineteenth century and continuing in the twentieth, social reformers began to question the claim that had defined charitable work for so long: that poverty was ineradicable. Instead, they pursued a "scientific philanthropy" designed to determine the root causes of problems such as poverty and crime. An image in the reform magazine *Survey* in 1914 demonstrated the shift. In the first frame of a drawing titled "The Old Way and the New," an older man with a careworn expression, representing "Individual Charity," rests on his knees at the edge of a precipice. He is lowering a rickety picnic basket labeled "food and drink" into a dark pit of grasping human hands meant to represent poverty. In contrast, in the second frame of the drawing, a young man bristling with strength and with legs firmly planted represents "Associated Charities"; he lowers a long sturdy ladder labeled "Scientific Charity" into the pit, where the desperate hands of poverty reach out for rungs labeled work, education, good cheer, encouragement, and health.[42]

Religious leaders were active in this reformulation of charity, joining social workers, journalists, and academics in pursuit of the "New Philanthropy."[43] Through organizations such as the National Conference of Charities and Correction, ministers promoted this scientific philanthropy, which in turn exposed them to hereditary explanations for human behavior. By 1899, Rev. A. O. Wright, secretary of the Wisconsin State Board of Charities, was warning of "knots of defective classes" of people who had produced "a whole population of criminals, paupers, idiots and lunatics." Later, as president of the National Conference of Charities and Correction, he offered a vision of the new philanthropy that would dispatch those "defective classes" to state-sponsored colonies, where they would no longer risk fouling the hereditary pool. "Unless we are prepared for drastic measures of wholesale death or equally wholesale castration," he said, "we must cut off defective heredity by the more expensive but more humane method of wholesale imprisonment."[44]

Expanded reform activities also brought closer contact among religious leaders of different faiths, as ministers, priests, and rabbis found themselves sitting together on the boards of reform organizations and charitable institutions, an experience that helped diminish the strength of denominational barriers. Liberal, reform-minded clergymen emphasized "deeds, not creeds" and formed an important part of the extended web of progressive social reform.[45] Unitarian minister John Haynes Holmes and Reform Rabbi Stephen S. Wise, both of New York, met through city reform circles and became longstanding friends who engaged in ecumenical experiments such as switching pulpits. Their numerous social reform commitments (and the size of their congregations) provided them both with high profiles. Though of different faiths, they were often of like minds on social questions, and in the 1910s they both endorsed eugenics.[46] This community of liberal religious leaders, active and usually well-known for their secular reform crusades, proved open to hereditarian thinking on social questions.

The religious leaders who became involved in eugenics included Protestants of nearly every denomination, Jews, and Catholics, and they overwhelmingly represented the liberal wings of their respective faiths. Many of them ministered in large churches or synagogues in big city parishes and fit historian Stow Persons's description of these religious institutions as centered on the "resonant personality of a pulpit orator who blended the elements of an innocuous theology with discussion of current interests."[47] They were the ministers, priests, and rabbis who were inspired by the developments of modern science and accepted much of the new historical criticism of the Bible. These "modernistic liberals" wanted to reconcile what they identified as the enduring principles of Christianity with the vagaries of modern experience and culture.[48]

Given their very different religious traditions, the liberalism (or modernism) of Catholic leaders was very different in degree and kind than that of Protestants, or of the Jewish religious leaders who expressed interest in eugenics. Liberalism in one church setting did not necessarily translate into liberalism in another; hence the importance of denominational and theological contexts. Nor did the liberal label always apply consistently to a religious leader's social strategy and theology. Presbyterian minister Charles Stelzle, an ardently liberal social reformer and head of New York's Labor Temple, was theologically a conservative Calvinist. Catholic priest John A. Ryan of Catholic University championed liberal causes like a living wage but never wavered in his adherence to Church doctrine.[49]

Walter Lippmann chronicled the complications and contortions of these modern theologies, noting their futile attempts to blunt the corrosive "acids of modernity." No longer could modern men believe that "the Secretaries of the Holy Ghost" took down the Bible and delivered it, free of error, to their doorsteps, Lippmann observed. Modern men were not atheists. They were something worse: uncomfortably disaffected quasi Christians. Although they searched earnestly, "with the best will in the world," for "a God whom they can worship," these moderns found themselves "not quite believing."[50] To the liberal or modernist mind of whatever denomination or tradition, however, their worldview was straightforward: they believed in finding a better way to believe.

That many religious leaders turned to social reform and science for personal inspiration as well as to motivate their flocks is not surprising, and no group did so with quite as much self-awareness as Protestants. Protestants proved the most enthusiastic and numerically powerful group of religious participants in the eugenics movement. Supporters ranged from high-ranking clerics to small-town ministers in the Methodist, Unitarian, Congregational, Protestant Episcopal, Baptist, and Presbyterian churches. Their participation had its roots in the movement for social Christianity that in many ways paralleled progressivism: the Social Gospel.

During the 1880s in both England and the United States, liberal Protestants pursued a "social Christianity" that had as its goal the creation of a "Kingdom of God on earth" through the efforts of Christian social service.[51] Social Gospel advocates were not simply religious social engineers, but their views were difficult to pin down. William Jennings Bryan spoke of the difficulty of locating any one representative figure, as they "differ widely, each being a law unto himself."[52] They were avowedly liberal or, more radically, modernist in their worldviews. Some, like liberal minister Rev. Harry Emerson Fosdick, appear in hindsight to be consistent only in their willingness consistently to rethink old creeds in light of new knowledge. Others, like modernist Shailer Mathews, were less concerned with accommodation than wholesale renovation of their Protestantism. Walter Rauschenbusch's 1917 classic, *A Theology for the Social Gospel*, was one attempt to reconcile doctrine with modern circumstances. Theology, Rauschenbusch argued, "must always embody the best thought of its age or its age will seek religion outside of theology." Their initial impulse was to take cues from secular culture, but they ended up facilitating their own capitulation to it.[53]

Whether pursued by liberals or modernists, however, the Social Gospel succeeded in creating space for Protestant ministers to participate in secular reform movements to usher in the Kingdom. Indeed, it was the duty of Christians to work for the "social salvation" of the world, since their teachings stated that human effort first had to perfect the earth to ensure Christ's return. It is easy to see why ministers of the Social Gospel would find eugenics appealing. The two movements shared certain assumptions. Salvation for Social Gospelers was a social matter; social redemption was as much a part of salvation as one's own personal redemption. In a similar vein, eugenicists argued that heredity should be a social matter, and they too supported intervention and reform to guarantee the preservation of the race. Both groups appealed to society's social conscience in the interest of reform.[54]

The sense of Christian mission that characterized the Social Gospel could also conform to ideas about racial uplift, as the career of Rev. Josiah Strong revealed. Strong, a Congregational clergyman and Social Gospel pioneer, is best known for his 1885 book *Our Country*, which praised Anglo-Saxons as the standard bearers of Christianity and civilization. "In modern times," Strong said, "the peoples whose love of liberty has won [civilization], and whose genius for self-government has preserved it, have been Anglo-Saxons." Strong argued that the Anglo-Saxon was the creator of an especially pure and spiritual form of Christianity that made him, "divinely commissioned to be, in a peculiar sense, his brother's keeper."[55] Strong was not the only Social Gospel leader to temper his Christian optimism with ethnocentrism. Rauschenbusch warned an audience at Rochester Theological Seminary in 1902 that the new immigrants from southern and eastern Europe were introducing "alien strains of blood" into American society.[56] A popular Social Gospel prayer for immigrants achieved the effect of simultaneously empathizing with and demonizing its intended recipients: "May we look with thy compassion upon those who have been drained and stunted by the poverty and oppression of centuries, and whose minds have been warped by superstitions or seared by the dumb agony of revolt."[57] The optimism of the Social Gospel coexisted with a fear of social unrest, a fear shared by supporters of the eugenics movement.[58]

Eugenics also fit well with social Christianity because Social Gospelers painted their theological canvas with broad strokes. While proponents of the Social Gospel agreed on the importance of the social teachings of Jesus, they did not reach uniform conclusions on their contemporary relevance or priority. Hence Walter Rauschenbusch emphasized Jesus' nonviolent radicalism, while Shailer Mathews noted Jesus' power to transform culture and Francis Greenwood Peabody presented the Son of God as a scientific philanthropist.[59] Ambiguity was common and provided ample room for socially minded ministers to include hereditary improvement in their litany of reform activities.

Between Protestant liberalism and full-fledged modernism there were differences of degree. Liberals were more anxious about their theological reformulations; modernists more intoxicated by the process of smashing idols. Of both impulses, not surprisingly, conservatives were wary. Conservative, evangelical Protestants believed in the inerrancy of the Bible (what critics referred to as their "paper Pope"), an experience of conversion or rebirth, and a commitment to proselytizing. They were not necessarily hostile to reform or to science, but as the materialistic philosophy of evolutionary theory grew, they became more intransigent in their insistence on Biblical infallibility. To liberal and modernist religious leaders, conservatives were the intellectual equivalents of canopic jars: full of the desiccated remains of their elders' views of culture and science, they were incapable of speaking to the concerns of modern believers.

Conservative Protestants also differed with their liberal and modernist counterparts in their enthusiasm for new reforms such as eugenics; they were usually premillennialist, evangelical Christians. The pre-and post-millennial distinction had a direct bearing on Protestant leaders' ideas about social reform. Premillennialists believed that Christ would return bodily to begin the millennium (the thousand-year period during which Christ would reign on earth, according to Revelation 20:1–7). Postmillennialists believed that the millennium would come through human effort.[60] Regarding social reform, premillennialists saw the world as merely a temporary lodging-place for Christians who awaited Christ's imminent return. Their goal was to save as many souls as possible before Christ's Second Coming, hence their designation as "evangelical" Protestants. Postmillennialists viewed the world as a place to change for the better to create the Kingdom of God on earth, and so reform was a vital part of their Christianity.

Protestant supporters of eugenics were postmillennialist Christians; their opponents were usually premillennialists. Premillennialists saw hubris in the assumption that human beings could usher in the Kingdom through their own efforts. To them, liberals and modernists such as Fosdick and Mathews were like the eager builders of Babel, too intent on their worldly tasks to realize they were neglecting their more important spiritual duties. Rev. Bernard Iddings Bell, Dean of St. Paul's (Protestant Episcopal) Cathedral in Fond du Lac, Wisconsin, expressed a common frustration when he noted, "One might as well admire the spectacle of Joan of Arc forsaking her place at the head of France's armies while she devoted her time to mending her soldiers' hosiery!"[61] Moreover, for evangelicals, premillennialism was the only appropriate worldview since it was the only one that squared with a literal reading of the Bible.[62] These disparate interpretations of Protestantism generated so much conflict during the decades between 1880 and 1930 that one historian has labeled it the "age of division."[63] Science was the proving ground for many of these conflicts. Social Gospel Protestants such as Josiah Strong believed that "the modern prophet, employing the methods of science, may again proclaim that the kingdom of heaven is at hand."[64] Evangelical Protestants were skeptical of the methods of a science that challenged Biblical doctrine on matters like the Virgin birth and bodily resurrection of Christ. If the warfare metaphor does not provide a wholly accurate picture of early twentieth-century science and religion, it does capture one element of the relationship: that of evangelical Christian opposition to many new scientific teachings, including evolutionary theory and its offshoots, such as eugenics.[65]

Although the influence of the Protestant Social Gospel would wane in the years following World War I—the disillusionment of world war dampening the reforming ardor of many leaders—the legacy of social service it left behind serves as the context for the story of Protestants and eugenics. Most of the Protestant leaders who supported eugenics found their way to the movement through their earlier social service work, which was initially an outgrowth of this Social Gospel impulse.

The same influences that inspired Progressives and Protestant Social Gospelers encouraged campaigns for social justice by Reform Jews, and Jewish leaders who became involved in the eugenics movement were overwhelmingly from this tradition. The Reform movement, which took root in America in the late nineteenth and early twentieth centuries under the guidance of Rabbi Isaac Mayer Wise, was largely the affiliation of Jews of German descent. They had settled in America during the nineteenth century, assimilated, and prospered. In contrast, the Jewish immigrants coming to America at the turn of the century were not educated or wealthy German Jews, but people of the *shtetl*— rural, Eastern European or Russian peasants who were usually Orthodox Jews. Many leaders of American Reform Judaism worried that these new immigrants were incapable of assimilation.

Adherents of Reform Judaism in America demonstrated openness to contemporary social questions and social reform that distinguished them from their Orthodox and Conservative co-religionists. Reform rabbis embraced Darwinian evolution and debated the finer points of biblical criticism.[66] Their liberal tendencies culminated in the formation, in 1899, of the Central Conference of American Rabbis, which would become an important forum for Reform rabbis; by the outbreak of World War I, there were approximately two hundred Reform rabbis in America.[67] Ecumenical activities increased during this era as well, as Reform Jewish and Social Gospel leaders attacked similar social problems. "Creed dwindles into insignificance," Reform Rabbi Emil G. Hirsch observed.[68] Another Reform Rabbi, Stephen Wise of New York, assessed his own reforming impulses as "not charity, but social service, building upon the rock of social justice," and in 1913 devoted 45 percent of his congregation's budget to social reform activities.[69] Rabbis such as Emil Hirsch and Stephen Wise, who lent their support to a wide range of social reforms, included eugenics in that orbit.

Jewish leaders' encounter with eugenics often centered on the unique qualities of the Jewish "race" and the vicissitudes of intermarriage with non-Jews. In their explorations, rabbis turned to centuries-old Biblical prescriptions for health as evidence of the compatibility of eugenic science and Jewish faith. In an essay on "Jewish eugenics," published in 1916, for example, Rabbi Max Reichler cited the Mosaic code as proof of Biblical strictures against defective marriages.[70] But racial distinctiveness proved to be a double-edged sword. Many eugenicists praised the Jewish people for their racial purity and historical attention to the power of heredity, and rabbis who supported the eugenics movement drew upon this history to demonstrate the compatibility of the two worldviews. However, this attention to cultural (and even physical) homogeneity made it easier for some eugenicists to condemn Jewish "clannishness" and to make invidious comparisons between Jews and non-Jews. In 1920, the periodical *Eugenical News* eagerly reported the findings of a recent book that declared "the Jews produce . . . a very much larger proportion of insane, idiots, and mental and physical defectives than any of the nations among which they live."[71] Eugenicists used their science—and Jews' discussions of Jewish racial distinctiveness—in the service of advancing their own anti-Semitism.

Numerically, rabbis' participation in the eugenics movement was far lower than Protestants, but they were, nonetheless, a significant presence, especially during the 1920s. Rabbi David deSola Pool, Rabbi Joseph Silverman, Rabbi Louis Mann, and others became members of the American Eugenics Society; other Jewish leaders sponsored eugenics lectures at their synagogues and served officially as speakers for the eugenics cause. Several rabbis were also central players in the American birth control movement, and they encouraged eugenicists and birth control advocates to campaign together for race betterment.

Catholic participation in the eugenics movement is perhaps the most paradoxical part of this story. The first few Catholics who wrote about eugenics expressed an abiding wariness about the movement, a fact that was never far

from the minds of later Catholic observers. Catholics were at times the movement's staunchest opponents; indeed, they offered some of the most rigorous
intellectual challenges to eugenics. Although most Catholics interpreted
Church teachings as disapproving of eugenics, the Vatican did not officially
weigh in on the matter until 1930. As a result, Catholic leaders carved their
own arguments out of existing Church doctrine and contemporary circumstances. During the course of these explorations, well-known Catholic leaders
expressed support for the *goals* of eugenics, though not always the *means* employed to achieve them.[72]

Catholic interest in eugenics began with Galton. In 1870, the periodical
Catholic World published a lengthy article assessing Galton's book, *Hereditary
Genius*. It was not an auspicious beginning for the relationship. The reviewer
methodically challenged every one of Galton's major claims about the heritability of genius, and with some relish decried the "insufficiency of method"
and "defective logic" of his research. Further, the reviewer said, while Galton
was correct that all men are not born with equal natural *abilities*, the conclusions Galton drew from this fact contradicted Catholic teaching that all men
are born with equal natural *rights*. Since science did not recognize this distinction, the reviewer argued, it could not claim to act as a social engineer. Men
such as Galton did a disservice to their science when they ask of it the answers
to questions "which confessedly lie not in its province."[73]

Eugenics did not appear again as a major topic of discussion in Catholic
periodicals until the 1910s. By that time, demographic changes and Church
encyclicals had altered the landscape of American Catholicism. By 1895, the
Catholic population in America had swelled to twelve and a half million people.
Many of these millions began to demonstrate a modern, reforming bent akin
to the Protestant Social Gospel movement, focusing their attention on social
problems. This new movement for social justice was sparked in part by Pope
Leo XIII's 1891 encyclical, *Rerum Novarum*, an antisocialist statement that outlined the Church's position on the conditions of labor and suggested a program
of reform. For many Catholics, the encyclical also emphasized that social problems had religious and moral, as well as secular and economic implications.
But American Catholic reform innovations were not met with unmitigated
praise. In 1899, Pope Leo XIII issued the encyclical *Testem Benevolentiae*, which
condemned "Americanism;" eight years later Pope Pius X's *Pascendi Dominici
Gregis*, also strongly condemned modernist trends, and called a temporary halt
to reform efforts.[74]

Catholics who explored the relationship between modern science and
Catholic teaching at the turn of the century walked on unstable doctrinal
ground. Yet, as one observer in those years went so far as to argue, "there is
no religious question which has excited more comment in our day than that
of the relation of the Catholic faith to the teachings of modern science."[75] This
included the science of heredity, and by 1900 the tone of Catholic writings on

the subject had shifted from the skepticism and hostility of the 1870s to wary acceptance of heredity's central principles.

This did not mean, of course, that Catholic writers immediately embraced eugenics. On the contrary, their willingness to accept the scientific laws of human inheritance always coexisted with an adherence to Church doctrine. This bred a certain caution. In 1904, for example, the Acting Dean and Professor of the History of Medicine at Fordham University Medical School, Reverend James J. Walsh, M.D., offered the readers of *The Ecclesiastical Review* a portrait of Father Gregor Mendel, conceiver of the central laws of inheritance whose work scientists had recently rediscovered. The Austrian priest offered Catholics a "new outlook" on heredity and belied the prejudice that the Catholic clergy lacked knowledge of science, Walsh said.[76] But Walsh also argued that science was not the only force that had informed Mendel's work; his Catholic faith was central to it as well. The lesson for contemporary students of heredity, Walsh said, was a warning "not to surrender their judgment to . . . theories, but to wait in patience for the facts in the case." Just as Mendel had toiled patiently in his pea patch, so, too, should modern Catholics be "working, not theorizing, while they wait."[77] Other Catholics were less cautious than Walsh in their enthusiasm for the newly revealed laws of heredity. "Every human being is the sum of his ancestors," William Seton wrote in the *Catholic World*, in language not unlike that of Galton himself. "If the rudder which the helmsmen holds in his hands is badly constructed, if the wood is decayed," Seton said, "it may fare ill with the ship he is steering."[78] Although they were not as enthusiastic about the social implications of the new science of heredity as their Protestant counterparts, Catholics nevertheless saw opportunities for good in its discovery. They also saw a chance to refute the prejudice, popular at the time, of Catholics as superstitious of science—after all, certain segments of American opinion felt that the Catholic Church had not yet completed proper penance for its treatment of Galileo in the seventeenth century.

Most Catholics eventually condemned the eugenics movement for its excesses, but it is revealing to trace the path Catholics took in coming to that condemnation. Their application of Catholic moral teaching and natural law to the question of eugenics was especially compelling during the decades before the Vatican officially weighed in on the issue in 1930. The more liberal Catholics who endorsed certain principles of the eugenics movement found its focus on the importance of marriage and the integrity of the family appealing, as well as the movement's goal of eliminating disease, disability, and other human suffering.

Few religious leaders became involved with every aspect of the eugenics movement. Instead, they promoted eugenics as they did the many other progressive reforms that drew their interest. They lent their names but not always a large portion of their energies to the movement, and it was not uncommon for a minister, priest or rabbi who supported eugenics to lack technical under-standing of the science of eugenics, or even to find himself confronted with a "eugenic" policy that he had not known existed. Nevertheless, given the degree to which these leaders controlled a captive audience in their congregations, as well as their often highly visible public profiles, their influence outweighed their numbers.

For other religious leaders in this story, eugenics became a modern Baal, zealously worshipped. In eugenics, these men found a faith stronger than their Christianity, fulfilling Francis Galton's hopes of replacing religion with eugen-ics. In 1934, for example, Congregational minister George Reid Andrews re-signed his Connecticut pulpit to become the Executive Secretary of the Amer-ican Eugenics Society. He justified his career change by arguing that he would have a far greater influence on society as a eugenicist than he would as a preacher. Another minister, Rev. Kenneth C. MacArthur, cut back on his pulpit duties to serve as a eugenics promoter, happily traveling around New England spreading the good news of heredity.[79] While the level of devotion of these two ministers is exceptional, the logic of their pursuit was familiar to many of their fellow religious leaders.

Religious participation in the eugenics movement provides a crucial ana-lytical vantage point for assessing the broader appeal of these ideas in American culture. How could a movement so irreverent in its meddling with marriage and procreation enjoy such support from the social arbiters of these functions? To practice eugenics was, in some sense, to play God. The excavation of the worldviews of religious leaders–the often-contradictory mix of education, the-ology, practical experience, personality—as well as circumstances, including the impact of rapid industrialization, immigration, urbanization, a more active state, and reform impulses that led to pitched battles over intellectual terrain, suggests the difficulty of imputing any one particular motive. As well, if preach-ers and rabbis too eagerly embraced eugenics, they also consistently challenged eugenicists' belief that scientists were the most qualified judges of human "fitness."[80] They were skeptical of eugenicists' intimations that the moral bur-den for alleviating social ills had shifted. Eugenicists might reason that the responsibility for improving the human race was theirs, but religious leaders were not so eager to see their flocks turned over to these scientific shepherds. The position of moral steward remained contested.

The religious examination of eugenics prompted broader questions: What was the place of organized religion in American culture? Were religious leaders supposed to serve as a bastion of stability amidst social change, questioning and skeptical of new social experiments? Or were they supposed to be respon-sive to change, perhaps even in the vanguard, leading the faithful into the modern age? By raising new ethical questions and demanding practical action, eugenics challenged preachers to respond more swiftly to trends that quietly had been bedeviling them for the past several decades. The inability of most religious leaders to foresee the ultimate consequences of eugenics policies does not necessarily point to either ignorance or disingenuousness on their parts.[81] However naive or unsophisticated the scientific beliefs of religious leaders (and of scientists themselves) appear today, they were taken seriously for a time. Similarly, however coercive or repressive the actions of eugenics supporters appear to contemporary historians, these were not necessarily the impulses they acted upon.[82] For many religious leaders, compassion, empathy, and a deep sense of social responsibility informed their judgment of the "feeble-minded." The intellectual inconsistencies we see plainly today come from the benefit of hindsight. Insofar as they supported eugenics earlier in the twentieth century, these men and women were consistent within the limits of their vision. Condemning that vision is easy; more challenging is understanding why they made the choices they did, and why eugenics had then—as it does now—the power to stir the human imagination.

I

Fervent Charity

And above all things have fervent charity among yourselves: for
charity shall cover the multitude of sins.

—I Peter 4:8

On a blisteringly hot day in July 1896, a preacher in Topeka, Kansas,
sat on his porch contemplating a way to increase attendance at the
Sunday evening services of his Central Congregational Church. By
month's end, Rev. Charles M. Sheldon's intellectual peregrinations
led him to write what would become one of the best-selling pieces of
inspirational fiction ever published. *In His Steps* eventually sold
more than 30 million copies worldwide, and its message, although
sometimes perfervidly presented, encapsulated the major impulses
of the Protestant Social Gospel movement.

   Sheldon's preacher asks his congregation to "pledge themselves
earnestly and honestly for an entire year not to do anything without
first asking, 'What would Jesus do?'" In doing so he became the fictional apotheosis of the Social Gospel leader Washington Gladden,
who argued that there could be "no adequate social reform save that
which springs from a genuine revival of religion." For Gladden, that
religion, like the pledge taken by Sheldon's characters, "must be a
religion less concerned about getting men to heaven than about fit-
ting them for their proper work on the earth."[1]

   As Sheldon's readers understood, the evocative question "What
would Jesus do?" implied, even demanded, a response: social action.
Characters in the novel who fail to keep the pledge, like slumlord
Clarence Penrose, experience near existential levels of anxiety about

their conduct. Their agitations are alleviated only by social action and well-timed interventions by the Holy Spirit (in the case of Penrose, this leads to an emotional breakdown in front of his bishop and a vow to refurbish his tenement properties). Edward Norman, the fictional editor of the *Daily News* in Sheldon's novel, responds to the prodding of the Holy Spirit by refusing to publish notices of prizefights in his paper, reasoning that Jesus would not want to see such bloody entertainments advertised.

Rev. Charles Sheldon practiced what he preached. An archetypical Social Gospel minister himself, he was known to masquerade as a tramp or laborer to gain firsthand experience of the average man's working conditions, and by the 1910s he had become an avid prohibitionist. In March 1900, he guest-edited the Topeka *Daily Capital* newspaper and, following his fictional editor Edward Norman, forbade publication of activities, such as prizefights, that he deemed immoral.[2] Sheldon was a typical Social Gospeler in another respect: He embraced science, including evolutionary theory, and encouraged its application to social reform.

The theology of the Social Gospel encouraged social action, and in the last decades of the nineteenth century, many Protestant ministers like Sheldon pursued it in campaigns to eliminate prostitution, raise the legal age of consent for sexual relations, and otherwise eradicate vice in cities that had become, in their eyes, modern-day Sodom and Gomorrahs. Purity reform in particular drew on the Social Gospel and embraced an ideal of perfectibility that meshed well with social Christianity.[3] Through local societies, national Purity Congresses, and the American Purity Alliance, reformers in the post–Civil War era promoted goals of "race regeneration" that presaged the rhetoric of the eugenics movement. Developing apace with this interest in purifying society was a move in the field of philanthropy toward hereditary explanations for social problems. Influenced by the emerging currents of thought on heredity, including Lombroso's theories of criminal degeneracy, charity and corrections workers confronted Herbert Spencer's claim that their work thwarted natural selection by stopping "that natural process of elimination by which society continually purifies itself."[4] Organizations such as the National Conference of Charities and Correction began to explore ways to *prevent* the spread of degeneracy by focusing on heredity as a probable cause and identifying those segments of the population most burdened by the scourge. As one contemporary observer noted, charity and philanthropic workers "had become persuaded that for the good of society and the rescue of unborn posterity such blighted lines of descent should be cut off."[5]

Ministers played a key role in these discussions, for they made up a large portion of the members of the Charities and Correction Conferences.[6] A 1906 survey conducted by the Institute of Social Service found that 92 percent of those working with associated charities, 88 percent working in social settlements, and 71 percent working with national reform organizations were church members.[7] Ideas about heredity found their way into the rhetoric of these contemporaries of Rev. Sheldon. At the National Conference of Charities and Correction in 1888, for example, Rev. S. J. Barrows, editor of the Boston-based magazine *Christian Register*, argued that the growing population of degenerates threatened the health of American society. "It is our duty," he said, "to prevent them from bequeathing this burden of imbecility to a future generation." A fellow cleric at the conference, Rev. M. Dana, echoed Barrows's assessment, noting that the overwhelming influence of heredity guaranteed that "idleness, thriftlessness, and vice propagate themselves," especially through the "excessive fecundity of the reckless classes in the population."[8]

Ministers lived among these "reckless classes," and one Congregationalist leader from Indiana, Rev. Oscar Carleton McCulloch (1843–1891), united a concern with their growth and a strong interest in heredity to produce one of the first eugenic family studies in the United States. His efforts reveal that the boundary between religion and science was remarkably fluid at the moment when eugenics began to filter into U.S. culture, fluid enough to facilitate the merger of Protestant Social Gospel theology and eugenics.

McCulloch's background reads like Rev. Sheldon's fiction. He began his career not as a man of the cloth, but as a traveling drug salesman for a large Chicago company. However, at the age of 24 and much to the surprise of the people who knew him, he quit his lucrative sales job to enroll in the Chicago Theological Seminary, graduating in 1870. Ordained as a Congregational minister that same year, he served at a church in Wisconsin before moving, in 1877, to the Plymouth Congregational Church in Indianapolis, where he would remain for the rest of his life. There he built one of the country's first "institutional churches" based on the principles of the Social Gospel and "applied Christianity." The church was tolerant in spiritual matters—McCulloch abolished the confession of faith as a requirement for membership—but demanding in social ones. This congregation of "friends associated for Christian work and worship" found that their leader viewed the sanctuary as a staging ground for his many social reform efforts.[9]

The citizens of Indianapolis were soon remarking on their pastor's zeal as a social reformer. In 1884, McCulloch created the Plymouth Institute as an offshoot of the church and through it offered lectures, classes, and even a savings and loan association for the congregation and the community. His skills as an organizer made him a prominent state and local figure, and he is credited with forming nearly all of Indianapolis's major philanthropic institutions in the late nineteenth century, including the Charity Organization Society, the Friendly Inn, the Children's Aid Society, and the Summer Mission for Sick Children.[10]

McCulloch's devotion to reform frequently brought him into contact with less fortunate members of Indianapolis society. In 1877, after a visit to a poverty-stricken household—a place of "extreme destitution," as he described it—McCulloch was inspired to study members of the extended family in the records of the township. Much to his surprise, he uncovered a trove of hereditary degeneracy. "I found that I had touched a family known as the Ishmaels," he said, "which had a pauper history of several generations." The Ishmael clan now numbered in the hundreds, McCulloch realized, having intermarried with other insalubrious families.[11] Spurred on by his discovery of the Ishmaelite family, he embraced a new hobby: tracking hereditary degeneracy. He spent the next ten years meticulously researching strains of degeneracy in other Indiana families. His work eventually covered the detailed histories of 250 families and 1,692 people, a remarkable feat for a full-time minister who did his research entirely during his leisure time.

McCulloch credited his chance visit to the pauper Ishmaelites with setting him on this investigatory course, but he later conceded that his work might have been influenced by the success of a book published that same year by Richard Dugdale. In *The Jukes: A Study in Crime, Pauperism, Disease, and Heredity*, Dugdale, a well-known reformer and secretary of the New York Prison Association whose work was widely read in charity circles, traced the misfortunes of seven generations of a degenerate family in New York. Prostitution, disease, and other licentious traits characterized the group, whose vices Dugdale claimed had cost the state more than "a million and a quarter dollars of loss" over just seventy-five years ("without reckoning the cash paid for whiskey"). Tapping into the growing concern among reformers for preventive measures, Dugdale urged his readers to determine if the courts and other social institutions were coping with the problems these families caused.[12]

Dugdale's verdict was clear: The laundry list of Juke turpitude he had compiled convinced him that existing social institutions had failed in their duty to protect the public. His suggestions for reform included tactics targeting *both* poor heredity and degraded environment; he viewed nature and nurture as inextricably linked. "In most cases," he noted, "the heredity is also accompanied by an environment which runs parallel to it, the two conditions giving cumulative force to a career of debauch."[13] In Dugdale's opinion, improving the environmental conditions of the degenerate classes was just as important as preventing their wayward reproduction.

Rev. McCulloch presented his Ishmaelite findings in 1888 at the annual meeting of the National Conference of Charities and Correction, and at that time admitted that his own work "resembles Dr. Dugdale['s] . . . and was suggested by that." But, he hastened to add, his Ishmaelite research "extends over a larger field." Moreover, McCulloch argued, the scope of the problem he outlined was much broader than Dugdale's reckoning; the Ishmaelites of Indianapolis were but the tip of an iceberg. "In all probability," he warned, "similar study would show similar results in any of our States."[14]

With the enthusiasm of the muckraker McCulloch uncovered a ready culprit on whom society could affix blame: charitable institutions that encouraged the feebleminded in their fecundity by providing unrestricted relief. McCulloch argued that a degenerate hereditary endowment, aided and abetted by well-meaning but unscientific philanthropy, had produced several generations of murderers, illegitimate children, prostitutes, beggars, thieves, and scores of "generally diseased" human beings. The "unlimited public and private aid" dispensed to the Ishmaelites—a shockingly maladjusted group of citizens, in McCulloch's rendering—encouraged them "in this idle, wandering life, and in the propagation of similarly disposed children."[15] To McCulloch's audience of professional charitable workers, this was akin to hearing that they were the foxes in their own henhouse.

McCulloch accepted some personal blame for this state of affairs. He confessed that he had married two young people from the extended, degraded Ishmaelite clan, naïvely convinced that he had done his small part to prevent the spread of illegitimacy. A short time later, when he asked how the newlyweds fared, a family member matter-of-factly informed him that the bride's "other husband came back," precipitating the hasty removal of husband number two, who died soon thereafter "in the pest-house." Although he quickly recovered from the shock of having sanctified a polygamous marriage, Rev. McCulloch told the conference participants that he felt it was his duty to prevent other men of God from making a similar mistake.[16]

Unlike Dugdale, who had given equal weight to environmental factors, McCulloch argued that heredity was the primary force with which charity workers now had to reckon. To Rev. Sheldon's fictional query "What would Jesus do?" McCulloch would have replied with an enthusiastic "Rid the world of indiscriminate benevolence." He expressed keen frustration with existing methods of charity, especially the practice of indiscriminate giving, which amounted to sending "the pauper out with the benediction, 'Be fruitful and multiply.'" To combat the powerful force of heredity in the "decaying stock" of families like the Ishmaelites, McCulloch said, society needed to transform philanthropy into a discriminating, scientific enterprise. His practical proposal had three elements: closing official "outdoor" (or public) poor relief; checking private, "indiscriminate benevolence"; and "get[ting] hold of the children."[17] The firm but humanitarian hand of the state was McCulloch's preferred method of implementing this three-step program, and he pursued legislation with alacrity. In 1889, he wrote and secured passage of a law creating the Board of State Charities for Indiana, as well as a Board of Children's Guardians for Center Township, Indianapolis. The latter organization had as its rather alarmingly worded purpose "to take charge of children of vicious or incompetent parents." The state later created similar boards for every county in Indiana.[18]

The shape of McCulloch's late nineteenth-century, local eugenics campaign—with its meticulous gathering of family histories, calls for scientific forms of charity, and use of the state's power to enforce eugenic beliefs—anticipated the tactics of organized eugenics movements by several decades.

The response of fellow residents also presaged later debates about eugenic methods. His calls for greater social control were met with consternation in a few quarters. *People,* an Indiana newspaper that championed the working man, decried McCulloch's efforts to eliminate indiscriminate public relief for the poor. "Who made Oscar C. McCulloch a judge of his fellows?" one editorial asked.[19] But McCulloch's fellow ministers at the National Conference of Charities and Correction buttressed his pleas for greater social control in their own work. Rev. William Frederic Slocum of Baltimore presented a paper on "Drunkards' Families," in which he argued that, once a home became a place of irredeemable degeneracy, "the State and Society have a duty in preventing it from training base citizens and degraded men and women, and must do for the children what the home has failed to accomplish." The "ideal of true charity," he argued, demanded this intervention.[20]

McCulloch's calls for charity workers to heed heredity and to practice scientific philanthropy brought him considerable prominence in the reform community. In 1891, the National Conference of Charities and Correction named him president, and he used the visibility of this position to call for a national registry of all dependent, defective, and delinquent persons. He would not live to see this reform enacted; later that year he died of Hodgkin's disease at the age of 48.[21]

Long after his death, McCulloch's work had a direct impact on the fledgling science of eugenics. Early disciples of eugenics in the United States pointed to his and Dugdale's family studies as the starting point for their own investigations, and both works became classics of eugenics literature (though Dugdale's work was by far the more well-known). The monikers "Ishmaelite" and "Juke" soon became synonymous with feeblemindedness in popular magazines, scientific journals, and newspapers. At the height of the eugenics movement's popularity, eugenicists quoted extensively from McCulloch's conference paper, and, in 1916, the *Eugenical News* declared him a eugenics pioneer.[22]

McCulloch's legacy—state and local reform organizations, early eugenics studies, a flourishing Midwestern church—reveals the strong link between his Social Gospel philosophy and the era's new embrace of social control, especially in the field of charity work. Although the Social Gospel encouraged ministers such as McCulloch to pursue "applied Christianity," it rarely defined the limits of those practical applications. McCulloch tested those limits by invoking the Social Gospel to justify reforms built on hereditarian thought and social control.[23] His activities also suggest the limits of those reform impulses when it came to serving the spiritual needs of his church; one biographer notes that his congregation often grew weary of overwrought Sunday morning sermons that examined in tedious detail the movement for an eight-hour workday.[24]

Yet, if McCulloch was overzealous in his pursuit of social causes, his emphasis on heredity and his calls for more widespread use of compulsory methods of reform were in keeping with the emerging philosophy of his Charities and Correction colleagues and many of his Social Gospel coreligionists. He and many of the other ministers who attended the annual National Conference of Charities and Correction brought to their philanthropic work certain assumptions about the people they were aiding—assumptions that were not always charitable. These ministers reasoned that the thoroughly degraded state of the feebleminded made social control not merely a necessity, but, as one of McCulloch's clerical colleagues noted, an expression of "Christ-like patience and devotion" in helping society's weaker members.[25] Not surprisingly, those devoting themselves to society's weaker members found they needed tools of greater strength. Prevention was becoming the byword of reformers; the year McCulloch died, one writer suggested that the misery caused by families such as the Jukes could have been avoided if the clan's patriarch had spent fifteen minutes on the receiving end of a surgeon's scalpel.[26]

Yet tensions over the place of Christian charity in this world remained. From a strictly hereditarian perspective, any social reform that targeted only environmental conditions—housing, nutrition, and the like—ultimately provided no eugenic benefits to society; on the contrary, as eugenicists often pointed out, some of these reforms worked directly against eugenics by encouraging the survival and propagation of the weak. Yet the charitable impulse, given institutional form and authority through the churches, took as a key dictum the biblical injunction to succor the weak. Rev. McCulloch tried to solve this contradiction by crafting charity programs that aided the weak while conforming to scientific standards. The language invoked revealed its Social Gospel roots: "Regeneration" and "redemption" were commonly used terms in ministers' descriptions of their goals.[27]

In 1908, Baptist minister and Social Gospel avatar Samuel Zane Batten of Lincoln, Nebraska, offered his suggestions for achieving the "redemption of the unfit" in the *American Journal of Sociology*. Batten praised the "Christian spirit" that informed modern society's charitable impulses, but, like Rev. McCulloch, he reminded his readers that "there are grave dangers in this modern philanthropic effort to care for the unfit, dangers that must be recognized and avoided or the race will pay the forfeit." If the goal of society was a world where "there will be no unfit and defectives to poison the blood and to hamper the march" of mankind, Batten said, charitable impulses needed redirecting.[28]

Rev. Batten's solution was to grant that environmental (i.e., nonhereditary) reforms could bring changes as permanent as those wrought exclusively by heredity. Alterations in a family's physical environment, he implied, were as central to improving the human race as modifications to their hereditary pool. Despite scientists' success in the late nineteenth century in disproving this Lamarckian notion of the hereditary permanence of environmental reforms, the idea of the inheritance of acquired characteristics had a continuing appeal for social scientists.[29] The same was true for religious leaders such as Batten. With Lamarckianism came *agency* and a measure of comfort about people's ability to change their world by acting on their charitable, Christian impulses. By promoting a form of "soft heredity" that allowed for the influence of experience and environment (and hence, Christian charity), Lamarckianism allowed Batten and other Protestant ministers to reconcile eugenics with the reform-minded worldview of the Social Gospel. Through a "definite, scientific, and Christian programme of action," Batten said, the redemption of the unfit would occur—not a redemption of individual souls, but an expiation of the social sin of feeblemindedness.[30]

While Batten focused his attention on redemption, a Baptist minister in England outlined a plan for race *regeneration.* Rev. Frederick Brotherton Meyer, chairman of the National Council of Public Morals for Great Britain, was well-known in the United States for his skills as a lecturer and for his good humor (at a speaking engagement during the Taft administration, Meyer raised eyebrows by insisting that Mrs. Taft join her husband on the platform, where he promptly introduced her as the real President of the United States). Meyer agreed with eugenicists' diagnosis of social problems; like them, he saw "symptoms of dry-rot in the foundation-timbers of the house of national well-being," including a race that was in a state of "national flabbiness," the birthrate in a free-fall. Meyer also agreed with eugenicists that "on the whole there are stocks that yield as there are stocks that do not yield the finest type of manhood."[31]

Yet Rev. Meyer did not see much hope in eugenicists' plans for regenerating the race. Their current methods, such as the segregation of the unfit in colonies and institutions, he deemed lacking in staying power, "impulsive, fragmentary, and fickle." For Meyer, only one force supplied its adherents with the inspiration and discipline necessary for achieving lasting race improvement: religion. This argument would have looked familiar to Francis Galton, for he, too, had wanted eugenics to incorporate the discipline, conviction, and zeal of a religious crusade. Unlike Galton, however, Meyer wanted to reconcile—not replace—his religious convictions with science. In doing so he did not reject the scientist's authority to tackle social issues; rather, he said: "All that we contend is that science is not capable of dealing finally and sufficiently with the problem of race-regeneration. She is the daughter and handmaid of religion, but her discovery of the primal laws of Nature needs to be supplemented by the endorsement and enforced by the sanctions of the spiritual realm, which is the special province of religion, before they can become universally recognised, operative, and permanent in the realm of human morality."[32] Science, in other words, could neither satisfactorily inspire nor maintain strong sentiments in its devotees. Only religion could do this. In an 1895 treatise on *Heredity and Christian Problems,* another minister had made a similar point, noting that Christianity "furnishes motives strong enough to inspire the individual and the race to constant effort toward better things."[33] Rev. Meyer's argument essentially stood Galton's position on its head. Most eugenicists believed that even if religion served some important functions, it was still a subordinate element in the movement for race betterment. Meyer insisted that *science* was subordinate to *religion*. "No discovery can emanate from mortal brain to replace or supersede" religion, he warned. Eugenicists neglected the spiritual element of mankind at their own peril, for without it, Meyer said, "the eugenesis of the race cannot be secured."[34]

Although Meyer viewed religion as a force superior to science, he still urged Christians to support practical eugenic programs. To ensure the "preservation of the race," it was the duty of the churches to spread the message of heredity in Sunday School classes, sermons, and individual counseling sessions.[35] Some of Meyer's fellow clergymen disapproved of his plan, with its intimations of sex and heredity being bandied about in the Sunday School room. A fellow Briton and the archdeacon of Coventry, Rev. James H. F. Peile, though sympathetic to the cause of eugenics, warned, "If we do not wish to court disappointment, we shall not expect the Church to lead in what is a very technical and hitherto a much controverted question." In an essay published in the British journal *Eugenics Review*, Peile explained the logic of a conservative, cautious approach to eugenics.[36]

Peile agreed with Batten and Meyer that eugenics did not require the elimination of religion. In fact, he told the readers of the *Review*, from his own study of eugenics, he had determined that the aim of the movement was, in principle, the aim of the churches: improvement of the human race. If eugenicists emphasized this common purpose, he argued, the clergy might find their message more appealing. Ministers did have a duty "to provide if possible that children of the generation to come shall be born with such equipment of qualities, physical, mental, and moral, as will make it reasonably possible for them to grow up useful and happy citizens."[37]

Peile's caution stemmed from his belief that eugenics was a science still in its infancy. Eugenicists had not yet defined their goals clearly or proven their scientific claims definitively. This situation bred misunderstanding and suspicion in the public mind and in the minds of clergymen, who, Peile noted, were far more likely to associate eugenics with the activities of the stockyard than with the duties of the pulpit. The public needed an intelligent educational campaign, directed by scientists, that would inform the world of the necessity and the practicability of eugenic measures. Once this occurred, the clergy could join scientific eugenicists in welcoming race improvement. For the present, Peile argued vigorously against ministers trying to teach eugenics in Sunday Schools or through sermons, and warned them not to wade into the murky waters of dictating fecundity to the "fit" classes.[38]

The cautious note sounded in Peile's 1909 *Eugenics Review* article was absent one year later when the Church of England held its Church Congress in Cambridge. There, several members of the Royal Commission on the Feeble-Minded delivered "brilliant" addresses urging the clergy to act along the lines proposed by Rev. Meyer. The National Church has "a very great responsibility towards the race," one speaker said, and "the future belongs to those nations whose religious leaders realise this responsibility." Responding to the comments of various medical professionals and asylum superintendents, the bishop of Ripon vowed to discourage marriages among the unfit and to inculcate a "higher sense of duty" toward reproduction among the eugenically healthy. The overall effect of the Congress, as an American observer noted with a trace of envy, was a sense that the Church of England "was ready, in matters of social action, to 'think biologically.' "[39]

Ministers' early musings on the subject of heredity coincided with a first period of institutional growth for the U.S. eugenics movement. In 1904, Andrew Carnegie's philanthropic tendencies and one biologist's determined campaign for research funds converged to create the Cold Spring Harbor Station for Experimental Evolution on Long Island, New York. The Carnegie Institution of Washington's grant was generous, superseding even the budget of the finest British eugenics research facility, and the Station's opening marked the first organized effort to study eugenics in the United States.[40] From the beginning, the mission of the Cold Spring Harbor Station was inseparable from that of its director, Charles Davenport. An outspoken apostle of Galton's science and a Harvard-educated biologist who early on grasped the importance of the new field of Mendelian genetics, Davenport dedicated himself totally to eugenics after meeting Galton and Karl Pearson on a trip to England in the early part of the century.

Davenport combined scientific training with a personal passion for tracing human ancestry and prided himself on his skills as an amateur genealogist. Colleagues at Cold Spring Harbor no doubt found tedious his frequent references to his earliest American ancestor, Rev. John Davenport (a noted English divine who reached North America in 1637), but Davenport quickly gained notice from the public for his efficient management of Carnegie's Cold Spring Harbor endowment.[41] A visitor to the Station in 1906 was duly impressed with the institution's plentiful acreage and tidy buildings, exclaiming over the pens of "demure-looking poultry" and "dignified goats of a somewhat questionable parentage" used for animal breeding experiments. Professor W. M. Wheeler, head of the Department of Invertebrate Zoology at New York City's Museum of Natural History, declared Davenport's early forays into eugenics to be work of the "utmost importance" that undoubtedly would yield practical results for mankind.[42]

Though Davenport's singlemindedness built an impressive scientific institution, many historians have shown how it led him to play fast and loose with his science. In evaluating his work it is impossible not to notice that at many points in his career he was uncritical in his assessments. Even in his early work, when he was at his most cautious in making claims about eugenics, Davenport's zeal often overshadowed good scientific judgment.[43]

Yet his achievements should not be overlooked. More than any other American scientist he was responsible for turning a relatively obscure British theory about human heredity into a successful U.S. scientific and reform enterprise. Moreover, he was blessed with a peculiar ability to convince potential patrons that the eugenics movement was in dire need of their munificence. In 1909, for example, he waged a campaign to persuade Mrs. E. H. Harriman, widow of the railroad magnate, to invest part of her husband's estate in eugenics research. Influenced by her daughter Mary, who had spent a summer under Davenport's tutelage at Cold Spring Harbor, Mrs. Harriman agreed to endow a Eugenics Record Office, complete with a fireproof vault for storing the family pedigrees collected by Davenport and his eugenics workers.[44]

Davenport struck a responsive chord in Mrs. Harriman (as he had earlier in the trustees of the Carnegie millions) with his argument that money devoted to eugenics was a far more effective exercise in giving than money donated to charity. Charity might alleviate human suffering in the short term, he said, but eugenics sought to eliminate it entirely by removing its cause, hereditary degeneracy.[45] "He who, by such a gift, should redeem mankind from vice, imbecility, and suffering," Davenport said in a 1909 lecture, "would be the world's wisest philanthropist."[46] Davenport's wise philanthropy, like Rev. McCulloch's scientific charity, required the wisdom of men steeped in the science of heredity.

Davenport's unwavering focus on heredity as a social and scientific force informed his understanding of religion. One cannot help but wonder, however, if the targets of his religious musings felt damned by his faint praise. In one of his earliest works, an analysis of family pedigrees published as *Heredity in Relation to Eugenics* (1911), Davenport conceded, "Religious teachers do a grand work for society." Nevertheless, he said, their work was limited because the effectiveness of religious and moral teachings depend on the nature of those who receive them. "While education and moral and religious instruction may do much to develop one's native traits," only "heredity can introduce the desirable determiner that will make such training useful or less necessary."[47] For Davenport, as for Galton, religion was a force to reckon with culturally, but one that did not necessarily aid eugenics; at times, in fact, organized religion's unscientific pursuit of charity threatened to undermine the overarching mission of eugenics.

Not all converts to eugenics in the early part of the century were as unforgiving in their assessments of organized religion's influence. In 1906, Willet M. Hays, assistant U.S. secretary of agriculture and president of the American Breeders Association (ABA), announced the formation of a Committee on Eugenics "to investigate all proper means of influencing heredity with the idea of encouraging the increase of families of good blood, and of discouraging the vicious elements in the cross-bred American civilization."[48] The ABA, formed in 1903 by scientists and professional plant and animal breeders to promote the study of heredity in their field, became the first national, membership-based group to promote eugenics research in the United States. Its chief concern was public education.[49]

The operating assumptions of Hays's Eugenics Committee were closer to Galton's utopian musings about eugenics than to Davenport's research- and science-oriented vision. The Committee invited "Science and Religion, cooperating with Government efforts," to participate in "an investigation at once conservative, careful, and possibly constructive." Speaking to a *New York Times* reporter about the Committee's plans in 1906, Hays invoked Galton's hope that eugenics would enter the public mind as a new religion.[50] The Eugenics Committee planned to enlist an eclectic mix of supporters in this effort: One early report suggested that information about eugenics "be set forth in popular magazine articles, in public lectures, in addresses to workers in social fields, in circular letters to physicians, teachers, the clergy and legislators."[51]

By 1910, the *American Breeders' Magazine*, official journal of the ABA, had published several opinion pieces urging the churches to join the eugenics crusade, including calls to help educate the public about eugenics. It was likely, the ABA argued, that certain portions of eugenic teaching (the editorial did not specify which ones) "can best be promulgated through the church," rather than through scientific channels. In this process the clergy had a special role to play because, the editors reasoned, "none should feel a more vital interest in research in eugenics than those who have been chosen to direct the moral and religious life of the community." Here, they said, was an opportunity for ministers to contribute to a practical, scientific reform movement. In subsequent editorials, the *American Breeders' Magazine* suggested that the churches could exert greater social pressure to prevent marriages among the "unfit" and thus help in the elimination of the "weak fibers" from the network of human descent.[52]

With its primary goals of education and promotion, the ABA was more eager than Davenport's Cold Spring Harbor Station to enlist the aid of religious leaders. Nevertheless, early expressions of interest in the links between religion and eugenics appeared more often outside fledgling eugenics organizations. At a speech before the Virginia State Conference of Charities and Corrections in 1911, Dr. H. E. Jordan spoke to an audience of professional social workers, penologists, and ministers about the churches' fading influence on their parishioners and on society as a whole. This decline, Jordan argued, could be reversed only by integrating modern biological teachings into the churches' traditional mission. The churches must "become suffused" with biological knowledge if they hoped to regain their influence over the group on which society depended for its survival: "virile men." He went on to argue, "Religion today is shaped too much to make its essential appeal to the sick and the unfortunate." The churches had directed all of their energies toward alleviating the misery of society's weaker classes with charitable programs rather than encouraging the development of the strong.[53]

This was an especially egregious error as it was the biologically healthy man, not the weak man, who "can best express the highest type of religion," according to Jordan.[54] In one sense, Jordan's argument harked back to Galton, who described eugenics as a "virile creed" that appealed to the "noblest feelings" of human nature.[55] But in another sense, it was a significant departure, for it suggested the need for organized religion's continued existence in a eugenic society, albeit in a modified form. That religion would be one that emphasized "health and bodily vigor" as much as prayer.[56]

It was the responsibility of church leaders to turn their flocks to this virile creed; however, eugenics enthusiasts saw little need to make similar accommodations for religious views. But this did not imply a lack of shared goals. Caleb W. Saleeby, a British physician, medical researcher, temperance advocate, and enthusiastic eugenicist whose work was widely read on both sides of the Atlantic, outlined the common ground in 1909. Eugenics "sets before it a sublime ideal, terrestrial indeed in its chosen theater, but celestial in its theme," he wrote. In Saleeby's view, Jesus' New Testament proclamation "I am come that ye might have life and that ye might have it more abundantly" should strike a responsive chord in any well-intentioned eugenicist; higher and more abundant life was exactly the eugenic ideal.[57]

Religion also served to remind eugenicists that they needed to take stock of moral as well as physical influences in their pursuit of this eugenic ideal. Saleeby offered an example of the integration of moral and physical traits he proposed: They "found their warrant and application in the unexamined riddle of the persistence and success, throughout more than two thousand years and a thousand vicissitudes, of the Jewish people." In Saleeby's telling, the survival of the Jews was a eugenic success story, one for which he offered three explanations. The first was the Jews' historical struggle to survive, which meant that the Jew who was a "weakling or a fool" suffered a swift dénouement. Persecution, working as a modified form of natural selection, guaranteed that only the strong lived to produce the next generation. The second factor, and the one Saleeby admired the most, was the emphasis on motherhood in Jewish culture. "The Jewish mother is the mother of children innately superior, on the average," he argued. The third factor was one that no doubt warmed Saleeby's teetotaling heart: The Jews "do not abuse alcohol." By avoiding this menace, the Jews guaranteed the strength and vitality of their race.[58] In the Jewish experience Saleeby found a compelling example of a group whose racial success rested on their continual adherence to the unwritten laws of heredity *and* an articulated code of moral behavior. These forces, working in tandem, produced an ideal race.

Saleeby was one of the first eugenicists to turn explicitly to biblical example to bolster his claims, and he was the first to engage in an extended discussion of the eugenic merits of Jewish laws and customs. Although he assumed the existence of a certain degree of physical and cultural homogeneity among Jews (enough, in any case, to warrant the connection he drew between their history and their current community), his characterization of Jews contained none of the thinly veiled anti-Semitism that marked many eugenicists' later work. Saleeby's rhetoric was presumptuous ("The present writer believes that eugenics is going to save the world"), but it captured the attention of the editors of eugenics periodicals, popular magazines, and academic journals, and thus introduced the question of the moral implications of eugenics and the eugenic significance of the Jewish race to a broader public.[59]

After 1910, eugenics became a more frequent topic in the pages of non-scientific magazines, journals, and religious periodicals, seizing the imagination of a broader scope of intellectuals. Writing in the journal *Religious Education*, psychologist G. Stanley Hall argued that eugenics was "simply a legitimate new interpretation of our Christianity." "Is it not all latent in our Scriptures?" he asked.[60] Coming from Hall, these were not idle queries. Born into a profoundly religious family, Hall had planned to enter the ministry and even briefly attended Union Theological Seminary in New York; he eventually found his niche in the fields of experimental psychology and education, publishing widely in both, and served as president of Clark University. As the country's recognized leader in the field of psychology, Hall trained a large number of the next generation of psychologists. He offered his thoughts on eugenics two years after he feted Sigmund Freud on the psychoanalyst's only visit to the United States.[61]

Although Hall's professional path led him to the secular world of social science, religion remained a constant influence on his work. He was representative of a transitional generation in U.S. social science, one that did not necessarily refute the religion of their youth (for most, a mildly evangelical form of Protestantism) so much as try to rethink its teachings in light of new discoveries. This elasticity of belief was an undercurrent in much of their work.[62] A significant portion of Hall's presumed audience was seminary professors, theology students, ministers, missionaries, and Sunday School teachers. He wrote a two-volume biography of Jesus that described him (in eugenic language) as "the best unipersonal exemplar of the race idea, the true superman."[63] In his *Religious Education* essay about eugenics, Hall made two proposals for encouraging eugenic-religious cooperation. The first was a radical reevaluation of the Bible: "The entire Old Testament from the myth of Eden to the latest prophets needs a new eugenic exegesis." A thorough reexamination of biblical teaching would reveal that "Jehovah's laws are at bottom those of eugenics."[64] Hall said explicitly what Saleeby had demonstrated by example: The teachings of the Bible and the teachings of Galton were complementary.

Hall's second proposal was practical: education. Information about eugenics "should be taught in week day and Sunday schools," he argued. Only through education would children overcome the tragic ignorance that led to the degeneration of the race. Moreover, Hall believed that this education should not come from parents; some couples might be able to educate their children about the laws of life, he said, but most were not plain-spoken enough with their young charges or left them with incomplete or misleading information. "It is up to the teacher and the clergyman," Hall argued, "to enlarge their function and fit themselves to be guides of the rising generation."[65]

For Hall, religion and eugenics reinforced each other. The Bible was not merely a collection of religious stories, but a text worthy of critical interpretation from the standpoint of eugenics. Ministers were the pulpit vanguard of eugenics educators. Such an explicit acknowledgment of the need for preachers' contributions was uncommon among eugenicists at the time. But for Hall, the key directive of Christianity, "Love and serve God and man," was easy to reconcile with eugenic goals: "We only need to turn a little larger proportion of the love and service we have directed toward God, who does not need it, to man who does, and we have eugenics."[66]

Eugenicists did not discourage explorations of eugenics by men such as Caleb Saleeby and G. Stanley Hall, respectable figures whose books and articles aided their cause. However, as with any wide-reaching reform, eugenics also gained converts who were less appealing to the movement's key scientific organizers. Even before the creation of the Cold Spring Harbor Station in 1904, eager reformers attuned to shifting public perceptions about the causes of degeneracy and criminal behavior incorporated eugenics into their proposed solutions to social problems. Jettisoning discussions of hard science in favor of accessible, advice-driven narratives, these amateurs often made fantastic claims about the power of heredity, something that did not go unnoticed by eugenicists. "Our greatest danger," Charles Davenport warned, "is from some impetuous temperament, who, planting a banner of Eugenics, rallies a volunteer army of Utopians, freelovers, and muddy thinkers to start a holy war for the new religion."[67]

Davenport was helpless to prevent this from happening. Earnest, well-intentioned reformers, amateur scientists, and nervous crackpots all had their say. Eugenics was still in its infancy, a science without thoroughly verifiable tenets or adequate gatekeepers.[68] This pliability, combined with a healthy public appetite for advice bearing the seal of science, encouraged nonscientists to link their work to eugenics. The language of linkage was often religious. Few of these amateurs had even a rudimentary understanding of the science that lay behind eugenics, but, like Saleeby and Hall, they saw many points at which eugenics and religion overlapped. In their accounts, written for the same market that found domestic advice books appealing, Bible stories became the basis for eugenic lessons.

Two of the eugenics movement's earliest amateur enthusiasts were Mr.

and Mrs. John Williams Gibson, authors of a 1903 book, *Social Purity*. What little is known about this husband-and-wife writing team suggests that they might have made a living peddling tomes about modern "science" packaged in the fusty yet familiar trappings of the advice manual; another title in their oeuvre was *Golden Thoughts on Chastity and Procreation*.[69] The Gibsons dedicated their book to "all who would bring into the world beautiful and healthy children"; their dogged refrain: "It is the right of every child to be well born." Yet if heredity's power was inescapable, so was God's. The Gibsons argued that the Creator's help was required if society hoped to attain social purity. After "a long-waged and desperate battle, supplemented by God's grace, the most potent factor," they wrote, the world would witness the end of degeneracy. For the Gibsons, religious conviction and eugenic sentiment formed a formidable duo.[70]

Like many amateur popularizers in this period, the Gibsons did not limit themselves to discussing eugenics; theirs was a more ambitious treatise on "sexual life" meant to provide readers with a broad range of valuable and, they hinted, previously unknown information about parenting, "the life of the home," and related subjects. They wrote in a didactic yet folksy style borrowed from earlier generations of domestic advice books, kept their science simple, and leavened their discussions of heredity with friendly suggestions about pregnancy, personal hygiene, and nutrition. Although familiar with the work of Francis Galton, whom they cited, the Gibsons avoided using complicated scientific language. Knowing that their target audience was not scientifically trained, they explained heredity in terms their readers would understand; they avoided the language of the laboratory and instead mined the Bible for revelation.

The Old Testament was the primary source of the Gibsons' inspiration, and after combing the Pentateuch, they found suitable material in the book of Exodus. Two edifying dramas emerged. The first was the compelling account of the Israelites' departure from bondage in Egypt, with Moses playing a leading role as the vigorous patriarch, the man chosen by God to deliver an important and timeless message about heredity. In the Gibsons' telling, while Moses was atop Mt. Sinai awaiting the Ten Commandments, he was also contemplating the force of heredity. God's dramatic dictum that He would visit "the iniquity of the fathers upon the children, and upon the children's children, unto the third and to the fourth generation," was unequivocal, biblical proof of the process of hereditary.[71]

The second lesson of Exodus was a warning for the fate of nations. For the Gibsons, a society that fouled its hereditary pool risked fulfilling the biblical prophecy that "the kingdom of God shall be taken from you and given to a nation bringing forth fruits thereof." They urged their readers to heed the unfortunate example of contemporary France, a nation whose citizens had "sinned away" their strong physiques, relegating the old "splendid type of

French manhood" to the dustbin of history. Not wanting to offend readers' sensibilities, the Gibsons offered few details as to how, precisely, the French had weakened their human stock (there were hints that venereal disease might be a culprit), but they predicted that Americans would suffer a similar fate unless they armed themselves with knowledge of heredity.[72]

In their retelling of Bible stories as parables of heredity, the Gibsons showed their readers that the laws of heredity had a historical—even an ancient—pedigree. They also made heredity familiar by linking it to something with which their readers were conversant, the Bible. The Gibsons' invocation of Scripture was not merely instrumental; they demonstrated sincere religious conviction throughout their work. They credited Jesus Christ, the "Great Teacher," with inspiring them to write the book, and were moved to action by the biblical directive "And ye shall know the truth, and the truth shall make you free."[73] This message, and the sense of religious purpose with which it was infused, found a ready audience among the consumers of Progressive Era advice manuals; the Gibsons' book went through many printings.

The Gibsons were not the only writers of the period to invoke Moses and the Old Testament God to bolster their arguments about heredity. The publication of their book coincided with the release of another, *Control of Heredity*. Subtitled *A Study of the Genesis and Evolution of Degeneracy* and written by Casper Lavater Redfield, the book argued that God had given human beings a new knowledge of heredity that must be used to right the wrongs committed by the human race. In the practical, can-do spirit of the engineer and inventor that he was, Redfield argued that "vicious or defective heredity" was not a mysterious dispensation. Rather, it was "the product of natural laws operating along certain prescribed lines" that humans could understand and control.[74]

Like the Gibsons, Redfield suggested that scientists had not developed these laws without assistance. Their discovery was part of a centuries-long process whereby God revealed His knowledge to mankind. Also like the Gibsons, Redfield fastened on Moses as one of the earliest students of God's hereditary lessons. The frontispiece of his book featured a reproduction of Michelangelo's imposing statue of Moses, the prophet's stern marble gaze likely meant to have a sobering effect on the reader. "In Moses," Redfield wrote, humanity had "an intellect surpassing anything that the world has ever seen." Not only had he organized the exodus of the Israelites from bondage in Egypt (a marvelous story of organizational efficiency, as Redfield told it), but in the process he had crafted the Mosaic laws, "the finest adaptation of morality to existing circumstances ever known."[75] These laws incorporated many of the lessons that eugenicists were now reteaching the public. The Old Testament thus provided ample evidence of the enduring power of heredity.

Neither the Gibsons nor Redfield offered serious, practical proposals for combating hereditary problems. Instead, they made readers familiar with the subject of eugenics, warned them of the growing problem of degeneracy, and encouraged the spread of further information. Their success in doing so came, in part, by wrapping their arguments in the respectable and familiar cloak of religion.

Not everyone appreciated their efforts. Eugenicists fretted over how to pursue an intelligent educational campaign while the public received a regular bombardment of silly theories and comforting Bible stories masquerading as eugenic science.[76] Even the eugenicists' emphasis on "well-born" children opened a Pandora's box. These years witnessed the creation of a eugenics subliterature devoted to the molding of good parents who would, presumably, bear and rear eugenically healthy children. Few of the authors of these tracts had scientific training, and eugenicists such as Davenport worried that although their intentions were good, these authors were presenting a distorted and misleading view of eugenics to the public.[77]

Like the Gibsons' and Redfield's amateur surveys of heredity, many of these child-rearing manuals were explicitly Christian in tone. The advice they offered linked children's spiritual and physical development to their obedience to both biblical teachings and the laws of heredity. In 1910, the American Baptist Publication Society, under the editorship of Social Gospel stalwart Rev. Shailer Mathews, published *The Child in the Normal Home* by A. L. McCrimmon. A professor at McMaster University in Toronto, McCrimmon instructed parents on how best to raise a healthy, God-fearing child—with the key to success identified as cultivation of a "normal" home. Employing the rhetoric of the Social Gospel, McCrimmon described this ideal abode of normalcy, this building block of society, as a miniature "Kingdom of God" through which "the character of civilization is largely determined." The child was central to this kingdom, in McCrimmon's view, for "upon him the future of the race depends."[78]

For McCrimmon, the future of the race was a concern both religious and scientific. Citing Galton, he reminded parents that interest in their child's spiritual welfare meant little if it was not joined by an understanding that we are all "dependent upon the forces of the biological world, and subject to its laws." Good parents had a duty to educate themselves about heredity so that they could produce "offspring who will understand aright its duty to God."[79] The cycle, when it operated successfully, was mutually reinforcing and linked the spiritual and physical responsibilities of parenthood.

Another widely sold child-rearing manual in this period, *Eugenics*, had as its slightly lurid subtitle *Nature's Secrets Revealed; Scientific Knowledge of the Laws of Sex Life and Heredity*. The author was a physician, W. J. Truitt, but the text included contributions from several unnamed "noted specialists" and bore the mark of authorship by committee. It contained an eclectic mix of material: detailed drawings of the male and female reproductive systems; advice on courtship; discussions of menopause and nutrition, the ethics of the unmarried, and the vagaries of twilight sleep; numerous photographs of cheerful women cavorting with their cherubic infants; and almost nothing specifically about the science of eugenics. A book titled *Eugenics*, the word emblazoned in fancy gold lettering across the top half of the cover, that nevertheless lacked any meaningful discussion of the subject suggests that even at this early stage of the movement, eugenics had significant popular appeal. Authors and publishers evidently believed that the novelty of the subject would attract readers, and so deployed the term indiscriminately.

Eugenics lacked specifics about science, but it did bear the stamp of religious approval in its introduction, written by Reform Episcopal Bishop Samuel Fallows. He did not employ the word "eugenics" explicitly, but Bishop Fallows's rhetoric, which warned of the dangers of feeblemindedness, was eugenic in tone and implication: "Our jails and penitentiaries and reformatories and insane asylums and institutions for the feeble-minded are filled with inmates who began the course thither because of their dense ignorance of the laws of their physical organisms." *Eugenics*, he said, was a weapon against such ignorance and a much needed reminder that "the destinies of the future race are held by the young men and women of today."[80] Child-rearing literature of this sort, with its religious overtones and sweeping recommendations, had its roots in late nineteenth-century purity crusades. Purity crusaders urged parents to be "co-workers with God" in the development of "little pilgrims"; descriptions of "well-born children" dominated the pages of their tracts. Authors ordered mothers to educate themselves about "pre-natal influences," physical nurturing, and, most important, "moral growth." The eugenic subcurrents in many of these child-rearing manuals helped prepare readers for more explicitly eugenic arguments in the future. Americans seamlessly incorporated eugenic science into this long-standing pursuit of well-born children.[81]

Eugenic child-rearing manuals were also the natural outgrowth of what historian Christopher Lasch has dubbed the "helping professions." New fields such as domestic science and home economics, as well as social work and psychiatry, altered the internal dimensions of the American family by encouraging parents to rely increasingly on outside, expert advice. Workers in these professions latched onto the degenerating quality of the family as a new source for the nation's social pathologies. Although many of these books focused on environmental factors (such as good hygiene, pure milk, and nutrition), treatises on heredity, especially the watered-down positive eugenic proposals meant to encourage the readers of advice manuals to reproduce, fit well in this context.[82]

It was the "popular" appeal of this new advice literature that concerned eugenicists such as Charles Davenport. He was horrified to find authors interspersing their "eugenic" advice with warnings to mothers about the dangers of "mollycoddling" their little boys. Even more worrisome was the fact that eugenicists were gaining allies from the radical fringe of the progressive movement, the sex reformers. These men and women celebrated a "new morality" that endorsed birth control and divorce, challenged prevailing sexual ethics, and even urged the abolition of some of society's bedrock institutions, including monogamous marriage.[83] They posed a significant challenge to eugenicists who were trying to gain credibility and security for their fledgling movement, and they likely succeeded in making eugenicists even more wary of welcoming nonscientists (including religious leaders) to their cause.

One of the noisiest of these sex reformers was Moses Harman, whose long, unruly white beard, zealot's stare, and apocalyptic rhetoric graced the front page of many of his publications (suggesting that he aspired to live up to his prophetic Old Testament namesake). The history of Harman's early life is sketchy, but by the time he reached his late fifties, he was fascinated by eugenics, making it a frequent theme of articles in the Chicago-based periodical he edited and published, *Lucifer the Light-Bearer* (1885–1906). This hodgepodge of reprinted articles, letters, and opinion pieces had as its main theme the destructiveness of the institution of marriage—or "sex slavery," as Harman preferred to call it.

Harman's avowed purpose in publishing *Lucifer* was the "lofty impulse to free woman from the sex slavery to which she is doomed by unjust marriage laws"; he believed that Church and State had conspired to limit women's ability to exercise full sexual freedom. He also linked his opposition to marriage to the problem of race improvement, arguing that once the restrictive institution was abolished, "maternity will always be honorable and no more innocent children will be called 'illegitimate,' 'bastards,' and a maimed, diseased, and crippled race will be succeeded by a race of noblemen."[84] Without the stifling institution of marriage to hamper them, Harman reasoned, men and women instinctively would choose the best mates—a free-love form of eugenics, if you will.

Harman soon ran into trouble with sections of the Federal Criminal Code dealing with the mailing of "obscene, lewd, or lascivious" materials,[85] but despite numerous warnings from the superintendent of second-class mails in Chicago, he continued publishing articles advancing his radical sex theories. Aphorisms such as "A woman who would not permit church and state to limit her love to one child, should not permit them to limit her love to one man," did not gain him allies among postal censors, and in 1906 he felt the sting of the Federal Criminal Code personally.[86] Prosecutors confiscated his journal and Harman served a short sentence in the federal prison near Leavenworth, Kansas, for publishing obscene materials. He emerged unrepentant, and soon after his release created a new forum to promote his cause. Whether he intended to bring the respectability of science to his new publishing venture or simply avoid the taint of the confiscated journal's title, in 1907, Harman (by then in his seventies) launched a new periodical called the *American Journal of Eugenics*.

Harman's eugenics bore little resemblance to the science of Galton. In fact, the use of "eugenics" in the journal's title appears to have been a device to lure readers (or lend authority) to Harman's continuing cause of ending marriage and challenging conventional sexual mores. He published few serious scientific discussions of heredity. Yet, like other amateur students of heredity, he sought support for his brand of eugenics in the Bible. Harman personally demonstrated only disdain for organized religion, viewing the churches as complicit in the attempt to stifle free love. Nevertheless, he included articles and supportive statements from ministers. In one issue, he published a lengthy essay outlining suggestions for a "Christian eugenics"; in another, a reader wrote of the need to see Jesus as a eugenic figure. "Not until Jesus is looked upon as a student of the science of eugenics will the world regard him as a genius, instead of a god or a myth," the correspondent wrote. "It is well to consider him the father, if not the founder, of the science."[87] Thus it was in the pages of a fairly obscure free-love journal that Jesus first emerges as a eugenic hero.

Although amateur eugenicists such as the Gibsons, Redfield, Mc-Crimmon, and Harman distorted or simply ignored the science behind eugenics, they were important contributors to the eugenics movement in its early years. They brought eugenics, albeit a bastardized version, to the public's attention in a way that Davenport and his fellow scientists did not, and eugenics would enter the public's vocabulary as much through this informal route as through the formal bulletins issued by Davenport and his colleagues at Cold Spring Harbor.

Such nonscientific presentations of eugenics were vital in influencing both mass culture and eugenicists themselves.[88] The proliferation of eugenics books by amateurs led some supporters of the movement to criticize scientists such as Davenport, blaming their cautious approach to eugenics for the steady stream of unscientific and misleading books and articles. If the experts would not discuss the subject in terms the public could understand, these critics said, then amateurs would fill the void. One supporter of eugenics expressed a prevalent fear when he predicted that eugenicists' caution "left the larger number of readers to receive the prophecy of eugenics indirectly, through unauthoritative writings of advocates whom Galton would hardly have wished as allies."[89] In this way the amateurs might have encouraged eugenicists to pursue public opinion more vigorously, in the belief that by doing so, they would prevent the spread of misinformation.

The Bible provided amateur promoters with their most comfortable and appealing cultural metaphors, and organized religion, through its centuries-long regulation of marriage, was given its due as an important force for preserving the health of the family and the nation. Amateur popularizers wanted the authority of science reflected in their work, but they used religious themes and stories to make this new science more familiar, and perhaps to assure their readers of the noble intentions of eugenics. The testing of these noble intentions was left to another group, the Catholic clergy.

It was perfectly obvious in the early years of the movement that eugenicists harbored suspicions about organized religion's willingness to bring its traditional practices into line with the teachings of their new science. Catholic clerical celibacy was perhaps the most frequently cited example of such premodern intransigence. In a paper read before a London audience and later reprinted in the U.S. periodical *Current Literature,* Francis Galton decried this practice the Catholic Church required of its priests and nuns.

Beginning in the Middle Ages, Galton said, the Church lured into its sanctuaries the gentle-natured men and women of Europe, often the sons and daughters of inconveniently large families. These men and women tended toward meditation, literature, or art and were on the whole moderately tempered. Yet, as a result of their celibacy, Galton argued, society would not see their traits passed on to future generations. In essence, "the Church drained off the cream" of society, leaving a rude residue behind to produce the next generation. In this way, "the Church brutalized the breed of our forefathers," practicing the arts that breeders would use if their aim were to create animals with "currish and stupid natures." European society, suffering from a dearth of the mild-mannered, lapsed into "ferocity." In a eugenic world, Galton said, monasteries would still exist, but they would be places "where the weak would find a refuge and a welcome" and where, presumably, their degenerate traits would die with them.[90]

U.S. eugenicists picked up on this theme in their work, though usually not in language as censorious as Galton's. A contributor to *Popular Science Monthly* suggested that some of the best specimens of the human race had been destroyed in times past by "religious intolerance." Though he did not name the Catholic Church specifically, this scientist blamed religious celibacy for a "decay of religious spirit" and, like Galton, concluded that such practices would lead to a race of men and women devoid of compassion and religious sense.[91] For eugenicists, celibacy (like Christian charity) was just one of the startlingly dysgenic practices that the churches encouraged. The normalcy and long-standing history of these practices, which bred nonchalance about them among the public, to the eugenicists' eyes presented a serious obstacle to the creation of a better human race.

While Protestants centered their debates around the issue of Christian charity, and popularizers heralded Moses as proto-eugenic biblical patriarch, Catholics focused their analyses on the eugenics movement's early methods, particularly sterilization. Catholic discussions of eugenics were different in tone than those of their Protestant counterparts, in part because eugenicists had already settled into the habit of singling out the Catholic Church for special criticism. The enthusiasm with which eugenicists denounced the rule of clerical celibacy prompted one Catholic priest to note defensively that the "strong and intelligent parents" of earlier ages "did not send *all* of their children into the cloister."[92] Moreover, in Britain in particular, fears about the differential birthrate often expressed themselves in subtle and not so subtle condemnations of the high fertility of working-class Catholics. Fabian socialist and eugenics supporter Sidney Webb noted with alarm that "children are being freely born to the Irish Roman Catholics" and that "this can hardly result in anything but national deterioration." Oblique references to the fecundity of Catholics also found their way into U.S. eugenics treatises.[93] The existence of such sentiments among eugenicists meant that Catholics who chose to discuss the eugenics movement were obliged to devote some of their time to a defense of the Church.

Catholic leaders had their own grievances with eugenics. Several Catholics writing in the earliest years of the eugenics movement criticized eugenicists for their overhasty applications of their new science, in many cases echoing the concerns of Protestant leaders such as Rev. J. H. F. Peile. The difference was the degree of caution called for by Catholics; it was much greater than that of Protestants and was in the main a reaction to a eugenic measure whose popularity was gradually growing in the country: sterilization. Catholic critiques of sterilization went to the heart of one of the central debates that emerged during the early years of the eugenics movement: the effectiveness of negative versus positive eugenic measures. Would society be better served by preventing the unfit from reproducing (negative eugenics) or by encouraging the fit to have more children (positive eugenics)?

Beginning in the 1840s and quickening in pace during the late nineteenth century, Americans built institutions dedicated solely to the care of the feebleminded. These state-supported "villages" and "colonies" were intended initially to segregate the feebleminded from the rest of the population, thus protecting society from men and women whose weak-mindedness might lead to criminal activities. They also, presumably, protected the feebleminded from the dangers of the outside world. This was a mild form of negative eugenics, as the superintendents of these facilities could discourage, but not lawfully prevent, the institutionalized inmates from having children.[94]

A combination of circumstances, including growing public concern over the cost of institutionalization, widely read studies of degenerate families such as Dugdale's *The Jukes* and McCulloch's *The Ishmaelites*, and advances in the surgical procedures for sterilization that made the operation safer, contributed to a shift in public attitudes about negative eugenic measures. Rev. McCulloch's home state of Indiana became the first in the nation to act on this change when, in 1907, its legislature passed a law "to prevent procreation of confirmed criminals, idiots, imbeciles, and rapists." The act stated plainly that "heredity plays a most important part in the transmission of crime, idiocy, and imbecility" and it applied to any of the above who were housed in state institutions and whose "condition had been determined to be 'unimprovable' by an appointed panel of physicians."[95] Other states, including Connecticut, Oregon, and California, soon followed with their own laws, though few of them were rigorously enforced.

Nevertheless, for Catholics, these legislative endorsements of sterilization were both a disturbing portent of future dangers and a practical problem of moral theology. In a series of articles published between 1910 and 1913 in the *Ecclesiastical Review*, Catholic leaders debated the "morality and lawfulness" of sterilization as it applied to convicted criminals. The discussants focused particularly on vasectomy, the procedure that severs the vas deferens in men, rendering them sterile (in 1897, Dr. A. J. Ochsner, a Chicago surgeon, was the first person to perform a vasectomy, and the practice quickly replaced castration as the preferred male sterilization technique because doctors could perform it without general anesthesia or substantial risk to the patient's life).[96]

Two Catholic writers emerged as supporters of punitive sterilization in the *Ecclesiastical Review* debate: Fr. Stephen M. Donovan, a professor at the Franciscan House of Studies connected with the Catholic University of America, and Theo. Laboure, O.M.I., a professor in the Diocesan Seminary in San Antonio, Texas. The most notable element of Donovan's and Laboure's stance was that they argued from the premise that heredity was *the* crucial factor in transmitting insane and criminal traits from one generation to the next. Citing contemporary statistics, they contended that the number of criminal and insane people in the United States was rising rapidly, posing a threat to society. In the interest of protecting society, they said, the state had the right to employ any means that were not immoral to check this spread. "Vasectomy is not only *not* intrinsically wrong," Laboure wrote, "but it is morally necessary for the protection of the body social against degenerate criminals."[97]

The second element of Donovan's and Laboure's argument engaged the question of whether vasectomy violated Catholic teaching regarding "grave mutilation" of the body. Citing the procedure's relative painlessness and brevity, they concluded that it did not. In fact, they offered anecdotal evidence that vasectomy produced "moral reform" in criminal individuals by fortifying their will power to resist sexual temptation and curbing their tendency to masturbate.[98] Donovan and Laboure mapped out for their fellow clergymen what they believed was a compelling argument for Catholic support for sterilization.

Opposition to this position emerged quickly and was led by Msgr. Jules DeBecker, rector of the American College at Louvain University and a professor of canon law. The salient point of DeBecker's opposition was the belief enshrined in Catholic moral law that "it is never lawful to do evil in order that good may result therefrom." Though he did admit that degeneracy was a problem and that the state's goal of eliminating it was a noble one, DeBecker rejected Donovan's and Laboure's argument that heredity was its primary cause. He claimed that heredity was merely one of many influences on human development; environmental factors, he suggested, loomed larger than those that were inborn. For DeBecker, this meant that sterilization legislation, no matter how noble its intentions, was morally misguided and incapable of totally eliminating crime and degeneracy.[99]

Msgr. DeBecker also disputed Donovan's and Laboure's second claim, that vasectomy was not a "grave mutilation" of the human body. He cited studies showing that the procedure could cause impotence. Because impotence was a serious impediment to a man's ability to contract marriage, DeBecker reasoned that the state could not impose vasectomy—even in the interests of protecting society from criminals—because man's spiritual right to marry was superior to the right of society to protect itself by legislating sterilization. Catholic teaching decreed that inferior rights must always yield to higher rights; thus, a surgical procedure such as vasectomy, which involved a "notable mutilation" but was not necessary for the conservation of life, was contrary to Catholic moral law. DeBecker linked this argument to the idea that the state could not impose as severe a punishment as sterilization until it had exhausted every other means at its disposal to deal with the problem of degeneracy. Anything less would be immoral.[100]

Other Catholic writers voiced similar concerns about the encroachment of state power. If sterilization laws proliferated, one critic hypothesized, "legislation would thus be degraded to a system of human breeding and natural selection as applied to animals in a stockfarm," opening the way to excesses.[101] Another Catholic writer argued that the function of the state was not to act as a "meddling busybody," but to protect the rights of men. Those "drivelers of social uplift," "underdone scientists," and "wry-brained politicians" who advocated sterilization pursued a policy that many Catholics believed had a "great influence for evil."[102]

Clear doctrinal differences existed between Catholic supporters and Catholic opponents of sterilization, but it is noteworthy that both camps accepted one of the underlying premises of the eugenics movement: "As for the good result intended, namely the prevention of hereditary disease, all will agree that it is desirable in itself."[103] None of the participants in this sterilization debate expressed qualms about the state's obligation and the Church's duty to protect society from the criminal degeneration of the race. They merely disagreed on what form that protection should take.[104] Nevertheless, Donovan and Laboure remained exceptions in the debate; the majority of Catholic clerics opposed sterilization.

The debate over the merits and evils of vasectomy would not be resolved to either side's satisfaction at this time, in part because vasectomy was a recent medical procedure and definitive proof of its long-term effects on men's sexual function did not yet exist. However, the *Ecclesiastical Review* debate did generate wider interest in eugenics among the Catholic clergy, paving the way for the publication of the first book-length Catholic treatment of the subject a short time later.

In 1912, Father Thomas Gerrard, a British priest and widely known author, published a lengthy examination of the relationship between the Catholic Church and eugenics. Although Gerrard, too, was concerned with potential misapplications of eugenic science, he took up a different problem in his work, one that several of his Protestant contemporaries already had raised: Eugenics neglected man's spiritual needs. As long as it continued to do so, Gerrard warned, it would remain an enervate science, incapable of succeeding in its quest for race improvement.

In an earlier essay, Gerrard had agreed with the eugenics movement's diagnosis of social problems: "To allow the feebles unrestrained liberty would appear to be a menace to the freedom of the community." Yet, he warned, "to subject them to all the remedies proposed would seem to be an unnecessary violation of their rights, and perhaps an infliction of unwarranted cruelty." Gerrard called for caution: "We must move warily and scientifically."[105] He was careful to point out that caution did not mean the wholesale rejection of eugenics. "In the modern eugenic movement there is much which is opposed to Catholic principles," he conceded. "But at the same time there is much in it which is in harmony with Catholic principles, and indeed highly conducive to the end for which the Church exists."[106] He did not specify what that common end was, but one can surmise from his work that it was similar to the end debated by participants in the *Ecclesiastical Review* exchange, namely, the worthiness of eliminating disease, criminal degeneracy, and human suffering.

Having noted the similarity of purpose eugenics shared with the Church, Gerrard focused on the significant differences that still divided the two. From the perspective of a religious leader, the eugenicists' pursuit of "fitness" emphasized physical and mental characteristics to the exclusion of moral and ethical ones. Gerrard's claim, like that of Protestant minister F. B. Meyer, was somewhat self-congratulatory, for it was an implicit criticism of eugenicists' obvious oversight. The Catholic Church taught that man was a spiritual as well as a physical creature, Gerrard said, possessed of an eternal and sacred soul. In this context, physical perfection was but a means to an end. The end "is another world, and this world is but a preparation for it." Reconfiguring a passage from Jesus' Sermon on the Mount, Gerrard wrote, "We have to seek first the kingdom of the spirit and then all the riches of the psychic and physical kingdoms are added unto us to aid us in our quest."[107]

For Gerrard, a true eugenics was one that recognized humans' essentially spiritual nature, their need for adequate *spiritual* forces to impel them to act on their *physical* conditions. Although a criticism of eugenicists' mission, Gerrard's eugenic ideal was of a less verifiable provenance. He did not deny the importance of physical health, but he believed that it and all other accomplishments "must be subordinated to the one supreme accomplishment, eminence in sanctity" and a "genius in morality" that sprung from man's ineffable, spiritual nature.[108]

Gerrard's attention to spiritual factors in man's eugenic development had an important practical implication. Like his Protestant counterpart, Rev. Meyer, Gerrard argued that the only force powerful enough to convince men of the need to live eugenically was a spiritual force, and the Catholic Church had at her "very essence and existence" a desire to "put the human will in the right direction" and to keep it there.[109] The Catholic Church was a powerful force for race improvement—more powerful, in fact, than that of Meyer's Anglican order. Gerrard argued that the "new discoveries" of science were nothing of the sort; rather, they were historic, essential Catholic teachings recast in the language of the laboratory.[110] The Catholic catechism, for example, taught "holy purity in looks, words, and actions"; the Church also followed—or presaged— Galton's recommendations for rational selection in marriage. The Church "promotes it and controls it more effectively than any other organisation on earth," Gerrard argued, by teaching that marriage was a sacrament.[111]

Not surprisingly, Gerrard's construction of a Catholic eugenics encouraged him to look within the Church for examples of superior human development. He found them in the lives of the saints. "In every age in the past," he wrote, "it is Catholicism which has produced the most and the greatest of the real supermen, the experts in moral excellence." In a 1912 essay for *Catholic World*, he argued that the men and women canonized by the Church were "the true regenerators of the race" and offered several examples of the "eugenic functions of the saints."[112]

To contemporary eyes, Gerrard's promotion of the Catholic Church and its saints as eugenic appears radical, even bizarre. But his tack was inherently conservative. By drawing on Catholic tradition to justify his measured support for eugenics, as opposed to crafting an entirely new theological argument to support it, Gerrard was in keeping with the tenor of his Church in the early 1910s. Writing in the wake of the Vatican's condemnations of "Americanism" in 1899 and "Modernism" in 1907, movements that had proposed significant alterations to existing theology, Gerrard adopted a more cautious approach, one that declined to stir the theological waters but instead pointed out, in quietly radical fashion, that eugenic solutions were nothing novel when compared to the historic teachings of the Catholic Church.[113]

Gerrard's Catholic eugenics was not greeted in a spirit of catholicity by eugenicists. A brief review of *The Church and Eugenics* in the British periodical *Eugenics Review* barely contained its disdain for the work, noting at one point that "the boldness of this amazing argument amply compensates for the thinness of its logic." The reviewer took special issue with Gerrard's claims about clerical celibacy. The "heroic attempt to defend the Church's practice of celibacy as 'the best possible thing for race culture'" rested on no evidence, the reviewer stated. His tongue-in-cheek conclusion was that the book, "of course, settles, it. Eugenics is dead."[114] Other eugenicists were less harsh in their judgments of Catholic critics, although they still found fault with the Church. A contributor to *Eugenics Review* urged the Catholic clergy to "utilise its two Sacraments of Confirmation and Marriage for their true purpose, namely, in the interest of an idealism which recognises the responsibility laid upon the present by the future." The writer assumed that clerics lacked the access to scientific knowledge that would allow them to become "a most important agent of selection in marriage" and blamed a benighted hierarchy for denying too many of its priests this education in modern science. While critical of the Catholic Church, the writer nonetheless seemed confident that, once Church leaders gained a modicum of knowledge about heredity, they would act in accordance with eugenic teachings.[115]

On the whole, eugenicists' reactions to religious assessments and critiques of their science were muted during these early years. When they did attempt to answer the questions raised by religious leaders, they did so defensively, citing Galton's 1904 essay, "Eugenics: Its Definition, Scope, and Aims," as proof that the eugenics movement should not become involved in debates over morality. In that essay, Galton urged eugenicists to "leave morals as far as possible out of the discussion, not entangling ourselves with the almost hopeless difficulties they raise as to whether a character as a whole is good or bad."[116]

A few eugenicists ignored their founder's advice and began to tap the movement's potential appeal to religious leaders. In a series of lectures on eugenics delivered at Oberlin College in 1910, eugenicist William E. Kellicott noted, "The Church could easily become a powerful factor in eugenic practice." Biologist John M. Coulter of the University of Chicago, writing in the journal *Religious Education* in 1911, argued that science and religion had much in common. "Both seek to produce better men physically and morally," he said, and although "it is sometimes thought that biology looks to the physical man alone, and religion to the moral man alone," both were now "weaving threads into the same texture."[117] That texture was growing ever thicker. Francis Galton died in 1911; by that time his science had secured enough of a foothold in the United States for one observer to claim that eugenics had "established its claim to recognition."[118]

Religious leaders underwent a more marked reorientiation in these years, as they began to understand just how far eugenicists intended to reach into their realm. When charity and child rearing, activities once understood to be under Christian influence, became "scientific," priests and ministers found themselves pressured to give way to eugenicists who had little obvious interest in engaging spiritual concerns. But religious leaders were not ready to leave the task of human improvement solely to science. As Fr. Thomas Gerrard argued, the eugenicist "above all things, professes to deal with the very fountains of good and evil."[119] Modest protestations notwithstanding, religious leaders viewed themselves as the most important tenders of those fountains. The terrestrial concerns of science would not overwhelm the need for their guidance in matters celestial.

2

Certifying Eugenic Purity in the Churches

Defraud ye not one the other.

—I Corinthians 7:5

It was not unheard of in 1912 for a wedding announcement to grace the front page of the *New York Times*, but it was unusual for a humble police telegraph operator and his bride to be the objects of such attention. On the evening of 11 April 1912, Albertus W. Bode married Ruth Palmer in the Protestant Episcopal Cathedral of Saints Peter and Paul in Chicago. It was the dean of the Cathedral who sparked controversy over their union and generated headlines. Less than one month before the couple exchanged vows, the Very Rev. Walter Taylor Sumner decreed that, beginning at Easter, no couple could be married in the church without first presenting a "certificate of health" from a reputable physician. Ruth Palmer and Albertus Bode were the first couple to comply with this new church regulation.[1]

The eugenic intentions of Dean Sumner's decree were clear. Prospective couples had to pass the inspection of a physician who could attest that they were "normal physically and mentally, and have neither an incurable nor communicable disease." No longer could he rely on civil authorities to monitor a man's fitness for marriage, Sumner said, noting the appalling ease with which even the most diseased and feebleminded person could acquire a marriage license. In Chicago, "all the man has to do is to visit the office of the clerk, and poke through the window a slip of paper with the name of a female written alongside his own." By adding to this meager

FIGURE 2.1 Rev. Walter Taylor Sumner, dean of the Cathedral of SS Peter and Paul in Chicago. Records of the Redpath Chautauqua, Special Collections Department, University of Iowa Libraries, Iowa City, Iowa.

municipal function the requirement of a health exam, "We will make the [marriage] certificate issued by the cathedral stand from this time on for absolute purity," he said.[2]

That a traditional arbiter of marriage was moved to take such an unconventional public stand in its defense suggests the extent to which the clergy felt the institution in jeopardy. That Dean Sumner and many of his fellow churchmen chose eugenics as their buttress reveals how quickly liberal religious leaders moderated their theologies to fit the tenor of the times. Sumner's activities were the logical outgrowth of his church's pursuit of social reform—a pursuit amenable to race improvement as much as to traditional revival. It was also indicative of the growing popularity and scope of eugenics; Sumner and his ilk collapsed under the rubric "social evil" their many fears about changing mores, venereal disease, and the challenges associated with urban growth, and turned to eugenics as their solution.

Walter Taylor Sumner was born in New Hampshire in 1873. After graduating from Dartmouth College in 1898, he headed for Chicago, where he went to work for the Western Electric Company, sharing "bachelor's quarters" with a dozen other young men. Almost immediately, he threw himself into the city's web of social reform organizations, and in time met and gained the respect of Jane Addams at Hull House, who recommended him to the dean of Chicago's Protestant Episcopal Cathedral. Sumner's enthusiasm and skill so impressed the city's Episcopal leadership that they offered to sponsor his theological training if he had even a glimmer of interest in the ministry. He did, reasoning that he could best fulfill his reforming zeal in the church. He graduated from Chicago's Western Theological Seminary in 1904 and soon became secretary to Bishop Charles P. Anderson of the Chicago Diocese. His rise through the church leadership was rapid; by 1906 he was dean of the Cathedral of Saints Peter and Paul in Chicago.[3]

From the beginning of his clerical career, Sumner made social reform his priority. The city of Chicago was a good proving ground for this impulse. One of the fastest-growing urban areas in the United States during the late nineteenth century and a center for railroads, stockyards, and other industry, Chicago was a hotbed of Progressive Era reform activities. The city served as the political backdrop for William Jennings Bryan's 1896 "Cross of Gold" speech at the Democratic Convention and the cultural landscape for Upton Sinclair's 1905 novel about the stockyards, *The Jungle*. Sumner's own reform efforts included continued work with Hull House, six years on the Chicago Board of Education, and numerous hours devoted to the Juvenile Protective Association, the United Charities, and the Wendell Phillips Social Settlement for Colored Persons. One historian of the Chicago diocese later claimed, "Never before had any of our clergy risen to such prominence and usefulness in the public life of our great city."[4]

Small of stature (he was called, affectionately, "the little father" by local bartenders), Sumner had an earnest, kindly countenance and wore his thinning hair smoothed back neatly from his high forehead. His unassuming appearance belied his reputation as a rousing speaker. One newspaper described him as "young, strong, perspicacious," and another dubbed him an "ecclesiastical Rock of Gibraltar" amid the city's "seething sea of evil." Sumner navigated that sea well. The *Chicago Tribune* recounted one yuletide pilgrimage made by the dean to the "darkest places" of Chicago's West Side, where he moved the assembled audience of prostitutes to paroxysms of emotion: "Tears plowed furrows through the rouge and powder on the painted cheeks," the *Tribune* reported, and "one girl burst out sobbing as if her heart would break."[5]

Dean Sumner's interest in the city's prostitutes was practical, not prurient. In 1910, he urged the mayor of Chicago to appoint a Municipal Vice Commission to study the problem of the "social evil in Chicago," broadly defined to include prostitution, drug use, massage houses, Turkish baths, dance halls, venereal disease, and numerous other expressions of crime and avarice. The mayor agreed, Sumner was named chairman of the Commission, and in 1911 he and the other commissioners released a report, *The Social Evil in Chicago*, which drew nationwide praise from reformers for its vehement opposition to the segregation (and de facto toleration) of vice in certain city districts in Chicago. *Survey*, a magazine of social reform, called *The Social Evil in Chicago* an "epoch-making" report, whose "influence is being registered, far and wide, in other cities throughout the entire country and abroad."[6]

The report was in keeping with the moralizing tone of late nineteenth-century urban exposés such as William T. Stead's *If Christ Came to Chicago* (1894) and Edward Everett Hale's *If Jesus Came to Boston* (1894). New York City's Committee of Fifteen report on prostitution, *The Social Evil* (1902), and a 1907 portrait of Windy City immorality by George Kibbe Turner in *McClure's* magazine were similar in spirit. These studies were a departure from the previous generation's techniques of moral reform. In the mid–nineteenth century, members of the New York Moral Reform Society were known to station themselves outside the city's houses of ill-repute, where they would loudly recite Bible passages and serenade with hymns the hapless customers who crossed their path. By the late nineteenth and early twentieth century, reformers were indicting municipal rather than individual hypocrisy, issuing calls for vice control by professional morals managers—although their reports still retained a whiff of that old-fashioned voyeuristic seaminess. Worries about the erosion of old-fashioned courtship rituals contributed to the general sense of connubial decay. As the movie theater replaced the Chautauqua tent as the preferred venue for an evening's entertainment, especially among the younger set, tradition-minded Americans fretted over the implications. Marriage was the pivotal institution, its rites deemed a bulwark against the growing scourge of social evil.

The "social evil" was the star of secular as well as spiritual exposés in this period, as the arrival on Broadway in 1913 of French playwright Eugene Brieux's *Damaged Goods* attested. The play, a dysfunctional domestic tableau about syphilis, tweaked sensibilities about scientific solutions and moral responsibilities, and its popular reception suggested growing public interest in both. American novelist Winston Churchill published in serial form *The Inside of the Cup*, a story about the awakening of a young minister's social conscience and the effect this "modern Savonarola" has on his prosperously staid, urban congregation. The story implied that it was not unusual for men of the cloth to spearhead municipal vice crusades.[7]

But a jurisdictional battle was brewing. The morality-based efforts of the churches were giving way to the scientific, professional efforts of the physician.[8] Some observers applauded the shift to secular oversight, seeing in it the death knell of a hectoring, Victorian judgmentalism. Walter Lippmann attacked Dean Sumner's Vice Commission report as blind moralism rather than sound scientific management. "The commission did not face the sexual impulse squarely," Lippmann wrote in *A Preface to Politics*. "The report is an attempt to deal with a sexual problem by disregarding its source."[9] But, as Sumner's actions demonstrate, this shift did not entirely eliminate religious leaders from these reform campaigns. Sumner and the clerics who followed his example employed the tactics of modern, scientific reformers while still retaining the cultural and moral authority of their pulpits.

Sumner's eugenic health certificate decree, though boldly stated, was not made without forethought or vetting. He told the press that he took this step "only after months of study of the situation and deliberations as to its advisability." He discussed the proposition at length with his superior, Bishop Anderson, who gave his approval to the plan before Sumner's public announcement. Anderson's approval was no small thing. Having served as Protestant Episcopal bishop of Chicago since 1905, Anderson was a "forceful personality" who often spoke on social and economic themes at the Church's General Conventions. His opinion carried weight both within the church and without in the secular world of reform, and he was not known as a man to succumb to the whims of public opinion. When a wealthy parishioner who had taken offense at some of the bishop's economic arguments threatened to withdraw his financial contribution to the church, Anderson responded with a brief letter: "Dear Sir: Your money be damned. C. P. Anderson." The bishop's support gave Sumner's health certificate plan legitimacy.[10]

From his experience on the Chicago Vice Commission, Sumner had learned the value of publicizing his reform message, and with this in mind he made the second half of his health certificate announcement a plea for clergymen of all denominations and creeds to make their own commitments to eugenic marriages. "We do not expect to bring about great good at once by this plan of ours," he said, "but we are hopeful that, standing as a protest [against lax marriage laws], it may encourage other clergy to take a similar stand."[11] Like the physician in Brieux's play, who upbraids the legislator-patriarch for failing to attend to the scourge of venereal disease—and whose own daughter contracts syphilis from her ne'er-do-well mate as a result—Sumner urged the clergy to show lawmakers the costs of their laissez-faire attitude toward marriage.

Dean Sumner's fellow clergymen needed little encouragement. Reaction from other liberal religious leaders was swift and largely supportive, revealing the breadth of support for reforms bearing the imprint of science in American churches in the 1910s. To the extent that Sumner's plan met clerical resistance from his fellow liberal Protestants, it was largely due to disagreement over strategy, not goals.[12] Bishop Samuel Fallows, of the Reformed Episcopal Church, Chicago, agreed with Sumner that "there is a great need for some step in the direction of purifying the marriage ceremony," but he placed his faith in the state to achieve this.[13] Others were less equivocal. Rt. Rev. Cortlandt Whitehead, bishop of the Protestant Episcopal Church in Pittsburgh, said, "No degenerates or those physically unfit in other ways should be allowed to marry and the step taken by Dr. Sumner is in line with what should have been done years ago." Interest in the proposal was not confined to the churches. The *New York Times* solicited opinions from a broad range of religious leaders and published the results in a feature story that ran in June 1913.[14]

When offering his endorsement of Sumner's proposal, Rev. John Haynes Holmes, the well-known liberal reformer and Unitarian minister at New York's Church of the Messiah, argued, "Nothing is more important, to my mind, in our modern treatment of the question of marriage, than to use our powers of social control to prevent many people from marrying—those, namely, whose marriage, for one reason or another, can be nothing but a tragedy." Later that month, Holmes and several other members of the Liberal Ministers' Association in New York (a group of Unitarian and Universalist ministers and Reform rabbis) formed a Eugenics Committee to study the issue further. Holmes hoped the Committee would agree "to perform nothing but health marriages" in their churches and synagogues. "Dean Sumner and the Chicago Cathedral have shown us the way," he said. It was now the "moral responsibility" of the rest of the religious community to follow. Another prominent American clergyman, Rev. Russell H. Conwell of Grace Baptist Church in Philadelphia, declared, "The stand so bravely taken by Dean Sumner commands the respect of all who believe that the way to serve God is to serve one's fellow men." Conwell, famous nationwide for the "Acres of Diamonds" sermon he claimed to have delivered more than six thousand times, went on to urge cooperation among clergymen in furthering Sumner's project for health marriages.[15]

Health certificates also earned the attention, if not the wholesale approval, of Reform rabbis. Rabbi Emil G. Hirsch of Sinai Congregation, Chicago, well-known for his own liberal championing of social causes (many of which he promoted in the pages of his periodical, the *Reform Advocate*), reminded the public that "the spirit of Dean Sumner's regulation has been observed in Jewry from time immemorial" through the disciplined and serious approach to marriage taken by Jewish rabbis and Jewish parents. Without invoking the "jargon of eugenics," Hirsch said, rabbis had done and continued to do their part to prevent unwise marriages.[16] In Pittsburgh, Rabbi Rudolph Coffee of the Tree of Life Synagogue was more enthusiastic about Sumner's plan. Like Sumner,

Coffee was an urban antivice crusader and a member of his city's Morals Efficiency Commission. He urged clergy of all creeds to unite in "refusing to marry persons who cannot bring a certificate of good health" to validate their marriage vows. In 1913, Coffee and the Pittsburgh Morals Efficiency Commission lobbied the Pennsylvania legislature for enactment of health certificate legislation. The language of these eugenic antivice crusades transcended denominational and theological boundaries; Rabbi Coffee wrote that tackling the social evil had "done more to batter down theological fences" in his own Pittsburgh religious community than any other issue.[17]

Just two months after Sumner issued his decree, two hundred ministers of the Federated Churches of Chicago adopted a resolution formally endorsing the eugenic health certificate plan.[18] As one national periodical described the situation, Sumner's plan was "exciting nation-wide controversy."[19] It did spark considerable debate in the press: the New York Times featured a steady stream of stories and editorials about Sumner, including several lengthy forums culling religious and medical opinion of his proposal. Asked to explicate his views in one of these forums, Sumner did not shrink from emphasizing the eugenic purpose of his proposal: "We seek to protect the integrity, sanctity and future health of the home by joining in matrimony only those who are fit to propagate a normal race." Sumner's listeners responded to his tone: "Mawkish sentiment must unquestionably yield to the high issues involved in eugenics," declared Rev. George C. Peck of St. Andrew's Methodist Episcopal Church, New York.[20]

While rhetorical support for Sumner's plan was plentiful, so was practical action. Many ministers crafted eugenic health certificate requirements for their own churches. With the blessings of their congregations, two Montclair, New Jersey, ministers, Rev. Henry E. Jackson of the Christian Union Congregational Church and Rev. Edgar S. Weirs of the Unity Church, announced in May 1913 that they would perform no marriages without receiving eugenic health certificates from all potential grooms.[21] At the New Jersey Baptist Convention in 1913, Rev. Robert Chipman Hull of the First Baptist Church in Summit introduced a resolution, which the Convention promptly passed, that read: "The Baptists should be the pioneers in eugenics, as they have been in other movements for social reform. We therefore recommend to the Board of Managers of the New Jersey Baptist Convention that it urge all our churches to give to this matter most careful consideration, looking toward the eventual requirement of a physician's certificate of good health from all those applying for marriage licenses."[22]

Individual Protestant religious leaders organized local, ecumenical campaigns to convert their communities to health certificates. Rev. C. Thurston Chase of the Central Congregational Church in Lynn, Massachusetts, persuaded the Methodist, Baptist, Episcopal, and Congregationalist clergy in the city to refuse to marry couples who could not produce evidence of physical and mental fitness.[23] And in New York City, in what was said to be the "first official

action by the officers of a church in this country in practically applying eugenics
to marriage," the officers of the Fort Washington Reformed Church passed a
resolution requiring couples to present health certificates before marriage. The
minister of the church, Rev. Abraham J. Muste, declared himself pleased with
the church officers' action and "glad that this church has the honor of starting
a movement in this city that is sure to be widespread."[24]

So great was the accumulated evidence for liberal clergy's support for
health certificates that the *New York Times* anointed ministers and rabbis the
new leaders of the eugenics movement. "It is a notable fact," one editorialist
said, "that clergymen are the leaders in proving sincere belief in the principles
which have developed from the observations of the Galton school and the more
definite and accurate deductions of the Mendelians." Hardly a week passes,
the editorialist stated, that a prominent minister does not announce his intention to solemnize only eugenically healthy marriages in his church.[25] One reporter was more effusive, gushing, "Sir Francis Galton, could he return to the
world he left only two years ago, would find that the light he lighted in his
youth had grown into a great flame."[26]

With this assessment Dean Sumner surely agreed. One year after issuing
his new marriage requirement, he declared victory for his health certificate
campaign. Despite the gloomy predictions of his critics, who expected a sharp
drop in the number of couples marrying at the Chicago Cathedral, Sumner
claimed to have performed *twice as many* marriages since his Easter 1912
edict.[27] In the process he had raised his own visibility in the Protestant Episcopal Church considerably.[28] In a widely attended speech on "The Church and
Moral Progress" which he presented at the Protestant Episcopal Church's General Convention in 1913, Sumner expanded on his marriage message to urge
his fellow clerics to broaden the church's reform horizon. We need "to take up
the questions and problems, not only of local needs," he said, "but of needs
nationwide in their importance—questions which involved the integrity of the
race, physical, social, and moral." He reminded his listeners that control of
marriage was the crux of this effort. The marriages of those who "pass on to
succeeding generations in an increasing geometric ratio the physical, mental,
and moral deficiencies which they possess" remained a serious barrier to maintaining the integrity of the race.[29] In their self-styled modernism, Greenwich
Village radicals might attack marriage as the last bastion of stifling bourgeois
morality, but ministers could not. Instead, Sumner said, they must incorporate
modern, scientific reforms while continuing to burnish their image as traditional arbiters of the institution.

Why did Sumner's plan excite such interest among liberal clergymen?
What did they find appealing in his calls for the clergy to exercise greater
control over marriage? A closer examination of Protestant liberalism in these
years, particularly the development of organized social service movements in
many denominations, reveals a climate of opinion openly eager to testing new

reform techniques. The social service movement in Sumner's own denomination, the Protestant Episcopal Church, offers a revealing case study of the way internal church institutions encouraged the exploration of new reform ideas and the embrace of modern scientific methods, including eugenics.

Dean Sumner made his health certificate decree in the years when the Social Gospel dominated the Protestant landscape; its message of ushering in the Kingdom of God on earth through reform and service permeated the rhetoric of liberal leaders. In 1911, two years before the General Convention at which Sumner delivered his health certificate speech, Rev. Charles Williams, Protestant Episcopal bishop of Michigan, leveled an "indictment against present-day Christianity" which accused the Church of dealing in "canned goods, stereotyped plans of salvation," and "crystallized and petrified orthodoxies." These methods had left the church ineffectual in the face of new social problems. It was time, Williams argued, for religious leaders to attack the roots of social problems and not waste energy on merely alleviating their symptoms.[30]

The Protestant Episcopal General Convention of 1913 answered this call with a large-scale mobilization of social service work. Reports from the Convention described an "awakened Church" that embraced "vital matters of the day" and appeared eager to follow the exhortation of their bishop that they "throw themselves into the living, breathing world" around them.[31] Other denominations engaged in similar undertakings. The Methodist Federation for Social Service, formed in 1907, was a voluntary organization whose members were occupied in fields that formed the Progressive Era's list of usual suspects: clergy, social workers, progressive educators, and businessmen.[32] The Protestant Episcopal periodical, *The Churchman*, claimed, "There is much to indicate that the Church is acquiring a new social vision" and an "awakening social conscience."[33]

This conscience, once awakened, required organized means for its expression. The Protestant Episcopal conscience had realized its earliest organizational impulse in local diocesan social service commissions, the first of which was formed on Long Island, New York, in 1903. By 1914, there were sixty such commissions, and many more parish-level organizations, with New York and Chicago boasting the largest and best-organized groups. The mission of these diocesan commissions—"investigating and taking measures" of their communities' reform needs—served as a model for the Protestant Episcopal Church's denominationwide campaigns. In 1911, the Church appointed a Joint Commission on Social Service to oversee the diocesan commissions, and in 1913 (the year Sumner delivered his marriage health certificate speech) the General Convention expanded the Joint Commission's membership and made it a permanent church institution. Among the clerical members of the Joint Commission were Dean Sumner and his superior, Bishop Anderson.[34]

The central features of the social service campaign, as described in an exhibit at the 1913 Convention, were "collective, preventive, and constructive" activities "aimed at social justice," which employed "methods based on modern social science." The latter required education, and through church-sponsored forums and "study classes," parishioners were expected to explore solutions to social questions under the guidance of their ministers.[35] It was this exploration of secular issues that provided an entry point for eugenic ideas. In Chicago, the Social Service Committee for the city's parishes organized a speakers series in 1913 that engaged a range of social questions, including "Social Ethics and Eugenics."[36]

Eugenics ideas were appealing to social service enthusiasts because they seemed to answer the charges leveled by Bishop Williams. Eugenics was a modern, scientific way of thinking about social problems, not the ineffectual methods of old. "Like secular agencies of social reform," one observer noted, "the church is beginning to recognize that something more than charity is necessary" to solve social problems. Just as their colleagues in professional charity organizations turned to science for guidance in modernizing their best philanthropic tendencies, so, too, church institutions began to model themselves after secular groups. This turn was, in some ways, a reactive rather than a proactive move on the part of the churches. Social settlements and related professional, secular reform movements, which directly tackled the new problems of the heterogeneous cities, forced the churches to change their message and tactics. To successfully pursue a social mission, the churches had to learn how to cope with the new problems in their communities.[37] And they had to do so in a way that rendered their efforts as relevant as those of their professional secular counterparts.

Marriage and the health of the family were central concerns in this context, and they became key issues for the social service commissions. As Rt. Rev. Thomas F. Gailor, Protestant Episcopal bishop of Tennessee, noted, marriage was "the fundamental social relation" because it served as the gateway to family life. "When the family fails and the home declines," he warned, "the Nation and the race are doomed to perish."[38] That the feebleminded posed a serious challenge to the health of the race was an assumption made even by religious leaders who had little direct connection to the eugenics movement or knowledge of its teachings on heredity.

John M. Glenn, director of the Russell Sage Foundation and a lay member of the Protestant Episcopal Church's Joint Commission on Social Service, outlined this connection between the health of the family and the fate of the race explicitly in a speech he gave just after the Church's General Convention in 1913. Glenn expressed concern over the rapid increase of the feebleminded population, whom he described as "the begetters of numerous degenerate children," and reminded his audience that it was the Church's duty to "consider the physical, as well as the spiritual well-being" of its members and of society. To this end he endorsed state-sponsored segregation of feebleminded men and women. "Should not the churches arouse themselves and their States to the horrors of this evil [feeblemindedness] and seek its prompt abolition by the Legislature?" he asked.[39]

Glenn's rhetoric soon had the force of an organized movement behind it. By the 1910s, liberal Protestants' socially minded, reforming zeal had generated an institutional structure of commissions, ecumenical organizations, and church programs that represented the high-water mark of the Social Gospel movement. With their emphasis on cooperation with secular reform organizations, these institutions were fertile ground for scientific reform ideas like eugenics. Indeed, in this context, it would have been surprising had the eugenics movement not garnered a significant number of Protestant sympathizers; a survey taken in these years by the American Institute of Social Service found that 85 percent of the country's social workers had ties to Protestantism.[40] In this context it is easy to see how the institutional framework of the Protestant churches, particularly the liberal, reforming bent of social service campaigns, could provide the structure for promoting eugenic solutions to social problems.

The social service movement's concern with the problems of marriage and feeblemindedness became clear at the Protestant Episcopal General Convention in 1913. There, the Diocesan Conventions from New York, Virginia, Maryland, Michigan, Kentucky, Oregon, and Pennsylvania reported to the General Convention resolutions they had drafted and passed in their annual diocesan meetings; appropriating the language of the eugenics movement, the resolutions required the presentation of health certificates before marriage.[41] The Virginia Diocesan resolution, for example, claimed that the churches could no longer ignore the "menace" to the race; the Maryland Convention endorsed "the movement for social and moral betterment" and encouraged the General Convention to craft "carefully drawn rules" and encourage legislation "to prevent the securing of licenses by those who are morally and physically unfit" to marry.[42] Rev. Dr. Tatlock, a delegate from Michigan, even asked the Convention to consider amending Canon 39 to require health certificates for marriage.[43] A survey conducted in the New York Diocese of the Protestant Episcopal Church by Rev. Charles K. Gilbert revealed additional Protestant Episcopal support for measures to control marriage. In 1913, the New York State legislature considered passage of a measure called the Duhamel Domestic Relations Bill, which would require health certificates of all couples before marriage—in effect, making Dean Sumner's plan the law in New York. Rev. Gilbert, the executive secretary of the New York Diocesan Social Service Commission, sent out a questionnaire soliciting clerical opinion of the pending bill. He received sixty-six replies, which he claimed represented the views of the rectors of the most important Protestant Episcopal parishes in the diocese. The results were revealing (see table 2.1).

In addition to the overwhelming support religious leaders offered for the

TABLE 2.1 Results of Questionnaire on the Marriage
Health Certificate Requirement

Do you regard this as a matter for legislative regulation? [66 responding]	
Yes	55
No	4
Doubtful	7

Do you regard the provisions of the Duhamel Bill as practicable and desirable? [55 responding]	
Yes	48
No	1
Desirable, but not practicable	6

proposed bill, ten of the clerics surveyed also urged the Protestant Episcopal Church (as Rev. Tatlock had at the Convention) to change the marriage canon to resemble the regulations in force at Sumner's Chicago Cathedral.[44]

The eagerness with which the social service commissions in Sumner's own denomination and religious leaders outside of it embraced his health certificate idea demonstrates just how amenable their Social Gospel philosophy was to hereditarian thinking about the control of marriage.[45] Theologically, liberal Protestants' support for health certificates was tenable because they believed that it did not significantly alter or challenge the sacredness of marriage as an institution. In fact, the favorable arguments made by many ministers reveals that, for them, the health certificate plan strengthened the sacredness of the institution by guarding it against anything that might lead to its degeneration, such as feeblemindedness and venereal disease. They still viewed themselves as society's best arbiters of marriage, and in their minds, support for health certificates offered them another means of monitoring the institution. Moreover, liberal ministers and rabbis easily incorporated eugenic health certificate proposals into their larger social service efforts because many of them were already actively involved in and familiar with a wide range of Progressive Era secular reforms. Eugenic proposals (or at least, popular conceptions of eugenic proposals) were neither alien nor unwelcome to religious leaders who read social work publications, sat on the boards of charity organizations, and grafted secular social services onto their churches and synagogues. Support for eugenic health certificates became another, logical building block in their Social Gospel fortresses.

Praise for eugenic health certificates did not come from all religious quarters, however. Catholics were the most vocal opponents. In the Catholic Church, marriage is a sacrament, whose regulation is the function solely of the Church. Cardinal Gibbons declared unstinting opposition to any proposals such as health certificates that tried to interfere with the Church's duties in this regard. "Marriage is a divinely ordered institution," he said. "It is a relation too personal and intimate to be interfered with" in this manner. He decried the "inquisitorial methods" proposed by Protestant and Jewish supporters of health certificates, arguing that they interfered with personal liberty.[46] Remarking on Cardinal Gibbons's opposition, the Catholic weekly *America* accused health certificate supporters of disregarding the "human soul, with its marvelous powers of intellect and free will," and treating conjugal relations as they would the "breeding on the stud-farm." The editorial ended with a cry of "Halt! to the ill-advised enthusiasts [who tampered with marriage] in violation of the laws of nature and of nature's God."[47]

Catholic opposition to health certificates stemmed not only from a belief in personal freedom and the sacredness of marriage; it was also an assertion of the Church's authority to regulate the institution. "The Church will not delegate its powers to medical practitioners or amateur dabblers in eugenics," one Catholic writer averred. Catholics were concerned with the considerable expansion of medical authority occurring at the time, particularly the "medicalization" of the home, and they did not believe that physicians or eugenicists should have the power to interfere with or prevent marriage.[48] Liberal Protestants might throw wide the doors to scientific and medical experts, but Catholics were more wary.

Catholic leaders leveled strong criticism against Protestant ministers for their embrace of eugenic health certificates. Jesuit Henry Woods penned a caustic denunciation in *America* in which he deplored the seemingly blind eagerness of the Protestant clergy who were following Dean Sumner's lead. "Ministers, like children, are always ready for a new toy," he observed. Questioning the validity of the eugenic science behind the certificate proposal, he offered the following warning to the Protestant clergy: Even if every minister followed Sumner's example by establishing this impediment to marriage, "the great Catholic Church, the mother of the weak as well as the strong, is ready to protect the former in their natural right, to make children, whatever the constitution of these may be."[49]

Contrary to Woods's suggestion, though, not all Protestant ministers approved of Sumner's actions. In fact, the social service impulse (and outgrowths of it such as health certificate proposals) was a serious point of contention within American Protestantism in these years. Rev. A. F. Campbell, a Methodist minister from Brooklyn, accused ministers of "running riot" with eugenic theories and declared the debate over health certificates notable for its lack of "sober thought." Like Catholic critics, Rev. Campbell believed that relinquishing control of marriage to physicians was a slippery slope; soon "every Tom, Dick and Harry" would have the power to regulate the institution, he said. For that reason, the churches should not allow marriage to be taken out of their "exclusive hands."[50]

Many Protestant ministers (especially those who did not embrace the liberal Social Gospel) were not pleased with the churches' seemingly overwhelming emphasis on social reform in the 1910s, of which the health certificate crusade was a part. These evangelical Protestants decried the churches' "dilettante concern with sociological minutiae" and the resulting neglect of spiritual concerns among the clergy. They worried that the Social Gospel emphasized social reform to the exclusion of all else, including the message of personal salvation. In exasperation, Rev. Bernard Iddings Bell, dean of St. Paul's (Protestant Episcopal) Cathedral in Fond du Lac, Wisconsin, noted the churches' misplaced priorities: "One might as well admire the spectacle of Joan of Arc forsaking her place at the head of France's armies while she devoted her time to mending her soldiers' hosiery!" Christians, especially Christian ministers, should concern themselves with the task of salvation, not solving social problems.[51] The Chicago White Stockings outfielder-turned-evangelist Billy Sunday criticized Social Gospel efforts as "godless social service nonsense" and told audiences at his revival meetings that they could "get right with God" only by establishing a personal relationship with Christ, not by becoming amateur sociologists.[52]

Although evangelical Protestants did not wholly reject social service (conservative denominations such as the Southern Methodists and Southern Presbyterians adopted social creeds in the 1910s, and the Southern Baptists created a Social Service Commission that investigated social problems in this period), between 1900 and 1930 a "Great Reversal" occurred among Protestants. Social reform, especially the zealous pursuit of social reform that characterized the Social Gospel, came under suspicion from evangelicals.[53] In their view, liberal ministers who devoted their ministries to social concerns neglected what the Bible instructed Christians to do: Save souls. What for liberal Protestants was a reasonable adaptation to new social conditions and recent discoveries of science was for evangelical Protestants a sure path toward heresy. In this context, health certificates represented Christian social service run amok.

The conservative publication *The Presbyterian* said as much in a July 1913 editorial. The editors declared marriage health certificates "an outrage upon decency and modesty" and argued that "there is no justice in forcibly subjecting decent people to any such ordeal" as the exams proposed by certificate supporters. Like some Catholic critics, they also saw health certificates as a threat to the sanctity of the institution of marriage. "The physical examination theory has a tendency to reduce the conception of marriage to a physical or animal basis," they said, and they "hoped that this well-meant delusion will proceed no further." In the 1920s, Rev. Phillips Osgood of Minneapolis would preach eugenics; his predecessor in the pulpit at St. Mark's Protestant Episcopal Cathedral, Rev. James E. Freeman, was wary of such movements. In 1913, he voiced caution against "worshiping as a fad the popular movement in behalf of social betterment." It should not be made "the whole end of religion," he said. Rt. Rev. David Greer echoed these sentiments at the New York Diocesan Convention in 1913, warning that social service of this sort lacked "spiritual vision" and seemed too concerned with "material aims." Similarly, in a discussion of "Heredity and Environment" at the Protestant Episcopal Church Congress in Charleston, South Carolina, another minister warned, "We are all in danger of attaching too much importance to outward cleansing" and not enough to inward spiritual growth.[54] Such sentiments reveal that the religious leaders who did embrace Sumner's eugenic health certificate plan were part of the more daring end of the liberal Protestant spectrum. They were eager to incorporate the discoveries of science and social science into their ministries. In the decades to come, as evangelical Protestants moved further away from the liberal Social Gospel, they would offer more pointed rebukes of the eugenics movement.

The zeal with which social service groups in the Protestant churches were pursuing marriage regulation in 1912 and early 1913 prompted one newspaper to point out that "the State is lagging behind the Church in its recognition of eugenic truths."[55] In fact, before Sumner's declaration, a number of states had laws on the books prohibiting or regulating the marriage of the insane, feebleminded, and epileptic. The clear intent of these statutes was not to prevent the marriage of these groups, but to thwart their reproduction; a few of the laws allowed marriage of a feebleminded woman if she was over the age of 45 on the presumption that she was past childbearing age and hence no longer a threat to society. States rarely enforced these laws, however, and with new evidence from eugenics studies showing a supposedly rapid increase in feeblemindedness, state legislators began turning their attention to strengthening and updating these marriage regulations.[56]

The United States was not the first nation to turn to health certificate legislation as a solution to the growing "menace of the feebleminded." As Dr. A. J. Mjoen reported in the British periodical *Eugenics Review*, the Women's Association of Stavanger, Norway, in 1908 proposed a waiting period and health certificate prior to marriage. Their suggestions, announced at a meeting of the League of Norwegian Women's Clubs, were heartily endorsed by Dr. Mjoen, who discussed them in public lectures in the United States over the course of the next few years. Unlike later U.S. proposals, however, Norwegian plans for health certificates made them a voluntary rather than a compulsory measure.[57]

A number of U.S. states proposed and passed legislation on marriage health certificates in the years immediately following Dean Sumner's decree. One such law in Wisconsin generated a controversy that revealed the contested meaning of eugenics among scientific eugenicists, legislators, public health advocates, and religious leaders in the 1910s. In 1913, state Sen. William L. Richards introduced a bill requiring medical certification of marriage for Wisconsin residents. The bill, clearly eugenic in intent, became law in 1913 and required that "all male persons making application for license to marry shall at any time within fifteen days prior to such application, be examined as to the existence or non-existence in such person of any venereal disease" and issued a physician's health certificate before being granted a marriage license.[58] The celebrations of reformers who had lobbied for passage of the law ended quickly, however. Just twenty days after the law went into effect, it was challenged; a state court declared it unconstitutional on the grounds that the tests required for assessing a man's health were expensive and technical and created an undue restriction on marriage.[59] To compound the problem, from the law's inception many physicians in the state refused to perform the "eugenic exams" for the maximum allowable fee of $3, insisting instead on charging upward of $25 to cover the costs of procedures such as the new Wassermann test for syphilis. "Although the theory of the eugenic marriage bill might well receive our hearty endorsement," the *Wisconsin Medical Journal* editorialized, "in its present form the act asks impossibilities of the medical profession."[60]

Supporters appealed their case to the State Supreme Court, though with little hope for success; even the law's defenders predicted defeat. Newspapers reported that popular opinion in the state assumed the law would either be declared unconstitutional by the high court or repealed by the state legislature. Rumors circulated that the governor might even call a special session of the legislature to discuss repeal. No special session materialized, however, and on 17 June 1914, in a surprise decision, the Wisconsin Supreme Court sustained the eugenics marriage law, stating that "the state may require of applicants for license to marry the submission of recognized tests to ascertain freedom from disease." "Wisconsin Ousts Cupid!" the *New York Times* front-page headline blared, in a story describing the victory for health certificate proponents.[61]

In the wake of the Wisconsin victory, supporters of health certificates in other states initiated their own legislation. Pennsylvania passed a similar law, although in place of a physician's health certificate the state required a sworn affidavit attesting to the applicant's freedom from imbecility, epilepsy, and transmissible diseases. In 1915, the Vermont legislature passed "an act providing for eugenic marriages" that included a fine of $500 for any person who wed without proof of physical and mental fitness. State activity on marriage regulation prompted a writer in *The Nation* to conclude that, "as embodied in a marriage license law, like those of Pennsylvania and Wisconsin, eugenics ceases to be a fantasy of magazine science and becomes an issue of distinct appeal to the minds and consciences of reasonable men."[62]

The appeal of eugenic marriage legislation was strong enough that in states where legislators did not immediately act, governors and local public health officials took up the cause. In New Jersey, health officials from the town of Paterson endorsed a model eugenic marriage law; at a meeting of the nation's governors in 1912 (the same year Sumner proposed the health certificates),

Idaho's Gov. Hawley called on all states to adopt health certificates as a requirement for marriage. Two years later, Gov. Mann of Virginia made a similar request in his message to the state legislature.[63] In Chicago, Judge Joseph Sabath of the Municipal Court refused to marry two couples in the Court of Domestic Relations because he deemed the prospective brides incompetent, with the mentality of children. In a similar vein, his colleague, Morals Court Judge Charles Goodnow, spoke frequently about the problem of "delinquent girls," telling the Woman's City Club, "The marriage license window is an open way to the destruction of the national health and morals, with the ultimate certainty of irreparable race degeneracy."[64]

The flurry of legislative activity on behalf of eugenic marriage demonstrates the idea's appeal in the 1910s. But the pace of action also blurred the distinction between eugenic and social hygiene campaigns. Supporters of health certificate legislation spoke in terms of "safeguarding" marriage, emphasizing their larger commitment to the preservation of race health. In much the way that eugenicists did, they viewed marriage as something people would approach intelligently, scientifically. But they often focused more on nonhereditary venereal diseases as the most important evil to expunge.[65]

Health certificate legislation did not meet with unmitigated success. In 1914 alone, Kentucky, New Jersey, New York, and Louisiana all failed to pass proposed eugenic marriage legislation, though New Jersey eventually did so in 1919.[66] Supporters of eugenic marriage legislation in Louisiana credited Catholic opposition with ensuring the bill's defeat, and Catholics were as vehement in their opposition to legislative health certificate proposals as they had been to Dean Sumner's nonlegislative efforts. Cardinal Gibbons directly attacked the 1913 Wisconsin marriage law and predicted, "Eugenics is a fad that is bound to pass with the rest of the fads." Catholic Thomas Gerrard, who had written extensively about eugenics, was also critical of health certificate legislation. Although recognizing that marriage was the medium through which the eugenic fate of the race was determined, Gerrard could not condone interference with a sacrament. "By the action of God's will moving man's will" (and not through legislation), Gerrard said, "man is able to resist and control his passions."[67]

During the debate following Sumner's Easter decree in 1912 and in the ensuing wave of legislative efforts on behalf of eugenic health certificates, the public paid little attention to leaders of the "official" eugenics movement. Though Charles Davenport and his colleagues received occasional mention in popular newspaper and magazine stories on the subject, they were by no means prominent in the early months of this debate. So forgotten were they that the *New York Times* could claim that Dean Sumner's actions were the *"beginning of a great campaign for human betterment,"* an assessment that eugenicists who had labored for more than a decade to educate the public likely found galling.[68] However, it is powerful evidence of the important position religious leaders such as Sumner had achieved in popularizing eugenic ideas.

Eugenicists' absence from popular discussions of health certificates was due in part to their skepticism about the efficacy of health certificate legislation. Though admitting that legislators were "well-meaning" in their intentions, eugenicists such as Davenport felt that the proposals, "at this stage of science, do more harm than good."[69] Likely informed by a degree of disdain for the churches' powers of moral suasion, Davenport followed the health certificate debate from its inception and knew of Sumner's proposal. At the First International Eugenics Congress, convened in London in July 1912, Davenport conceded that the physician's certificate, "which some clergymen are requiring in the States," had "eugenical bearings." But he believed that such proposals were ultimately futile, "for so long as a feebleminded person is at large he will find another feebleminded person who will live with him and have children by him. The reproduction of the feeble-minded will not be diminished by laws forbidding the issuing to them of marriage licenses." He pessimistically concluded that, given the "weak sex-control" of the feebleminded, "it would be as sensible to hope to control by legislation the mating of rabbits."[70]

Prof. Samuel G. Smith, a sociologist from Minnesota University also in attendance at the Congress, agreed with Davenport, arguing that although the intent of health certificates was good, the consequences could be disastrous. "Whenever marriage is made more difficult, either by law or by a high standard of living," he said, "immorality increases." Eugenicist Caleb Saleeby echoed these sentiments, raising the specter of illegitimacy in *The Method of Race Regeneration*. Far from preventing dysgenic marriages, Saleeby said, health certificates would prove so burdensome that the feebleminded would simply avoid the institution of marriage altogether. Eugenicist Edwin Grant Conklin of Princeton also urged caution. Noting that eugenics was still an "infant industry," he warned readers of *Science* in 1913 that "giving advice regarding matrimony is proverbially a hazardous performance, and it is not much safer for the biologist than for others." All three eugenicists called for more public education about eugenic science and for the segregation of the feebleminded.[71]

Dean Sumner's plan and proposed state legislation received warmer treatment from eugenicists at the *American Breeders' Magazine*. During the early years of the eugenics movement, the editors of the magazine had decried society's lack of attention to marriage. In one lamentation they noted their anticipation of the day when "society and the church would increase their approval of good marriages" and, through the "possession of facts" about heredity, discourage dysgenic unions.[72] Just a few years after publishing this hopeful statement, Sumner made his announcement, and although the editors confessed that his proposal had taken them by surprise, they credited him with having "broken the ice so far as cooperation of the church with other social agencies is concerned." In this spirit, the ABA issued an invitation to "all clergymen to become members of this organization."[73]

This initial burst of enthusiasm from the ABA was replaced by a strong dose of skepticism after the Association reorganized in 1913 to become the American Genetic Association (AGA).[74] The primary reason for this shift was the AGA's concern that popular measures deemed "eugenic" in fact flouted science and misinformed the public, a sentiment shared by eugenicists like Davenport. Over the course of several months in 1914, readers of the AGA's new periodical, the *Journal of Heredity*, saw criticism from the medical community ("The provisions of the law have far outrun the results of scientific investigation"), the professional charity community ("The popular conception, formed through flippant references to eugenic marriages, eugenic babes . . . and eugenic novels, has resulted in its falling into more or less disrepute"), and from the scientific community, who claimed that eugenic marriage proposals "prostituted" their science and misled the public.[75]

One of the most fervent rebukes came from Dr. W. C. Rucker, the assistant surgeon general of the U.S. Public Health Service and an outspoken eugenicist. In an article in the *Journal of Heredity* in 1915, Rucker complained that "most of the measures which the public hails as eugenic have nothing to do with eugenics." Rucker, who was also the secretary of the AGA's Committee on Education, denounced eugenic marriage laws. "Eugenics is a science," he said. "It is a fact, not a fad . . . At present, it cannot countenance any attempt to interfere with marriage by law."[76] Most eugenicists agreed with Rucker that state laws were premature and ill-advised. Davenport lost his temper over the issue: "Oh, fie on legislators who spend thousands of dollars on drastic action and refuse a dollar for an inquiry as to the desirability of such action!"[77]

Eugenicists' objections were not merely a rearguard effort to protect their own intellectual terrain; they also identified several real weaknesses in eugenic marriage statutes. One problem was that most states did not require women to receive the health examinations. This was a real dilemma in the reasoning of health certificate supporters. Men like Dean Sumner, who cut their reforming teeth on antivice crusades, often linked their support of eugenic marriage to an attack on the moral double standard that allowed men to "sow wild oats" and, hence, contract disease, without public censure. Their eugenic marriage proposals excluded women on the assumption that they were pure and free from disease. The "new woman" might flirt with convention, but Sumner and his colleagues assumed she didn't fornicate. Eugenicists had no such illusions; because they were concerned with all hereditary traits, not just venereal disease, they believed that health certificate legislation had to cover all forms of hereditary feeblemindedness and had to include both men and women.[78]

Another concern was that people who could not fulfill the requirements for gaining a health certificate would either procreate without the benefit of marriage ("like rabbits," as Davenport had fretted) or simply avoid the regulation altogether by getting married in a state that did not have a health certificate requirement. Evidently the latter had become a serious problem in Wisconsin. After passage of the 1913 eugenic marriage law, the nearby city of Waukegan, Illinois, became a boom town for marriages, with local officials and ministers reaping substantial profits by marrying out-of-state couples. States such as Illinois, which did not have health certificate requirements, became the preferred place for the nuptials of couples who feared they could not obtain a clean bill of health in their own state. Legislators condemned these "marriage mills," and some states (including Wisconsin) amended their marriage laws to declare null and void these unions.[79]

By far the most frequently made criticism of health certificate laws was that prospective brides and grooms could go to "unscrupulous quacks" who would willingly exchange a health certificate for cash, regardless of the candidate's fitness. Eugenicists suspected that even legitimate physicians did not always perform thorough, "eugenic" examinations. Their suspicions gained sanction soon after the passage of Wisconsin's marriage law. In what became known in eugenics circles as the "infamous Ralph Kirwinio episode," a physician in Milwaukee examined and found fit prospective groom Ralph Kirwinio. He received his health certificate, his marriage license, and Miss Dorothy Klinowski's hand in matrimony—only to be revealed soon thereafter to be a woman (Miss Cora Anderson) masquerading as a man.[80] News of this blunder traveled quickly through eugenics circles, providing more evidence of the weakness of marriage examinations. Indeed, such occurrences prompted many eugenics supporters to retreat from their initial stand in favor of health certificates. Psychiatrist G. Alder Blumer, for example, claimed to have undergone "a certain process of 'deSumnerization' as the years have rolled by and experience has given pause and poise."[81]

Though eugenicists remained less than enthusiastic about health certificate proposals, voluntary plans such as Sumner's and state laws like Wisconsin's forced them to take stock of the public debate over regulating marriage. Health certificates remained popular with the public in this period, which linked them to broader efforts to improve public health.[82] The Chicago Society for Social Hygiene had two divisions, one to fight venereal disease and the other to prevent the propagation of "irresponsibles" who were the target of eugenic campaigns. Although measures such as health certificates were not technically eugenic, the common vocabulary of heredity that eugenics and social hygiene groups shared and their emphasis on protecting unborn children allowed them to meld easily in public discourse.[83]

In popular culture, particularly entertainments for immigrant and working-class audiences, health certificates suffered a few skeptical blows. A vaudeville romp composed by Aaron Hoffman in 1915 featured a song, "Eugenic Marriage," that pilloried the pretensions of high-minded, highly educated purveyors of the science of eugenics. The song, sung from the perspective of a man who has agreed (in response to an advertisement) to marry a "eugeni-cally fit" woman named Annabel Schmidt, traces the travails of a man caught in a medicoscientific farce:

> Every scientific—tiffic—stiff, who could afford a carriage,
> Attended the Hygienic church where occurred our eugenic Marriage.
>
> While we stood beside the altar, on a fumigated spot,
> An antiseptic minister tied the disinfected knot.
> Deodorized and pasteurized and sterilized we two.
> On a sanitary bible we swore we would be true.

Much to the narrator's alarm, however, things don't go quite as planned with regard to the fitness of their offspring. His score of children are riddled with ailments, from stuttering to St. Vitus dance, leading him to conclude: "Many a time when I look at that gang, the tears roll down my cheeks. How can a man as eugenic as me, be a father to so many freaks?"[84]

Eugenicists were more sympathetic to certain other proposals to regulate marriage. Many states attached to health certificate laws provisions requiring the publication of banns (a public announcement of a proposed marriage). Such a plan to prevent "hasty marriages" came before the Georgia state legis-lature in 1916, and eugenicists gave their support to the bill by noting that it might prevent "ill-considered," dysgenic marriages.[85] They also recognized that health certificate legislation, though not eugenic, in their estimation, did at least serve an educational function by making the public aware of the need to safeguard marriage. An article in the *Journal of Heredity* called for a new "prop-aganda of marriage" and asked why society had "ardent crusaders against vice" but few "propagandists of one of its antidotes, marriage." Efforts such as Sum-ner's, and even those of state legislators, though not wholly scientific, at least encouraged the public to think of marriage as a "social sacrament."[86]

These efforts also bolstered a long-standing assumption of the eugenics movement: Implicit in the movement from its origins and explicit in Galton's calls for the creation of a eugenics religion was an understanding that eugen-icists' scientific plans ultimately relied on people's willingness to adhere to certain codes of behavior. Without a broadly accepted and consistent enforce-ment of certain codes, particularly those relating to marriage, the eugenics enterprise collapsed. For their science to succeed, eugenicists required a means for monitoring human behavior; the institution of marriage provided a ready-made scaffolding on which they could construct their plans to control repro-duction. This explains, in part, why scientific eugenicists such as Davenport denounced so vehemently the usurpation of eugenics rhetoric by free-love ma-vens and sex reformers like Moses Harman, but also why they were alarmed by the public's impulsive pursuit of health certificates.

Most eugenicists, while registering their disapproval of health certificate laws, did not necessarily call for their wholesale repudiation. In fact, one can begin to see eugenicists responding more readily to the public's concern with safeguarding marriage. Though no doubt spurred in part by their fears of misinformation emanating from "that underworld of quacks and fakirs," eugenicists did begin to recognize that on the subject of marriage, the public had strong convictions and even displayed an "emotional tendency" with which their movement had to contend. A contributor to the *Journal of Heredity* urged scientific eugenicists to emerge from their laboratories to tackle "problems of human interest," like marriage, which dominated public debate.[87]

Such suggestions came at a time when scientific eugenicists were broadening their educational campaigns. Science departments at Harvard, Columbia, Cornell, Brown, Northwestern, and Clark Universities all offered courses on eugenics, and the ABA reported that "eugenics societies" were springing up across American college campuses. To encourage this trend, the Eugenics Record Office in 1914 created an extension department that began offering the services of its eugenics lecturers "to all organizations of an educational nature," including women's clubs, local societies, and churches.[88]

During the 1912–1913 academic year, a number of eugenicists traveled to colleges and universities to deliver lectures on eugenics. The intention of the lecturers, a group that included leading eugenicists Charles Davenport, H. E. Jordan, and Charles Ellwood, was to explain eugenics in a nontechnical fashion and from a wide variety of intellectual perspectives. Matrimony emerged as the common theme. Dr. Lewellys F. Barker, a professor of medicine at Johns Hopkins University, claimed that "the cultivation of a healthy public opinion regarding marriage and parenthood will, it seems probably, be more efficient in promoting eugenics than anything that can be done by way of legislation."[89]

Barker and other lecturers hoped to educate their audiences about the need for eugenic standards in marriage. Despite harboring doubts as to the scientific merits of health certificate proposals, more than half of the eugenics lecturers chose to highlight Dean Sumner's cathedral decree as a positive example. Zoologist Robert H. Wolcott of the University of Nebraska suggested that Sumner's declaration "will accomplish quite as much as legal enactment," and Dr. H. E. Jordan, an embryology professor at the University of Virginia, believed that "many more churches should follow the courageous example set by the authorities of the Cathedral of SS. Peter and Paul of Chicago, under the leadership of Dr. Sumner." Sociologist Charles Ellwood of the University of Missouri and economist Morton Aldrich of Tulane University also praised the dean's proposal.[90]

It is clear, then, that leaders in the eugenics movement found Sumner's activities useful as an educational tool—despite personal qualms about the plan's effectiveness. The university lectures, delivered at the height of the publicity surrounding Sumner's decree, produced no direct criticism of Sumner or any other religious leader who might enter the debate over eugenics. The only misgivings present in these speeches concerned hasty marriage *legislation* in the states. These eugenicists seemed prepared to welcome the initiative of a religious leader such as Sumner, but they hesitated to endorse the proposals of state legislators. Voluntary efforts by respectable religious leaders met with their tentative approval; crusades by fringe reformers or state legislators did not.

Fears about social and familial decay akin to those that prompted Sumner's marriage decree informed a broad range of other religious reform movements. Since the late nineteenth century, several religious denominations had created and sponsored settlement houses in the growing cities to tackle urban social ills. By 1910, there were more than four hundred settlements, religious and secular, in the country. Settlement house workers, like eugenics fieldworkers, were overwhelmingly Protestant, usually idealistic young men and women who believed that, through proper application of the latest social science methods—information gathering, statistical analysis, edifying educational programs—they could eliminate social evils (Dean Sumner had apprenticed under the most redoubtable doyenne of settlement work, Jane Addams). If settlement house workers did not always gauge correctly the sensibilities of their intended audience, they nevertheless made an earnest effort to expand their horizons. Hull House sponsored performances of Beethoven and lectures on Epictetus by John Dewey, for example.[91]

Social service–minded Protestants working in the teeming cities in the 1910s sometimes expressed sympathy with the eugenics movement's diagnoses of social problems. One minister and settlement house worker in Brooklyn, Rev. William E. Davenport, became actively, if not wholeheartedly, involved with eugenics. At one level, his connection to the eugenics movement could not have been closer: he was the brother of Charles Davenport, the chief of the Eugenics Records Office (ERO) and the country's leading eugenicist. His intellectual connection to eugenics was more tenuous, however, and his correspondence with Charles captures the struggles the eugenics movement had with social reformers, both religious and secular. Reformers such as William Davenport were willing to support the eugenics movement, but only so long as it did not interfere with the Christian charity that they believed was so important for eliminating human suffering. Reformers—whether motivated by religion, science, or social concern—could not pursue one at the expense of the other.[92]

Rev. William Davenport directed the Italian Settlement House Front Street in Brooklyn, which listed among its activities "Clubs, Classes, English, Gym, Cooking, Sewing, Counsel, Shelter, Study, Outings, and Naturalization Aid," all fairly standard offerings in the nation's urban settlements. Italians were a large percentage of the immigrants entering the United States at this time, and some of the poorest. As well, their language, appearance, and customs alarmed many native-born Americans. An Italian in Brooklyn was an exotic, the Hottentot of the outer boroughs, and settlement workers cottoned to the notion of "civilizing" these new arrivals.

Although William Davenport shared his peers' assessment of Italians, he remained optimistic about their ability to assimilate and become productive members of American society. Their efforts to do so became fodder for his own inquiries into the interplay of heredity and environment among immigrant populations. Settlement house workers went beyond traditional charity work in that they not only sought to help poor city dwellers by living among them, but hoped to learn from them as well, amateur anthropologists embedding themselves in the mores of transplanted foreign cultures.[93] Encouraged by his brother Charles, who sent him blank copies of the ERO's *Record of Family Traits*, William turned the Italian Settlement into a laboratory, measuring and questioning the many immigrants who availed themselves of the settlement's services.[94]

In 1912, the ERO published *The Family History Book*, which Charles Davenport compiled from records and family schedules furnished by ERO fieldworkers, fellow eugenicists, and his brother. Charles reproduced in full William's assessments of the Italian families that passed through the Front Street settlement, praising his brother's work as "a model of such studies." Like other eugenic family studies, William's analysis of "The A—Family from Sicily" mingled general remarks on physical traits, illnesses, and marriage patterns with opinions of the character and morals of the subjects under observation. William described "Alfonso A—," for example, as "large-bodied, strong," of "good sexual habits," and "socially inclined" but "superstitious and lacking in initiative, reflection and mental force." Another family member possessed a "cheerful disposition" but "gambled inordinately."[95]

Rev. Davenport expressed caution in the conclusions he drew from his family studies. "I believe the study of men and races can never be without pertinence," he wrote to Charles, but the publication of "poorly demonstrated conclusions" is "fraught with frightful consequences." Unlike his brother, or his family studies predecessor in the clergy, Oscar C. McCulloch, William emphasized the results achieved by environmental reform efforts like settlement house work, frequently challenging Charles's negative assessments of immigrants by reminding him of the many young men who had been "rated very low mentally by competent examiners" yet who nevertheless demonstrated "excellent capacity in their home relations and social obligations." William also viewed his religious reform work as similar in spirit, if not always in kind, to Charles's eugenics studies. In one letter to Charles he expressed his desire to "run down to Cold Spring Harbor soon and learn more of your work there, as of course it has the closest relationship with the sort of work our settlement houses are trying to do."[96] Like earlier religious students of heredity, such as

Rev. Samuel Zane Batten, William Davenport reconciled his faith in Christian social service with the new findings of science through a qualified embrace of eugenics. He tempered his conclusions about the importance of heredity with his experience as a settlement house worker. Having witnessed firsthand the changes a positive environment could bring, he did not adopt the pessimistic hereditary determinism of his brother.

Most eugenicists, however, embraced hereditary determinism, and in the 1910s began delivering their proof in a popular form: sensational accounts of degenerate families. Just as Richard Dugdale and Rev. McCulloch had tapped into public fascination with tainted generations with their Juke and Ishmaelite family studies in the late nineteenth century, eugenicists traced the diseased branches of American family trees to prove the heritability of a range of traits, extrapolating from these few studies to the population as a whole.[97]

Arthur H. Estabrook, a fieldworker at the ERO, offered a typical example of this method. Estabrook intrepidly set out in 1913 to investigate a feeble-minded family in upstate New York. As he reported back to the reform magazine *Survey*, he was surprised to have his friendly knock on the family's front door answered by a decidedly "animal-like grunt." Alas, Estabrook's ears had not deceived him; one of the two "apartments" in the family's shack was a pigpen inhabited by a sow and her litter. Of the two rat-infested apartments he said, "Filth abounds everywhere, the two families rivals in this respect, the humans being slightly in the lead." Estabrook described the several illegitimate children in the family as feebleminded and the seven-month-old as "puny, underfed, syphilitic, and neglected." He ended his report by revealing that this feebleminded flock were descendants of the notorious Jukes clan, whose misfortunes Richard Dugdale had famously traced in the late nineteenth century.[98]

Perhaps the most well-known eugenic family study of this period was Henry H. Goddard's *The Kallikak Family: A Study in the Heredity of Feeble-mindedness*, which appeared in 1913. Goddard, director of the Training School for the Feebleminded at Vineland, New Jersey, was one of the first psychologists to promote the use of the Binet-Simon intelligence tests. He and his acolytes went about their work with evangelical fervor; contemporaries referred often to the energetic "Vineland Spirit." In the 1910s he began studying one of the Vineland School's more recalcitrant inmates, a "high-grade feebleminded" delinquent girl named Deborah Kallikak. Goddard traced Deborah's hereditary troubles to the unfortunate sexual escapades of her Revolutionary War–era ancestor, Martin Kallikak. According to Goddard, Martin's brief affair with a feebleminded tavern maid spawned generations of paupers, criminals, and imbeciles, and his later marriage to a eugenically fit Quaker woman produced generations of prominent, respectable citizens. Goddard concluded from this bifurcated lineage that heredity was of far greater importance than environment in determining which traits would be passed to offspring. He also interpreted his findings as a warning of the havoc just one feebleminded woman could wreak: despite Martin Kallikak's good hereditary material, the tavern girl's dysgenic traits were the ones passed on to their progeny.[99]

Eugenicists' growing concern with the threat posed by feebleminded families was perhaps best demonstrated by the studies of Goddard's assistant at the Vineland Training School, Elizabeth Kite. Much of Goddard's work, including *The Kallikak Family*, would not have been possible without the contributions of Kite, a writer fluent in French who translated the Binet-Simon intelligence test. Kite was also a convert to Catholicism, and although she left no direct discussion of the connections she made between her faith and her eugenic research, her published articles reveal a serious concern with moral and ethical issues, particularly as they related to heredity.[100]

In addition to writing major portions of *The Kallikak Family*, Kite published a well-known family study of her own in *Survey* in 1913. Called "The Pineys," the study described the hereditary misfortunes of native residents of New Jersey's Pine Barrens region. Kite traced the Pineys back to colonial times, constructing a "moron family tree" whose branches were heavy with "sowers of wild oats." According to Kite, the typical Piney had existed for generations: "lazy, lustful, and cunning," a "degenerate creature" whom she likened to a barnacle, feeding off of society. Yet her focus was not primarily on physical traits. Instead, she noted that although the "question of physical degeneracy" was important, it was the "moral element which entering in makes the human degenerate such a profound menace to social order." In this vein she expressed her desire to "draw out [the] ethical ideas" of local residents.[101]

Kite wore "spotless white dresses as she rode in a horse-drawn wagon through the woods" in search of degenerate Pineys.[102] Her chaste attire contrasted markedly with the questions she posed to her quarry. In her many interviews with the feebleminded residents of the region, she took special care to ask probing questions about illegitimacy and polygamous unions. She even reprinted a question-and-answer session she conducted with a feebleminded Piney woman named Beckie, whose responses likely fulfilled Kite's expectations of her subject: "Tell me, Beckie," Kite asked, "you people don't think of it as wrong to marry a man when he has another wife?" Perhaps responding to Kite's leading tone, Beckie promptly retorted, "No, we don't think it wrong."[103] Kite embodied the impulses of progressive social reformers at this time. Earnestly, even idealistically committed to improving society, they nevertheless viewed themselves as superior strangers in the land of feeblemindedness and degradation, reporting back to others the goings-on of this underclass, often in a tone of high adventure. Kite was the kind of person who could travel through the poorest stretches of North Africa and later depict its inhabitants as "indescribably picturesque beggars."[104]

Kite's impulses were not entirely investigatory; she ended her study of the Pineys with a call to arms: "The time has come for us as an enlightened community to set about clearing up these 'backdoors of our civilization' and to save from the worst form of contagion what remains of moral health in our rising generations."[105] The moral health of future generations evidently concerned New Jersey's governor. After reading Kite's exposé he visited the Pine Barrens region and recommended that it "be somehow segregated from the rest of New Jersey" to preserve the health and safety of the state's population.[106]

Contained in the family studies of the 1910s is another shift in the eugenics movement's rhetoric about degeneracy. The feebleminded, formerly a problem, had now become a palpable threat to society, a "menace" that must be eliminated. This new tone emerged in part through the efforts of professional eugenicists such as Goddard who were using more sophisticated tests for diagnosing feeblemindedness—and claiming that diagnosis was the task of experts. In describing the feeblemindedness of a young woman from a degenerate family, for example, Kite noted, "She is attractive, and only a trained eye could readily detect her deficiency." Another researcher from the Vineland Training School, Alexander Johnson, made a similar point about this new class of the "invisible" feebleminded: "Their defectiveness is seldom recognized without careful scientific tests, so that, although they constitute a far greater danger to the social order than their feebler brothers and sisters, comparatively few of them get into institutions for defectives."[107]

Although the authors of eugenic family studies focused new attention on the supposed heritability of moral traits and the "invisible" face of feeblemindedness, they overlooked the inherently paradoxical nature of their findings. If moral traits were heritable and desirable, as the eugenic family studies purportedly proved, how could eugenicists reconcile this with the fact that these same moral impulses encouraged churches and social reformers to succor the weak, an inherently dysgenic practice? One eugenicist touched on this dilemma. In his textbook, *Heredity and Environment*, biologist Edwin Grant Conklin of Princeton University noted that moral strictures limited the scope of the eugenics enterprise. "Human ideals of morality" acted as a brake on the more extreme eugenic proposals, he noted, hence, "mankind will probably never consent to be reduced to the morality of the breeding-pen."[108] Conklin himself considered this a positive development, but his views were exceptional among eugenicists.

Despite the continued challenge posed to the eugenics mission by religiously motivated charitable impulses, religious-eugenic cooperation and mutual interest grew steadily in this period. Among the vice presidents of the First International Eugenics Congress, for example, were British religious leaders such as the bishops of Birmingham, Oxford, and Ripon, and the General Committee of the Congress contained three clergymen. Religious participation in the formal eugenics movement, if not yet numerically strong, was recognizable.[109]

In 1913, the *American Breeders' Magazine* published an editorial that explicitly called on religious leaders to join the eugenics crusade. In the editors' view, ministers had a strong motivation to support eugenics: Once eugenics had cleared degeneracy and feeblemindedness from the "network of human descent," the clergy would find their spiritual mission easier to pursue because the eugenically fit were more likely to absorb and apply the messages of religion. Employing religious rhetoric, the editors described eugenics as a "racial religion" that strove to achieve "eugenic righteousness."[110]

Although the editors were prepared to employ the language of religion in their appeal, they were not fully convinced that the nation's ministers were schooled enough in science to preach eugenics in their pulpits. The editors recommended further education in the form of eugenics courses at all theology schools and "summer courses in eugenics for preachers, Y.M.C.A., Y.W.C.A. workers, and other leaders in religion." They even provided a "Ministers' List" of recommended readings on eugenics, which included books by Charles Davenport, H. H. Goddard, Havelock Ellis, and Caleb Saleeby.[111] Girded with scientific knowledge, ministers could deliver homilies on heredity to their congregations.

Perhaps more noteworthy than the specific attention the eugenicists at the *American Breeders' Magazine* gave to ministers was the tone they adopted in doing so. Assuming that ministers were interested in eugenics (a sensible assumption given the spate of recent publicity of their support in the wake of Dean Sumner's announcement), they also carefully distinguished them from the "sensation-mongering" amateurs whom they believed had muddled the public's understanding of their science. They placed ministers alongside philanthropists, teachers, and practical scientists as the "conservators of society" who were responsible for spreading the eugenics message. More important, and for the first time, eugenicists acknowledged the need for religious guidance in crafting eugenics philosophy. "The assistance of all churchmen," the editors said, "will be greatly needed to aid in developing the philosophy along wholesome lines, and in carrying to all the people those facts and rules of practice which will best serve the race." The preachers are needed to give eugenics "an ethical, altruistic, and religious turn."[112]

Such an admission by eugenicists was a clear departure from earlier discussions, which, if they mentioned ministers at all, usually relegated them to a subordinate or innocuous role. Up to this point, eugenicists had not suggested that religious leaders might have something vital to contribute to the development of eugenic philosophy. In essence, eugenicists at the *American Breeders' Magazine* recognized what religious leaders such as Rev. Meyer and Fr. Thomas Gerrard had remarked on earlier in the century, but which the public's enthusiastic response to Sumner forced them to reckon with: A eugenics crusade that failed to recognize the crucial dynamic of man's spiritual nature and the importance of religious support was likely to fail.

Writing in the *Nineteenth Century* magazine in 1913, Canon Edward Lyttelton (of the Anglican Church) offered similar sentiments about the future of religious-eugenic collaboration: "The eugenist and the Christian are really so near together that there should be no difficulty about co-operation between them." In fact, Lyttelton suggested, the eugenics movement owed intellectual homage to Christianity for first articulating the idea that the human race could work to perfect itself. What concerned Lyttelton, however, was the eugenics movement's apparent unwillingness to recognize an important distinction: "The first truth for the scientific eugenist is the second truth in the Christian series; it is the unspeakable value of human life; the eugenist starts with it, the Christian treats it as a corollary of something deeper and more mystic which the eugenist may or may not understand."[113] This "mystic something" was the spiritual world, and eugenicists' inattention to it was the source of nearly every religious leaders' hesitation in fully embracing the eugenics movement in this period.

There was evidence that that hesitation was fading, however, especially among Protestants. In addition to supporting the call for eugenic certification of marriages, ministers in several prominent churches launched educational campaigns about eugenics for their parishioners. In the 1910s, Fordham Methodist Episcopal Church in the Bronx sponsored eugenics lectures for its congregation, and the Mount Morris Baptist Church in Harlem offered eugenics classes modeled on those taught in colleges and universities across the country. In June 1913, Rev. A. Edwin Kelgwin of the West End Presbyterian Church in New York City held a Sunday evening "platform meeting" on eugenics. Four speakers, including Kelgwin and Rev. Walter Laidlaw of the New York Federation of Churches, spoke to a "congregation which taxed the capacity of the edifice," according to newspaper reports; in their presentations the ministers noted the "fearlessness" with which the Presbyterian Church was treating the topic of eugenics. Rev. Kelgwin paid particular attention to marriage in his speech, urging men and women to use eugenics to release themselves from the "shackles of ignorance" and "effect a reform that is vital to the whole human family."[114]

Although the content of most of these eugenics lectures, classes, and forums is unknown, the participants' rhetoric, particularly their keen focus on marriage, suggests that, like Dean Sumner's efforts, these "eugenic" meetings blurred the distinction between eugenics and social hygiene campaigns. At Rev. Kelgwin's forum, for example, he was joined on the platform by Richard Bennett, a well-known American actor recently famous for his portrayal on Broadway of the lead role in *Damaged Goods*.[115] Eugenics could serve as a means for justifying greater church control over courtship as well. In 1913, Rev. John Gunn of New York credited the "present awakening of interest in eugenics" with inspiring his proposal for scientifically informed courtship; he turned his church into a social center where "worthy young men and women" could meet each other in a controlled and safe setting. Gunn's intentions were explicitly eugenic: "Love, courtship, and marriage have too long been regarded as merely sentimental and accidental matters. Cupid should familiarize himself with the facts of science."[116]

Finally, these years witnessed continuing interest in eugenics among Reform rabbis. In 1913, the Free Synagogue of New York announced a series of lectures to be given at Synagogue House, the church's social service department, on many current social issues, including eugenics.[117] The Free Synagogue was an ideal forum for such discussion. Founded in 1907 by Rabbi Stephen S. Wise, its stated purpose was to "broaden the spirit and form of the synagogue, expound Judaism in the light of the present, uphold liberty of thought and speech, and promote social service."[118] The growing number of churches and synagogues debating eugenics suggests the ease with which liberal congregations embraced the new science; they viewed it as no more radical than settlement house work.

For a time in the 1910s, the debate over health certificates dominated public discussion of marriage and eugenics. Dean Sumner's plan, and the state laws that resembled it, appealed to Protestant ministers and Reform rabbis because of their emphasis on safeguarding marriage and the health of the American family. Health certificate proposals and legislation also succeeded in disrupting the distinction between eugenic reforms (which targeted hereditary traits) and social hygiene campaigns (which emphasized nonhereditary diseases such as syphilis). Although eugenicists remained skeptical of health certificates' effectiveness, the popularity of the measures among social reformers and religious leaders forced eugenicists to examine more closely these marriage regulation proposals. In addition, the publicity provoked by the issue offered points of entry for religious leaders who were eager to explore eugenics questions or pursue eugenic reforms in their own churches and synagogues.

Dean Sumner was the first prominent religious leader to craft and carry through a eugenics program of his own making. Although he didn't decamp to Greenwich Village and embrace radical ideas, and likely would have been scorned by readers of the Village's voice, *The Masses*, in his own way Sumner challenged traditional thinking about marriage by merging it with modern science. At the most basic level of human psychology, health certificates satisfied a certain need. Certification imbued marriage with a sense of seriousness and lent to the novices embarking on their great connubial experiment a feeling of participating in a broader mission: contributing to the health of the race and nation. With the young in full-blown cultural revolt, at least by their own assessment, confusion over changes in home-grown mores and the fate of marriage as an institution loomed large. "It seems as though everywhere, in that year of 1913, barriers went down and people reached each other who had never been in touch before," wrote the Village's éminence grise, Mabel Dodge. "The only enemies were tradition and timidity."[119] There is no little irony in the fact that farm girls would soon be yearning to be flappers—and the flapper embraced, as part of her modern sensibility, a movement that applied the breeding techniques of the farm to her fellow citizens.

Dean Sumner's rise in the Protestant Episcopal Church hierarchy continued, as did his enthusiasm for eugenics. He left Chicago in 1913 to be consecrated bishop of Oregon. Asked about his support for eugenic reforms seventeen years after he had announced his health certificate plan, Sumner said, "No problem is more worthy of our time and attention."[120] The public agreed. As an editorial in the *Medical Times* said of Sumner, "His name will always be associated with eugenics in this country, for his determination to regulate marriage in his own parish has given the science an impetus that all good men will endeavor to assist."[121]

3

Protestant Promoters
and Jewish Eugenics

For he that soweth to the flesh shall of the flesh reap corruption.
—Galatians 6:8, text of Rev. Newell Dwight Hillis's
speech to First National Conference on Race
Betterment, 1914

When health reformer and eugenics supporter Dr. John Harvey Kellogg delivered his welcoming address to the First National Conference on Race Betterment in 1914, he credited a Protestant minister with inspiring the meeting. "If you esteem it a privilege to gather here for the discussion of great questions which concern the welfare of the race," he said, "you are most of all indebted to our greatly esteemed friend, the eminent Dr. Hillis, of Plymouth Church, for it was he who last summer suggested to me and to other members of the Central Committee the idea of this Conference."[1]

Hillis and Kellogg were unlikely allies. The Race Betterment Conference where they joined forces mirrored the eclectic philosophy of its host institution, the Battle Creek Sanitarium in Michigan, and its director. Raised a Seventh-Day Adventist (though he was excommunicated in 1907), John Harvey Kellogg (1852–1943) incorporated into his Battle Creek program Adventist leader Ellen G. White's philosophy of treating health reform as a religious obligation. Kellogg was a physician and skilled surgeon—he loved to regale correspondents with tales of his success in removing patients' penetrating stomach ulcers and intestinal blockages—with boundless energy and a slightly quirky personality; later in life he took to wearing all-white clothing, among other affectations. By the 1910s he had built a sanitarium with an excellent reputation, an impressive roster of former patients (including Upton Sinclair, Amelia Earhart, Thomas Edison, and Admiral Richard Byrd), and the motto "Health through Right Living." The Battle Creek program required plenty of exercise, water cures, and a diet void of most animal products and stimulants; one 1914 advertisement promised patients "the most thorough-going physical examination possible," including close inspection of "kidney and bowel excretions, the blood and stomach contents . . . a complete and accurate 'inventory' of the whole body." The testimonial juxtaposed this fairly graphic text with sunny pictures of patients playing golf and tennis and a view of a placid lake.[2]

Rev. Newell Dwight Hillis (1858–1929) was the minister of the Plymouth Congregational Church in Brooklyn and by the 1910s was already a well-known and highly regarded religious leader, his prestige derived in part from the rich pedigree of his pulpit. Hillis's predecessors at Plymouth Church were Lyman

Newell Dwight Hillis
Preacher, Lecturer, Author.

FIGURE 3.1 Rev. Newell Dwight Hillis, Plymouth Church, New York. Records of the Redpath Chautauqua, Special Collections Department, University of Iowa Libraries, Iowa City, Iowa.

Abbott and Henry Ward Beecher, the latter of whom had made the church famous in antebellum times through his charismatic preaching and strong denunciations of slavery. Hillis graduated from McCormack Presbyterian Theological Seminary in Chicago in 1887 and was ordained that same year; he was called to Plymouth Church in 1899. Early in his Brooklyn ministry, in *The Influence of Christ in Modern Life* (1900), he outlined his hopes for a church oriented toward solving modern problems. "The time has come when the preacher must be a universal scholar," Hillis said. "He must make himself an expert in social reform," including knowledge of "physiology and hygiene."[3] By the 1910s, Hillis's Plymouth Church embodied this philosophy of expanded church service rhetorically and architecturally: a generous endowment from Brooklyn coffee merchant John Arbuckle made possible the raising of the Plymouth Institute adjacent to the main sanctuary. The Institute's art gallery, gymnasium, bowling alley, clubhouse, and classrooms became, by one contemporary account, "a vital part of the church's mission in helping to improve standards and conditions, moral, social, and physical, for all over whom its influence falls."[4]

A highly regarded speaker and favorite on the Chautauqua lecture circuit, the bristly, dark-haired Hillis's pulpit mien was undemonstrative, a "curbed animation" that nevertheless earned him enough fans to secure hundreds of speaking engagements across the country every year.[5] Rev. Hillis also demonstrated an early interest in heredity. Along with thoughts on John Ruskin, the "New Germany," and "Self-Help: The Golden Secret of Success," Hillis traveled the Chautauqua tent circuit preaching about better breeding. In 1913, the *New York Times* reported that he was "cooperating" with actor and eugenics promoter Richard Bennett "in a eugenics crusade."[6] One year later he was serving on the Eugenics Record Office's Expert Advisory Committee, charged with investigating the moral and ethical issues raised by eugenics and gauging the general attitude of the churches on eugenics.[7]

Hillis was deeply serious about the importance of heredity. At the Race Betterment Conference that he was credited with organizing and where he served as vice president, he delivered a wide-ranging speech on race degeneracy that deployed wrathful, Old Testament imagery to drive home dire warnings about humanity's precipitous racial decline. "The time has gone by when we can any longer say that race degeneracy is simply a bugaboo created by pessimists and alarmists," Hillis said. "A tide of degeneracy is rolling in upon us," and "for the individual and the nation, it is true that 'he who soweth the wind shall reap the whirlwind.'" That whirlwind was taking form. Hillis cited the work of eugenicists in England and the United States to demonstrate that the population of insane and feebleminded persons was growing. Paraphrasing from the New Testament book of Galatians, Hillis warned, "It is for the people of this nation to remember that he who sows to the flesh shall of the flesh reap corruption."[8]

The solution Hillis offered to conference-goers drew as much on his religious training as on his considerable enthusiasm for eugenics. Society must place its hopes for the future on that part of the population that was "God-fearing, law-loving, pure-living," he said. For Hillis, eugenics offered hope not only for the long-term physical well-being of the human race, but also for its spiritual health. Sounding the same theme other Protestant ministers had touched on, he argued that a race made *physically* strong by eugenics would be better equipped to receive and promote the *spiritual* message of Christian salvation. In an artful melding of Congregationalist and eugenics rhetoric, Hillis called this hoped-for future race "the elect." The Puritan intonations of the phrase were deliberate. Hillis insisted that such a group would be physically and spiritually superior, a Christian "aristocracy of health."[9]

It was typical of Hillis to make grandiose leaps from Protestant theology to practical reform. As one contemporary noted, "He is not a theologian in the ordinary sense, for he loves flowers more than botany."[10] Like Dean Walter T. Sumner of Chicago, who had recently announced his proposal for eugenic health certificates, Hillis also worked backward from reform to bedrock principles, his energies always focused first on practical action and only secondarily on finding biblical justifications for it. Not all of his religious colleagues were pleased with this intellectual dance, nor with Hillis's outspokenness on matters related to reproduction. The editors of the conservative Protestant magazine *The Presbyterian* took him to task over an article he published in the *Christian Work and Evangelist* in 1913 on "The Social Diseases and Heredity." In it, Hillis criticized the pinched silence that had marked discussion of sexual matters, especially venereal disease and hereditary degeneracy, and urged more widespread public education.[11]

The editors of *The Presbyterian* were aghast. In fact, they wrote, "There is probably no subject upon which the American people are really better informed" than on sexual matters, for socially minded clergy such as Hillis insisted on an unseemly amount of "promiscuous publicity" on the issue. It was in 1913, after all, that the journal *Current Opinion*, commenting on the contemporary candidness about such matters, claimed that it had struck "Sex O'Clock" in America. The editors of *The Presbyterian* urged religious leaders to "quit the damnable practice of conceiving sin to be chiefly social" and turn their attention to the one remedy "which in all the history of our race has ever been able to check the evil and remove the sin, that is, repentance toward God and faith in Jesus Christ."[12] The Protestant Episcopal Church periodical *The Churchman* offered a similar critique of the Battle Creek Race Betterment Conference as a whole, claiming that it had "lost sight of the one most hopeful element in any effort for racial betterment," namely, "God and the gifts which God imparts to men through His church."[13] Hidebound in their insistence that salvation was more important than social reform, they urged the clergy to focus on the souls of their congregants, not the social (and sexual) ills of the nation.

Judging by the continued popularity of Hillis personally, and the Race Betterment Conferences generally, criticism from conservative evangelical Protestants had little impact. Hillis was playing to a broader audience. Unlike the gatherings sponsored by the ERO at Cold Spring Harbor or the International Eugenics Congresses, whose delegates were largely scientists and social scientists, the Race Betterment Conference hosted a more diverse range of participants. The president of the Conference, Dr. Stephen Smith, worked for the New York State Board of Charities, and the vice presidents (in addition to Rev. Hillis and eugenicist Irving Fisher) were Indiana State Commissioner of Health Dr. J. N. Hurty and U.S. Sen. Robert L. Owen from Oklahoma. Social workers were well-represented by Jacob Riis and Graham Taylor, among others, and the list of local cooperating organizations included the Battle Creek Ministers' Association, the YWCA and the YMCA, the Ladies' Aid Societies of the Nine Churches of Battle Creek, and the Women's Christian Temperance Union. Dean Sumner sat on the Conference's General Committee and presented a paper, "The Health Certificate: A Safeguard against Vicious Selection in Marriage," that was, according to Kellogg, one of the most widely attended sessions of the whole conference.[14]

The summary of "constructive suggestions" presented at the conference reflected the diversity of the "race betterment" rubric: calls for the prohibition of alcohol, anti-spitting ordinances, nationwide better babies contests, more

FIGURE 3.2 Banquet for delegates to the First National Conference on Race Betterment, Battle Creek Sanitarium, 1914. American Philosophical Society, Philadelphia, Pennsylvania.

widespread eugenic education efforts, stricter immigration laws, advice on how women could "suppress" brothels, calls for women's suffrage, and better meat and milk inspection all gained a hearing. The wide array of topics evidently attracted public interest; reports from the Conference noted that audiences at each session numbered between 1,500 and 2,000 people, with up to 200 turned away at the doors due to lack of seating.[15]

Hillis's alter ego at the conference, Dr. Kellogg, was no less committed to understanding heredity, but his understanding of "race betterment" included more than a commitment to the eugenics promoted by biologists such as Charles Davenport. It involved health and environmental reforms as well. Unlike the amateur eugenicists whose claims so incensed the high priests of the organized eugenics movement, Kellogg cultivated cooperative relationships with leading eugenicists and regarded his health crusades as complementary measures in the latter's campaign. He paid for Davenport to travel to Battle Creek for the First Race Betterment Conference in 1914, for example, and frequently wrote him flattering letters filled with questions about eugenics.[16]

Religious questions also occupied Kellogg. Indeed, the Adventist religion within which he was raised, and which emphasized the connections between spirituality and health, permeated his life's work and likely served as a bridge to religious leaders such as Rev. Hillis. In an 1886 address delivered at Battle Creek, Kellogg sounded a theme that Francis Galton had first composed when he suggested, "Religion affords a means by which the beasts of appetite and passion may be subdued and chained—yea, even slain." It was the "one radical cure" and "the most essential of all aids" in battling degeneracy.[17] Kellogg, like Galton, admired the disciplinary power of organized religion and hoped to harness similar sentiments for his own crusade for race betterment.

Kellogg and Hillis also succeeded in luring other clerics to the gathering. Many ministers attended the 1914 Race Betterment Conference, and each session opened with prayer. The Battle Creek Ministers' Association deemed the Sunday during the Conference "Race Betterment Day" in the city's churches and "selected their topics accordingly" for their morning services. On Sunday evening Rev. Thornton Anthony Mills of the Independent Congregational Church of Battle Creek went one step further and used his church as a forum for a discussion of race betterment. In his presidential address, Dr. Stephen Smith noted "the power of Christian consciousness, when awakened to activity, to change the most savage tribes into highly civilized communities" and, like Galton and Kellogg, suggested the need to apply this consciousness to the campaign for race betterment.[18]

The success of the first conference was followed by a Second National Race Betterment Conference in 1915, held in San Francisco as part of the Panama-Pacific International Exposition. Moral questions took center stage at the gathering, where more than five thousand conference attendees crowded into the Oakland Civic Auditorium to witness a "morality masque" aptly titled *Redemption*. Two years earlier, Frenchman Eugene Brieux's play about venereal disease, *Damaged Goods*, had debuted on Broadway, slightly scandalizing the matrons of Manhattan. *Redemption* posed no such danger for social guardians on the West Coast. Heavy on moralizing and low on titillation, with a *Pilgrim's Progress*–style allegory as its centerpiece, *Redemption* was numbingly earnest. The masque's main characters included "Mankind," "Womankind," "Neglected Child," "Science," "Pity," "Unseen Spirit," Faith," and "Religion"; minor characters included "Pleasure," "Scoffer," and "Ignorance, Poverty, Vice—the companions of Disease." The plot followed Mankind and Womankind as they pursued pleasure at the expense of their children and ignored the warnings of Unseen Spirit, who appeared at opportune moments to warn the couple of the imminent disasters awaiting them. Tragedy, predictably, strikes, but it is only when their son, Neglected Child, is crippled by disease and prone on his deathbed that Mankind and Womankind finally realize the error of their ways. With belated penitence they call on Art, Science, and Religion to aid them in saving his life but find that "Art fails unless the race is strong physically," Science was brought in too late to help, and "Religion can give comfort to the soul, but cannot alone save the body from death." Neglected Child dies. The "redemption" of the play's title comes in the form of a new, eugenically healthy child named "Fortunate," whom Mankind and Womankind vow to rear correctly. As the drama ends, the couple offers a prayer of thanks to Unseen Spirit and summon Art, Science, and Religion to usher in "the salvation of the race."[19]

Redemption was not overtly religious, despite its drawing on religious themes, but its evangelizing message was clear: Eugenics was star and savior of this production called life. No amount of clever staging would give religion (or art or old-fashioned science) anything other than a supporting role in the cast. As Prof. Irving Fisher of Yale University reminded his audience at the Second Race Betterment Conference, eugenics was "the foremost plan of human redemption."[20] Religion, a necessary but unscientific force, was secondary, and eugenicists continued to view religious leaders as a Conference of Bishops might view a chemist who offered them his views on theodicy: with a gracious but bemused tolerance—and with assurance of the superiority of their own knowledge.

Nevertheless, the Race Betterment Conferences provided a venue for preachers interested in exploring eugenic ideas. Under the rubric of "race betterment," many religious leaders felt comfortable offering their support to the eugenics movement, even in a formal capacity. At the 1915 Conference, for example, Bishop John W. Hamilton of the Methodist Episcopal Church, San Francisco, served on the Advisory Board.[21] The wider reach of the Race Betterment Conferences, extending as they did into areas of social reform with which liberal Protestant ministers were familiar, also provided a less rigorously scientific environment in which to discuss race improvement. The Conferences thus offered scientific and nonscientific supporters of eugenics an opportunity to explore common ground.

It was a brief window of opportunity for the two. By the time the Third Race Betterment Conference convened on 2 January 1928, most of the delegates were health reformers, physicians, and nutritionists, not ministers and social reformers, and the emphasis was less on eugenics than on health reforms more amenable to Kellogg's offbeat nutritional philosophies. The "Morality Masque" of 1915 was replaced in 1928 by the musical stylings of "Seven Vivacious Vegetarians," children of a local herbivorous family who presented a light program of musical solos, duets, and choruses.[22]

Nevertheless, Dr. Kellogg continued to cultivate relationships with eugenicists, and in the process encouraged their study of religious matters. Ever on the lookout for potential sources for eugenical family studies, Charles Davenport wrote to Kellogg in 1914 to inquire after missionaries who had gone to the Battle Creek Sanitarium while on furlough from their evangelizing in foreign countries. "I would suggest that a number of studies should be made upon these missionaries," Davenport wrote, including an examination of the existence of the following traits: "interest in theology, piety, love of natural history, love of travel, love of language, and love of outdoor life." Davenport hoped to untangle "the 'why' of a foreign missionary as opposed to a home missionary or a home clergyman," surmising that people drawn to foreign missions might have an inborn restlessness and piety that made such work particularly appealing to them. He furnished blank ERO family schedules for Kellogg to pass along to his visitors.[23]

Two years later, Kellogg convinced Davenport to travel to Battle Creek to deliver a lecture for the Golden Jubilee of the Sanitarium. It is unclear if Kellogg recommended a particular topic, but the one Davenport settled on suggests an understanding of his host's interests, "Eugenics as a Religion." For a man not noted for his enthusiasm or skill as a speaker (the "aromatic acid phenylaline" and descriptions of "wild allelomorphs" marked the heights of his hortatory prowess), the subject of eugenics and religion inspired Davenport to summon his inner orator. With a nod to Francis Galton, he argued that the chief strength of organized religion was its ability to suppress humanity's baser instincts. Religion was able, he said, "to train the inhibitions" and "to supply those whose inhibitions are weak with a different means of control." Religion, in other words, offered far more powerful deterrents; hell and eternal torment, he noted, were harsher goads to maintaining good behavior.[24] Although his was a more crudely stated version, Davenport's argument resembled that of Protestant minister F. B. Meyer and Catholic priest Thomas Gerrard, both of whom had remarked on religion's disciplinary features in their discussions of eugenics a few years earlier.

Yet, just as Meyer and Gerrard had criticized eugenicists for neglecting the

FIGURE 3.3 Charles B. Davenport, 1929. American Philosophical Society, Philadelphia, Pennsylvania.

inspirational force of religion and the spiritual element of man's nature, Davenport faulted religious leaders for not giving heredity its due. Religions "fail to regard the importance for society of inheritable racial traits," he said. Only eugenics recognized this need, for it had as its primary objective the development of a social order of the "highest, most effective type." In this, Davenport, like Galton, ultimately rejected the need for organized religion. The achievement of the "most effective type" was an aim guided by the discoveries of science, not religion. If one accepted what science had proven, Davenport told his audience, then eugenics became the "religion that may determine your behavior." He closed his speech with a eugenic replacement for the Apostle's Creed: an eleven-point "creed for the religion of eugenics" that included statements such as "I believe that I am the trustee of the germ plasm that I carry" and "I believe in repressing my instincts when to follow them would injure the next generation."[25] Davenport's eugenics was a *replacement* for organized religion; nevertheless, it was still a religion, complete with creed (hereditary science), sanctuary (the laboratory), texts (family studies), and, as Davenport himself surely demonstrated, high priests. Soon enough this cosmology would spawn heretics.

The implicit themes of degeneration and decline raised by Davenport in his speech and touched on explicitly by participants in the Race Betterment Conferences became more prominent in the eugenics movement after 1914. With the outbreak of war in Europe, eugenicists' thoughts turned to the implications of war for the human race. They explored the biological implications of war, including its effects on what they viewed as an alarming differential birthrate. Threats to the security of democracy abroad also sparked reevaluations of the health of such ideas at home, including the state of the American character. Authors of eugenics textbooks began to make distinctions among physical, mental, and moral defectives and adopted a new vocabulary that included the seemingly self-explanatory descriptor "moral imbecile," for example.[26]

As a rule, most eugenicists believed that war of any kind was dysgenic (harmful to the race) because nations enlisted the physically strongest young men to fight wars, losing many of them on the battlefield and leaving behind only the old and feeble to produce the next generation. As eugenicist Irving Fisher told the *New York Times* in 1915, war is "a waste of germ plasm."[27] In *War's Aftermath*, a study published just after conflict erupted in Europe, brothers David Starr Jordan of Stanford University and Harvey Ernest Jordan of the University of Virginia made the eugenic implications of warfare explicit through a case study of the biological implications of the Civil War. They concluded that the Civil War had "seriously impoverished this country of its best human values," and that the current conflict would do the same. War "destroys men who are superior," leaving "the relatively inferior to perpetuate the race."[28]

Eugenicists did not translate their worries over the fate of America's germ plasm into a stout pacifism. Instead, they joined the others whose concerns over the country's preparedness for war led them to the U.S. Army training camps. Between 1917 and 1918, the Army became a proving ground for the social schemes of many a reformer. The training camps were a microcosm of Progressive Era tinkering: Anti–venereal disease crusaders, psychologists intent on measuring military minds, YMCA leaders, and a happy host of others descended on the camps. The Army's Commission on Training Camp Activities (CTCA), headed by former settlement house worker Raymond B. Fosdick, established a comprehensive program of recreation, education, and entertainment whose consistent message was a pseudo-eugenic insistence on keeping U.S. troops healthy and "fit to fight" through avoidance of prostitutes, alcohol, and other "race poisons."[29] The result was an amalgam of reform activities, many of which resembled the moral-scientific eugenic marriage certificate crusade of Dean Sumner in that they attacked "racial poisons" such as venereal disease using a vocabulary furnished by the eugenics movement.[30] Psychologist Robert M. Yerkes's success in initiating Army-wide mental testing of recruits yielded the most startling results for eugenicists, results that would fuel fears of feeblemindedness well into the 1920s: Testers found the average mental age of white recruits to be only 13 years.[31]

Religious leaders were not immune to the pull of these forces; they too responded to the swelling patriotism and jingoistic rhetoric of wartime, eager to cleanse the country of imported radicalism and race degeneration. Their efforts were not modest. Historians have noted how Protestant, Catholic, and Jewish leaders of all theological stripes "lifted their voices in a chorus of support for the war."[32] The chorus, more often than not, was shrill. Protestant evangelist Billy Sunday warned large crowds in 1917 and 1918, "If you turn hell upside down, you will find 'Made in Germany' stamped on the bottom" and helped raise money for the Liberty Loan fund by painting a portrait of "pretzel-chewing, sauerkraut spawn of blood-thirsty Huns" overtaking the world. Rev. Cortlandt R. Myers of the Baptist Temple in Brooklyn expressed a common sentiment when he told his congregation, "If the Kaiser is a Christian then the devil in hell is a Christian, and I am an atheist."[33] Wartime fervor left little room for detractors, even among religious leaders. Pacifists such as the Unitarian minister John Haynes Holmes were scorned as "passivists" and found themselves regularly flayed in the press by boosters for the war.[34] Few religious leaders passed up opportunities to denounce Germany with "hymns of hate."[35]

Eugenic and anti-German sentiment achieved a startling symmetry in the rhetoric of Race Betterment Conference veteran Hillis. An avid lecturer who had traveled extensively in Germany before the war, Hillis had been speaking for years about the excellent qualities of German political and social institutions. Nevertheless, his good feelings evaporated after the United States' entry into the conflict, and, not content to sit idly by, he became the cross-country-stumping darling of the American Bankers Association, which was sponsoring the Liberty Loan drive. His new position as war propagandist required him to recant much of his prewar public praise of the "genius of the German people," a process he undertook with swiftness and enthusiasm. By 1917 he was eagerly condemning German militarism. Speaking more than four hundred times in 162 cities in 1917–1918, Hillis was credited with raising more than $100 million in forty-six days. He electrified crowds with stories of the atrocities supposedly committed by German soldiers, which he catalogued in print under such lurid titles as *German Atrocities* and *The Blot on the Kaiser's 'Scutcheon*. In the latter work, Rev. Hillis combined his enthusiasm for eugenics with his newfound loathing for the German people, whom he described as "brutes" who "must be cast out of society." His solution called on "statesmen, generals, diplomats, and editors" to pass an international decree modeled on the state of Indiana's eugenic sterilization law. One can imagine the anticipatory glee of a Liberty Loan audience as Hillis intimated that implementation of his plan was drawing nigh. "Surgeons are preparing to advocate the calling of a world conference to consider the sterilization of 10,000,000 Germans soldiers and the segregation of the women," Hillis said. "When this generation of Germans goes, civilized cities, states and races may be rid of this awful cancer that must be cut clean out of the body of society."[36]

Rev. Hillis's inflammatory statements placed him squarely in the mainstream; war fever infected a substantial portion of U.S. religious leaders during the years of the conflict. Indeed, Hillis's vitriolic denunciations of the Germans heightened his appeal as a Liberty Loan crusader. The rapid adjustments these ministers made to their beliefs suggests a degree of malleability in their theologies, Hillis's intellectual about-face on Germany being only one of many examples of this process. In the hothouse of wartime, many ministers, priests, and rabbis adjusted their public statements to suit the times and used their pulpits to promote the war. But this process of adaptation was not new, merely unusually swift. In a compressed fashion it resembled the adjustments liberal religious leaders had been making for decades as they stippled their theologies with ideas that conformed to the demands of modern times: historical criticism of the Bible and evolutionary theory, for example. Their worldviews proved tractable long before they began to accommodate warmongering.

Extreme patriotism proved a more seductive lure than other causes, of course. Unlike the eugenics movement, which drew religious support almost entirely from liberal leaders, the war garnered a broad spectrum of religious devotees; conservative evangelist Billy Sunday and liberal leader Newell Dwight Hillis likely never again served as spokesmen for the same social cause. Still, they shared a willingness to reinterpret long-held convictions in light of recent events (or even simply to marshal biblical evidence to justify participation in a cause). In this context, men such as Hillis, who gave eugenics and war boosterism equal enthusiasm, departed from their coreligionists only in the degree of their conformity to modern circumstances, not in their willingness to engage in conforming altogether.

If demonizing the Germans assuaged the worries of pulpit leaders, it did not do the same for eugenicists. The world war raised a more worrisome question for them: What was happening to America's best people? Drawing on new studies of the original *Mayflower* families, eugenicists located a disturbing trend: If the present low birthrate of the Pilgrim descendants continued, in the near future it would be possible to load all surviving descendants back onto a *Mayflower*-size ship "with no overcrowding." Embedded in the germ plasm of the Pilgrims had been the traits that ensured the moral health of future generations of Americans—the best the Old World had to offer the New, in eugenicists' view. A sharp decline in the birthrate of Pilgrim descendants threatened the survival of these qualities in the American population. "Considering the role which the *Mayflower* descendants have played in the history of our nation," two eugenicists wrote, "this result is certainly one to be greatly deplored." The linchpin of the *Mayflower* studies was the congruence of religious belief and fecundity: Whereas religion still exercised an influence over Jews and Catholics ("families are unusually large in certain sects"), it no longer held sway over Protestants. "Religion," the same study warned, "has largely ceased to make itself effective among Protestants."[37]

Worse, the replacement population for these hardy Pilgrims was unlikely to match its forebearers' good works. As "the old New England families are dying out," Prof. Edwin Grant Conklin said, "their places are being taken by recent immigrants."[38] For eugenicists, who viewed southern and eastern European immigrants as inferior types, this trend posed a threat to the nation's race health. In the country at large, fears of imported radicalism, fueled by wartime fervor, had changed the tone of U.S. efforts to assimilate immigrants. Americanization in the war years became "the civilian side of national defense."[39] The campaign for "100% Americanism" that emerged in these years resembled earlier glorifications of Anglo-Saxonism (such as Rev. Josiah Strong's hymns of racial uplift), but the mood of the country in the 1910s was becoming more pessimistic. A few social critics saw the real danger of immigration as accelerating already nefarious cultural trends. The melting pot brewed "a tasteless, colorless fluid of uniformity," Randolph Bourne said. Immigrants became "the flotsam and jetsam of American life, the downward undertow of our civilization with its leering cheapness and falseness of taste and spiritual work."[40] But most observers did not worry that the vaunted American melting pot was producing a cultural gruel; they feared it was boiling over, the country incapable of assimilating such untoward stock. Writer Andrew Siegfried observed that the old Protestant majority "have a vague uneasy fear of being overwhelmed from within, and of suddenly finding one day that they are no longer themselves."[41]

This depleting Protestant majority surely was uneasy, as Siegfried suggested, but they were not all vague in their assessments of the situation. Eugenicist Madison Grant declared that in the United States, "the melting pot is an absolute failure."[42] For eugenicists, immigration, like war, had serious implications for the future health of the race. The public might view it as an economic or political problem, but these aspects of immigration "are temporary and insignificant as compared with its biological consequences," as eugenicist Conklin warned. Only immigration restriction, a necessary form of world eugenics, could keep superior races geographically separated from inferior races.[43]

Eugenicists' pessimistic prognostications about immigration were summarized well by University of Wisconsin sociologist Edward A. Ross in 1915. Asked by the *American Journal of Sociology* to answer the question "What is Americanism?" Ross described a nation governed by eugenic social policies, including stricter control of immigration to "forestall the weakening of our social and political democracy by ignorant superstitious people from the backward lands, many of whom not only lend themselves readily to exploitation, but can also be employed politically as instruments for the exploitation of others." Rather than note the immigrants' potential for success in the New World, Ross focused on what he saw as their easily exploitable natures, which, he concluded, posed a threat to democracy.[44]

The most vitriolic denunciation of the new immigrants came from that maligner of the melting pot, Madison Grant. A wealthy lawyer and amateur naturalist from New York City and a founder and president of the New York Zoological Society, Grant combined his belief in Nordic racial superiority with alarmist sentiments about immigration to produce *The Passing of the Great Race* in 1916. Grant's adoration of Nordicism rather than Anglo-*Saxonism* was motivated by the circumstances of the current European conflict. Like Rev. Hillis, Grant had to reformulate his theories to conform to the country's condemnation of Germans. His book was a paean to the physical and mental characteristics of the Nordic race and a plea to halt the process of race mixing (Grant subscribed to a theory of reversion that posited that race mixing led to the reemergence of latent characteristics of earlier, primitive types, and hence to race deterioration). Like Ross, he saw eugenics as the solution and proposed applying negative eugenic measures "to an ever widening circle of social discards," beginning with criminals and the mentally ill, but "extending gradually to types which may be called weaklings" and eventually "to worthless race types."[45]

Eugenicists' calls for immigration restriction pitted the Protestant establishment against arriving Catholic and Jewish immigrants, and the anti-immigrant philippics of this period contain strong currents of religious bias. Grant saved the worst of his accusations for Polish Jews. Old-stock Americans were "today being literally driven off the streets of New York City by the swarms of Polish Jews," he wrote, "whose dwarf stature, peculiar mentality, and ruthless concentration on self-interest are being engrafted upon the stock of the nation." His paranoia elevated, Grant charged, "These immigrants adopt the language of the native American; they wear his clothes; they steal his name; and they are beginning to take his women, but they seldom adopt his religion or understand his ideals, and while he is being elbowed out of his own home the American looks calmly abroad and urges on others the suicidal ethics which are exterminating his own race." He urged his readers to put aside the "maud-lin sentimentalism" surrounding immigration and stop the nation's sweep "toward a racial abyss."[46]

Eugenicists were not the only members of the Protestant social order who viewed Jewish and Catholic immigrants as a threat. Protestant ministers were not immune to such fears. In *The New Opportunities of the Ministry*, Rev. Fred-erick Lynch characterized southern and eastern European immigrants as "full of superstitions and with a very childlike apprehension of religion." He asked, "Can the Christian Church transform this seething pot of Jews and Slavs and Latins into Christians, convert the Jew and redeem the former Christian?"[47] Similarly, British cleric F. B. Meyer, author of *Religion and Race-Regeneration*, lamented the high birthrates of Jews, Catholics, and the feebleminded, lumping them together as a collective menace to society.[48]

Not all religious leaders agreed with these dire pronouncements. Writing in the *North American Review* in 1912, Rev. Percy Stickney Grant dismissed the immigration restrictionists by noting, "Every race considers itself superior; its diatribes against other races are sheer vanity." He recommended a reconstruc-tion of the U.S. understanding of democracy, one that could include a broader range of peoples.[49] Catholic and Jewish leaders also defended the new immi-grants, though not always to the satisfaction of the native-born workers who felt their livelihoods jeopardized by the arrival of so many low-paid laborers. After listening to a university president and a Catholic archbishop both de-nounce immigration restrictionists, one observer mused: "I wonder what they would say if two shiploads, one of college presidents and another of archbish-ops, had landed last week, and the foreign-born college presidents and arch-bishops were now trying to get their jobs."[50]

Anti-immigrant grumbling did prompt government action, but none as sweeping as the restrictive legislation that would appear in the 1920s; for the most part, the public remained guardedly optimistic about assimilation. At-tempts by Congress to require a literacy test for admission of immigrants were thwarted by presidential vetoes in 1911 and 1915, for example.[51] Writing in *The Nation* in 1915, essayist Horace Kallen likened the new immigrants not to a menacing, swarming horde, but to instruments in an orchestra, each with its specific timbre. Unlike a symphony, however, which is written before it is played, "in the symphony of civilization the playing is the writing, so that there is nothing so fixed and inevitable about its progressions as in music." For Kallen, this meant that the variety of American harmonies "became wider and richer and more beautiful" as a result of the new tones.[52]

This was the theme of British dramatist Israel Zangwill's 1908 play, *The Melting Pot*. Zangwill (1864–1926), the son of Jewish immigrants, was raised in the Whitechapel ghetto of London's East End and his experience there shaped the themes that marked his work: assimilation and toleration of Jews, world peace, social reform, and Zionism. *The Melting Pot* focused on the issue of assimilation through the fictional experiences of David Quixano, a young Jewish immigrant and violin player from the Russian Pale who lives in New York with his uncle and his uncle's mother. In the story, David meets and falls in love with Vera Revendal, a fellow Russian immigrant who, in preternaturally perfect progressive fashion, is both a Christian and a settlement house worker. Despite David's faith in America as a "race crucible," capable of assimilating all those who come to her shores, however, he and Vera are unable to overcome their religious differences and marry. The tone of the play is, nevertheless, optimistic. Zangwill used the character of David to argue that, in the United States, opportunities for immigrants of all creeds were limitless; the play was promoted as a "drama of the amalgamation of the races." "The real American has not yet arrived," David tells his uncle, an irascible fellow who scoffs at David's optimism. "He is only in the Crucible, I tell you—he will be the fusion of all races, perhaps the coming superman."[53]

The subtext throughout Zangwill's play is the strain intermarriage between Jews and non-Jews added to the already great challenge of assimilation. When young David expresses his desire to marry the Christian Vera, his uncle accuses him of rejecting "the call of our blood through immemorial generations" and throws him out of the house. David remains firm in his rejection of his religious heritage, emphasizing instead his and Vera's common identities as Americans. The image of the melting pot is his guide, and the play closes with David ecstatically praising what it stands for: "There she lies, the great Melting Pot—listen! Can't you hear the roaring and the bubbling? There gapes her mouth—the harbour where a thousand mammoth feeders come from the ends of the world to pour in their human freight. Ah, what a stirring and seething . . . How the great Alchemist melts and fuses them with his purging flame!" As the curtain falls, the audience hears the piping strains of "My Country 'tis of Thee" and David predicts, "Here shall they all unite to build the Republic of Man and the Kingdom of God."[54]

Zangwill captured well the clash of culture and faith sparked by assimilation, but his work reveals that he was also sensitive to the disruptions that immigration could create for a society. Unlike eugenicists, however, he argued vociferously against restricting immigration. "The notion that the few millions of people in America have a moral right to exclude others is monstrous," he said, and in his nonfiction writing he characterized the vetting procedures at Ellis Island as unreasonably cruel.[55]

Zangwill's version of the American melting pot was at odds with the pessimistic posture of most eugenicists. Invoking the language of Zangwill's play, the *American Breeders' Magazine* editorialized, "We have in most unjustifiable and unscientific fashion been assuming that in this great 'melting pot' the best qualities of all nations and all races are being run into one great flux from which there would be cast one superior individual—a superman—the American." Such optimism about race mixture was unwarranted and dangerous, they concluded, because the new immigrants were of inferior racial types.[56] "Mental, spiritual, and moral traits," Madison Grant reminded the public, "are closely associated with the physical distinctions among the different European races." Unrestricted immigration by the wrong racial types would lead to spiritual and moral, as well as physical, deterioration.[57]

Zangwill's play debuted during a period of increased immigration by Jews. Between 1880 and 1921, over 2 million Jews arrived in the United States. Most came from eastern Europe (immigration to the United States during these years represented 33 percent of the Jews living in eastern Europe), and most settled in New York City's Lower East Side. By 1915, Jews made up 28 percent of the city's population. These immigrants were largely Orthodox Jews, fleeing the persecution of the Russian pogroms that had begun in the 1880s. Unlike their Americanized, German Jewish counterparts, most of whom were Reform Jews, the new immigrants raised questions in the minds of the native-born about their ability to assimilate. Most of the new immigrants spoke Yiddish, a mixture of Russian, Hebrew, and High German, and appeared both to non-Jews and to many American Reform Jews insular and unwilling to adapt to American culture.[58]

Abraham Cahan's novel *The Rise of David Levinsky*, published in 1917, recorded the immigrants' struggle and offered readers an entry into the broad sweep of Jewish immigrant life on the Lower East Side of New York. Cahan, a Russian Jewish immigrant who founded and edited the Yiddish newspaper, the *Jewish Daily Forward*, drew on his own experiences to craft the character of David Levinsky, a Russian immigrant whose assimilation was not rendered with as much optimism as Zangwill's enthusiastic David. Cahan's David discovers that, despite achieving material success in the United States, spiritual and personal fulfillment elude him because he sacrifices his faith to mammon. The closing pages of the novel find Levinsky despairing, "My sense of triumph is coupled with a brooding sense of emptiness and insignificance. There are cases when success is a tragedy."[59]

The often difficult process of assimilation that Cahan depicted in his novel was a point of serious discussion among leading Jewish intellectuals at this time and was linked to their concerns about growing levels of anti-Semitism in the country. It is no coincidence that during these years of heavy immigration, Jews organized two major defense organizations, the American Jewish Committee, founded in 1906, and the Anti-Defamation League of B'nai B'rith, founded in 1913. The murder trial and vigilante-style execution of Leo Frank, who was president of the local B'nai B'rith chapter in Atlanta, in 1913–1915, exposed the virulence of the nation's, and particularly the South's, anti-Semitism.[60]

Concerned as they were with the general problem of immigration, eugenicists nevertheless gave special attention to the issue of Jewish immigration and assimilation. Two questions dominated their discussions of Jews during

these years. First, were the Jews a distinct race? Although much of the groundwork for this debate had been laid in the nineteenth century by European race
theorists such as Joseph Arthur de Gobineau, Ernest Renan, Georges Vacher
de Lapouges, Werner Sombart, and Houston Stewart Chamberlain, U.S. eugenicists sought to craft a response to this question that incorporated the vagaries of the recent U.S. experience.[61] The second question followed from the
first, and was something eugenicists were asking of all new immigrants: What
effects might assimilation, particularly intermarriage among different immigrant groups, have on American society?

On the first question, most eugenicists agreed, though with some equiv-
ocation, that the Jews were a distinct race. As early as 1909, eugenicist Caleb
Saleeby had argued that the Jews were a separate race whose adherence to the
hygienic dictates of their religion helped ensure their survival.[62] In one sense,
questions about racial distinctiveness stemmed from eugenicists' tendency to
equate national and racial identity and to assume, for example, that Germans,
Greeks, Italians, and Irish were each biologically different groups.[63] In this
rendering, Jews were a separate race as well, whom eugenicists sometimes
referred to as Hebrews. What eugenicists could not agree on, however, was the
criteria for determining racial distinctiveness.

In a lecture on immigration, Charles Davenport suggested that Jewish
distinctiveness stemmed from a history of isolation. Not surprisingly, his interpretation of the Jewish experience in Europe was historically misguided and
filled with stereotypes. "For centuries the peoples of Europe . . . have established Ghettoes where Jews were segregated, partly by their own preference,
much as the negroes are segregated in many Southern states," Davenport told
his audience. "Isolated by their instincts and their greed, [and] by their Yiddish
language," they formed "an alien people in the country where they dwelt and
reproduced so unrestrictedly."[64] A letter from H. B. Hayden, a member of the
Washington, D.C. Army and Navy Club, to Davenport demonstrated a similar
anxiety about Jews. In the correspondence, Hayden asked about the advisability
of a marriage between a friend's son, who was "a practically pure Nordic type,"
and a woman whose ancestry included one Jewish grandparent; Hayden was
concerned about the offspring of such a union. "Will they be a good addition
to society or will they be queer?" he asked. Davenport's response was equivocal.
Although the "Jewish type" was dominant in any intermarriage, he said, and
this was not necessarily desirable from the standpoint of eugenics, these
mixtures were becoming more common and at least "seem to be socially adap-
tible [sic]."[65]

British physician Redcliffe N. Salaman, writing in the Eugenics Review, also
concluded that the Jews were a distinct race, but he emphasized their identi-
fiable physical characteristics. Through an analysis of intermarriage case studies, Salaman concluded that a "Jewish facial type" existed that was "subject to
the Mendelian law of Heredity" and was, among the children of intermarried

couples, a dominant trait. He described the facial expression thus: "a long and heavy nose, eyes somewhat close together with long upper eyelids, rounded angles to the jaw, prominent and rounded chin, and rounded and spacious forehead." Salaman's methods for gathering this information eerily foreshadowed the Nazis', including intense genealogical excavation to find Jewish ancestors in supposedly non-Jewish families. Although Salaman was confident that such physical distinctions existed among world Jewry, he refrained from making judgments about Jewish mental traits. "At present," he wrote, "one is in entire darkness as to whether the physical features that one recognises as Jewish are allied with any peculiar psychical qualities." When he did venture a personal opinion on this question, he admitted that he had only a "strong feeling"—but no evidence—that there existed a "distinctive mental attitude which is Jewish."[66]

Like Salaman, Prof. Louis Covitt of Clark University also argued that a distinct "facial expression" characterized Jews and served as evidence of their racial distinctiveness. However, he went further, speculating as to the causes of this trait. He identified as important "the pathos and tragedy of ages of persecution and martyrdom" and, in a willing embrace of the negative stereotypes common in this era, "the cunning and shrewdness that is characteristic of all people who have to live by their wits." Covitt also argued that the Jews shared a common "psychic personality," a "race consciousness" that was "fully alive" and growing in intensity in the modern era.[67] This amorphous "race consciousness," or "race solidarity," as it was also called, was central to eugenicists' understanding of Jews. Eugenicists were convinced that it existed as a dominant trait, and they were even more certain that it was ineradicable. As one writer put it, "No amount of Americanization will be able to get it out of the system." It was the factor that spelled doom for assimilation.[68]

The distinctiveness and, hence, the unassimilability of the Jews, like their supposedly excessive "shrewdness and cunning," became stereotype staples for eugenicists who assumed that such qualities were heritable traits, bred over the course of centuries. Prof. Covitt matter-of-factly told readers, "These elements have by long use and repetition fused and become hereditary."[69] In a triumph of circular logic, the negative stereotypes held individually by many eugenicists became the basis for "scientific" arguments purportedly proving Jewish inferiority. Samples of statements from just a few of the country's prominent eugenicists suffice to prove the point. Just after World War I, one of anti-Semitism's incarnations came in publicly announced quotas for Jewish students seeking entry into prestigious universities such as Harvard and Yale. In a letter to a colleague, biologist Raymond Pearl explained his support for quotas by pointing to the Jews' "high survival rate." "There is a complete absence [in Jews] of any inhibiting sense of morals or decency," he said. Pearl went on to express paranoid fears of a race confrontation between Jews and Gentiles, asking fearfully, "Whose world is this to be, ours, or the Jews?"[70] Eugenicist Madison Grant (whose extreme racism Pearl, oddly enough, publicly criticized) warned Americans of Jewish plots to steal their women, an anti-Semitic paranoia ERO chief Charles Davenport candidly returned in a letter to Grant in 1925. Vexed over the country's unwillingness to take action on immigration restriction, Davenport wrote, "Our ancestors drove Baptists from Massachusetts Bay into Rhode Island, but we have no place to drive the Jews to."[71]

Not all eugenicists expressed such extreme views. When they focused strictly on physical traits, such as susceptibility to diseases or infant mortality rates, a few eugenicists reported statistics that were favorable to Jews.[72] Dr. Lester Levyn of New York, for example, catalogued the many ailments to which Jews proved less susceptible than non-Jews, including tuberculosis, pneumonia, smallpox, typhoid, and intestinal disorders. He attributed this physical hardiness to a process of selection "that has lasted two thousand years, and has been the most severe and most painful which living beings have ever had to endure."[73]

Nevertheless, eugenicists often paired favorable statistics on physical health with unfavorable ones that purported to reveal higher rates of mental illness among Jews, particularly among eastern European Jewish immigrants. Dr. Levyn claimed that Jews were a disproportionate number of the nation's sufferers of nervous disorders such as hysteria, idiocy, apoplexy, and neurasthenia; as he had with physical diseases, he viewed the disorders as the logical outcome of centuries of persecution.[74] Likewise, in a 1917 survey of arriving immigrants at Ellis Island, Henry H. Goddard classified 60 percent of Jews as morons. An even higher number, he claimed, were high-grade feebleminded. These statistics proved their inferiority as a race, Goddard concluded, and offered further fodder for his calls for stricter immigration laws.[75]

Still, there was dissent among scientists and social scientists over eugenicists' arguments about Jewish racial distinctiveness. Writing in the *Journal of Heredity* in 1916, Maynard Metcalf of the Orchard Laboratory at Oberlin College argued that, despite centuries of social ostracism, a "racial fusion" had occurred between Jews and their neighbors. A Jew in Syria, Germany, or Spain "resembles his local neighbor more than he resembles his brother Jew of another country," Metcalf noted. To speak of Jews as a distinct race was, therefore, misleading.[76] Picking up on this theme, psychiatrist A. A. Brill of New York Medical School argued that any claims (such as Levyn's and Goddard's) that Jews suffered higher rates of mental illness only because of inborn racial flaws was incorrect. Instead, he blamed the "past environment" of the Jews and their current struggles with assimilation. "A gradual transition from eastern to western civilization intelligently guided by a sound mental and social hygiene," he wrote, "will prevent such abnormal reactions as neuroses, psychoses and criminality in the adjusting Jew." Although Brill did assume that such a thing as the "sensitive Hebraic nature" existed, his emphasis on Jews' current environmental conditions challenged the eugenicists' static portrait of heredity-based Jewish inferiority.[77]

It was left to a physician, anthropologist, and Russian Jewish immigrant named Maurice Fishberg (1872–1934) to mount a definitive defense of the Jews against claims of racial inferiority. Dr. Fishberg recognized the danger inherent in claiming that the Jews were a distinctive race, and he stated it explicitly in his work. Anti-Semites attempted "to put a pseudo-scientific veneer on their agitation" by propounding "a theory that the 'Jewish race' constitutes a branch of the Semitic race" that is "incapable of assimilating European standards of morals and fair-play." Instead, he concluded in his 1911 study, *The Jews: A Study of Race and Environment,* there were "no differences between Jews and Christians which can solely be attributed to racial causes, and which depend solely on hereditary transmission." His own statistical findings revealed that Jews produced a higher percentage of "physical and mental defectives" *and* a higher proportion of "persons of marked ability" than other groups. In Fishberg's telling, the Jews were not an example of a distinct race made purer through a rigorous process of natural selection-by-persecution. They were a conglomeration of "various racial elements" whose history demonstrated the force of religious, environmental, and social conditions.[78]

Following the lead of anthropologist Franz Boas, whose research demonstrated the decisive influence of environment on the supposedly intractable racial qualities of immigrants, Fishberg rejected the hereditarian interpretations of eugenicists. Rather, he claimed that observable differences between Jews and non-Jews were due to social factors—mainly differences in religious beliefs and practices—that he called the "separative tenets of Judaism."[79] Fishberg himself did not believe that all of these practices were good. In a series of articles published in the *American Hebrew,* he noted that although Jewish marriage and divorce laws were "more in accordance with the principles of eugenics than the Christian and Mohammedan marriage laws," the Achnoses Jaleh (societies that provided dowries for marriage to poor Jewish women regardless of their physical or mental fitness) and Jewish charities sometimes exercised a dysgenic influence.[80]

On the whole, Fishberg's portrait of Jewish immigrants undermined eugenicists' claims of racial inferiority by arguing that cultural conditions, not heredity, explained differences. Rather than responding directly to the challenges Fishberg posed, however, eugenicists selectively reprinted his findings in their own journals. The *Eugenical News,* for example, reported the results of Fishberg's study on the high proportion of Jews with mental defects but gave no mention to his larger conclusion that such traits were the result of environmental rather than hereditary influences.[81]

In his defense of Jewish immigrants, Fishberg hoped to combat the misleading science of eugenicists and to counter the negative stereotypes of Jews that made regular appearances in the popular publications. Magazines and newspapers continued to promulgate stereotypes of Jews as the parasitic masterminds of worldwide financial conspiracies.[82] These stereotypes found a permanent home in Henry Ford's newspaper, the *Dearborn Independent*, which serialized passages from the notoriously anti-Semitic *Protocols of the Elders of Zion* in 1920. Replete with spurious claims about a Jewish plot to take over the world, the articles (which appeared at the height of the Red Scare) tapped into Americans' fears of Jews as adherents and potential importers of the radical doctrines of the Russian Revolution.[83]

Like eugenicists, Protestant clergymen sometimes flavored their public statements with anti-Semitic rhetoric in these years. An unnamed Episcopal clergyman, writing in the *American Citizen* in 1912, argued that the Jew's "chauvinism, his race-pride, race conceit, race-exclusiveness, [and] race aloofness," and not anti-Semitism, were causes of prejudice against them.[84] Another anonymous Protestant minister, responding to a poll sponsored by the *American Hebrew* magazine, spoke of Jewish "snobbishness" and asked, "Have you not held yourself apart from the life of this New World in a nook of your own . . . looking down from your fancied eminence as the chosen race?"[85]

These ministers' accusations of "race pride" and "race exclusiveness" echoed those made by eugenicists, but among Jewish leaders, a related debate had been raging about race distinctiveness and the effects of intermarriage on the contemporary Jewish community. The lightning rod in this debate was Israel Zangwill's play, *The Melting Pot*. In a speech delivered at the Free Synagogue in New York, Reform Rabbi Leon Harrison of Temple Israel in St. Louis claimed that Zangwill's message of assimilation was dangerous to Jews. "The Hebrew race has nothing to bind it together and preserve it, except its religion," Harrison argued, "which is in turn dependent on its refusal to intermarry." Lest anyone accuse Jews of extreme separatism for this prohibition, Harrison reminded his audience that the Catholic Church also condemned intermarriage. Invoking "holy traditions, sacred memories, and transcendent ideals," he ended his speech with a plea to Jews to "fulfill your racial destiny from within" and reject intermarriage.[86]

Five months later, the leader of the Free Synagogue, Reform Rabbi Stephen S. Wise, joined Harrison in condemning intermarriage. According to the *New York Times*, Wise took "emphatic ground against the intermarriage of Jews and Christians" in his weekly sermon.[87] Evidently, Rabbi Harrison's and Rabbi Wise's stance was not universally accepted by their Reform Jewish coreligionists, for a heated debate broke out over the question of intermarriage at the 1909 meeting of the Central Conference of American Rabbis. Newspaper reports noted frayed tempers, especially among older rabbis in the conference who opposed intermarriage (one asked why the supporters of intermarriage, "in their denial of Jewish authority, did not all go over to Unitarianism"). The foes of intermarriage eventually triumphed and the Conference passed a mildly worded resolution declaring "mixed marriages between Jews and non-Jews contrary to the traditions of the Jewish religion" and urging the U.S. rabbinate to discourage such unions.[88]

Even the prosperous, assimilated character of David Levinsky in Abraham Cahan's novel harbored doubts about intermarriage. Considering marriage to a non-Jewish woman with whom he had developed a strong friendship, Levinsky says, "I saw clearly that it would be a mistake. It was not the faith of my father that was in the way. It was that medieval prejudice against our people which makes so many marriages between Jew and Gentile a failure." Levinsky goes so far as to tell the object of his affection, "It's really a pity that there is the chasm of race between us. Otherwise I don't see why we couldn't be happy together."[89]

In contrast, many secular Jewish leaders did not consider intermarriage a threat. Speaking also at the Free Synagogue, Charles Zueblin, a former sociology professor at the University of Chicago and editor of *Twentieth Century* magazine, responded to the opposition of Rabbis Harrison and Wise by arguing that intermarriage was desirable because it encouraged race mixing, and "strength comes from mixture." Unlike eugenicists, who viewed this type of amalgamation with extreme skepticism, Zueblin optimistically predicted that the resulting mixture would "retain the best traits of both" and contribute to "the common racial good."[90] Dr. Fishberg had encouraged intermarriage for similar reasons, viewing it as the best means for ending the social and cultural isolation of the Jews in the United States.[91]

The intermarriage debate highlighted how the concept of race informed nearly every discussion of Jews in these years. Supporters of intermarriage encouraged "race mixing" and denied that a pure Jewish race even existed. Opponents of intermarriage justified their stance by calling on Jews to fulfill their "racial destiny" and maintain that supposedly nonexistent race purity. And many eugenicists continued to insist that the Jews harbored hereditary traits that threatened the nation's future. The "chasm of race" so clear to David Levinsky in Cahan's novel was felt in this debate as well.

Rabbi Max Reichler (1886–1957) attempted to bridge this chasm in a copiously annotated essay that outlined the common ground between Jewish teachings and eugenics. In "Jewish Eugenics," a paper read before the New York Board of Jewish Ministers in 1915, Reichler argued that "eugenic rules" were "incorporated in the large collection of Biblical and Rabbinical laws." Through a thorough excavation of those parts of the Talmud that engage the questions of marriage and reproduction, Reichler made his case.[92]

Rabbi Reichler brought a unique perspective to the eugenics movement. As an active Reform rabbi, serving first at the Sinai Temple in the Bronx and later at the Beth Sholem Peoples Temple in Brooklyn, as well as in numerous religious and civic organizations, he was connected to a wide web of secular and religious reformers. His interest in eugenics likely grew out of his experiences in this milieu. But Reichler was also an eastern European immigrant, having come to the United States from Presburg, Hungary, when he was 9 years old. Like Maurice Fishberg, another Jewish immigrant who examined the eugenics movement, Reichler was particularly sensitive to the anti-immigrant prejudices of the day.[93]

Reichler began his presentation to the Board of Jewish Ministers by noting the seriousness with which Jewish leaders approached the issues of marriage and reproduction. "The Rabbis, like the eugenists of to-day," he wrote, "measured the success of a marriage by the number and quality of the offspring." According to Talmudic teachings, the main objects of marriage were *leshem piryah veribyah* (the reproduction of the human race) and *lethikun havlad* (the augmentation of the favored stock). The latter occurred in part through strict adherence to the prohibitions against the marriage of "defectives" such as lepers, epileptics, the deaf and the dumb, and the lame and the blind.[94] As interpreted by Reichler, these teachings were the central principles of what he called "Jewish eugenics."

Eugenicists such as Caleb Saleeby had praised these hygienic rules, and popular eugenics books written by amateurs earlier in the century had made mention of them. The authors of *The Science of Eugenics and Sex Life* (1904), for example, noted, "The Jews as a race are singularly free from the contaminations arising from the sexual diseases" because they followed "the law of Moses on sex-hygiene."[95] Yet Reichler went one step further. He argued that Jewish eugenics had a "distinctive feature" lacking in the current eugenics movement: an emphasis on "psychical" as well as physical well-being. Rabbis had recognized that "both physical and psychical qualities were inherited," Reichler said, endeavoring "by direct precept and law, as well as by indirect advice and admonition, to preserve and improve the inborn, wholesome qualities of the Jewish race."[96]

Reichler was sensitive to the perception that his construction of a Jewish eugenics and his claims for the purity of the Jewish race might appear "narrow and chauvinistic," but he justified his support for racial distinctiveness by turning the arguments of eugenicist William E. Kellicott in his favor. In his 1911 book, *The Social Direction of Human Evolution*, Kellicott argued that a "natural aristocracy" formed by the propitious pruning that Reichler said the Jews had undertaken "can become the guardians and trustees of a sound inborn heritage, which, incorruptible and undefiled," can be preserved "in purity and vigor throughout whatever period of ignorance and decay may be in store for the nation at large." Reichler argued that the Jews were just such a natural aristocracy, possessing three traits "unique to Israel": sympathy, modesty, and philanthropy.[97]

Rabbi Reichler was clearly well versed in eugenics literature, citing, in addition to Kellicott, Galton, Davenport, and others to bolster his claims. His work did not go unnoticed by eugenicists; an excerpt of his essay, absent the annotations, appeared in the *Journal of Heredity* in February 1917. Nor did secular Jewish leaders ignore it. Physician Maurice Fishberg cited the study and readily agreed with Reichler's conclusion that "rabbinical teachings are teeming with positive eugenic suggestions." Indeed, Fishberg claimed that "the rabbis anticipated Galton by about sixteen hundred years." Although Reichler's work emphasized the distinctive qualities of the Jewish race and Fishberg argued against that distinction, they did agree that Jewish religious dictates had hygienic benefits, or, as Fishberg put it, Judaism "utilized piety for the preservation of health."[98]

Rabbi Reichler's work marked the first attempt by a rabbi to reconcile eugenics with the Jewish faith, but he was not alone among Jewish leaders in his interest and measured support for eugenics. Two years earlier, in November 1913, Rabbi Wise sponsored a series of lectures on eugenics and mental hygiene through Synagogue House, his congregation's social service department. Speakers included notable eugenicist Alexander Johnson of the Vineland Training School in New Jersey.[99] Although it is impossible to assess the turnout for such events (or, for that matter, to assess the tenor of the discussions), it is nevertheless revealing that one of the country's most well-known Jewish leaders used his synagogue to sponsor discussions of eugenics.

The efforts of liberal-minded religious leaders such as Rabbis Wise and Reichler, as well as those of Rev. Hillis, mark a shift in the relationship between eugenicists and churchmen. The public's and, increasingly, the eugenics movement's own desire to find answers to the questions sparked by immigration and world war created space for pulpit leaders to fill. During these years eugenicists demonstrated a greater willingness to grant religious leaders a venue, whether at their national conferences or in the pages of their journals. This impulse to include the views of religious leaders in the eugenics movement would reach full flower in the 1920s with the creation of a new organization, the American Eugenics Society, which actively recruited religious leaders to the cause of race improvement.

4

Eugenicists Discover Jesus

Yea, I have a goodly heritage.
> —Psalm 16:6, inscription on the medals
> given to "Grade A" individuals in the Fitter
> Family Contest at the 1924 Kansas Free Fair

"Selling the idea of Better Health." This was the mission of the in-
defatigable Dr. Almus Pickerbaugh, public health advocate and bane
of Martin Arrowsmith in Sinclair Lewis's 1925 novel. "Let's every
health booster, crow just like a rooster," advised Pickerbaugh. "What
the world needs is a really inspired, courageous, overtowering leader—
say a Billy Sunday of the movement—a man who would know how
to use sensationalism properly and wake the people out of their
sloth." Pickerbaugh was a caricature, but in the 1920s, eugenicists
followed his lead and began exploring ways to sell the idea of Better
Breeding to a curious public. The seeds of this new, popular eugenics were planted at the Second International Eugenics Congress,
held at the American Museum of Natural History in New York City
in 1921. There, eugenicists such as Irving Fisher of Yale University
challenged colleagues to organize a vigorous, popular educational
program to promote eugenics throughout the country. An Interim
Committee was soon formed, and by 1922 this small group was on
its way to becoming the American Eugenics Society.[1]
　　Unlike the Eugenics Record Office, whose main purpose was
scientific research, the American Eugenics Society (AES) from its inception emphasized propaganda and public education. In the late
1910s, a few scientists had proposed popular campaigns for race bet-

terment. In his presidential address, read before the Eugenics Research Association at Cold Spring Harbor in June 1917, physician Adolf Meyer noted that the eugenics movement "has so far worked mainly by its appeal to natural human meliorism, and that very largely negatively." Although "it may have raised the *fear* of tainted families," only to a lesser extent had it provided "a wider and clearer knowledge about them." Fellow eugenicist A. E. Hamilton urged his colleagues to "positivize our negative eugenics" to gain wider approval of the movement's goals.[2]

Eugenicists' desire to improve their movement's public image by "positivizing" their message fit the tenor of the times. The 1920s witnessed the extraordinary growth of the field of advertising, with its corporate "ad men" intent on peddling products to the public in a manner that often emphasized image over substance. As one ad writer in the 1920s described his trade, "You do not sell a man the tea, but the magical spell which is brewed nowhere else but in a tea-pot."[3] The new AES would soon have its own version of ad men: professional, nonscientific promoters who ginned up popular interest in eugenics through an accessible, sometimes sensational style. These new tacticians had larger pretensions than the average advertising agent, however; they compared their task to the "founding and development of Christianity."[4]

The cultivation of this new eugenic faith required an accessible credo. Like all good self-promoters, the leaders of the AES understood that the success of their goals required simplification of their message. Lengthy, arcane scientific treatises would not whet the public's appetite for eugenics. In 1926, Leon F. Whitney, a farmer and dog breeder who served as the AES's secretary, constructed the *Eugenics Catechism* to meet this need.[5] The *Catechism* was quintessential AES propaganda. In a commonsense, positive tone and a question-and-answer catechetical style, it summarized the principles of the eugenics movement:

Q: What is the most precious thing in the world?
A: The human germplasm.

Q: How may one's germplasm become immortal?
A: Only by perpetuation through children.

When the *Catechism* hinted at negative eugenic plans such as sterilization, it did so innocuously:

Q: Is vasectomy a serious operation?
A: No, very slight, about like pulling a tooth.

The *Catechism* even anticipated its audience's religious concerns. As to the question of whether eugenics contradicted the Bible, it reassured readers, "The Bible has much to say for eugenics. It tells us that men do not gather grapes from thorns and figs from thistles."[6] The *Eugenics Catechism* became one of the most frequently requested pieces of AES literature. Thousands likely read its simplified sketch of eugenics. After writer and lecturer Albert E. Wiggam suggested in his book, *The Next Age of Man*, that readers request copies of the tract, hundreds of petitions poured into the Society's offices from lawyers, journalists, homemakers, dentists, accountants, and even an entire Grand Lodge of Masons from Reno, Nevada.[7]

In February 1923, the AES had a hundred members; within seven years it would have more than twelve hundred.[8] This rapid growth was a testament to the propagandizing prowess of its leaders. One of the AES's most successful early campaigns was a series of eugenics exhibits at state fairs and regional expositions. In their booth at the Sesqui-Centennial Exposition in Philadelphia in 1926, for example, the AES display included a twelve-foot-long blue board with juxtaposed flashing lights, one flashing every 16 seconds to note the birth of a person in the United States and another flashing every 7.5 minutes to mark the birth of a "high-grade person." The exhibit helpfully reminded the viewer that the latter constituted only 4 percent of the total population.[9]

The AES also participated in state fairs across the country, where, working with local health officials, they sponsored competitions for eugenic families. These "Fitter Families for Future Firesides" contests had their origins in "better baby" contests held sporadically at state fairs during the 1910s. Whereas these earlier contests emphasized infant health, the Fitter Families competitions sought to stimulate "a feeling of family and racial consciousness and responsibility." Examiners combed the pages of family Bibles and other documents to construct hereditary histories. They probed participants' physical and mental health by measuring posture and strength, peering into eyes, ears, and throats, and taking blood and urine samples.[10]

The promise of poking and prodding did not deter participants. Contest organizer Mary T. Watts, who explicitly equated the judging process with livestock examinations going on in nearby tents, reported, "Parents come from miles around bringing their little broods and spend most of a hard-earned holiday securing an examination for every member of the family." Fitter Families officials staged elaborate pageants at the conclusion of the festivities; winners at the 1925 Kansas Fair competition, for example, were paraded around in automobiles under lavishly decorated banners emblazoned "Kansas' Best Crop."[11] Held at state fairs throughout Texas, Michigan, Oklahoma, Kansas, Massachusetts, Arkansas, and Georgia in the 1920s, the Fitter Families contests became one of the most popular methods for spreading information about eugenics to a large audience.[12] This was particularly important given that the institutional eugenics movement was concentrated geographically along a narrow corridor stretching from New York City to Long Island and into Connecticut. Fitter Families contests at expositions and fairs exposed ordinary Americans to the somewhat rarified world of eugenics and made it familiar.[13] So familiar, in fact, that even country parsons participated. At the Kansas Free Fair in Topeka in September 1929, Rev. Henry Apel and his family, who hailed from Delia, tied for first place with another eugenically fit brood. Honorable mention went to the family of Rev. Clarence Broadfoot of Burlingame, whose six children scored exceptionally high in their eugenic examination.[14] Rev. Kenneth C. MacArthur of the Federated Church in Sterling, Massachusetts, and his family were the winners of the trophy for the average-size family (four children) at the Eastern States Exposition in 1925.[15]

Although local public health and hygiene officials often managed such competitions, national standards drafted by the AES governed the judging. The AES also chose the design for the medals awarded to "Grade A" individuals at the fairs. Turning again to religion for guidance, Prof. Irving Fisher assigned eugenicist Madison Grant (author of *The Passing of the Great Race*) the task of "search[ing] the Scriptures for an appropriate motto" for the medals. The resulting bronze "Capper" medals (named for U.S. Sen. Arthur Capper) featured a portrait of a eugenically fit family holding aloft a torch and inscribed, "Yea, I have a goodly heritage." Just as the *Eugenics Catechism* referenced Scripture, so, too, the Capper medal's motto would have been familiar to Bible readers; it was from the book of Psalms, chapter 16. The medal later served as cover art for the AES journal *Eugenics*, and eugenics promoter Albert E. Wiggam chose it as the frontispiece for his best-selling book, *The Next Age of Man*.[16]

Fitter Families contests encouraged public participation in the eugenics movement, but they also invited parody, in itself evidence of the AES's success in spreading its message. Sinclair Lewis's novel *Arrowsmith* included the dénouement of an award-winning "eugenic family" at an Iowa State Fair. The fictional Fitter Family turns out to be a notorious criminal gang headed by an unwed couple; during the health examination one of their children has an epileptic seizure.[17] Nevertheless, the success of these contests demonstrates the public's concern with the health of American families and their eagerness to live by the standards that science was setting for their perpetuation.

That the AES often relied on biblical imagery and language to make its arguments was evidence of a shift in eugenicists' awareness of organized religion. Since the earliest years of the eugenics movement, Francis Galton's injunction to make eugenics itself a religion had been a common reference point for his intellectual heirs, although one to which they paid homage largely in the abstract. That changed in the years immediately preceding the creation of the AES. More eugenicists began to recommend that their movement enlist the direct support of religious leaders in their crusade. In their 1918 text, *Applied Eugenics*, Paul Popenoe and Roswell Hill Johnson argued that, "without abandoning their appeal to reason, eugenists must make every effort to enlist potent emotional forces on their side. There is none so strong and available as religion, and the eugenist may turn to it with confidence of finding an effective ally, if he can once gain its sanction."[18]

FIGURE 4.1 Fitter Family Medal of the American Eugenics Society. The inscription reads, "Yea, I have a goodly heritage," from Psalms 16. American Philosophical Society, Philadelphia, Pennsylvania.

The organizers of the AES sought that sanction vigorously. While drafting a list of potential members for the organization's Advisory Council, they included a separate list of nationally known clergymen whom they planned to approach for support.[19] The minutes of these early meetings show that AES organizers assumed from the beginning that religious leaders should play a role in the Society. Whether that role would be merely symbolic or active was a detail the eugenicists left to work itself out. The only evidence of disagreement came after one eugenicist (there is no mention of whom) recommended that the group extend invitations to Reform Rabbis Stephen S. Wise and Sidney E. Goldstein to join the evolving Advisory Council. A cryptic note in the minutes of the 9 June 1922 meeting reads: "It was voted to postpone the election of a Jewish representative."[20]

Currying favor with clergymen was not an easy task, especially because the fledgling Society hoped to attract representatives from Protestant and Catholic (and eventually, Jewish) traditions. A temperate tone characterized the earliest recruitment efforts. The general letter of appeal sent to potential Advisory Council members in 1922 stressed the social rather than the scientific message of eugenics and called on its recipients to stand with eugenicists "against the forces . . . [of] racial deterioration and for progressive improvement in the vigor, intelligence, and moral fiber of the human race."[21] Here was language familiar to secular and clerical social reformers. Not surprisingly, the letter was successful in convincing a few religious leaders to join the organization, churchmen whose influence far outweighed their numbers. By 1927, the Advisory Council of the AES listed among its ranks Rev. Harry Emerson Fosdick, Bishop William Lawrence, Fr. John M. Cooper, and Rabbi Louis Mann.[22]

Of the four, Baptist minister Harry Emerson Fosdick (1878–1969) was likely the most well-known. Fosdick joined the AES Advisory Council on the heels of a very public and contentious struggle with the First Presbyterian Church in New York City, where he had preached by special arrangement since 1919 and where, in 1922, he delivered a sermon, "Shall the Fundamentalists Win?", that marked him as one of Protestantism's most outspoken proponents of theological liberalism.[23] Rev. Fosdick's motivations for joining the AES are difficult to assess. He made few public statements about eugenics, and those he did were cautious. "Few matters are more pressingly important than the application to our social problems of such well-established information in the realm of eugenics as we actually possess," was a typically restrained encomium. "The failure to do this is almost certainly going to put us in the position of endeavoring to cure symptoms while basic causes of social degeneration and disorder go untouched."[24]

The liberal Protestant theology that guided Rev. Fosdick clearly informed his assessments of modern science, which he believed offered opportunities to improve mankind. He praised the "humanitarian desire to take advantage of this scientific control of life so as to change social conditions that mankind may be relieved from crushing handicaps which now oppress it," for example. Yet on the particulars of this view of science he remained frustratingly vague. Remarking on the contortions of Fosdickian theology, Walter Lippmann concluded, "No painter who ever lived could make a picture which expressed the religion of the Rev. Harry Emerson Fosdick. There is nothing there which the visual imagination can use." This was manifest in the architecture of the Riverside Church over which Fosdick presided. Modeled after a thirteenth-century Gothic cathedral in Chartres, France, it was filled with busts of spiritual and secular heroes, from Aquinas to Einstein. Fosdick's worldview was more ambiguous than his church's Gothic modernism. His joining of a secular, scientific crusade like eugenics could be read as a way of marking his distance from the Fundamentalist critique of science, or merely (with his many other social reform pursuits) as another point in his journey of becoming, as he put it, "both an intelligent modern and a serious Christian."[25] Nevertheless, his participation on the AES Advisory Council, even if token, is notable because his influence and prestige were considerable. His contemporaries consistently named him one of the most important Protestants of his age, and after 1922 his weekly radio addresses, *National Vespers Hour*, reached 2 to 3 million listeners.[26] His endorsement was a promotional coup for the AES.

The other Protestant leader on the Advisory Council, Bishop William Lawrence (1850–1941), also enjoyed a high profile. Ordained a Protestant Episcopal priest in 1876, Lawrence was named bishop of Massachusetts in 1893 and filled the post for the next thirty-four years.[27] A liberal minister active in social reform, Lawrence, like Fosdick, praised "discoveries in geology, biology and history" as ideas that "are not to be feared or evaded but to be met and welcomed with exhilaration and confidence."[28]

Prominent Protestants such as Fosdick and Lawrence found themselves in good company on the Advisory Council. Secular members included conservationist Gifford Pinchot, Stanford University president David Starr Jordan, and eminent scientists such as Robert Yerkes and H. S. Jennings. Council members were expected to live up to their description as advisors. As the minutes of the earliest AES meetings attest, the organizing committee did not want the Council merely to rubberstamp proposals; they expected them to play an active role: "No important educational program or propaganda shall be conducted by this Committee without giving opportunity to members of the Advisory Council to object," one resolution stated. Another resolution effectively gave the Council veto power if a "substantial number" of them objected to a Society proposal.[29]

In October 1925, officers of the AES cast a vote to "authorize the establishment of three committees, namely the Committee on Cooperation with Physicians, Committee on Cooperation with Social Workers, and Committee on Cooperation with Clergymen." Of the three, it was the last that would become one of the largest and most well-funded of the fourteen standing committees of the Society. The AES named Rev. Henry Strong Huntington, brother of Yale University geographer and eugenicist Ellsworth Huntington, to head the clergymen's committee.[30] Because AES officers had provided precious few guidelines for how this new clergymen's committee should take shape, it was left to Rev. Huntington to develop a program and draft religious leaders. Huntington was an unusual man for the job. The staid sensibilities of his WASP upbringing warred with an innate intellectual restlessness that saw him through exotic travels and many odd jobs before he landed as an associate editor at the *Christian Work* magazine in the early 1920s. Known as "Harry," Rev. Huntington had an insatiable interest in experimental reform ideas; in the 1930s he embraced nudism, for example, describing his forest frolicking with similarly minded friends as "poetry incarnate."[31]

Huntington had been interested in eugenics for some time, and (perhaps under the influence of his brother Ellsworth) had devoted considerable time to studying the major theorists of the movement. He wrote *Baptist Babies*, an educational tract published by the Northern Baptist Convention and sent to every minister in the Baptist fold. The pamphlet described the eugenics program and made a plea for child allowances (payments given per child to defray the costs of bearing and raising children) specifically for the clergy.[32] While in Palestine with the Red Cross Commission in 1916, he wrote to Charles Davenport to request copies of the Eugenics Record Office's *Record of Family Traits*, noting that he was "intensely interested in the practical implications of eugenics" and believed that "we can educate the people here and educate them within a generation" about its importance.[33]

In a letter to potential committee members, Rev. Huntington repeated these educational hopes and described the committee as a forum to "work out methods of forwarding the teaching of eugenics through the churches" and to locate "new opportunities for the usefulness of the churches" in the eugenics campaign.[34] This message fell on ready ears. By 1927, Huntington had convinced thirty-nine prominent ministers to join the Committee on Cooperation with Clergymen.[35] Like the ministers who signed on to the AES Advisory Council, these men were prominent figures in their faiths, as a few examples suggest: Rev. Charles Clayton Morrison (1874–1966), a minister in the Disciples of Christ Church since 1892, exercised considerable influence over Protestant leaders through his stewardship of the *Christian Century*, the leading journal of nondenominational Protestant opinion in the twentieth century; Rev. Guy Emery Shipler (1882–1968), an Episcopal clergyman who served as editor of *The Churchman* for more than forty-five years, was also a committee member, as was Methodist Episcopal Bishop Francis John McConnell (1871–1953).[36] A popularizer of his teacher Borden Parker Bowne's philosophy of personalism and the author of a book on theodicy, McConnell, a president of the activist Methodist Federation for Social Service, was an outspoken liberal who often clashed publicly with conservatives in his denomination. Bishop McConnell succeeded another member of the new committee, Rev. S. Parkes Cadman, as president of the Federal Council of Churches of Christ in America in 1928.[37]

Although Protestants were the dominant presence on the committee, Jews were represented by Reform Rabbis Louis Mann and David de Sola Pool. Pool (1885–1970), who was born in London and educated at Heidelberg and the University of Berlin, became rabbi of the Spanish and Portuguese Synagogue Shearith Israel in New York City in 1907, where he remained until his retirement in 1955. He had served as president of the New York Board of Jewish Ministers when Rabbi Max Reichler presented his essay on "Jewish eugenics" to the group in 1915.[38] Catholics were represented on the committee by two priests from the Catholic University of America, Rev. John A. Ryan and Rev. John M. Cooper; Rev. Huntington also enlisted the support of well-known Quaker historian and social reformer Rufus M. Jones (1863–1948), a scholar of mysticism who taught at Haverford College.[39] The Committee even included

Social Gospel pioneer Rev. Samuel Zane Batten, who had first written about eugenics in 1908.[40]

Committee members were well-known liberals in their faiths, and seven of them were among the twenty-five "American Pulpit Leaders" selected by *Christian Century* in 1925 as "men of prophetic vision, of pulpit power, whose message seems most vitally to interpret the mind of Christ" (another of the top twenty-five was the well-known supporter of eugenics, Rev. Newell Dwight Hillis of Plymouth Church in Brooklyn).[41]

The willingness of these prominent religious leaders to join the Committee on Cooperation with Clergymen reveals the mainstream, progressive appeal of eugenics in the 1920s. But it also raises questions about what, specifically, motivated these men to join the eugenics crusade. The available evidence suggests that all of them, regardless of creed, shared a background in and commitment to social reform, along with reputations as outspoken leaders (and occasionally, dissenters) in their faiths. Only a handful of these ministers, priests, and rabbis ended up devoting significant amounts of time and energy to the eugenics crusade. The others were content to appear on the Committee letterhead, answer the occasional query from the chair, and attend the irregular Committee luncheons at the Town Hall Club in New York City. Still, men of their stature, by the very act of affixing their names to the Committee, brought inestimable influence to the eugenics movement. In joining, they also (perhaps unwittingly) signaled to eugenicists that their endorsement could be used to promote and justify the AES's mission.

Early on, the mundane details of running the Committee on Cooperation with Clergymen fell to a smaller executive committee that met to develop specific plans for spreading the eugenic message in and through the churches. A typical executive committee session elicited educational proposals such as Rev. Benjamin Winchester's suggestion to lobby the International Sunday School Committee to include eugenics lessons in its curriculum. Often, before dispersing, one minister or another would make a general plea to the others to use every means at their disposal to publicize the eugenics message; one such plea was directed toward those ministers with access to the airwaves, asking them to devote some portion of their radio broadcasts to discussions of the topic.[42]

The research projects pursued by the Committee also provide clues as to how ministers differed from scientists in their interpretations of eugenics. One clear distinction emerged: Unlike most eugenicists, the clergymen were not strict hereditarians. In 1928, the Committee assessed the ancestry of 106 contemporary "eminent clergymen" in the United States (including several members of their own Committee) to determine the frequency of religious leaders in families. Their results revealed that 40 percent of the clergymen surveyed were themselves sons of clergymen, and another 40 percent were sons of church officers. To a strict hereditarian, these findings suggested the existence of a distinct trait—"religious sense" or "spiritual sense," for example—that traveled through successive generations much like eye color. Indeed, eugenicist Charles Davenport suggested the existence of just such a trait in his own work.[43] Rev. Huntington and his fellow Committee members declined to draw such a conclusion from the survey, however. "As to whether heredity or environment explains why these men went into the ministry, this study throws no conclusive light," they said.[44]

The early organizational efforts of the Committee on Cooperation with Clergymen included a fairly constant level of interest in eugenics promotion, and by 1928, the *Eugenical News* reported that "the Committee feels that its work is beginning to do something toward making church leaders a little familiar with the idea" of eugenics.[45] The larger Society encouraged the Committee's efforts. If money was any measure of a committee's worth, the success of the Committee on Cooperation with Clergymen was one of the AES's top priorities. In the 1927 budget, for example, that Committee was second only to the Committee on Popular Education in funding, receiving over $5,000 for the year. In contrast, the Committees on Cooperation with Physicians and Social Workers (born of the same resolution that created the Clergymen's Committee) received only $100 and $300, respectively. Combined, the Committee on Popular Education and the Committee on Cooperation with Clergymen utilized all but $5,375 of the Society's total annual budget.[46]

The Committee's use of its generous portion of the AES budget would end up exposing countless Americans to eugenics, for the ministers devoted most of their funds to the promotion of a eugenics sermon contest. The origins of the contest idea are murky, but its emphasis on popular outreach and the active participation of ordinary ministers bore the mark of Rev. Huntington. The AES announced the first contest in 1926 by placing advertisements in 180 religious newspapers and magazines and in numerous secular publications. The competition was open to all ministers, priests, rabbis, and theology students, and the rules were straightforward: The sermon had to be preached to a regular congregation in a church or synagogue, and the minister had to take as his or her topic "Religion and Eugenics: Does the church have any responsibility for improving the human stock?" The prizes were substantial: $500, $200, and $100 for the first-, second-, and third-prize sermons, respectively.[47]

The contest was appealing because it offered an ideal opportunity to publicize the eugenics message. Indeed, the AES was explicit about its propagandistic purpose, as an advertisement for the contest revealed: "Since the churches are in a measure a natural selective agency and since a large percentage of the intelligent classes are church members, it is hoped that the message of eugenics will be received by thousands of people in the United States who otherwise would not hear it."[48] The sermon contests were an example of the skill with which the AES pursued propaganda. By making this event a sermon contest, as opposed to an essay contest, and by insisting that it be preached to a regular congregation, the AES gave clergy the opportunity to use their strengths (pulpit oration and a knowledge of Scripture, for example) while promoting eugenics to thousands of worshippers in churches and synagogues across the country.

The first contest elicited an enthusiastic response from the religious community. One month after its announcement, the AES reported that it had received nearly 150 requests for the printed rules of the contest. One AES official speculated that more than two hundred sermons were preached for the 1926 contest, of which approximately seventy arrived at the offices of the AES for judging. Presbyterians, Baptists, and ministers of the Methodist Episcopal Church submitted the largest percentage of sermons, but entries arrived from ministers of nearly every major Protestant denomination and even a few rabbis. Geographically, the participants were spread evenly across the country and from a range of demographic settings: large cities, small towns, and rural districts.[49]

If the AES's propagandistic purpose was clear, the motives of those who participated in the contests are more difficult to ascertain. Only a few ministers included with their contest entries any explanation for their participation. Rev. A. Nelson Willis of Union Baptist Church in Poindexter, Kentucky, wrote that he was inspired by "a study of the birth rate of the local church community." A few others expressed a general enthusiasm for the subject of eugenics. In a letter accompanying his 1926 entry, Rev. Kenneth R. Close of the Congregational Church in Miami Beach, Florida, wrote, "I believe strongly in eugenics and hope that I may be of some service to the movement." A participant in the 1928 contest, Rev. R. Homer Gleason of the First Universalist Church in Rochester, Minnesota, was even more effusive: "Please allow me to add that I have greatly enjoyed my preparation for this work. I have thought for years that I was somewhat of a eugenist, but five months of intensive study have thoroughly convinced me . . . Surely this is a great cause."[50]

The ministers' correspondence with the AES also provides few clues as to how their congregations received the sermons, but the available evidence suggests positive responses. Rev. D. W. Charlton of the First Baptist Church of Altavista, Virginia, wrote that his sermon on eugenics "met with a favorable response on the part of our people," and another contestant, Rev. Duncan P. Cameron of the First Presbyterian Church of Cottage Grove, Oregon, noted that his sermon was "repeated by request." Other ministers recorded that they preached the sermons in special services or to their local ministers' association, in addition to the required delivery at a regular church service.[51]

The sermons themselves offer a rare opportunity to examine how ordinary religious leaders understood eugenics. The men (and two women) who entered these contests in 1926, 1928, and 1930 were not the highly visible pulpit leaders of the AES Advisory Council or the Committee on Cooperation with Clergymen. They were ministers and rabbis who were virtually unknown to those outside their immediate communities. They did not sit on the editorial boards of major religious publications or have nationally broadcast radio shows, but as the leaders of local congregations they had a significant impact on the lives of their parishioners. Their perceptions of the eugenics movement, as outlined in their sermons, reveal how the average minister reconciled his or her theological training with the new discoveries of science. The sermons also offer insights into eugenicists' successes and failures thus far in publicizing their science.

One clear element that emerged in the sermons was the participants' focus on the social message of eugenics rather than its scientific details. Although most of the contest participants demonstrated some knowledge of the available literature on eugenics, they tended to cite popular works such as those by eugenics promoter (and nonscientist) Albert E. Wiggam, rather than the scientific treatises published by the ERO. The closest most participants came to citing scientific work was their frequent mention of the eugenic family studies, which had, in fact, been popularized in newspaper and magazine articles since the 1910s. The Jukes, Kallikaks, and Ishmaelites appeared often on the pages of the sermons, along with the alarmist sentiments fueling the notion that such groups posed a new "menace" to the nation. Francis Galton also received mention and dutiful praise, and one minister even noted the irony that although celibacy was a dysgenic practice, it was the state in which the key theoretician of heredity, Austrian priest Gregor Mendel, lived his entire adult life.[52] For the most part, however, the sermons offered no rigorous discussions of the science of heredity, only its social and religious implications.

Several other common themes emerge from the eugenic sermons. The first and most prevalent was the compatibility of religion and science. These ministers, writing in the immediate aftermath of the 1925 Scopes trial over the teaching of evolutionary theory in Tennessee, embraced neither William Jennings Bryan's fiery fundamentalism nor Clarence Darrow's atheistic scientism. Instead, they carved out a middle path based (in the case of Protestants) on the liberal goal of ushering in God's Kingdom or (in the case of Jews) a Reform commitment to improving man's capacity for spiritual understanding. Sermon contestants faulted the fundamentalist position because, in its rejection of the discoveries of modern science, fundamentalism stifled society's opportunity for progressive development; at the same time, a purely scientific, "mechanistic" worldview was equally unsatisfactory because it denied men the necessary comfort and fulfillment of an inner spiritual life. The resulting compromise between these two poles was a faith that understood eugenics not as the ultimate answer to society's problems, but as a *tool* for achieving a better moral and spiritual consciousness for mankind, a means, in other words, of achieving God's will on earth. As one Protestant contestant put it, "Surely the Kingdom can never come in all its fullness among a people descended from the Jukes." Another minister suggested that the animating principles of the eugenics movement might hold the key to transcending denominational and doctrinal differences: "No matter how we word our creeds, or whether we are Liberals or Fundamentalists, I am convinced that the Christian must be guided by the eugenic ideal."[53]

The importance of Scripture in illuminating the truths of eugenics was another frequent theme in the sermons. Many contestants cited passages that had become favorite fare among eugenicists, including Jesus' Sermon on the Mount and the Parable of the Talents. Other contestants were more creative in stocking their scriptural arsenals. Rev. H. Arndt of the Montgomery Presbyterian Church in Montgomery, Ohio, claimed that the Bible sanctioned severe methods for maintaining the purity of the human race, as the Old Testament account of Noah and the Flood revealed. "When, after about fifteen hundred years, the race had degenerated so far as to be beyond redemption, God eliminated them through the deluge," Rev. Arndt noted approvingly. Rev. James L. Smiley of St. Luke's Protestant Episcopal Chapel in Eastport, Maryland, expressed similar sentiments in his contest sermon, noting that "a very merciful God" had destroyed Sodom and Gomorrah and the Canaanites to prevent "a race, reeking with corruption, from propagating a vicious progeny."[54]

Scripture also provided a reference point for a third theme developed in the sermons: solving the problem eugenics posed to the ideal of Christian charity. One minister argued that eugenics compelled the biblical Good Samaritan (who stopped to aid the victim of a theft) to "assume new functions." Once, he sermonized, the Samaritan simply befriended the victim on the road to Jericho; in the early part of the twentieth century, he would have provided "better policing and lighting of the road" to discourage the thieves who preyed on travelers; now, with eugenics, the Good Samaritan knew that his duty was to prevent those thieves from ever being born in the first place. Thus was the Good Samaritan reinvented as an aggressive promoter of preventive philanthropy.[55]

A final theme to emerge from the sermons was the ministers' sense that the churches and synagogues had an important obligation to spread the message of modern science, a sentiment that surely pleased the members of the AES. "The church can help popularize the knowledge now in possession of the scientists," said Rev. George C. Fetter of the First Baptist Church in Ottawa, Illinois. Taking a cue from Galton, Rev. Fetter went on to note that the church "can also help unite the zeal of religion with the accurate knowledge of science." Contestants frequently emphasized the uniqueness and importance of this function. Eugenicists might have the scientific knowledge to improve the human race, but they lacked the ability to compel adherence to it. "Religion alone can lead the coming generations to see that a man and a woman are cooperating with God in building a spiritual universe when they carefully plan and prepare for a happy eugenic parenthood," Fetter concluded.[56]

The idea that the churches and synagogues performed a special function, namely, inculcating faithful belief and discipline, and that that function could be used to promote eugenics was taken as a given in the sermons. Such sentiments reveal the extent to which these ministers accepted eugenics as a necessary and normal part of modern reform. It also suggests how ministers solved the larger dilemma of reconciling their faith with contemporary culture: by highlighting the common elements (rather than the differences) between their experience-based, liberal Christianity or Judaism and a culture in thrall to science. Eugenics was an ideal reconciler, for its purpose, "bettering humanity," evoked much that was central to many leaders of organized religion.

The task of judging the sermons for the 1926 contest fell to eugenicist Charles Davenport, Prof. William Lyon Phelps of Yale University, and Ozora S. Davis, president of Chicago Theological Seminary; in 1928, the judges were Dallas L. Short, a professor at Boston University, Edmund D. Soper, president of Ohio Wesleyan University, and eugenicist Harry H. Laughlin. They were to judge each sermon for scientific quality (30 percent of score), literary quality (30 percent), and "convincing quality" (40 percent), a task not all of them found easy. In a letter to Committee on Cooperation with Clergymen chair Henry S. Huntington in 1928, Dallas Short admitted, "The lack of originality both in matter and manner [in the sermons] is rather appalling." Still, he thought, "the frankness, the vigor, and the excellent logic and good writing in all of them certainly speak well for the American pulpit and its technical training."[57]

The sermons deemed worthy of prizes did not demonstrate a better grasp of the science of heredity than their competitors. They did, however, evince considerable fervor for eugenics and an elevated rhetorical flair. Some of that enthusiasm had been honed through practical experience; several prizewinners already were engaged in eugenics movements in their local communities. In 1926, the judges awarded the first prize to Rev. Phillips Endecott Osgood (1882–1956), rector of St. Mark's Church in Minneapolis, whose oratorical skills shone in his sermon, "The Refiner's Fire." Rev. Osgood's offering combined a Social Gospel vision of ushering in the Kingdom with practical recommendations for eugenic legislation; the latter was something very few contest participants discussed with knowledge or detail, but with which Osgood had firsthand experience.

The good reverend was involved in the Minnesota Eugenics Society, a state organization unaffiliated with the AES. Osgood's friend, Minneapolis physician and socialist Charles Fremont Dight, founded the Minnesota group. With Dight, Osgood pushed for passage of a bill that would broaden Minnesota's existing voluntary sterilization law to make the procedure compulsory for feebleminded inmates of state institutions. When calling for "legislation against the possibility of criminal or diseased childbearing" in his prize sermon, Osgood spoke as an informed lobbyist.[58] He was also staunchly liberal; indeed, his theological liberalism was such that it warranted few restraints. Ordained in the Protestant Episcopal Church in 1908, he eventually resigned from the

FIGURE 4.2 Rev. Phillips Endecott Osgood, rector of St. Mark's Church, Minneapolis, and winner of the 1926 American Eugenics Society's Eugenics Sermon Contest. Minnesota Historical Society, Saint Paul, Minnesota.

Episcopal ministry to become a Unitarian. This combination of practical experience in a state eugenics organization and liberalism from the more daring end of the theological spectrum was what made Osgood's sermon a winning statement of religious support for eugenics. Calling Christians the "God-appointed guardians of the gate of new birth," he urged the churches to ensure that their members kept their "birthrights" pure. Only then would the Kingdom of God on earth be realized. "Blood will tell" was Osgood's constant refrain.[59]

The second-prize winner in the 1926 contest was even more explicit in linking his liberal Protestant theology to his support for eugenics. Rev. Kenneth C. MacArthur of the Federated Church in Sterling, Massachusetts, argued in his sermon that "if we take seriously the Christian purpose of realizing on earth the ideal divine society, we shall welcome every help which science affords." For Rev. MacArthur, eugenics was the best available means for achieving that "ideal, divine society." In its appeal to the public to produce healthier families, the eugenics movement fit well with the Social Gospel understanding

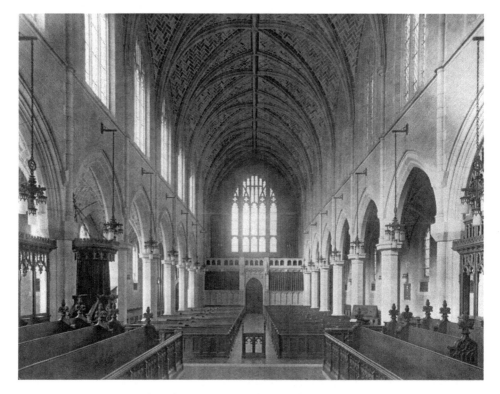

FIGURE 4.3 St. Mark's Church, Minneapolis. Minnesota Historical Society, Saint
Paul, Minnesota.

of the family as the "working model of the Kingdom," he noted. Healthy, eugenic families were a particular concern of his. Just a year earlier he and his
brood had entered and won a eugenic Fitter Families contest at the Eastern
States Exposition. Perhaps thinking of his own "Grade A" progeny, MacArthur
concluded, "Eugenics offers great assistance in this effort to establish a race of
people who approximate the Christian ideal."[60]

In viewing eugenics as a means for ushering in the Kingdom, Osgood,
MacArthur, and other liberal ministers simply treated it as the most recent and
most effective in a long line of social reforms that would bring about its realization. As Rev. William A. Matson, pastor of the Methodist Episcopal Church
in Livingston, California, noted in his first-prize sermon in 1928, "We have
assumed that if we could sufficiently advance education, sanitation, and social
surroundings the Kingdom of God would come." But these tools had not
brought success. "That is like trying to strengthen the pillars of society by
painting them," Matson argued. Eugenics, which proposed to strengthen the
pillars by replacing the fissured stone with stronger material, was simply a
more scientific and, hence, more effective solution.[61] Liberal religion and well-

meaning science were partners. Rev. MacArthur even argued that eugenics was itself a peculiarly Christian enterprise, "a means of peopling the Earth with Christlike men and women."[62] The appeal of linking eugenics to the Christian mission is clear. Doing so gave these ministers' beliefs the desirable patina of science while still leaving them with a measure of control over the direction the Christian-eugenic mission would take.

They were not the first group of eugenics enthusiasts to make such a claim. After all, eugenic sensibilities were found more often than not among native-born Protestants, the "Protestant establishment" whose fears for the fate of their Christian civilization were already well known. Writing in the *Journal of Heredity* ten years earlier, Maynard Metcalf of the Orchard Laboratory in Oberlin, Ohio, argued that the success of eugenics in fact *depended on* the success of Christian civilization because only Christian societies could foster eugenic ideals. Other cultures were dominated by religions that Metcalf found to be lacking the necessary altruism (Islam) or motivating force (Shintoism, Buddhism) to make eugenics a success.[63] Eugenicists Paul Popenoe and Roswell Hill Johnson made a similar claim in their widely sold text of 1918, *Applied Eugenics*. "Theoretically," they wrote, "there is a place for eugenics in every type of religion." In practice, however, Christianity was the "natural ally of the eugenist" (they judged Buddhism "too contemplative to do anything"). This was never so true as in contemporary times, they said. Popenoe and Johnson were heartened by what they saw as Christianity's "rapid change in ideals," a change that brought to believers' attention the need for effective secular solutions to social problems. They concluded that this shift in priorities would make it impossible for Christians to remain "as ignorant of and indifferent to eugenics as they have been in the past."[64]

Indifference did not appear to be a problem among religious leaders, even those who did not participate in the eugenic sermon contests. Evidence of considerable religious interest in eugenics could be found outside the formal structure of the AES in the 1920s. At the Episcopal Church Congress in San Francisco in June 1927, for example, Rev. Henry Lewis of Ann Arbor, Michigan, told his audience, "The church should cooperate with the findings of modern science and urge the use of scientific discoveries which tend to the upward development of the race." One such developmental strategy he advocated was the "sterilization of mental defectives."[65] Rt. Rev. Ernest W. Barnes, bishop of Birmingham, England, also encouraged eugenicists to continue their appeals to Christian listeners. Barnes, a controversialist described by one biographer as a "thorn in the flesh to four successive archbishops of Canterbury," urged eugenicists to present their evidence with Christian concerns in mind: "When religious people realise that, in thus preventing the survival of the socially unfit, they are working in accordance with the plan by which God has brought humanity so far on its road, their objections to repressive action will vanish." If eugenics was understood as a tool for pursuing the larger goal of creating the

Kingdom, accepted as merely another part of God's plan for society, religious men and women would not resist its entreaties. Appeal to them as Christians, Barnes said, and they will eagerly join the eugenics crusade.[66]

No one was more persuasive in describing eugenics as God's plan than Albert Edward Wiggam (1871–1957). A modern self-promoter who often invoked his old-fashioned roots (he was "born on a Southern Indiana farm" and "attended an actual little red schoolhouse"), Wiggam became a best-selling author, essayist, and favorite on the Chautauqua lecture circuit.[67] In 1928 alone he traveled to Cleveland, Buffalo, Toledo, Los Angeles, Fresno, Portland, Tacoma, Seattle, Salt Lake City, Cleveland, Rochester, and Atlanta to participate in debates and to lecture about eugenics. Awkward in appearance—one observer described him as a "skinny, shambling tower of bones"—Wiggam nevertheless charmed audiences with his vigorous presentations about eugenics.

FIGURE 4.4 Albert Edward Wiggam. Records of the Redpath Chautauqua, Special Collections Department, University of Iowa Libraries, Iowa City, Iowa.

He brought a certain sensationalism to his task, at least enough to stir his audiences to action. "Following in the wake of his lectures," one testimonial noted, "parents are crowding the physicians' offices with defective and backward children which were not before suspected to be such."[68] Like the amateur eugenicists who wrote popular tracts in the 1900s and 1910s, Wiggam tried to make eugenics intelligible to the average American, in part by glossing over the hard science of heredity in favor of sensational warnings written in religious language.

His first eugenics book showcased this style. In *The New Decalogue of Science* (1922), Wiggam argued that the discoveries of modern science required a new set of moral imperatives, and he invoked Jesus to justify his own revision of them. He argued that the time had arrived "for a new Decalogue, a new Sermon on the Mount, a new Golden Rule." This new guidance would not come from the spiritual sources of old, but from "the New Mount Sinai—the Laboratory" and were "just as divine, as sacred, as inspired as the old." Wiggam's Sinai, like Moses', produced Ten Commandments, though ones that bore little resemblance to the originals.

Wiggam's Ten Commandments:	The original (Exodus 20):
The Duty of Eugenics	Thou shalt have no other gods before me
The Duty of Scientific Research	Thou shalt make no graven images
The Duty of Socialization of Science	Thou shalt not take the name of the Lord in vain
The Duty of Measuring Men	Remember the Sabbath day and keep it holy
The Duty of Humanizing Industry	Honor thy father and mother
The Duty of Preferential Reproduction	Thou shalt not kill
They Duty of Trusting Intelligence	Thou shalt not commit adultery
The Duty of Art	Thou shalt not steal
The Duty of Internationalism	Thou shalt not bear false witness
The Duty of Philosophical Reconstruction	Thou shalt not covet

"Eugenics means a new religion, new objects of religious endeavor," and a "new social and political Bible," Wiggam said. It was "the final program for the completed Christianizing of mankind."[69] As his swift dispatch of the Ten Commandments suggests, Wiggam had little patience for the doctrines of traditional religion. Blasphemy, adultery, and the other prohibitions of the original Decalogue seemed to him minor concerns compared to those that animated eugenicists. Moreover, he reasoned that improving the human race through eugenics meant eliminating the traits that led to this prohibited behavior in the first place.

Nevertheless, Wiggam had a keen sense for the appealing tone of religious rhetoric. Rather than citing the work of scientists to bolster his arguments, he relied on a more familiar figure: Jesus. "Had Jesus been among us," he wrote, "he would have been president of the First Eugenics Congress." With the knowledge of eugenics at his disposal, "He would have cried: 'A new commandment I give unto you—the biological Golden Rule, the completed Golden Rule of science. *Do unto both the born and the unborn as you would have both the born and the unborn do unto you.*'" "This is the real Golden Rule," Wiggam informed his readers. "This, and only this, is the final reconciliation of science and the Bible."[70]

Although Wiggam's portrayal of Jesus as eugenic champion was one of the most colorful in eugenics literature, it was not the first. Others had examined Jesus' life for clues to its eugenic significance. Jesus was a fascinating figure to those of a eugenic bent because he posed something of a conundrum. How could a man of such humble beginnings—born in a lowly manger, at that—be the son of God? So asked Rev. Amory Bradford in 1895 in his essay on the "heredity of Jesus." Several decades later, a professor at the Hartford School of Religious Pedagogy argued that Jesus "came from a stock of priestly and prophetic men" and was "the highest product of religious and moral selection in the history of the world."[71] Wiggam focused more on Jesus as a promoter, a depiction in keeping with the times. From 1925 to 1926, the best-selling nonfiction book in the country was Bruce Barton's *The Man Nobody Knows*, which portrayed Jesus as a superlative businessman. Christ was a popular cultural symbol, and saving souls became as understandable a challenge as selling soap; after all, Barton told his readers, Jesus "would have been a national advertiser today." Depicting Jesus as a supporter of one's particular social cause was a favorite tactic of reformers, with churchman and professional activist alike adapting him to the promotional demands of the age. In these times it is "impossible for the moralist to command," Walter Lippmann observed. "He can only persuade."[72] Jesus offered a powerful tool for persuasion.

Although Wiggam admired Jesus, he offered withering indictments of his contemporary followers. The "Catholic and Protestant churches have, in the main, used all the threats of the orthodox hell to prevent men from thinking freely and bravely about life," he noted. Just as Wiggam had proposed to replace the biblical Ten Commandments with a new scientific decalogue, he also sought to replace existing religious institutions with enlightened organizations based on the "new universe" of science.[73] Not surprisingly, the new religion he envisioned was one that invested scientists, and especially eugenicists, with a great deal of power.

Wiggam took Galton's injunction to make eugenics a religion to its logical (and extreme) conclusion. Ironically, he did so by invoking the language (biblical) and the leader (Jesus) of the worldview he sought to replace. In this way, Wiggam's work was more inventive and more radical in its prescriptions than that of any other eugenicist.[74] At the same time, it was some of the most popular eugenics literature ever published. Wiggam relied on a certain intellectual alchemy in his readers: an understanding of and commitment to Christian principles and a curiosity and hopefulness about modern science that, when combined, produced a willingness to restructure society along eugenic lines. "The social organization of science," he explained, "is simply the technical administration of the love of God."[75] That ministers from across the country glowingly cited Wiggam's work in their eugenic sermons suggests that this message of reconciling God's will and science—not Wiggam's desire to replace Christianity—was what they took from his work.

Despite its populist tone, Wiggam's work drew praise from a few professionals in the social sciences. Clark University psychologist G. Stanley Hall, no stranger to the study of religion and science, recommended *The New Decalogue of Science* by saying, "One lays it down with the feeling that biology is the basis of a new decalogue as important and as authentic as the old one." Support came from across the Atlantic as well. "I wish we had a man like Wiggam in England," British eugenicist Leonard Darwin remarked after reading the book.[76] But Wiggam's zeal for his cause also invited ridicule. In a two-part essay in *The Century* titled "The New Testament of Science," writer Walter B. Pitkin served up a parody of *The New Decalogue of Science* that depicted eugenicists like Wiggam as a scheming "Biological Block" of society bent on eliminating defective people. Pitkin urged "charity toward all freaks and fanatics, who, like ourselves, are products of that same Nature which brings forth maniacs, newspaper columnists, deaf-mutes, aldermen, saxophone players, thugs, priests, statisticians, contortionists, and all the rest of that hurly-burly which calls itself the human race."[77]

More serious criticism came from AES Advisory Council member Rev. Harry Emerson Fosdick. In "The Importance of the Ordinary Man," a sermon preached at the Park Avenue Baptist Church in New York in December 1928, Fosdick took Wiggam to task for suggesting in his book *The Next Age of Man* that "the average man has nothing to do with progress except to hold it back," a claim Wiggam made to emphasize the need for the eugenically fit to hold the reins of progress. For Fosdick, the idea that eugenicists were an enlightened cadre leading the dull masses revealed a dangerous hubris. As he perceptively noted, "The question is not whether changes will occur." Fosdick and other liberal religious leaders already agreed with eugenicists that science made change inevitable. The question was "how they will occur, under whose aegis and superintendence, by whose guidance and direction, and how much better the world will be when they are here."[78] Though sympathetic to science, Fosdick feared that eugenicists, in their headlong pursuit of race betterment, prematurely dismissed the important contributions of other social leaders, including the clergy.

Wiggam was the most prolific and outspoken eugenicist discussing religion, but his lack of scientific training and popular style made his claims suspect in the eyes of some of his more established colleagues. Charles Davenport, ever cranky about the efforts of nonscientific promoters of his science, expressed his concern for the "consequences of propaganda ahead of knowledge."[79] Others were somewhat more welcoming of explorations of religious influence on their science. Biologist Edwin Grant Conklin of Princeton University was perhaps the most qualified eugenicist to explore these links. He had earned a lay preacher's license from the Methodist Episcopal Church in 1885 and taught at Rust University, a Southern Methodist institution in Holly Springs, Mississippi, before earning his credentials as a biologist.[80]

Conklin's attempts at reconciliation were evident in his widely sold *Heredity and Environment in the Development of Men*. Although the bulk of the book was a standard biology text, one section, "Genetics and Ethics," was atypical in its choice of themes. Like many religious leaders who wrote about eugenics, Conklin criticized eugenicists' purely mechanistic conception of humanity, rejecting the notion that physical, mental, and moral capacity were immutably fixed in the germ plasm. Just as Francis Galton had many years earlier, Conklin turned to the New Testament Parable of the Talents to support his claims; unlike Galton, however, he argued that the parable's real lesson was its emphasis on man's *use* of his talents. Although it is true that "men differ in hereditary endowments," Conklin wrote, this does not prevent the feebly endowed from using their talents to the best of their abilities. Social reform, whether secular or religious, still served a purpose in society by aiding those less fortunate in fulfilling their potential. Conklin also found backing for his claims in the Old Testament story of the writing on the wall at Belshazzar's feast ("Mene, Mene, Tekel, U-pharsin"). Focusing on the third word of the supernatural missive, "Tekel," Conklin asked, "May we not surely predict that if we continue to put individual freedom and luxury and selfishness above social obligations our race and civilization will also see the writing on the wall, 'Thou art weighed in the balances and art found wanting'?"[81]

An increasing number of Conklin's colleagues were asking the same question—and with an eye to religious leaders' answers to it. In their original mission statement, the organizers of the AES had expressed interest in broadening the scope of their research efforts. As part of that process, they noted, "research is needed to answer the question whether religion, philanthropy . . . and medical progress are really eugenic."[82] Answering this question required eugenicists to expand their connections to religious leaders on two fronts: First, they began to make more frequent overtures to their existing religious allies; second, they began to make religious topics the specific focus of eugenic research. Both of these developments occurred at the same time that the AES was trolling for religious leaders to fill its membership rolls, but they happened in a different context, one somewhat removed from the propagandistic tone of the AES campaign. Nevertheless, these developments, like the eugenic sermon contests, ensured that religious participation remained relevant to the eugenics movement.

One of the earliest of these efforts came in May 1925, when the Galton Society, a group of New York City–area eugenicists who met regularly at the American Museum of Natural History, invited a special guest from England to speak to them about eugenics: Rev. William Ralph Inge (1860–1954). Inge was dean of St. Paul's Cathedral and a well-known liberal cleric whose bouts of depression and pessimistic social forecasting had earned him the sobriquet "the gloomy Dean."[83] He was also one of the few well-known religious leaders in the United States and Britain who wrote frequently about the relationship between religion and eugenics. In earlier essays, he had unabashedly proclaimed himself a eugenicist, pointing to the common purpose of eugenics and religion. "The Christian conception of a kingdom of God upon earth teaches us to turn our eyes to the future, and to think of the welfare of posterity," he wrote.[84] He later extended this argument to the realm of morals, arguing, "Since the object of all social morality is the good of the human race, and since eugenics also has no other end in view, it is plain that social morality and eugenics are indissolubly connected."[85]

Eugenicists in England and the United States were pleased with Inge's praise of their science, no doubt in part because of the prestige he brought to the movement as a high-ranking cleric. While organizing the Second International Congress of Eugenics in 1921, eugenicist Henry Fairfield Osborn praised Inge's "wonderful mind" and recommended to Charles Davenport that they invite the dean to speak. When Dean Inge agreed to participate in the Congress, Osborn secured speaking engagements for him at four "leading churches" in New York.[86] Thus it was as a friend and admired colleague that Dean Inge returned to New York in 1925 to talk about religion and eugenics. In his presentation, he focused on religious opposition to the eugenics movement, taking particular aim at a favorite target of his, the Catholic Church. The Church jealously guarded its intellectual borders, Inge said, and this "suspicion attached by all religious bodies to any ethical teaching not started by themselves," aided and abetted by "the old theory of the natural rights of man," proved harmful to the acceptance of eugenics. Eugenicists must combat these prejudices with an organized educational program "to prepare the public mind" to receive the teachings of modern science.[87] An educated Protestant clergy and an informed public could, Inge predicted, overcome any dissenters. One well-known churchman agreed. In 1927, Shailer Mathews, Social Gospel stalwart and dean of the Divinity School at the University of Chicago, edited a book about religion and science in which he included an essay by Davenport and argued himself that "it is hard not to see how sympathetic Augustine might have been with our modern knowledge of evolution and eugenics."[88]

While religious leaders such as Dean Inge were educating members of the Galton Society, research of a religious nature was appearing with greater frequency in the programs of other eugenics organizations. At a joint session of the Eugenics Research Association and the AES held at the American Museum of Natural History in June 1929, for example, William Grossman of Passaic, New Jersey, presented a paper on "Eugenics in the Talmud and Its Effect," which touched on many of the same themes that Rabbi Reichler had outlined in his 1915 speech to the New York Board of Jewish Ministers. In the discussion immediately following Grossman's paper, Rabbi David de Sola Pool (a member of the AES Committee on Cooperation with Clergymen) noted that the important element of Talmudic teachings to bear in mind was "its setting up breeding for character as the paramount eugenic consideration," rather than breeding for physical traits. "Perhaps in a complete and scientific history of eugenics," he said, "Moses, Amos, and the rabbis of the Talmud will be recognized as intuitive and extraordinarily influential primitive eugenists even before the days of Galton and Karl Pearson."[89] Rabbi Pool's comments, while demonstrating his general interest in the links between eugenics and Jewish teaching, also offer an example of how religious participation in the eugenics movement at the organizational level pushed debate toward questions of a spiritual nature.

Other, previously unexplored religious traditions came under scrutiny by eugenicists in these years as well, including Mormonism. At one eugenics conference, a fieldworker who had studied the inheritance of intellectual ability among Mormon families pronounced founder Joseph Smith's family "of mediocre ability, simple, honest, and very few defectives among them." After examining the family of Mormon leader Brigham Young, another eugenicist declared the Latter-Day Saints an untapped trove of useful hereditary information.[90] An underlying curiosity about the eugenic effects of polygamy marked these first examinations of Mormons, but by 1928, Roswell Johnson, a member of the AES's Board of Directors, began his study of the Latter-Day Saints by noting that polygamy in Mormonism was "now of little importance" as it was no longer officially sanctioned by the Church. Instead, Johnson argued that the Mormons added to traditional Christianity "some theological positions and some practices of great moment to eugenics."[91]

The most important of these practices was the Mormon doctrine of "Eternal Progression," which (among other things) insisted on marriage on earth in order for the spirit to reach the highest "Celestial Realm" and the possibility of attaining Godhood. Citing a Mormon leader, Johnson noted that this encouragement of marriage included one notably eugenic exception: "those who through infirmities of mind or body, are not fit for marriage." To Johnson, this disclaimer was an implicit recognition of the importance of limiting defective offspring. Mormon theology went further, Johnson noted, to argue that because the progression of the soul depended on the fitness of the body it entered, Mormons believed they had a "religious duty to see to it that no defective bodies are provided" for the soul's housing. Mormonism, in Johnson's accounting, was a religion that had "not only eugenic but survival value."[92]

Eugenicists predicted survival for the Mormons; their assessments of Protestant clergymen were far less rosy. Research into the reproduction of Methodist clergymen, for example, found that despite their temperament as "marrying men," they had a "dangerously small birth rate." Studies of the Protestant clergy in this period echoed the alarm produced by earlier research into the survival rates of the *Mayflower* descendants.[93] Yet, although this research produced concern, it was a concern that stemmed from a positive assessment of clergymen. Eugenicists were worried about the low birthrates of clergymen because they believed that clergymen, as a group, were eugenically desirable. As eugenicist Clarence Campbell noted, "The offspring of clergymen produce more leaders than any other social class," a fact that suggested the "importance and value of the religious life and attitude in human affairs, as well as of its eugenic value." Campbell and other eugenicists viewed ministers as important contributors to the national germ plasm, albeit ones in need of some reproductive encouragement.[94]

This sense of religious leaders' importance to the eugenics movement was captured well in a special issue of the AES's magazine, *Eugenics*, in 1928. The editorial of this "preachers' issue" claimed that between the covers was "an impregnable battalion of proof" that "eugenics is an ally, not a foe of religion." It also demonstrated how savvy eugenicists were in first gaining the imprimatur of religious leaders and then ceaselessly promoting it. Directing the reader's attention to the membership rolls of the AES, the editorial claimed, "The most eminent leaders of religion in America are already alive to the salvation inherent in the eugenics programme."[95]

Two themes emerged from the "preachers' issue." The first was the most remarkable: recognition by eugenicists of the genuine social influence of the clergy. Ministers are "the sentinels at the gates which lead to the minds of the masses of citizens," one essay proclaimed. In her article, "The Preacher's Part," eugenics promoter Florence Brown Sherbon suggested that "the average, well meaning, law abiding citizen depends upon his pastor to put things together for him and iron out incongruities and philosophical difficulties, like harmonizing religion and science." Sherbon concluded her essay with a gentle reminder that this influence required the clergy to continue to educate themselves about modern science. In a significant departure from the lackadaisical attitude that characterized earlier evaluations of religious participation in their movement, eugenicists were stating explicitly what the AES sermon contest had revealed implicitly, namely, that eugenicists needed and wanted religious leaders to promote eugenics by employing the most effective methods of their calling.[96]

The second theme that emerged in the "preachers' issue" was the familiar problem that stemmed directly from liberal ministers' embrace of science: the challenge science and its methods posed to Christian charity. Liberal religious leaders had been grappling with this question already, but by the late 1920s, many were now willing to collapse Christian charity into eugenics and argue that both had interchangeable goals. In an essay on "Eugenics and the Church," AES sermon contest winner Rev. Kenneth C. MacArthur revealed just how far some religious sentiment had shifted in his discussion of Christianity and the "survival of the fittest." "Eugenics," he said, "gives us a synthesis between these two laws in upholding the Christian principle of ministry to the feebleminded and wrong-willed and at the same time in preventing them from pouring their corrupt currents into the race stream." In MacArthur's rendering, eugenics assured a race progress free from "anything contrary to the love of Christ" because it allowed society to aid existing generations of the feebleminded while also actively preventing them from passing on their hereditary taints.[97] A similar argument about the eugenics movement's conformity to the principles of Christian charity came from Dr. Harry F. Ward, a professor of Christian ethics at Union Theological Seminary and founder of the Methodist Federation for Social Service. Writing in *Eugenics*, Ward said that Christian morality and eugenics were compatible because both pursued the "challenge of removing the causes that produce the weak."[98]

Only one religious leader challenged the assumption that underlay this supposedly ideal partnership, the assumption that society should eliminate the feebleminded. Rev. John A. Ryan, a member of the AES Committee on Cooperation with Clergymen and director of the Social Action Department of the National Catholic Welfare Conference, offered a brief but withering indictment of the idea that "the weaker members of society ought to be left to perish in order that society as a whole may reach a higher average of welfare or achievement." His understanding of Christian charity was at odds with the other contributors to the magazine, and he viewed some eugenics proposals as slippery slopes toward a world where "the 'welfare of society' will come to mean the welfare of a few supermen, namely those who have been powerful enough to get themselves accepted at their own valuation."[99] To Ryan, these ministers had convinced themselves of the harmony of Christian charity and eugenics not because the two were, in fact, interchangeable, but because they had failed to consider fully the underlying principles of the eugenics movement.

Aside from Rev. Ryan's brief but trenchant criticism, the "preachers' issue," with its reprinted eugenic sermons and praise-filled articles by eugenicists, was a mutual hymn to eugenic-religious cooperation. "We want ministers everywhere to understand," the editors noted at the conclusion of the special issue, "that eugenics does not menace piety, but coincides with it; that it does not deny the Bible but finds therein many of its most eloquent texts; that it does not reject Christian pity but intertwines with it, that it is the engine, the device, the practical plan by which the sweet vision of faith may be attained."[100] On its face, the new AES appeared to embody this spirit of cooperation. Ministers, rabbis, and even a few priests had given their approval to eugenics; eugenicists were exploring religious questions in their research and publicly praising the preachers' influence. Unlike the pitched battles over evolutionary theory, in the eugenics movement, religion and science met on common ground.

But that ground was beginning to shift. In 1927, a theologian named Reinhold Niebuhr asked, "Does civilization need religion?" To many, it appeared not. A younger generation increasingly expressed skepticism about spiritual solutions to their problems. In "A Flapper's Appeal to Parents," Ellen Welles Page limned the concerns of her cohorts. "We are the Younger Generation," she said. "The war tore away our spiritual foundations and challenged our faith. We are struggling to regain our equilibrium." Others were not convinced that the clergy was the appropriate group to restore those foundations. Heywood Broun, a well-known columnist for the New York *Telegram*, claimed, "The ministry is the only learned profession in which a man may close his mind forever at the moment of ordination." Learning mattered for little; on the contrary, "as long as he maintains a sufficiently sanctified look [a minister] can dodder on till death releases an all-too-patient congregation."[101]Others agreed. With an air of definitiveness, Walter Lippmann declared men of science "ever so much superior to churchmen" at inspiring human beings. His contemporary, Joseph Wood Krutch, argued that only "weak and uninstructed intelligences take refuge in the monotonous repetition of once living creeds." Lippmann, Krutch, and other critics did not unequivocally embrace science (Krutch warned that science's findings offered only a "phantom of certitude"), but they felt it more capable of wrestling with the questions sparked by modernity. For them, of course, the stakes were lower. Although science posed certain challenges— while completing his *Principles of Psychology*, William James wrote, with frustration, to his brother Henry: "I have to forge every sentence in the teeth of irreducible and stubborn facts"—conformity still meant readjustment, not possible extinction, as it did for religious leaders.[102]

But science, too, was beginning to breed uncertainty. In 1927, the same year Niebuhr asked after the need for religion in modern civilization, German physicist Werner Heisenberg outlined his uncertainty principle, which made the laws of physics statements of relative rather than absolute certainties. Science, like religion, now operated to some extent on faith. Closer to home, geneticists began voicing serious criticisms of eugenic science, posing a challenge to eugenicists' cultural authority in the process. Delivering the Lowell Lectures at Harvard University in 1925, British philosopher Alfred North Whitehead warned that, without religion, "human life is a flash of occasional enjoyments lighting up a mass of pain and misery, a bagatelle of transient experience."[103] Those who had turned to the science of eugenics to alleviate the confusion caused by modern transience soon found their new faith shaken.

5

Sterilization, Birth Control, and the Catholic Confrontation with Eugenics

But the seed of the wicked shall be cut off.

—Psalm 37:28

Hindsight can grant to groups clarity of purpose and a consistency of thought that they often did not enjoy in fact. Doctrinal bickering, personality conflicts, and the arguments exchanged during feverish correspondence gradually recede, replaced by narratives that, in their convenience more than anything else, shape our understanding of how people came to hold the beliefs that they did.

Any history of the U.S. eugenics movement would be incomplete without reference to the sustained opposition it received from Catholics. Indeed, most historians of eugenics have noted how the organized efforts of Catholics led to the defeat of many eugenics legislative proposals in the 1910s and 1920s.[1] Contrary to the secular worldview embraced by eugenicists, Catholics argued that natural, divine law—not the laws of biology—governed human behavior and protected, among other things, the indissolubility of marriage, the sanctity of procreation and human life (born and unborn), and the family. By interfering with these things, eugenicists violated natural law, and thus earned the censure of most Catholics.

But Catholics did not arrive at this denunciation of eugenics as quickly or neatly as historians have suggested. During the decades before the Vatican took an official position on the controversy, a spectrum of Catholic opinion existed. Though never as broad as the one that governed Protestant participation in the movement, this spectrum ranged from staunch opposition (the most heavily

weighted end) to wary acceptance of some eugenic methods, to active participation in the American Eugenics Society by two prominent clerics. Exploring
the range of Catholic thought on eugenics reveals a great deal about the shape
of the American Catholic community and its approach to science and social
reform in the 1920s. Two developments in particular had resonance for Catholics: the resurgence in the late 1920s and early 1930s of public support for
eugenic sterilization legislation and the increasing visibility of the birth control
movement, which in personnel and philosophy eventually overlapped with the
eugenics movement. Both of these developments posed a challenge to the
natural law philosophy that undergirded much Catholic thought on social issues and sparked debate over the legitimacy of eugenic methods and aims.

Catholic clerics and laymen had engaged in debates over eugenics since
Francis Galton's time, but not until the 1920s and the creation of the AES did
any prominent Catholics become members of a eugenics organization. The
two who did, Fr. John A. Ryan and Fr. John M. Cooper, were not laymen flirting
with heresy, but priests whose adherence to Church doctrine was unwavering.
Their participation occurred within a dual context: the realization of the Catholic social reform impulse in the years following the First World War, and the
attack on eugenic science launched by geneticists. The former was responsible
for exposing many Catholics to the eugenics movement; the latter (in combination with the Church's own natural law doctrine) colored that exposure with
serious misgivings about the movement's methods. Catholic clerics approached the eugenics movement with a wariness and skepticism absent in
most of their liberal Protestant or Reform Jewish counterparts.

They also came with a different experience of social reform. Pope Leo
XIII's 1891 encyclical, *Rerum Novarum* (On the Condition of Workers), inspired
a new era of Catholic social campaigns by carving a middle way between socialism and laissez-faire capitalism and outlining the Church's position on the
conditions of labor. But it had even broader implications. What many Catholics
drew from the encyclical was an understanding of their responsibility to craft
moral responses to secular problems. *Rerum Novarum* affirmed that natural
law was the foundation of Catholic social ethics and served as the blueprint
for Catholic reform well into the twentieth century.

Catholic natural law doctrine rested on the teachings of medieval philosopher St. Thomas Aquinas (ca. 1225–1274) and understood the universe as
governed by laws that were the reflection of divine reason and, hence, un-
changeable. Aquinas reconciled faith and reason by arguing that the two were
never actually in conflict. Reason seeks knowledge from experimental and logical evidence, whereas faith seeks understanding through revelation, using the
knowledge provided by reason. Both, according to Aquinas, come from and
reveal God as the source of truth. Perhaps most important, the Catholic interpretation of natural law, known as Thomism, stresses the dignity of the individual.[2] Thomism gave Catholics an entry point and guidelines for their en-

gagement with contemporary culture and an "intellectual cement" that was not always perfectly adhesive.[3] Problems arose in the application of natural law to specific social questions, because natural law could produce competing solutions. Sympathizers and opponents of social programs could invoke its claims to argue for their respective causes.

Rerum Novarum also encouraged the flowering of a Catholic reform impulse akin to the Protestant Social Gospel. Catholics channeled these energies through organizations such as the National Catholic Welfare Council, later called the National Catholic Welfare Conference, formed to continue the work begun by the National Catholic War Council during the First World War and to coordinate Catholic activities at the national level. The Conference's Bishop's Program of Social Reconstruction (1919), which called, among other things, for a Christian ethics of industry, captured this spirit well.[4] At the same time, reformers among the Catholic clergy encouraged the Church to improve clerical education by exposing priests to new intellectual currents in the natural and social sciences. In this way, they predicted, the Church would be better equipped to face the problems of the twentieth century.[5]

No Catholic embodied the Rerum Novarum–inspired reform impulse as well as John Augustine Ryan (1869–1945). A priest widely known for his work on economic issues (the argument he made in his doctoral dissertation, published as A Living Wage in 1906, reappeared in the 1912 platform of the Progressive Party), Ryan served as the head of the National Catholic Welfare Conference's Social Action Department, taught at the Catholic University of America, and participated in numerous secular crusades, including the American Civil Liberties Union. Fr. Ryan's often acerbic opinion carried great weight; he was considered the U.S. spokesman for the Vatican on public policy issues.[6]

In 1925, Ryan added the eugenics movement to his list of secular commitments when he joined the AES's Committee on Cooperation with Clergymen. In a letter to eugenicist Irving Fisher, Ryan wrote, in typically blunt fashion, "While I have no reason to think that my participation will be of any particular value to the Committee, I am glad to accept the appointment on account of the general interest which I have in the subject."[7] Ryan's interest in eugenics was not especially keen or consistent; given the broad range of liberal secular causes he championed—so many that at times he lost count, his biographers note—this is not surprising.[8] Nevertheless, by agreeing to add his name to the AES letterhead, Ryan, like other prominent religious leaders, signaled the movement's increasing significance.

This signal, whether intentional or unwitting, was ironic in Ryan's case for he rarely made supportive statements about eugenics. On the contrary, even his earliest musings on the subject demonstrate a strong streak of skepticism. Writing in the Ecclesiastical Review in 1904 in response to the alarm recently raised by Theodore Roosevelt over "race suicide," Ryan questioned whether a society was "justified in instituting a comparison between quality and quantity

in respect of beings endowed with human souls, each of which has conse-
quently an intrinsic and, in a sense, an infinite value."[9] His participation in
the eugenics movement is best understood within the broader context of Catholic campaigns for social reform; like other reformers in the Church, Ryan
wanted Catholics to join forces with secular crusaders to achieve social justice.

The second Catholic priest to join the AES, Fr. John M. Cooper (1881–
1949), was also familiar with the currents of secular thought, but in their
scientific guise. His approach to eugenics owed much to geneticists' growing
critiques of the eugenics movement. By the 1920s, geneticists had begun to
cast doubt on eugenicists' bold claims. It was not possible to ferret out "feeblemindedness" in a generation or two, as eugenicists suggested, because science could not locate a single gene for such a trait. These and other deleterious
markers were part of a far more complex equation of human heredity than
eugenicists suggested, as geneticists such as Herbert S. Jennings and Raymond
Pearl frequently reminded the public.[10] Eugenicists' claim that they could eliminate feeblemindedness might still make for good propaganda, but it could no
longer pretend to be good science.

The scientific credibility of the eugenics movement became Cooper's consistent concern. A priest, anthropologist, and educator from the Department
of Sacred Theology at Catholic University who joined the AES in 1922, Cooper
was actively engaged in the eugenics movement for nearly a decade. At a time
when anthropologists, most famously Franz Boas, already had repudiated eugenics for its denigration of cultural forces, it is remarkable that Fr. Cooper,
the author of a study of the tribal peoples of Tierra del Fuego and founder of
the Catholic Anthropological Conference, responded to a solicitation from the
Society with enthusiasm, writing that it would be "a pleasure to serve" on the
Advisory Council. By 1925, Cooper had also signed on to the Committee on
Cooperation with Clergymen and the Committee on Birth Regulation.[11]

Why would someone whose religious and professional callings were generally hostile to eugenics become involved in the movement? Although Cooper
published no books or substantial articles on eugenics, in his personal papers,
especially his nine-year correspondence with AES executive secretary Leon
Whitney, he stands revealed as a man genuinely interested in the links between
religion and science. In a series of radio talks delivered in 1926, Cooper outlined their common purpose: "Religion, like science, is deeply concerned with
all that concerns human welfare. In particular it is deeply concerned in all that
prevents or allays human suffering, in all that builds up and maintains human
health."[12]

Cooper approached eugenics with an attitude similar to the one he advised
his students at Catholic University to adopt at the beginning of each semester:
"Don't be a sponge that soaks up everything, nor a porcupine that erects his
bristles at everything, simply because new," he cautioned. "Like the Church go
slowly, select, discriminate."[13] If the Church was moderate and selective, it was

also, in Cooper's rendering, an agent of race betterment. In 1917, during a High Mass at St. Matthew's Catholic Church in Washington, D.C., where he served as assistant pastor for thirteen years, Cooper took as his topic "The Church and Eugenics." "In her teaching and practice," he told the assembled faithful, "[the Church] has made and is making great contributions to the betterment of humanity through the betterment of parents."[14] Like British priest Thomas Gerrard's eugenics, Cooper's version began with a recognition of the Church's long-standing, special efforts at race improvement.

What Cooper's early explorations of eugenics do not reveal, but what became clear once he joined the movement in 1922, was his primary concern for the credibility of eugenic science. In his correspondence with Leon Whitney and in his contributions to published debates in AES periodicals, Cooper consistently challenged eugenicists to defend their scientific claims. Like the geneticists whose critiques his mirrored, he singled out the eugenics movement's nonscientific propagandists for particular censure. In a letter to Whitney, he denounced the "Nordic presuppositions" of eugenicists such as Madison Grant and argued that their views created "an internal problem in the American Eugenics Society which is alienating interest from the eugenics movement not merely on the part of those unfamiliar with its aims but also on the part of many who are thoroughly familiar and sympathetic with the eugenic movement as such." Writing to a Catholic colleague about this problem, he was more candid, describing "the present clique controlling the American Eugenics Society" as just "a little short of being a crowd of 'nuts.' "[15]

Cooper occasionally aired these concerns publicly. In a *Eugenics* symposium on the question "Is Eugenics Racial Snobbery?" he argued that the eugenics movement was "still steeped in the doctrine of superior races." "If we interpret eugenics as an applied science rather than as a clan velleity," he said, "we must base both its theories and its program upon carefully established facts rather than upon chauvinistic folk tales."[16] His criticisms echoed those made by geneticists just a few years earlier. In a 1924 letter to eugenicist Irving Fisher, for example, geneticist H. S. Jennings argued that eugenics societies were no place for "men of pure research, the strength of whose work lies in as complete a freedom as is possible from prejudice and propaganda."[17] Later that year, Jennings resigned from the AES.

Cooper found the geneticists' stance appealing for several reasons. Geneticists readily admitted the complexity and, to some degree, the mystery of the hereditary process, a feature of their science that Cooper, who was sometimes appalled by eugenicists' lack of humility, admired. Geneticists also based their conclusions on research that took many years to accumulate and that rested on such careful, unglamorous laboratory study as the minute hereditary vagaries of thousands of generations of fruit flies. As an anthropologist who, between 1925 and 1940, took thirteen field trips to study the Native American tribes living in northern Ontario, Cooper had a respect for such thorough and painstaking research.[18] Sweeping conclusions based on an undergraduate eugenics fieldworker's day trip into the Piney Woods did not impress him.

Cooper's uneasiness about the AES's scientific credibility did not prompt him to resign from the organization, as it had geneticists such as Jennings. Rather, he remained internally vigilant, writing often to Executive Secretary Whitney of his concerns and lobbing the occasional intellectual grenade at eugenicists in the pages of *Eugenics* magazine. As he said in a letter to Whitney in 1930, six years after geneticists' public attacks on eugenic science, "I can see no particular good coming out of the work until we put the whole thing on a real scientific basis and work out our policies in the light of our known facts rather than on the basis of emotional attitudes."[19] Unlike geneticists, who found little worth saving in the eugenics movement by the late 1920s, Cooper was still optimistic that the AES could shift its priorities to conform more closely to unimpeachable standards of science.

Cooper occupied a paradoxical position in the eugenics movement. As a Catholic and an anthropologist, he was clearly an outsider. This was a role he did not necessarily reject; as the above examples suggest, he enjoyed acting as the movement's scientific conscience, cautioning eugenicists when they appeared to be overstepping their bounds. But it was also a position that bred misunderstanding. Although his Church did not compromise Cooper's intellectual freedom, eugenicists sometimes insinuated that when he or any Catholic cleric spoke, what the world heard was, in fact, an act of papal ventriloquism. Whitney said as much in a letter to Cooper in 1925, when he asked, "Tell me, is it true that you can't have freedom to think as you want?" Cooper assured Whitney that "in matters 'not of faith' as we say, we are free to hold what views we wish and to discuss them as we please."[20] He included eugenics among these matters "not of faith," and despite his contentiousness on matters scientific, he clearly saw himself having a stake in the future of the AES. The language he used in his correspondence reveals this: To other eugenicists he spoke of his concern for "our Society" and "our eugenics movement," and the records of the AES reveal that he was one of the most active religious participants in the Society.

His participation, like that of other religious leaders, was a valuable asset to the AES. As a Catholic priest and educator, Cooper assured that his eugenics activities had an impact on a constituency normally hostile to eugenics. It even led some of his fellow clerics to reconsider their initial wariness about the subject. Writing to Cooper in 1928, Rev. Joseph C. Flynn of Creighton University in Nebraska noted that he recently had received a solicitation from the AES. "To be frank with you," he told Cooper, "my first reaction on receipt of this communication was one of suspicion, but the presence of your name on the Advisory Council made me feel that I would like to know more about the Organization expecially [sic] from the ethical and Catholic standpoint."[21] Internally, Cooper's vigilance regarding the scientific claims of the movement earned him the respect of several eugenicists. He wrote to Rev. Henry Strong Huntington, chair of the AES Committee on Cooperation with Clergymen, about this in 1927. Rev. Huntington turned to his brother, eugenicist and geographer Ellsworth Huntington, for advice in responding. "Dr. Cooper is more or less right about part of the people who run the Eugenics Society," Ellsworth wrote. "There is great zeal in running things, but often not quite enough thought." Ellsworth found that, "for a Roman Catholic, Dr. Cooper takes quite a progressive attitude," and told his brother that "letters like that of Dr. Cooper's will tend to produce greater thoughtfulness" in the eugenics movement.[22]

In joining the AES, both Cooper and Ryan took advantage of the intellectual freedom the Church provided, a freedom expansive enough to allow support for a movement that was, if not expressly forbidden, certainly inimical to many Church teachings. By formally joining the AES, Ryan and Cooper put into practice the sentiment expressed by one of Ryan's students, whose 1926 doctoral dissertation tackled "The Catholic Church and Eugenics": Because eugenics was "not likely to pass away as a temporary fad," the student wrote, it was "the duty of Catholics to see that this influence will be for good, and not for evil."[23]

Frs. Cooper and Ryan were exceptions among the Catholic clergy in that they formally joined a eugenics organization and, in doing so, offered a measure of support for eugenic goals. Even without a papal condemnation, most Catholic clergy and laymen opposed eugenics; throughout the 1910s, 1920s, and 1930s, they organized to defeat eugenics-inspired legislative proposals such as marriage health certificates and compulsory sterilization laws. Writing to Whitney in 1928, a genetics professor and eugenics organizer in Lexington, Kentucky, complained about this "Catholic influence," noting that it had stalled passage of a compulsory sterilization measure in the state legislature. In New Orleans, Catholics formed a coalition with fundamentalist Protestants to thwart legislators' attempts to pass a compulsory sterilization law.[24]

Catholic opponents of eugenics found sanction for their views in the work of a diverse group of Catholic laymen and clerics who wrote about eugenics in the 1910s and 1920s. A marked difference in approach distinguished the lay Catholic writers from their clerical counterparts. Lay writers, focusing on the weaknesses of eugenic science, tended to dismiss the movement in its entirety: Eugenic science was questionable, ergo, no application of the theory was viable. Clerical writers, on the other hand, while implicitly recognizing some limits to eugenic science, usually drew a clear distinction between eugenic means and ends. In this reckoning, the aim of eugenics—the improvement of the human race—was a worthy goal that could enjoy Catholic approval as long as the means employed in its pursuit were legitimate. To put it another way, for the laymen engaged in this debate, eugenics was already a real and visible threat, a movement unlikely to change for the better; to the clerics, the movement was something still in the making and thus in theory was responsive to criticism and capable of change.

One of the earliest contributors to the lay debate was Lawrence F. Flick (1856–1938), a highly regarded Catholic physician. In a lecture delivered at a Catholic summer school in Philadelphia, Flick brought his experience as a tuberculosis crusader to bear on the subject of eugenics. In his view, the most dangerous and scientifically unsound principle of the eugenics movement was the claim that heredity was a more powerful force than environment. Proving the opposite was Flick's life work. A study he conducted in the late nineteenth century in a poor section of Philadelphia convinced him that, contrary to the prevailing wisdom of the day, tuberculosis was a contagious, rather than a hereditary disease. His 1903 book, *Consumption: A Curable and Preventable Disease*, drew on a meticulous collection of evidence to prove this theory.[25]

This belief in the power of environment over heredity also informed Flick's assessment of the eugenics movement. Eugenicists' evidence, he argued, did not withstand close scrutiny. Of the Jukes family study, for example, he wrote, "The merest tyro in logic must see at a glance the absurdity of trying to draw deductions on heredity from these two lines of progeny." Flick understood the appeal to the public of a movement such as eugenics—a movement that reduced society's myriad problems to a single cause (bad germ plasm) and offered a seemingly swift and permanent solution to that problem (sterilization)—but he reminded his audience that it was a movement driven by inconclusive evidence and tainted by a questionable agenda.[26]

Another Catholic physician, Sir Bertram Windle, president of University College in Cork, Ireland, also justified his rejection of eugenics by pointing to the inferior quality of eugenic science. Windle was well qualified to make this assessment; he was a widely respected scholar on both sides of the Atlantic who was also well-known for his grasp of Mendelian genetics. For Windle, the shoddiness of eugenic science compelled opposition even to the movement's milder schemes, such as segregation of the unfit. He described colonies for the feebleminded as "concentration camps under armed guardians and surrounded by barbed-wire inclosures." Sterilization he dismissed as utterly uncivilized.[27] Layman Henry Somerville, anticipating by several years secular critiques of IQ tests, denounced as "detestable tyrannies" the Binet intelligence tests eugenicists relied on to assess feeblemindedness and joined Windle in his opposition.[28]

Among the laymen writing about eugenics, British writer and Catholic convert G. K. Chesterton offered perhaps the most scathing assessment of the movement. "That it ought to be destroyed I propose to prove in the pages that follow," he stated in his book, *Eugenics and Other Evils*. Like other lay contributors to this debate, Chesterton argued that eugenic proposals were illegitimate because eugenicists lacked a consistent body of provable scientific theory on which to base them. The weakest link in the chain of eugenic thinking, Chesterton claimed, was the inability to prove conclusively that heredity exercised as powerful a force over human existence as eugenicists claimed. "I am willing to pay the scientist for what he does know," Chesterton said. "I draw the line at paying him for everything he doesn't know."[29]

Chesterton was particularly concerned with eugenicists' use of state power to achieve their goals. Legislators, under the sway of the "modern craze for scientific officialism," had gone too far. In their efforts to control feeblemindedness they trampled individual rights and ethical boundaries, all the while exhibiting "that creepy simplicity of mind with which the Eugenists chill the blood." Although he did not deny "the right of the State to interfere to cure a great evil," he believed that if state power were used to promote eugenics, "it would interfere to create a great evil."[30]

Not all Catholics considered eugenics a great evil. Several Catholic clergymen writing in these years tried to navigate a path between more extreme eugenicists on the one side and the wholesale rejection of the eugenics movement called for by Catholic laymen such as Chesterton on the other. They found the eugenics movement's aim of improving the human race appealing, but they coupled their endorsement of that end with a strong skepticism about the means many eugenicists favored in pursuing it. British priest Thomas Slater demonstrated this approach in his book, *Questions of Moral Theology*. Slater began his examination of eugenics by noting the significant similarities between its stated goal and the goals of the Catholic Church. "If the spiritual good of mankind be added to the list of objects," he wrote, "the end of Eugenics would be identical with that for which the Catholic Church exists and works." That end was the improvement of the human race and the alleviation of human suffering. In this, Slater was in agreement both with the earlier work of Fr. Gerrard and the sentiments expressed by Fr. John Cooper in his 1917 Mass on the Church and Eugenics.[31]

Nevertheless, the existence of similarities did not negate the Christian's duty to examine scrupulously the means eugenicists employed to reach their goals. "Theology is quite at one with Eugenics as to the end to be aimed at," Slater remarked, but "it very cautiously scrutinizes the means proposed for the attainment of that end." For Slater, as for earlier Catholic observers of the eugenics movement, the "end to be aimed at" was a general notion of an improved humanity, one free from diseases and so, presumably, from much suffering. The eugenic method Slater could not abide was sterilization; like many Catholics, he deemed it "physiologically and morally . . . a serious mutilation of the human body." He also challenged the hubris of eugenicists' claim that they should be entrusted with determining the human qualities that should and should not exist in future generations. Such a task belonged only to God. "To exist even with a taint is better than not to exist at all," he said.[32]

Aside from these points of contention, however, Slater endorsed the eugenics movement. "Moral theology would have no insuperable difficulty in allowing other means which have been proposed by eugenists to improve the race and to remedy degeneration," he pointed out, and "many of them it would cordially approve." Among those he listed was segregation of the feebleminded. In contrast to Bertram Windle's portrait of frightening concentration camps for the feebleminded, Slater viewed segregation as a form of "kindly detention" that served the best interests of society without violating the natural rights of the feebleminded.[33] A eugenics movement that understood its limits and relied on means other than sterilization could, in his estimation, enjoy Catholic support.

Rev. Charles P. Bruehl, a professor of dogmatic theology at the Seminary of St. Charles Borromeo in Overbrook, Pennsylvania, drew a similar distinction between means and ends in his exploration of eugenics. In 1926, he transformed the *Pastoralia* column of the *Homiletic and Pastoral Review* into a forum for examining the ethical implications of the eugenics movement. "Instead of simply condemning the movement in its entirety," he wrote, "we will try to separate the grain from the chaff, and see to what extent it can be made to serve good purposes." For Bruehl, the grain of the movement was its admirable aim of improving the human race. He felt that it was "perfectly legitimate to speak of a menace of the feebleminded" and praised eugenicists for arousing society "to a realization of the grave peril in its very midst." Unfortunately, in their pursuit of that goal, he said, eugenicists often employed unscrupulous means, the "chaff" of his metaphor.[34]

Like Slater, Bruehl found an egregious example of this in eugenicists' support for compulsory sterilization. And like the lay Catholic critics who condemned sterilization, he based his assessment of the practice on the science that purportedly sanctioned it. Before the state legitimately could compel a person to be sterilized, he said, "it would have to be shown that this particular individual will be responsible for a defective progeny, and thus become a menace to the community." However, eugenic science did not allow for such certainty: "It is just at this point," the point of causality, "that our knowledge of heredity breaks down lamentably." It is notable that this conclusion did not prompt Bruehl, as it had his lay counterparts, to reject the eugenics movement in toto. "The only point we wish to make now," he said, "is that our present state of knowledge concerning the laws of heredity does not warrant the passing of legislation that would deprive large groups of the population of a basic human right."[35]

The willingness of Catholic clerics such as Slater and Bruehl to refrain from rejecting the eugenics movement in its entirety despite its scientific and ethical lapses represents another form of the same impulse that motivated Revs. Ryan and Cooper to join the AES: a sense, first of all, that eugenics was an idea worth pursuing and, second, that the existing eugenics movement was amenable to redirection and intellectual reshaping by critics such as themselves. Cooper and Bruehl in particular saw promise in the movement's aims—its optimistic hopes for breeding out disease and other sources of human suffering, as they interpreted them—and felt that once it had met rigorous scientific standards and conformed adequately to Christian principles, it would (and should) gain wide acceptance. As Bruehl put it, "In the matter of eugenics, everything depends on the spirit in which the movement is conceived and on the means that are adopted by its sponsors . . . eugenics will either be a noble and commendable thing or a thing inutterably vile and loathsome."[36] Although theirs were the views of a minority of Catholics, these priests hoped that their contributions might succeed in pushing the eugenics movement toward those nobler aims.

In the work of nearly every Catholic who engaged in a discussion of the eugenics movement, compulsory sterilization was the practical eugenic proposal that served as a flash point for debate; soon birth control emerged as one as well. The contentiousness sparked by both of these methods gradually upset the intellectual balancing act being performed by Catholics such as Ryan, Cooper, and Bruehl. Their efforts to craft a "true eugenics,"[37] one based on adherence to strict standards of scientific evidence and respectful of Christian ethics, appeared increasingly hollow in the face of a movement that praised and promoted compulsory sterilization and artificial contraception.

Catholic concern with sterilization stretched back several decades. The first wave of compulsory sterilization legislation, enacted in eighteen states between 1907 and 1922, had sparked a series of exchanges among priests in the pages of the *Ecclesiastical Review*.[38] During that debate, a minority view emerged from the arguments of contributors such as Fr. Stephen Donovan that sterilization did not, in theory, violate Catholic moral teachings. In practice, however, clerics and laymen in these years nearly all opposed sterilization. The archbishop of Milwaukee expressed a common sentiment in 1913 when he condemned sterilization as "an interference with personal independence and individual liberty."[39]

Opponents challenged the laws in court, claiming that they violated constitutional protections against cruel and unusual punishment and standards of due process and equal protection. In 1919, Indiana's Supreme Court overturned the nation's first sterilization law; by that time, the disputatious aura of these laws meant that many states had, for all practical purposes, ceased enforcing them.[40] The 1920s witnessed a reversal of this trend, due in large part to the efforts of ERO superintendent Harry H. Laughlin. His 1922 book, *Eugenical Sterilization in the United States*, became the bible of sterilization supporters. In addition to drafting a supposedly challenge-proof "model sterilization law," Laughlin marshaled evidence to prove that "there is every reason to believe that great benefit would accrue to the natural hereditary qualities of future generations, from laws providing for the eugenical sterilization of certain hereditary degenerates and defectives."[41] In 1924, he applied this reasoning to Carrie Buck, an inmate at the Virginia Colony for Epileptics and Feebleminded in Lynchburg, when he evaluated her as a candidate for the state's newly enacted compulsory sterilization law.[42] After a quick glance at Buck's file, Laughlin pronounced her "part of the shiftless, ignorant, and worthless class of anti-social whites in the South"; soon thereafter, Lynchburg Colony superintendent John H. Bell, acting in accordance with the recent state law, sterilized her. Buck sued, and the test case that emerged reached the Supreme Court in 1927 as *Buck v. Bell*.[43]

In upholding the Virginia sterilization law, the Supreme Court, in an opinion written by Justice Oliver Wendell Holmes Jr., declared that because Carrie Buck was the "probable potential parent of socially inadequate offspring," it was within the police power of the state to sterilize her. Holmes's opinion was a succinct and, to contemporary ears, chilling summary of eugenic sentiment: "It is better for all the world, if instead of waiting to execute degenerate offspring for crime, or to let them starve for their imbecility, society can prevent those who are manifestly unfit from continuing their kind. Three generations of imbeciles are enough."[44]

The Supreme Court's decision in *Buck v. Bell* unleashed a torrent of new compulsory sterilization laws. In the two years immediately following the decision, eleven states passed new legislation that incorporated the safeguards (outlined in the *Buck* decision) necessary to withstand constitutional challenges. Between 1925 and 1935, with the avid support of physicians and reformers, these laws resulted in the quadrupling of the number of men and women sterilized in state institutions. The increase is even starker when a broader span of time is examined: In 1917, approximately 1,422 people in institutions were sterilized; by 1941, that number had reached 38,087.[45]

Although the spectrum of Catholic opinion on sterilization was never broad (the *Ecclesiastical Review* debate participants who had supported the practice were always in the minority), it shrunk considerably after *Buck v. Bell*. Many in the Catholic community viewed the Court's decision as a dangerous example of the extremes to which the state could extend its power in the name of eugenics. The ruling encouraged Fr. Bruehl, who was already on record as an opponent of sterilization laws, but who had conceded that such measures might be necessary in the future, to make a more forceful condemnation of the practice. He credited *Buck v. Bell* as the major impulse behind his decision, in 1928, to publish *Birth Control and Eugenics in the Light of Fundamental Ethical Principles*. An expansion of his earlier *Homiletic and Pastoral Review* essays, the book unequivocally stated, "As Catholics, we absolutely repudiate the principle that the end, however good and exalted in itself, has the power to justify the means, unless they are themselves good or at least indifferent."[46] Sterilization as upheld by the Supreme Court was not, in Bruehl's estimation, an indifferent practice. Condemnation came from the Catholic press as well. A priest writing in the *Catholic Daily Tribune* decried the Court's failure to recognize that Carrie Buck "has rights which the state has not given her, but which she possesses by the very fact that she is a human person." The *Ecclesiastical Review* called the decision a "sustained legislative encroachment upon a purely personal right of liberty" that deprived the feebleminded of "a natural function."[47]

What these comments reveal is a coalescing of Catholic opinion about sterilization around two points: first, the incontrovertibility of natural law, as revealed in phrases such as "rights . . . which she possesses by the fact that she is a human person," and second, a growing concern with the encroachment of state power. Catholic opponents of sterilization began to articulate these themes more clearly in the wake of the Court's decision. In Colorado in 1927, for example, the governor vetoed a sterilization law passed by the legislature after receiving substantial opposition from the Denver Knights of Columbus and the Catholic Holy Name Society. The Knights argued that the proposed legislation "would deprive certain persons of a natural right and hence is fundamentally immoral," and the Denver Diocesan Holy Name Union stated, "No matter how much we lament the human deformities of society," the proposed legislation "is against the natural law."[48] *Buck v. Bell* served as a wake-up call for the lay and clerical Catholic community, alerting those who previously had given only lukewarm attendance to the issue of the threat a pro-eugenic state posed to individual liberty.

Yet the *Buck* decision did not alter official Church doctrine on sterilization. The fact that the great majority of Catholics by 1927 opposed eugenic sterilization did not make that opinion binding on all Catholics, as Fr. Ryan pointed out to a fellow priest in 1928. Asked by Fr. John F. Doherty, the director of the Bureau of Catholic Charities in St. Paul, Minnesota, about Church teaching on sterilization (Doherty's state legislature recently had enacted a compulsory sterilization law), Ryan noted that although he personally disapproved of sterilization, "a Catholic is not compelled to hold that this operation is necessarily forbidden by the moral law."[49] Ryan's opinion of the *Buck* case demonstrated a similar logic. A great fan of Justice Holmes's jurisprudence, Ryan conceded to a correspondent that "all Catholic authorities admit that such persons as the one whose case came before the Court may be segregated and prevented from becoming parents in state institutions and colonies." He had hoped to see Buck's attorneys mount a stronger Fourteenth Amendment case, but as they did not, "I do not see how the Court could have rendered any other decision in view of the facts before it."[50]

Ryan's musings in his personal correspondence were but one expression of alternative Catholic views of sterilization in the late 1920s. In 1927, Joseph Mayer, a priest who was associated with the Institute for Social Work at the University of Freiburg, Germany, published *Gesetzliche Unfruchtbarmachung Geisteskranker* (The legal sterilization of the mentally diseased), which claimed that, in principle, eugenical sterilization was necessary and suitable in many cases to prevent the spread of feeblemindedness. Mayer's approach to this issue was as shocking to most Catholics as the conclusions he drew from it: "From the wonderfully clear and penetrative consideration that Thomas Aquinas gave to legal castration and to the death penalty which in the middle ages often followed it and which he held to be justified for offenders against morality, I tried to derive a new theoretical justification for official restraint of the blind and irresponsible propagation of hereditarily defective, anti-social criminals and also of asocial psychopaths."[51] Drawing on the natural law teachings of Aquinas, Mayer concluded that "various details of the program of negative as well as positive eugenics are indispensable aids to meet the many emergencies of our time, and that they follow simply from the old laws of life and of nature."[52]

Natural law was one of the points around which Catholic opposition to sterilization coalesced. How could it also support Mayer's endorsement of sterilization? The answer lay in which elements of Thomism one chose to emphasize. Unlike the arguments of sterilization opponents, which emphasized the integrity of the individual, Mayer's argument rested on Aquinas's teachings on the nature of social power and the maintenance of the common good. In Mayer's interpretation, if conflict arose between the individual good and the common good, the common good prevailed. Just as a person might have to sacrifice a diseased limb for the good of the whole body, so there were times when the rights of a few (in this case, the feebleminded) had to be sacrificed for the greater good of humanity.[53]

Mayer's support for sterilization was more equivocal than one might glean from the parts of his work that received English translation, however. Eugenicist Paul Popenoe, a staunch supporter of sterilization (he was founder of the Human Betterment Foundation, based in California, the state that sterilized more people than any other during this period), interpreted Mayer's work for the readers of *Eugenics* magazine and thus had a strong motive to emphasize Mayer's support for sterilization. In a more circumspect study of eugenic sterilization published in 1936, a committee of physicians of the American Neurological Association translated several pertinent passages of Mayer's original book that Popenoe had chosen to omit in his version. These passages revealed that Mayer's assessments of eugenic sterilization were closer to those of his fellow Catholic clerics than to eugenicists like Popenoe. The Mayer that emerges from this translation urged sterilization only as "a last remedy if all other measures are inadequate or impossible" and concluded that legal sterilization at the present time would be "premature, useless, and unworkable, and therefore, from a practical point of view prohibitive and morally objectionable."[54] Until this corrective appeared in 1936, however, many readers of *Eugenics* accepted Popenoe's contention that in Mayer the eugenics movement had a Catholic ally. That Popenoe felt the need to promote Mayer's work in the first place suggests awareness among eugenicists that their movement faced growing opposition from Catholics.

If the Catholic discussion of sterilization in the 1910s and 1920s produced feuding interpretations of natural law and significantly different levels of enthusiasm for eugenic measures, the Catholic position on birth control was notable for its clarity and unanimity. Fr. Bruehl stated unequivocally, for example, "If birth control is to be made an essential feature of the program of the eugenists, we can have nothing at all to do with it."[55] His warning proved accurate. Even more than sterilization, eugenicists' support for artificial contraception tested the ties Catholics had formed with the eugenics movement.

As members of the AES, Ryan and Cooper had been ardent and outspoken opponents of artificial contraception for years. Their opposition centered on two arguments. The first stated that the use of contraceptives (or any other unnatural means of controlling births, including abortion) "constitutes the immoral perversion of a human faculty." The second deemed birth control a symbol of the growing selfishness and "decadence" of modern existence. Families that "speak much of aiming at quality rather than quantity in offspring" to justify their use of contraception, Ryan argued, in fact inculcate the worst materialistic values by doing so. Artificial restriction of the family "makes for enervating self-indulgence and perverted moral notions in parents, a morally and physically enfeebled generation of children, a diminishing population, and a decadent race."[56]

Fr. Cooper held similar views on artificial contraception. His 1923 pamphlet, *Birth Control*, published by the National Catholic Welfare Conference, emphasized that the practice was a perversion of natural faculties, but drew a distinction between birth control and artificial contraception. The Church's quarrel was not with the idea of limiting offspring, Cooper noted; contrary to some claims, she does not instruct believers to bring on an "avalanche of babies" through indiscriminate reproduction. Rather, the Church opposes the *artificial* means of limiting offspring advocated by birth control supporters. "Limitation of offspring by artificial prevention of conception is of its very nature immoral, and immoral means are not justified by ends however good," Cooper concluded.[57]

The intersection of the birth control movement, the eugenics movement, and the Catholic Church in the 1920s and early 1930s reveals the degree to which the ideas of members of all of these groups were in flux. To contemporary eyes it appears strange to find Catholic priests such as Ryan and Cooper strongly condemning contraception while also participating in the eugenics movement. The seeming paradox is dissolved given two facts: First and most important, Catholics such as Cooper drew a distinction between eugenic means and eugenic ends. Cooper could agree with eugenicists' goal of improving mankind while simultaneously disagreeing on the means proposed to achieve that end. In the absence of an official Vatican pronouncement on eugenics, this was a tenable position. Birth control was merely another means that could be employed to pursue eugenic ends (and one not even all scientific eugenicists agreed was good), hence Cooper could remain consistent by condemning artificial contraception (an immoral means) while supporting the improvement of the race (a eugenic end).

Second, the position of the birth control movement vis-à-vis the eugenics movement in the 1920s was that of the young upstart to the established clique. Although the birth control movement in the United States unofficially began in October 1916, when Margaret Sanger opened her birth control clinic in the Brownsville section of Brooklyn, it did not gain sustained public attention until Sanger formed the American Birth Control League (ABCL), an educational and lobbying group, in 1921.[58] Those years were also formative ones for the AES, but other eugenic institutions such as the ERO had existed for more than a decade, and eugenicists enjoyed the support of a broad swath of public opinion. Eugenics had become more mainstream; at a 1926 meeting in New Orleans, the Protestant Episcopal House of Bishops favored eugenic measures but thoroughly rejected birth control, for example.[59]

Birth control advocates, in contrast, led a fledgling movement whose doctrines many people considered more radical than eugenics. Since the passage of a federal obscenity statute in 1873, referred to as the Comstock Law for its most zealous enforcer, Anthony Comstock, the law of the land prohibited "every article, instrument, substance, drug, medicine, or thing which is advertised or described in a manner calculated to lead another to use or apply it for preventing conception or producing abortion." Before Sanger's deliberate flouting of Comstockian imperatives, a subterranean market in contraceptives had existed, usually advertised in magazines under euphemisms such as "feminine hygiene," but contraceptives were neither safe nor standardized. Sanger's very public birth control campaign, with its links to radical ideas about women's equality and sexual freedom, resulted in a birth control movement that emanated a distinctly scandalous aura to many in the 1920s.[60] As Sanger's contemporary, Walter Lippmann, summed things up, "Whether or not birth control is eugenic, hygienic, and economic, it is the most revolutionary practice in the history of sexual morals."[61]

Catholics were not the only group skeptical of the birth control movement. Many eugenicists opposed it for scientific and practical reasons. On scientific grounds, they were concerned that contraception might have a dysgenic impact on society. In theory, contraception was a eugenic measure when used to prevent births among the unfit. In practice, however, eugenicists feared that those segments of society that should be reproducing at the highest rates—the "fit," educated, native-born classes—in fact were the group most likely to read about and practice contraception. The steady numerical decline of the *Mayflower* descendants suggested to many eugenicists that such a dysgenic practice was already widespread. Legalizing contraceptives surely would only make the situation worse.

Eugenicist Henry Fairfield Osborn's salvo against birth control was typical. Drawing a distinction between "birth selection," which eugenicists encouraged, and the new doctrine of "birth control," Osborn argued that the latter posed a serious risk to society. "I am very doubtful about birth control," he said. "In fact, on eugenic as well as on evolutionary lines I am strongly opposed to many directions which the birth control movement is taking." In language akin to that used by Catholics, Osborn pronounced birth control "fundamentally unnatural." Charles Davenport expressed skepticism as well, saying that he was "not convinced that, despite their high motives, the movement will not do more harm than good." Ellsworth Huntington agreed, noting that "like charity and religion," birth control was "a 'two-edged sword,' which may be used most effectively to fight the enemy, but may also cut the man who wields it." Edwin G. Conklin's opposition to birth control sounded very much like the "decadence" charges leveled by Catholics: "No one denies that the chief motive for limiting the size of families is personal comfort and pleasure rather than the welfare of the race."[62]

Eugenicists also had practical concerns about the public relations damage their own movement might sustain if formally allied to Sanger's ABCL. Some of the birth control movement's tactics seemed to them too confrontational. For example, the cover of the October '1921 issue of the *Birth Control Review* (the ABCL's official publication) featured a graphic image of a nude woman, doubled over on her knees; the woman's hands are bound behind her back with thick ropes and her face is averted as an infant nurses at her left breast, a less than subtle pictorial interpretation of women's fate without contraception. Eugenicists themselves were adept propagandists, of course, but they were more prudish practitioners of the art.

Eugenicists' wariness about the birth control movement had come to the fore during the formation of the AES in the early 1920s. In organizational meetings, eugenicists made a distinct effort (as one internal memo noted) to "try to steer clear of Birth Control movement, and Venereal Disease movement" so as to avoid tainting their own cause. A later proposal to combine the *Birth Control Review* and *Eugenics* magazine was also deemed "unwise."[63] But eugenicists sympathetic to the birth control movement and Sanger herself gradually whittled away at this reserve. Sanger aggressively promoted the eugenic features of birth control and actively recruited biologists and other scientists to her cause. At the 1921 International Eugenics Congress in New York, for example, she outlined the eugenic logic of her crusade and argued, "The most urgent problem today is how to limit and discourage the overfertility of the mentally and physically defective." Legalization and distribution of contraceptives would aid in this pursuit, she said.[64] The ABCL's publications encouraged ties to the eugenics mission as well; one early volume of the *Birth*

Control Review featured the phrase "Birth Control: To Create a Race of Thoroughbreds" prominently displayed under the masthead.[65]

Sanger also gained key early converts to her movement from within the eugenics movement. Eugenicists such as biologist Clarence Cook Little and geneticists Edward M. East and Leon J. Cole announced their support for birth control in the early 1920s. They were joined by AES executive secretary Leon F. Whitney, who was behind several of the unsuccessful attempts to link officially the AES and the ABCL in the late 1920s. Whitney's enthusiasm for birth control was such that he even nobly offered to get himself arrested for passing out birth control literature because, as he wrote to a friend, "it would make a trial such as they had in the Scope [*sic*] case in Tennessee and it would quickly settle the matter as far as the public was concerned."[66]

In their opposition to birth control, Revs. Cooper and Ryan were the notable exceptions among the AES's religious supporters. Most of the liberal Protestants and Reform rabbis active in the AES supported Sanger's crusade. AES Advisory Council member Rabbi Louis L. Mann (1890–1966), of Sinai Temple Congregation in Chicago, was one of the founders of the ABCL. At a crowded luncheon at a 1923 birth control conference in Chicago, Rabbi Mann spoke about "The Morality of Birth Control," telling his audience at the Drake Hotel that "even in the days before the Christian era, the wise men of Israel had realized the necessity of checking the multiplication of the unfit." Reform Rabbi Sidney E. Goldstein (1879–1955), the associate rabbi under Stephen S. Wise at the Free Synagogue in New York, also explicitly linked birth control and eugenics, declaring that with their combined force, "we can prevent the defectives from bringing forth abundantly and peopling the earth after their own kind." Protestants such as Advisory Council member Harry Emerson Fosdick agreed. He declared himself an "ardent advocate" of birth control and in 1928 preached to an audience of more than thirteen hundred about its benefits.[67]

Liberal ministers and rabbis responded to the birth control movement's message because its refrain was similar in tone to that of the eugenics movement: Birth control was just another example of man harnessing and applying scientific knowledge to solve social problems. Those who opposed such methods opposed progress. As the *Birth Control Review* put it, "Why then, should men and women be condemned for trying to use common sense and scientific methods in regulating the reproduction of their kind?" One physician directed his comments even more specifically to religious leaders: "If religion does not assist man to use his reason to adapt to his environment, but rather tends to make it more difficult for human beings to coordinate their activities and to develop health and aspiring views of life, it becomes one of the chief forces that block progress, and increases human suffering and misery." Turning to Scripture, the doctor paraphrased Matthew 13:25, "Why should they be encouraged to sow tares and wheat ignorantly together?"[68] Despite the charge that the churches had lost control of "family issues" (there is "no longer any compulsion to regard the sexual life as within the jurisdiction of the commissions of the Lord," one critic said), these commissioners still pursued control of families vigorously.[69]

Margaret Sanger's efforts to link birth control and eugenics, combined with the growing number of eugenicists who gave their support to the new movement, produced a gradual migration away from the AES's earlier skepticism about contraception. By 1928, the Society's legislative program included two provisions promoting birth control, one calling for "state authorization" for physicians to prescribe "contraceptive materials or devices to their married patients" and another making the sale of such materials legal by druggists. The growing prominence of the issue also encouraged the AES to form a small Committee on Birth Regulation, which Fr. John Cooper joined and which was charged with assessing the birth control movement's effects on eugenics.[70] By 1931, these efforts had given way to more explicit cooperation with birth control activists. A promotional pamphlet distributed by the AES that year listed birth control alongside standard eugenic programs such as immigration restriction and compulsory sterilization as one of the Society's principle legislative concerns. In his history of the AES, eugenicist Frederick Osborn described the Society as maintaining "close contacts" with the ABCL beginning in 1931.[71]

This move left Frs. Cooper and Ryan increasingly marginalized within the AES and subject to withering indictments from birth control supporters outside of it. This shift was one-sided. Catholic participants in the eugenics movement remained consistent in their sustained criticism of artificial contraception; it was the eugenics movement that lost its initial skepticism and slowly migrated toward the birth control movement. This migration, combined with the eugenics movement's continued insistence on the need for compulsory sterilization laws, eventually left the AES's two Catholics with few ways of justifying their participation in the formal eugenics movement.

In an implicit recognition of Cooper's unique position, the AES called on him in 1929 to clarify the Catholic position on birth control for readers of the AES's magazine, *Eugenics.* The impetus for commissioning the essay was the public denunciation of eugenics made by Catholic priest John A. McClorey of the St. Joseph Mercy Hospital in Detroit; McClorey's key accusation was that the eugenics movement was in league with birth control proponents. *Eugenics* gauged reaction to McClorey's comments in a symposium on the question of "The Birth Rate of Genius: Does Contraception Curb It?"[72] In his brief essay, Fr. Cooper avoided altogether discussing either Fr. McClorey's statement or the Catholic Church's position on contraception. Instead, he made an argument for which he was well-known in the AES: that eugenicists' scientific evidence was insufficient at present to answer the symposium's query. "Maybe, perhaps, possibly, probably, if—that is about all we can say" about genius and contraception, he wrote. Genetics professor Edward M. East of Harvard University was not nearly so restrained. He reaffirmed the importance of birth control to eugenics but also left room for an attack on the Catholic Church, reminding readers that Fr. McClorey was "a priest of that organization which is horrified at sterilizing imbeciles, yet castrated thousands of healthy boys to furnish sopranos for its choirs."[73]

In 1930, the AES's support for birth control prompted an informal loyalty test when the Committee on Birth Regulation requested that all committee members formally endorse a measure calling for legislation "that would permit physicians to prescribe contraceptive materials or devices to married patients."[74] In a letter to Committee secretary Guy Irving Burch, Fr. Cooper explained that although he had joined the Committee due to his interest "in the ethical issue involved" in birth control, he was "loathe to enter the political phases of the subject, where the issues are very far from being clear cut and certain." He tendered his resignation from the Committee. Still, Cooper's differences with the Committee did not preclude continued involvement in the AES. He reassured Burch that his break did "not mean any lack of interest in the work of the Society as such or cessation of participation in its activities."[75]

But there were other signs that the few Catholics who had participated in the eugenics movement were growing increasingly disenchanted with it by 1930. One Catholic who had granted his approval to sterilization twenty years earlier in the *Ecclesiastical Review* almost entirely recanted that position in 1930. In a symposium on sterilization in *Eugenics*, Fr. Stephen M. Donovan, a professor of moral theology at the Franciscan College at Catholic University, offered a more tentative clarification of the support he had given to sterilization in the 1910s. Noting the Vatican's continued silence on the subject and the division of opinion among the clergy, Donovan assessed his own position by noting, "I am not quite so sure now, as I was, or seemed to be, in 1910, that compulsory sterilization is lawful." The initial analogy he had used to justify his earlier stance—the state's right to engage in capital punishment for the common good—now seemed to him less than convincing. "What is meant by the public welfare, the common good?" he asked. Eugenicists did not have a satisfactory answer. Donovan ended on a speculative note. As to the question of whether sterilization of defectives was "forbidden by the law of God," he said, "I venture to predict that it will eventually be decided in the affirmative."[76]

Fr. Donovan's "eventually" came very soon. Seven months later, on 31 December 1930, Pope Pius XI issued *Casti Connubi*, an encyclical on Christian marriage. As for eugenics, the encyclical statement read:

> For there are some who, over solicitous for the cause of eugenics,
> not only give salutary counsel for more certainly procuring the
> strength and health of the future child—which, indeed, is not contrary to right reason—but put eugenics before aims of a higher order, and by public authority wish to prevent from marrying all those

who, even though naturally fit for marriage, they consider, according to the norms and conjectures of their investigations, would, through hereditary transmission, bring forth defective offspring and more, they wish to legislate to deprive these of that natural faculty by medical action despite their unwillingness . . . Those who act in this way are at fault in losing sight of the fact that the family is more sacred than the State and that men are begotten not for the earth and for time, but for heaven and eternity. Although often these individuals are to be dissuaded from entering into matrimony, certainly it is wrong to brand men with the stigma of crime because they contract marriage, on the ground that, despite the fact that they are in every respect capable of matrimony, they will give birth only to defective children, even though they use all care and diligence. Public magistrates have no direct power over the bodies of their subjects, therefore, where no crime has taken place and there is no cause present for grave punishment, they can never directly harm, or tamper with the integrity of the body, either for the reasons of eugenics or for any other reason.

On birth control the Pope was equally straightforward: "Any use whatsoever of matrimony exercised in such a way that the act is deliberately frustrated in its natural power to generate life is an offense against the law of God and of nature, and those who indulge in such are branded with the guilt of a grave sin." The passage from Scripture that the Pope chose to illustrate both of these positions was Romans 3:8: "Evil is not to be done that good may come of it."[77]

The Pope's condemnation of the eugenics movement and birth control were not of a piece. Although the encyclical thoroughly rejected birth control, its disapproval of eugenics suggested a rejection of the *methods* eugenicists employed (such as sterilization and birth control), but not necessarily eugenic *aims*. Indeed, in the opening sentence of the passage dealing with eugenics, the Pope stated, "What is asserted in favor of the social and eugenic 'indication' may and must be accepted, provided lawful and upright methods are employed within the proper limits," and, as noted in the excerpt above, he conceded that the eugenicists' efforts to ensure the health of future generations "is not contrary to right reason." Nevertheless, the encyclical harshly criticized the eugenics movement not only for its use of objectionable means, but for its misplaced priorities. The papal pronouncement firmly stated what many Catholic critics and even a few sympathizers had noted about eugenics: In its headlong pursuit of physical perfection, it forgot that "men are begotten not for the earth and for time, but for heaven and eternity." Eugenics had lost sight of the soul.[78]

The encyclical's message—that eugenics was materialistic in its aims and immoral in its methods—received a wide hearing. According to the Catholic weekly *America*, "Never before has a document issued by a Pope been reprinted as much or discussed as widely as the recent encyclical of Pius XI on 'Christian Marriage.'" The National Catholic Welfare Conference issued it in pamphlet form, and another edition published by *Catholic Mind* reached a circulation of over 150,000. That a papal encyclical garnered such attention suggests that the larger public shared Catholics' concern with issues related to marriage and the family.[79]

As for its clarification of the Catholic position on sterilization or birth control, *Commonweal* summarized the encyclical's spirit best: "Rome has spoken, and the case is closed." But what, exactly, had Rome said? The Catholic press interpreted the encyclical as a complete repudiation of eugenics; the *Homiletic and Pastoral Review* stated, "The said theory [eugenics] is to be absolutely rejected and to be considered as false and condemned."[80] Within months, most major Catholic periodicals were applying the new encyclical to current affairs. In March 1931, the editors of *America* denounced a recent ruling by the Nevada Supreme Court upholding the validity of the state's compulsory sterilization law. The editors also wondered "just where the *vox populi* may be when legislation of this sort is being discussed, and why especially Catholic men and women seem so apathetic."[81] They interpreted the encyclical to mean that Catholics, laity and clergy alike, should not simply reject eugenic sterilization as a matter of individual conscience, but actively work to prevent its legislative enactment in the states.

Other Catholics, particularly Fr. Cooper, who still retained official ties to the eugenics movement, did not view the encyclical as such a watershed. One of the few comments he made about it came after Leon Whitney wrote to tell him that he himself was, with a few notable exceptions, "quite delighted with the encyclical." Cooper remarked only that the encyclical "did not bring out any new points except the rather strong stand on sterilization." Nowhere did he suggest that the Pope's message barred him from continuing to participate in the AES.[82]

Fr. Ryan, who had conceded just a few years earlier that sterilization was a debatable question, stated firmly that the encyclical utterly eliminated the need for further discussion. "Sterilization is authoritatively declared to be intrinsically wrong," he said, and Catholics "will know that they are not permitted to promote such legislation, nor to take part in its execution." To this he added a scientific condemnation of sterilization, arguing that "recent scientific opinion is almost unanimous in rejecting sterilization as an effective preventive of feeblemindedness." Eugenicists who nevertheless continued to carry on "propaganda in its favor" were "emotional persons who are ignorant of the most recent findings of science."[83] Although his tone everywhere implied it, Ryan, like Cooper, never explicitly conceded that the encyclical's rejection of eugenic sterilization entailed a rejection of eugenics itself.

In the wake of the encyclical, eugenicists faced harsher scrutiny of their methods not only from Catholics, but from formerly supportive secular observers as well. The *New York Times*, which over the years had promoted the eugenics cause in its editorial pages, was less enthusiastic by 1931. Eugenicists "must admit the possibility that in a hundred years or more their theories will have proved inadequate, so that then more plausibility and force may be seen in the view expressed by the Holy See," noted one editorial.[84] Eugenicists themselves had little comment on those papal views. The most extensive published assessment, an editorial in the *Eugenical News*, noted that the Pope's "pronouncements and admonitions on the sanctity of marriage will find a hearty response in all circles which value virtue and human happiness," but expressed disappointment that the papal letter "gives no consideration for the demonstrated laws of human heredity" and simply "casts aside the most fundamental biological truths." But this was as far as the eugenicists' critique went. The brief article ended on a conciliatory note, expressing a hope that "perhaps in the not too distant future some Pope will commend the demonstrated laws of human heredity."[85]

Birth control advocates were harsher in their assessments. Unitarian minister John Haynes Holmes of the Community Church in New York characterized the encyclical as evidence of "a tenth-century mind at work on twentieth-century problems." Mrs. F. Robertson Jones of the ABCL was equally forceful in her denunciation. "In unconditionally condemning birth control the Roman Catholic Church sets itself squarely against social progress," she stated. Other birth control advocates issued cries of papal hypocrisy. "The Pope seems to lay the most stress on the statement that contraception is contrary to nature," said Humanist Society founder Charles Francis Potter. "Then let us respectfully suggest that he be consistent and lay aside his spectacles and stop shaving."[86]

In the chronology of Catholic participation in the AES, the edict that elicited the strongest reaction from the movement's Catholic participants was not the Vatican's December 1930 statement on Christian marriage, but the Society's own spring 1931 clarification of its official program. Included in the pamphlet, called *Organized Eugenics*, were endorsements of birth control for the unfit, compulsory eugenic sterilization, and an expansion of the grounds for divorce to include hereditary ailments such as feeblemindedness. This triumvirate proved too much for Fr. Cooper. On 9 April 1931, he wrote to his frequent correspondent Leon Whitney, informing him that because he found "a great many of the basic provisions of this new program" both "scientifically unsound and socially undesirable," he was tendering his resignation from the AES effective immediately.[87]

Judging by his statements, the impetus for Cooper's withdrawal from the AES was not the recent encyclical (he did not even mention the papal document in his resignation letter), but his long-standing concerns about the eugenics movement's scientific credibility. Three years earlier he had written to a friend, "I have been on the point of resigning at least half a dozen times in the last five years" over the movement's questionable scientific reasoning. What had prevented him from following through was "the feeling that there is such a thing as sane eugenics and the feeling too, that we can do perhaps just a little more from the inside than we could do from the outside towards directing the present society into more sensible ways."[88] But by 1931, Cooper felt that he could no longer have an impact on the movement. If the new *Organized Eugenics* program was any guide, he told Whitney in his letter of resignation, then his years of wrangling with other eugenicists over their science evidently had produced little lasting effect. For Cooper, the new program "appears to make it clear that such 'advising' as this one member of the Advisory Committee may make in the future would likewise be fruitless."[89]

Cooper's resignation was not, however, a repudiation of eugenics in its entirety. "I shall continue to be keenly interested in the program of the international eugenic movement and shall participate wholeheartedly in its activities wherever I find it operating on a scientific basis," he told Whitney. By his own reckoning, Cooper's resignation was not a rejection of eugenics, but a rejection of eugenics as the AES practiced it.[90]

Was Cooper's pledge of continued support for eugenics merely an excuse to facilitate a more graceful exit from the AES? If it were, it would not have been in keeping with his nearly decade-long relationship with the organization. One of the unique features of Cooper's support for the Society was his boldness in constantly criticizing eugenicists for their lack of scientific rigor and for their support of methods such as birth control; he was not shy about expressing his views. His resignation earlier from the Society's Committee on Birth Regulation revealed his willingness to take unpopular stands. Moreover, although he did not usually engage it as a first defense (preferring scientific arguments), he was willing to cite Church doctrine to argue a point with eugenicists.[91] It seems highly unlikely that he would fail to do so if violation of those doctrines was his primary reason for leaving the AES.[92] Rather, it appears that the encyclical encouraged him, in the wake of the AES's new 1931 program, to reassesses his long-standing doubts about eugenic science.

In his letter of resignation, Fr. Cooper told AES executive secretary Leon Whitney that he had discussed the matter of leaving the AES with Fr. John Ryan, his colleague at Catholic University and a fellow member of the Society. Though Ryan was still technically a member of the Committee on Cooperation with Clergymen, his participation in the AES had fallen off in recent years, so much so, in fact, that when he, too, decided to withdraw from the Society, he claimed not to have realized that he was still a member. Unlike Cooper, who had written privately to Whitney informing him of his decision to leave—and had taken the opportunity to reaffirm his support for eugenics—Rev. Ryan condemned eugenics in a strongly worded letter that he issued simultaneously as a press release through the National Catholic Welfare Conference's news service.[93]

Like Cooper, Ryan cited the proposals contained in the new AES pamphlet,

Organized Eugenics, and not the papal encyclical, as the reason for his resignation. Unlike Cooper, Ryan's letter suggested a thorough repudiation of eugenics. He deemed the AES's proposals for sterilization, birth control, and expansion of the grounds for divorce "abhorrent for religious, moral, and social reasons," and added to that rebuke a nod to the weaknesses of eugenic science. "As regards the scientific aspect of some of the objects of your organization," he wrote, "perhaps the less said the better."[94]

Fr. Ryan's public departure from the AES is not surprising viewed from the perspective of his seven years as a member of the organization. Unlike Fr. Cooper, who was actively engaged throughout his tenure, Ryan's interest in the eugenics movement was intermittent and always laced with skepticism. His primary concerns lay elsewhere. Ryan biographer Francis Broderick has argued that Ryan's departure from the AES was an example of one of the rare times that his alliance with secular liberalism did not hold, and this seems an accurate assessment.[95] By 1931, with scientific evidence of eugenicists' missteps mounting (thanks to geneticists) and the Vatican on the record as opposed to much of what the AES stood for, Ryan reasonably could argue that the eugenics movement was no longer a suitable cause to support, even for progressive Catholics such as himself.

Cooper and Ryan's departures had an ambiguous impact on the eugenics movement. In one sense, Catholic opposition such as theirs reaffirmed eugenicists' opinion of their movement as thoroughly modern and scientific. In their assessment, if Catholics (whom they generally viewed as superstitious and reactionary) opposed them, then they must be doing something right. In another sense, however, Catholic departure from the AES robbed the movement of perhaps its most rhetorically powerful religious allies. Unified Catholic opposition gave the lie to eugenicists' claims that theirs was a movement that enjoyed broad support in the religious community.

Throughout the 1930s, Catholic writers continued to reinforce the papal denunciation of eugenic sterilization with arguments about the eugenicists' shoddy science. One thing was certain, *America* editorialized, "and that is that the sterilization laws of our States are not based on the tested conclusions of science." Another Catholic critic reaffirmed this: "Seeing that the science of eugenics is still in so crude a state, what right have they to influence our legislatures to adopt the most dramatic measures in behalf of a problematic improvement of the race?" Catholic writer Jerome Blake deemed sterilization supporters "hysterilizationists," and admitted that although they "fairly ooze good intentions . . . they are the kind used for highway ballast in Hades."

Sterilization supporters countered in kind. The virulently anti-Catholic Mariann S. Olden, founder of the sterilization lobbying group Birthright, claimed (with conspiratorial inflection) that Catholics engaged in widespread political blackmail to ensure that state legislators would not pass sterilization laws. "Facts must be squarely faced." she wrote. "The unalterable ambition of the Church of Rome to dominate in temporal affairs is vigorously at work in America today."[97] Despite the vitriol of this back-and-forth, the criticisms made by Catholics were important in helping "delegitimate the 'science' of racist eugenics" in the 1930s.[98]

Fr. Charles Bruehl began one of his 1926 *Homiletic and Pastoral Review* essays with a warning to eugenicists that if they wished to win and, presumably, to keep the support of Catholics, they would ensure that their cause would not be associated with "anything that conflicts with the principles of Christian morality, that would deprive man of his basic and inalienable rights, or that could be used as an instrument of oppression."[99] By the early 1930s, Catholics who had been involved in the eugenics movement found it a failure in all three respects. Geneticists' discoveries and Pope Pius XI's encyclical had exposed scientific and ethical fault lines severe enough to warrant their opposition to the movement. This opposition anticipated the public's turn away from eugenics. By the mid-1930s, as the country lay in the grips of a severe economic depression, the movement that had enjoyed widespread support in the 1910s and 1920s was struggling to maintain its financial solvency, its members' loyalty, and its social relevance.

6

Twilight Converts

Every reform, however necessary, will by weak minds be carried to
excess, that itself will need reforming.

—Samuel Taylor Coleridge,
Biographia Literaria, 1817

In 1933, with the country suffering under the weight of a severe economic depression, the city of Chicago hosted the World's Fair.
Deemed the "Century of Progress Exposition," the fair, with its sky
ride and Hall of Science, studiously avoided unpleasant economic
realities in favor of an image of a vital nation, teeming with experts
from government, business, and science, working diligently to find
solutions to America's problems. The tone, if somewhat forced, was
optimistic, and attendance was high. This image of scientific-
industrial progress was not uncontested, however. One year earlier,
British writer Aldous Huxley published his novelist's vision of a
Brave New World, a futuristic society that grew human embryos in
bottles and bred them for passivity and collectivism. When a "savage" enters this world—a person who had read Shakespeare and believed in freedom and moral choice—he ends up going mad and
killing himself. In Huxley's view, such a world represented the possible cost humanity would pay for its scientific "century of progress."[1]

Huxley's dystopian vision of eugenic breeding-in-bottles might
have granted that movement too much influence. Judging by the
four modest panels that composed the movement's place in the 1933
Exposition's Hall of Science, eugenics was in a state of decline. In

1932, the number of delegates to the Third International Congress of Eugenics, held at the American Museum of Natural History, totaled a paltry seventy-three, and one conference participant presented a paper that took as a serious question "Is Eugenics Half-Baked?"[2] The country's major eugenics organization, the American Eugenics Society, was listing under the weight of sustained criticism from geneticists and the impact of the Depression (the winter of 1932–1933 was the worst economically in U.S. history).[3] The departure of prominent geneticists and Catholics from the movement in the 1920s was an early harbinger of distress, and by the early 1930s member attrition was high and new debts were accruing.[4] To add insult to injury, arbiters of mainstream opinion had turned their censorious glance on eugenicists. The *New York Times* editorial page, once an avid booster of eugenic sentiment, by 1932 spoke for a growing number of Americans when it reflected, "Eugenics seems to have become a disguise for race prejudice, ancestor worship, and caste snobbery." The movement substitutes "fear and emotion for science and reason." Editors now lauded geneticists, whose scientific sinecures and "earnest experiments" struck them as more worthy of praise.[5]

A few stubborn souls chose to ignore the clamor of the movement's critics and the vagaries of the contemporary economic situation. At a meeting of the AES in 1932, eugenicist Clarence C. Little saw a silver lining in the cloud cast by the Depression. In these times of economic strain, he said, "the public was getting more and more of a grievance against the defective," something the AES could turn to its advantage. The methods of eugenics, particularly compulsory sterilization, were cost-effective, protective of the dwindling public coffers. Sterilization supporters like Little juxtaposed the cost to taxpayers of lifelong segregation of the feebleminded (usually an exorbitant figure, in their estimation) with the relatively inexpensive cost of sterilization, which allowed the state safely to release the feebleminded back into the community.[6]

But if the Depression encouraged a few eugenicists to extol the frugal features of sterilization, it led many more people to question the movement's underlying assumptions, most notably the idea that class status and material success were connected somehow to the quality of one's hereditary material. The Depression cut a broad swath through society, affecting rich and poor alike, and prompted people to look at environmental rather than hereditary forces as the cause of social ills. In this context, science was no longer viewed as having definitive solutions to social problems. As an editorial in the Catholic weekly *America* noted, "Is it anything short of remarkable how the sacred name of Science is being reviled in these depression days?" Where once "that arrogant lady bestrode the world," now "people are beginning to notice that she is slightly cockeyed, frequently a liar, extraordinarily changeable in her dogmatic utterances, and never very reliable anyhow."[7]

Assessing this situation in 1933, Frederick Osborn, nephew of eugenicist and American Museum of Natural History director Henry Fairfield Osborn, declared the eugenics movement "at a low ebb" and lacking "any sense of direction."[8] He vowed to change that. After retiring at the age of 40 from a successful career in banking, Osborn spent several years under his uncle's tutelage studying eugenics. He emerged with a different formula for eugenic success. With public sentiment turning away from the hereditary determinism of the eugenicists' position, Osborn called on the leaders of the movement to adjust their rhetoric to better suit the times. He took his cues from mainstream opinion. "If eugenics has made little progress in democracies," the New York Times noted, it was because its promoters were too willing to make it "a cloak for class snobbery, ancestor worship and race prejudice." However, "a gospel which teaches that the right social environment is as important as the right germ plasm . . . will probably be more widely acceptable because it is obviously more democratic."[9]

Osborn was soon linking eugenic science to the social environment in just this way. A Time magazine profile contrasted him favorably with his uncle, deemed an old-school eugenicist and embodiment of the "class snobbery" decried by the Times. Writers at Time praised young Frederick for jettisoning his uncle's notion that Anglo-Saxons were "God's special gift to earth," and instead promoting a form of eugenics that denied coercion. "Doctors should be educated to urge voluntary sterilization of persons known to be carriers of serious hereditary defects," Frederick advised, and Time commended him for his emphasis on "voluntary population control" and "freedom of parenthood."[10] Osborn and others also attempted to banish from their rhetoric any traces of pro-Nordic prejudice and spoke of eugenics in terms of its usefulness for families and individuals rather than racial groups. In a discussion of sterilization, for example, Osborn emphasized its social as well as its eugenic benefits, noting, "Mentally deficient or defective parents cannot provide a home environment suitable for rearing children." Eugenicists now touted negative eugenic methods as a means of stabilizing the crisis-laden institutions of home and family, not for eradicating the "menace of the feebleminded."[11]

By 1935, Osborn and his supporters had staged what amounted to a takeover of the AES, a feat made possible in part by the fact that many of the old guard eugenicists by that time either had died or retired.[12] Osborn quickly made changes to the structure of the organization, including revising the by-laws and eliminating the Advisory Council. His business acumen also helped move the Society's finances into the black (it was noted that Osborn was the grandnephew of J. Pierpont Morgan). From the mid-1930s on, Frederick Osborn was the prime figure in the AES. He was also, briefly, that movement's savior; by the end of the decade, membership in the AES had increased significantly (though not to pre-Depression levels), and eugenicists were promoting the Society's new kinder, gentler message in a range of venues.[13]

This internal restructuring altered the eugenics movement's approach to religious leaders. With Osborn at the helm, the AES should have been more hospitable to ministers and rabbis, as the "reform" eugenic message it now promoted incorporated many of the same ideas that religious observers of the eugenics movement had been emphasizing for years. "We are all environmentalists, and we are all hereditarians, too," Osborn said, a sentiment that echoed religious leaders' long-time emphasis on the importance of reconciling Christian charity and scientific reform. Moreover, Osborn encouraged eugenicists to build connections with nonscientific reformers in a variety of fields, including sociology and nursing, and among religious leaders in various denominations and faiths.[14]

But the same external pressures that challenged the AES in the 1930s— the Depression, the growing threat of war in Europe—occupied religious leaders as well, so much so, in fact, that few found time for rumination about race improvement. Protestant Social Gospel optimism was giving way to realism in theology, as seen most clearly in the work of brothers Reinhold and H. Richard Niebuhr. Reinhold Niebuhr's *Moral Man and Immoral Society*, published in 1932, called for a reevaluation of liberal Protestantism's uncritical embrace of secular (including scientific) solutions to social problems. A fellow theologian, Walter Marshal Horton of Oberlin College, in 1934 published *Realistic Theology*, his choice of title suggesting that the theology that had come before had not been quite realistic enough. His was a blunt indictment: Theological liberalism was "politically inept, sociologically shallow, psychologically stupid." The old terms no longer applied, and "the old faiths and hopes no longer carry conviction." Secular versions of this lament had been circulating. Walter Lippmann's concern for the corrosive effects of the "acids of modernity" was similar in tone, if not target. "However self-sufficient the eugenic and perfectly educated man of the distant future may be," Lippmann wrote, the evaporation of religious and moral certainties meant that, already, the "need to believe haunts him."[15]

For his part, Frederick Osborn had little patience or enthusiasm for preachers. "The task of the clergy is a difficult one," he conceded, but "one for which they are perhaps the least prepared." He spoke condescendingly of the clergy's lack of "real understanding" of social and scientific problems and urged them to "turn student and scientist" to correct these deficiencies.[16] Internal developments in the AES did not encourage such a transformation. The group responsible for promoting religious participation, the Committee on Cooperation with Clergymen, had started out the decade of the 1930s on a positive note. Rev. Guy Emery Shipler, a Committee member and editor of *The Churchman*, presided over the group's annual meeting in 1930, where the featured speaker was Albert Wiggam, the eugenics promoter well-known for his attention to religious themes. Turnout was good, and Committee members announced their sponsorship of another eugenics sermon contest. Within a few years, however, the Committee was functionally nonexistent. Lacking a chairman and with a rapidly dwindling membership roster, it fell victim to the same financial constraints and lack of interest that plagued the AES as a whole. By 1938, the AES still had not paid the prize money owed the winners of the 1930 sermon contest.[17]

General meetings of the Society drew some religious participants, though fewer than they had in the past. At a 1934 meeting in New Haven, Connecticut, Dr. Robert E. Speer (1867–1947), a Presbyterian layman, presented a paper about the successes of missionaries. Missionaries happened to be Speer's forte; he oversaw more than sixteen hundred of them as secretary of the Foreign Missions Board of the Presbyterian Church, USA, a position he held from 1891 to 1937.[18] "The children of missionaries rank very high from the eugenic standpoint," Speer noted. Such superiority made sense because "missionaries are selected because of superior qualities of health, intelligence, general ability, adventurous spirit, and training, as well as moral character and religious fervor."[19] In 1936, at an AES Round Table Conference, Methodist Episcopal Bishop Francis J. McConnell, a former president of the Federal Council of the Churches of Christ, presented a paper on "The Relation of Religion to Eugenics," and in the afternoon, Rabbi Sidney Goldstein, chairman of the Social Justice Commission of the Central Conference of American Rabbis, offered his thoughts on "Birth Control and Eugenics."[20] These few examples notwithstanding, the AES by the mid-1930s lacked a coherent plan (and an active committee) for encouraging religious participation; in truth, the Society was barely able to sustain the interest of the religious leaders who were already members.

Eugenicists' most significant insight into their relationship with religious leaders in these years came too late to be of any benefit to the movement. At a 1937 Conference on Eugenic Education sponsored by the AES, one participant wondered "how we can convince our fundamentalist and Roman Catholic friends that while there may legitimately be diversity of opinion as to the use of certain methods, there can be no reasonable disagreement as to the basic tenent [sic] that the trend of reproduction ought to be altered." The conference-goers considered crafting a eugenic educational program "which will appeal equally to Catholics and Protestants, Fundamentalists and Liberals."[21] Had this debate occurred a decade earlier, it might have had a chance of attracting religious converts. As it was, the intellectual demarcation lines were drawn too deeply to be erased now. No Protestant fundamentalist ever joined the eugenics movement, and by 1937, the two Catholics who had been members of the AES, Frs. John M. Cooper and John A. Ryan, had long since departed over eugenicists' support of compulsory sterilization, birth control, and the liberalization of divorce laws. Attempts to win back their support would require an overhaul of the eugenics program far more radical than the one enacted by Frederick Osborn. The Catholic retreat from eugenics in particular was complete by the 1930s. In a neat intellectual turn, Rev. Edgar S. Schmiedeler of the National Catholic Welfare Conference appropriated the language of eugenics while condemning the movement's aims. "The Church had in her own way done much to promote race betterment," Schmiedeler told conferees at the AES gathering, but "her views and her methods have differed . . . from those of the modern eugenist." The Church "makes bodily and mental culture subservient to morality, while modern eugenics tends to make morality subservient to bodily and mental culture."[22] With a public far less trusting of eugenicists' pronouncements on bodily and mental culture, and many former religious allies in retreat from the movement, few echoes of the religious enthusiasm of the previous decade could be found now.

Still, troubled causes gain converts. In the 1930s, eugenicists gained the loyalty of two preachers whose commitment to the movement rested on willful ignorance of its waning fortunes. Rev. Kenneth C. MacArthur was a beneficiary of the AES's earlier outreach efforts: With his family, he had been the recipient of a trophy at the Fitter Families Contest at the Eastern States Exposition in

FIGURE 6.1 Rev. Kenneth C. MacArthur and family after winning the trophy for "Average Family Class" at the American Eugenics Society's Fitter Families Contest at the Eastern States Exposition, 1925. American Philosophical Society, Philadelphia, Pennsylvania.

1925; in 1926 and 1928 he entered the Society's eugenic sermon contests, garnering second prize in 1926.[23] Rev. MacArthur told AES officer Clarence Cook Little in 1928, "I have been for years deeply interested in Eugenics and I have frequently spoken before various groups on this subject." He even sought practical experience in eugenics by "breeding purebred cattle in a small way" to learn more about the process of heredity.[24] MacArthur, who did his undergraduate work at Harvard and graduated from Union Theological Seminary in 1908, ministered in several churches in the years following seminary, including Tremont Baptist Church in the Bronx, the Old Cambridge Baptist Church in Cambridge, Massachusetts, and for nearly a year as a chaplain in the U.S. Army. By the late 1920s, when the record of his interest in eugenics begins, he was living in Sterling, Massachusetts, and serving as the rural secretary of the Massachusetts Federation of Churches.[25]

From the beginning, MacArthur's participation in the eugenics movement was marked by a consistent emphasis on the compatibility of Christian and eugenic goals. In his 1928 AES sermon contest entry, he argued that eugenics "has a direct bearing upon the Christian purpose to make a good world, inhabited by good people. There is nothing in it that is opposed to Christian ideals but much that is helpful to their realization."[26] Yet MacArthur always grounded his enthusiasm for eugenics in his identity as a minister. Eugenics was important chiefly as a means of achieving the Kingdom of God on earth, and not as an end to be pursued for its own sake. In an article he contributed to the special "preachers' issue" of *Eugenics* magazine in 1928, he argued, "The more fully [eugenic proposals] are adopted, the more rapidly will the ends for which the church exists be furthered." Eugenics, after all, promoted the development of the "best possible human material." This was "the very material from which to recruit the citizenry of the commonwealth of Christ among men."[27] If MacArthur saw himself as a eugenicist, then he was one whose promotion of the science came second to his role as a recruitment officer for the Kingdom of God.

In 1928, Rev. MacArthur became secretary of the Massachusetts State Eugenics Committee.[28] Within two years, he had added to those duties the position of secretary of the AES's Committee on Cooperation with Clergymen, cutting back to part time his responsibilities at the Massachusetts Federation of Churches to accommodate this new commitment. Within a few months, he embarked on a minor whirlwind of activities for the AES, lecturing on "Eugenics and the Church" to a joint meeting of the AES and the Eugenics Research Association in New York, contributing to a symposium in *Eugenics* magazine, and outlining for AES members his plans for the Committee on Cooperation with Clergymen.[29]

One of those plans was a monthly column in *Eugenics* magazine, called "Eugenics and the Church," and in 1930 it became MacArthur's forum for promoting his vision of religio-eugenic cooperation. That vision was occasionally quirky. In a July 1930 installment, for example, he praised the efforts of a minister in New York City whose new church would include "courting parlors," where, under the watchful eyes of religious leaders, "the lads would have an opportunity to meet the ravishing girls of the parish" and, presumably, make eugenically felicitous marriages.[30] He also promoted his pet causes, including church federation. His was a simple formula: Federation and interdenominational cooperation made the churches more efficient. "When the funds and energy now expended on sectarian competition are released for more constructive activities," he claimed, "there should be available a large amount of personal and financial resources for race betterment."[31] Once internecine squabbling among the churches ceased, he reasoned, more productive projects, such as eugenics, could be pursued.

MacArthur was also an enthusiastic promoter of child allowances for the families of superior clergymen. Charges of self-interest might be leveled against him for promoting these cash payments from churches and synagogues to defray the cost of raising children (of which he himself had four), but his justification for the plan was thoroughly eugenic: "Since the ministers, who constitute only four-tenths of one percent of the men in the United States, are the fathers of eleven percent of those leaders whose names are found in *Who's Who in America*, it is desirable from the standpoint of the public welfare that ministers' families be larger."[32] Child allowances were not a form of charity, but a "service to society" that ensured the promulgation of certain important spiritual traits in the population. People of a religious bent were usually "self-controlled, thrifty, industrious, and possessed of social instincts of helpfulness," MacArthur said, as his own lineage revealed. His maternal grandfather, great-grandfather, and uncle were ordained ministers, as was a paternal cousin; and his father, Robert Stuart MacArthur, was for forty-one years pastor of Calvary Baptist Church in New York City.[33] If Rev. MacArthur's championing of child allowances demonstrated his efforts to combine his Christian and eugenic crusades, it also revealed his fairly simplistic understanding of science. He took as a given the heritability of certain personality traits, despite the fact that he wrote at a time when geneticists had exposed that assumption as fraudulent.

MacArthur's *Eugenics and the Church* column was something of a vanity venue, one that allowed the avuncular reverend to promote his personal theories of race betterment and ecumenical resolution. But it also served as a useful, if lone, bulwark against religious criticism of the eugenics movement. In December 1930, when a critic told the AES to stop "bribing the parsons" with cash prizes for eugenic sermons, MacArthur fired back in his column with a defense of religious participation in the movement. Pointing to the list of "numerous American religious leaders [who] are backing the program of the American Eugenics Society," he reminded the malcontent, "Control of human heredity offers a very powerful weapon for fighting the battle of the Lord to destroy the strongholds of evil."[34]

MacArthur was also unsparing in his criticism of church institutions, a fact that surely pleased some eugenicists. He devoted column space to delineating the deficiencies of religious education, echoing Frederick Osborn's critique that if religious educators "leave out of account the hereditary factors in character, they are destined to be disappointed." MacArthur wryly noted that knowledge of the Bible alone did not preclude the development of antisocial tendencies; the sterling childhood Sunday School attendance records of some notorious criminals attested to that. Rather, he reminded his clerical readers, they must reckon with heredity as a powerful influence on human character as well.[35]

Although eugenicists composed the majority of MacArthur's audience, he wrote also to persuade his clerical colleagues of the benefits of eugenics. He delivered his enlightenment with a strong dose of scolding about the uselessness of certain church methods. Eugenics presented society with "an approach to the solution of the age-long problem of poverty with which the church has unsuccessfully wrestled for 2,000 years," he said in one essay. In another, he urged clergymen to exercise their influence over wealthy church members, advising them to alter their usual bequests to give money "to eugenics rather than to hospitals for sick cats . . . or even to worthy palliative charities."[36]

In a sense, MacArthur was the last of the line of religious converts to eugenics, and he is a good example of how some adherents to liberal Protestantism could easily incorporate eugenic thinking into their worldviews—even in the realist climate of the 1930s. His enthusiastic dispatches were short-lived. The *Eugenics and the Church* column ran for a little less than a year; in 1931, the magazine *Eugenics* ceased publication. Around the same time, MacArthur lost another of one his forums when the Committee on Cooperation with Clergymen lapsed into inactivity.[37] He eventually landed at Andover Newton Theology School as an instructor, and as late as 1939 the AES was promoting him as a eugenics lecturer for the New England region.[38]

Unlike Rev. MacArthur, who defined himself primarily as a minister, the eugenics movement's second major religious devotee in the 1930s, Rev. George Reid Andrews (1886–1941), put eugenics above spiritual commitments. Indeed, he made eugenics his religion, at least for a time. His rapid rise and swift dénouement in the AES in the late 1930s proved the truth—at least, in eugenicists' view—of the warning to beware the zeal of the convert.

Rev. Andrews, a native of Montgomery County, North Carolina, attended Columbia University and graduated in 1914 from Union Theological Seminary (nearly a decade after Rev. MacArthur had been a student there). He was ordained a Congregationalist minister that same year, served as assistant minister at the West End Presbyterian Church in New York, and then moved to St.

Paul's Congregational Church in Brooklyn, where he remained until 1921. His ambitions were not fulfilled in normal pulpit duties, so he turned to religious drama, serving as chairman of the Committee on Educational and Religious Drama of the Federal Council of Churches of Christ in America (1925–1930) and as executive director of the Church and Drama League (1926–1930). His skills in this capacity attracted the attention of filmmaker Cecil B. DeMille, who, in 1925, hired Andrews to serve as a consultant and scene writer during production of his epic Jesus biopic, *King of Kings*.[39]

It was in 1930, toward the end of his involvement with the Church and Drama League, that Andrews first publicly entered the eugenics fray. At the time minister of the Park Street Congregational Church in Bridgeport, Connecticut, he submitted a brief response to a symposium in *Eugenics* on the eugenic implications of divorce.[40] Evidently a great deal of enthusiasm for eugenics lay behind this small contribution, for within a year he had initiated a correspondence with Leon Whitney, executive secretary of the AES, wherein he frequently expressed his desire to become more actively and formally engaged in the activities of the AES. "I do not think any social enterprise of today can surpass it in its social significance," he wrote. Given the waning financial fortunes of the organization, Whitney told Andrews, "We all want you to take an active part," but he was unable to find an administrative position for him in the AES.[41]

Two years passed until Rev. Andrews again pressed his case. Whitney by then had resigned as executive secretary, and Andrews sent the AES Board of Directors an unsolicited application for the job. Although the Board viewed Andrews favorably, financial constraints again prevented them from offering him a job. This time, Rev. Andrews would not be put off. So enthusiastic was he that he contacted the Society again to let them know of his willingness to act as executive secretary on an unpaid basis, "in the hopes that if he was successful he would be elected to such an office with a salary to be arranged later." Coming at a time when the Society's financial resources were stretched thin, Rev. Andrews's offer was too good to pass up. With a warning about the difficulty of the task he was about to undertake, the Board passed a motion "accepting Mr. Andrews's offer with the understanding that the Society could not be committed to remunerate Mr. Andrews."[42] Through sheer persistence, Rev. Andrews, a man with no scientific training or experience and no record of interest in eugenics prior to 1930, secured for himself a position as an officer of the American Eugenics Society.

Andrews's first act was to resign his post as minister of Park Street Congregational Church. Dining with his new eugenics colleagues soon thereafter, he explained that he had done so because he believed "that education, religion, political and social reforms, and every other method of improving mankind are not having a fair chance because we exercise no intelligent control over the reproduction of the human race." As an officer of a eugenics organization,

Andrews believed he could have a more significant impact on society than he had been able to as a minister.[43] This neophyte eugenicist quickly used his position to promote his own ideas for the Society, ideas a bit bolder in their execution than was considered prudent by some members of the AES Board. Linking his previous incarnation as religious drama expert with his new role as a eugenics promoter, Rev. Andrews told a reporter for the *Charlotte News* (North Carolina) that he favored "birth control, sterilization of the socially unfit, and the 'cleaning up' of the movies." In 1934, addressing the ninth annual meeting of the AES, he announced a plan to woo wealthy women to the eugenics cause, "an active campaign to interest certain influential and wealthy persons, especially women, in the purposes of the American Eugenics Society." Andrews was unbothered by the current gloomy economic forecast; in fact, like eugenicist Clarence Cook Little, he viewed it as an opportunity for the Society, noting that "the time is distinctly favorable for the realization" of eugenic goals, "since men and women are awakening in this time of economic depression to the desirability of smaller families in the impoverished and unemployed group and encouragement of births by the healthy and educated groups." In addition to planning this new appeal, he spent his first year as executive secretary helping to revise the *Eugenics Catechism* and traveling to Washington, D.C., to lobby for federal birth control legislation.[44]

Rev. Andrews knew whom to court closer to home as well. He titled one speech "Tomorrow's Children," an homage to AES chairman of the Board Ellsworth Huntington's recent book by the same name. "Human sympathy urges us to care for the weak and fallen; human intelligence should demand that we prevent the birth of children where they cannot be well born and bred," Andrews said. But if his tone was conciliatory, even fawning at times, his delivery often favored his roots in melodrama. "The graduates of our women's colleges are giving us a half baby each!" he was moved to exclaim in one speech. "Every time we graduate a student from college we put three people in jail, one in an insane asylum, and one in an institution for the feebleminded," was another typical offering.[45] Jettisoning explicit references to church and faith, like those that characterized Rev. MacArthur's work, Andrews played the role of promoter, not preacher.

Nevertheless, by May 1936, Andrews appeared firmly ensconced as a member of the eugenics movement, enjoying (along with other officers of the Society) a feast at Delmonico's in New York City to celebrate the organization's annual meeting. The featured speakers were Tennessee Valley Authority director Arthur E. Morgan and philosophy professor E. C. Lindeman of the New York School of Social Work. This would be Rev. Andrews's last supper with the AES, however. A few weeks later, at a Board meeting, "the question of continuing Mr. Andrews as Executive Secretary of the Society was brought up by the president and discussed at length." He was allowed to give a "lengthy statement of his position," but after he retired from the meeting, the remaining group voted unanimously to adopt a resolution "to take such steps as they may think best for the purpose of terminating the service of the Executive Secretary." For the duration of the summer of 1936, Rev. Andrews remained in limbo, meeting occasionally with AES Board members to plead his cause. By early fall, however, it was clear that he would not have enough support to remain in his position, and so he offered his resignation, which the Board immediately accepted, in October.[46]

The reticence of the Board meeting minutes offers few clues as to why Andrews was, effectively, forced out of the AES. Eugenicists had praised his work early in his tenure; Board member Guy Irving Burch described him as a man of "interest and ability" whose work with the Society undoubtedly would lead to "a year of greater activity" in 1934.[47] But Andrews's letter of resignation suggests that his unusual ideas and often bombastic presentations did not please everyone. "For some time there has been apparent a fundamental difference of opinion respecting the program and policy of the Society between me and certain members of the Board which makes further tenure of the office by me inadvisable," he wrote. He tendered his resignation "with much regret and reluctance."[48] The ouster might also have been over money. Rev. Andrews had joined the AES as a volunteer and there is no mention of his ever receiving a salary, but he traveled frequently for the Society and likely generated some expenses. On accepting his resignation, the AES Board agreed to pay him $4,000 and, on the recommendation of their attorney, to note that the sum was "in full settlement of all claims against the American Eugenics Society, Inc., for services, expenses, or otherwise."[49]

It is more likely that Andrews's lack of scientific training did not sit well with Frederick Osborn, who was attempting to put the Society on firmer footing financially and scientifically. In Osborn's ongoing effort to distance the organization from well-meaning but reckless amateurs, Andrews was a logical target. Andrews's activities after leaving the AES suggest that he was an avid supporter of sterilization, often employing just the sort of rash rhetoric that Osborn was seeking to purge from the AES's public vocabulary.

Rev. Andrews's exit from the AES did not end his career as a eugenics advocate. A few months after his removal, he spoke at a luncheon conference of the New Jersey League of Women Voters as part of that organization's educational campaign in support of sterilization; the League was at that time active in lobbying the state legislature for passage of a compulsory sterilization law.[50] A short time later, in December 1937, he gave another speech in support of sterilization before the New Jersey Health and Sanitary Association. In the latter presentation, Andrews touched on some of the same themes he had promoted while at the AES, arguing, for example that "unless we mix biological science with our altruistic sentiment, we shall soon fill the world with incompetents beyond our power to care for them." In his exposition of solutions, however, he debuted a more rhetorically aggressive style. The mission of eugenics supporters with regard to this excess of "idiots, imbeciles, and morons" was clear, he said: "Get these people out of circulation" through sterilization.[51] He became particularly exercised over Catholic opposition to sterilization, accusing the Church of subsidizing "the birth of idiots, imbeciles, and morons." As his speech suggests, Andrews's approach to eugenics did not incorporate the modulated tones recommended by eugenicists such as Frederick Osborn; on the contrary, it resembled the anti-Catholic rants of the very fringe of pro-sterilization forces. Whether Andrews's removal from the AES was a matter merely of financial limits or a deeper problem of conflicting views and promotional styles, we cannot say definitively, but it did mark the end of active religious participation in the formal structure of the AES.

The experiences of both Rev. MacArthur and Rev. Andrews, though separated by several years, nevertheless share certain features. Both men lacked scientific training, and if either of them was aware of the impact of genetic science on the eugenics movement, the records do not reveal it. They did not engage scientific critics of the movement, as some eugenicists did, nor did they try to push eugenicists to defend their scientific claims, as Catholic AES member Fr. John Cooper had done in the 1920s. Instead, they tended their particular fields of interest—MacArthur his *Eugenics and the Church* column and Andrews his administrative duties—with little recognition of the external scientific debates. They did so because the most appealing element of the eugenics program for them (as for most liberal religious participants) was its social message. MacArthur believed religious leaders should have a hand in delivering that social message, and so he devoted his time to building links between the churches and the eugenics movement. For Andrews, the dissemination of that social message required a well-run eugenics organization, and so he contributed his administrative skills to the cause.

By the 1930s, the AES was one of the few organizations still hospitable to amateur eugenic enthusiasts such as MacArthur and Andrews. Despite his amateur foray into cattle breeding, MacArthur was unlikely to have found a comfortable home in the American Genetics Association, for example. By that time, it and other genetics organizations were peopled by professional scientists; the same was true for eugenics organizations such as the ERO.[52] Despite the AES's internal discord, or perhaps because of it, in the 1930s it was the only organized outlet for the eugenic sympathies of preachers.

In May 1939, representatives from the AES and a bevy of prominent religious leaders gathered at the Society's favorite meeting spot, the Town Hall Club in New York City, to convene a conference on the Relation of Eugenics and the Church. Although the title of the conference suggested an inattention to ecumenism ("the church"), in fact, the organizers were careful to ensure that the four featured speakers were a eugenicist, a Catholic priest, a Protestant minister, and a Jewish rabbi. Albert Wiggam, the eugenics promoter who a

decade earlier had reconfigured the Ten Commandments and insisted on Jesus'
enthusiasm for eugenics, served as conference chairman, and former AES
Advisory Council member Rev. Harry Emerson Fosdick opened the round table
discussion.[53]

The invitation to the 1939 gathering, mailed to approximately 150 clergymen, described it as the final conference in a series that included explorations
of the relation of eugenics to recreation, nursing, education, medicine, and
related fields. "The American Eugenics Society believes," the invitation read,
"that it is for those already engaged in the work of improving human conditions
to tell us whether their efforts can also include training in those motivations,
interests, and desires, which make for love of children, interest in family life,
and a desire to participate in proportion to one's abilities in the highest of
human functions, the bearing and proper rearing of children." This statement
provides a suggestive synopsis of the AES's new reform image in the late 1930s.
No mention is made of that staple of previous eugenic lore, the feebleminded.
Nor is there any discussion of sterilization, birth control, or other controversial
subjects.[54] Instead, the Society's invitation to clergymen emphasized the organization's concern for families and children. Only two phrases suggested
standard eugenical thinking on these topics: "to participate *in proportion to one's
abilities*" and "the bearing and *proper* rearing of children," value-laden statements that suggest the AES had firm ideas about what "abilities" were necessary if prospective parents hoped to raise their children "properly."[55]

More than 135 religious leaders, largely from New York, New England, and
Washington, D.C., attended the conference (with a few ministers traveling from
Michigan, Iowa, Nebraska, and even California to participate). Many of the
religious leaders who had been formally affiliated with the AES in the 1930s
were in attendance, including Bishop McConnell, Rev. Kenneth MacArthur,
and Rabbi DeSola Pool (Rev. George Reid Andrews was noticeably absent).
Prominent leaders who had spoken of their support for eugenics in the past,
such as Rabbi Sidney Goldstein and Rabbi Stephen S. Wise, also attended.
Perhaps most revealing of the conference's broad reach, however, was the presence of two conferees from the Catholic University of America whose opposition to eugenics and the AES had been clear for many years: Fr. John M.
Cooper and Fr. John A. Ryan. Several other prominent Catholics, including Fr.
John LaFarge (a founder of the Catholic Interracial Council) and Fr. Edgar
Schmiedeler of the National Catholic Welfare Council, were also present. The
conference included a host of representatives from divinity schools, religious
charities, and even "power of positive thinking" pastor Norman Vincent
Peale.[56]

The minimal extant evidence makes it impossible to assess the reactions
of most of those who attended the conference, but it is clear that neither the
AES nor the religious conferees came to the meeting expecting conversions to
the other side's cause.[57] Instead, they gathered to see if any common ground

still existed between organized religion and organized eugenics. Religious leaders might have been excused for wondering if the organized eugenics movement itself still existed; the same year the conference convened, the Carnegie
Foundation, which oversaw the ERO, shut it down after several years of struggle with its employees (including H. H. Laughlin) over their production of what
the Carnegie trustees viewed as unscientific, political propaganda.[58]

Propaganda was mostly absent from the conference on the Relation of
Eugenics and the Church. Catholic priest Fr. Francis J. Connell tried to set a
tone of cooperation for the meeting with his opening presentation: "In the
presence of this friendly gathering, sincerely anxious for light on the question
under discussion, I have no intention of employing polemics." Rather, he
sought to outline the "chief tenets of the Catholic Church bearing on the subject of eugenics."[59] Connell (1888–1967) was eminently qualified to explore the
Church's moral concerns with the eugenics movement. Ordained a Roman
Catholic priest in 1913, he had been, since 1924, a professor of dogmatic theology at the Mt. Saint Alphonsus Seminary and, since 1930, a frequent presence on the radio as a contributor to the "Catholic Hour" on the *Church of the
Air* program. He was clearly comfortable in the role of interpreter of Church
teachings, outlining ably three fundamental principles of Catholic teaching on
eugenics: first, "the soul of man is immeasurably more important than his
body"; second, "the purposes of marriage are both social and individual"; and
third, "the Catholic Church holds that there is an objective code of morality
established for the regulation of human conduct by the Almighty, and made
known to men by their own reasoning powers and by positive divine revelation"—a reminder of the importance of natural law. As for possible points of
cooperation between the Church and the eugenics movement, Fr. Connell offered little encouragement. He utterly rejected birth control (by now a staple
of the eugenics program) and compulsory sterilization of the feebleminded.
He did, however, make a pitch for his own faith. "If the instructions of the
Catholic Church were followed," he claimed, "the human race would make
notable eugenic progress." Its teachings—and, by implication, *not* the measures of organizations such as the AES—represented the "promotion of true
eugenics."[59]

There was little room for agreement between this "true eugenics" and the
eugenics practiced by the AES in the late 1930s, as Frederick Osborn noted
with frustration during the discussion following the papers. After listening to
all of the presentations, he declared himself "more bitterly discouraged than I
have ever been in the years I have been working and thinking about eugenics."
The root of this bitterness was his feeling that none of the presenters seemed
to recognize the transformation the eugenics movement had undergone.
"There is nothing that has been said here that might not have been written, or
said, twenty years ago," Osborn noted with exasperation, but "since that time
the whole movement of eugenics has changed." Turning to Wiggam, the con-

ference chairman, Osborn expressed embarrassment over his outburst, confessing, "I did not mean to make this kind of speech." Nevertheless, he asked, "If the churches cannot teach us the true values of life and the beauties of life, where are we going to learn this lesson?"[60] His complaints about the tone of the conference discussion suggest that few of the religious leaders assembled understood that eugenicists in the AES had made considerable effort in the prior five years to change the direction of their movement. Ministers, priests, and rabbis equated eugenics with the aggressive pursuit of birth control and sterilization legislation. They still viewed Osborn's eugenics as a wolfish science in sheepish reform clothing. In this climate, there were few opportunities for rapprochement with eugenicists.

About the other papers presented by religious leaders the historical record is silent, but the conference discussion yielded at least one expression of optimism about the reconciliation hoped for by Osborn. Rev. George Hall of St. Thomas Church in New York saw great possibilities in the eugenics movement. The Church faced "a turning point in its life," he said, and in the next quarter of a century it would either "become the greatest force that exists on the face of the earth" or merely "something intelligent people refer to as nonsense." It could be a leader or a follower: "The Eugenics Society offers an opportunity for us to be leaders. I hope we will not fail."[61]

Hall's remarks likely appeared quaint to many in the audience. Regardless of creed, many religious leaders' views of social engineering on the scale proposed by eugenicists had been chastened by a long and severe economic depression and a growing uneasiness with the way Germany was pursuing such social engineering. Times were very different from the heady days of the 1920s. The same year that the conference on the Relation of Eugenics and the Church convened, the *Christian Century* published a series of essays by prominent religious leaders on the topic "How My Mind Has Changed in the Last Ten Years." Their responses reveal the extent of the theological migrations that had occurred. Reinhold Niebuhr's contribution, "Ten Years That Shook My World," was the starkest example; in it, he wrote of the "rejection of almost all the liberal theological ideals and ideas with which I ventured forth in 1915." For Niebuhr and many others, the attempt to mold their Christianity to modern culture had produced "grievous errors" in their theology, errors all the more apparent as the culture in which they had placed their hopes hurtled toward another world war.[62]

This theological shift was accompanied by a larger cultural shift away from theories that emphasized nature and heredity to those that emphasized nurture and environment. This change was slow but seismic, and it had a significant impact on the public's perception of eugenics.[63] These many developments forced a recalibration of the cultural and intellectual dial by which many ministers, priests, and rabbis had measured movements such as eugenics. If the Zeitgeist of the late 1930s is amenable to characterization, the spirit was one that had a stronger sense of humanity's limits than the era that had witnessed the birth of the eugenics movement. The 1939 New York World's Fair, whose theme was "The World of Tomorrow" and whose symbols were the futuristic trylon and perisphere, tried to tap into a much depleted reservoir of human optimism about mankind's ability to control nature. The exposition's booster-ish promotion of science and technology (fairgoers left the exhibit hall sporting "I have seen the future" buttons) was a far less inspiring message in 1939 than it had been in 1933 at the "Century of Progress" Exposition in Chicago.[64] Fairgoers might have seen the future, but they were no longer as optimistic about its possibilities as they once were.

On 1 September 1939, Hitler invaded Poland and World War II began. The war brought to light Hitler's extreme and terrifying version of eugenics; in the decades that followed, it was consigned by many people to the dustbin of discredited scientific theory, a biological "reform" movement thoroughly and justifiably tainted.[65] Still, as the zeal of Revs. MacArthur and Andrews suggests, eugenic ideas could appeal even as the movement itself sustained serious criticism of its methods and aims. The story of the American Eugenics Society in decline would be little more than a miniature were it not for the fact that the ideas that fueled it still excite the human imagination. The impulse to control nature and to improve the species was not quenched by the circumstances of the 1930s. For much of the eugenics movement's existence in the United States, a significant number of religious leaders from many creeds shared eugenicists' conceit that man was capable of controlling and directing nature to produce a better race of human beings. Although they often justified that conceit by cloaking it in Scripture or in appeals to the traditions of religious charity, and although many ministers, priests, and rabbis sincerely believed that their pursuit of that eugenic utopia was consonant with the principles of their faith, theirs was an error so profound as not to be forgotten.

Conclusion

> Man is an ironic creature because he forgets that he is not simply a
> creator but also a creature.
> —Reinhold Niebuhr, *The Irony of American History*

Delivering the Lowell Lecture at Harvard University in 1925, British
philosopher and mathematician Alfred North Whitehead predicted,
"When we consider what religion is for mankind, and what science
is, it is not exaggeration to say that the future course of history depends upon the decision of this generation as to the relations between them." An influential segment of that generation—the ministers, priests, and rabbis described in these pages—did not so much
reach a point of decision as craft an uneasy compromise. They did
so in part through an embrace of hereditarian explanations for human behavior. Eugenics offered religious leaders a modern, scientific way to grapple with the questions of their age, including the
usefulness of charity and social service, the health of marriage as an
institution, the ability of new American immigrants to assimilate,
and the broader challenge to religious authority posed by changing
cultural norms. Although mindful of the necessity of religion,
Whitehead himself offered a bleak snapshot of its place in the modern world: "Religion is tending to degenerate into a decent formula
wherewith to embellish a comfortable life," he told his audience.[1] By
embracing eugenics, some religious leaders hoped to forestall this
process of degeneration.

Organized religion and organized eugenics shared certain features. Both encouraged the belief in a better world, whether that was

eugenicists' vision of a perfect human race or the clerics' vision of heaven. Both also insisted on enforcing social codes, whether biological or ethical. Both had clear notions of sinfulness, although for the eugenicist, these transgressions were biological. Both had catechisms and rituals to define their faiths, and both, of course, had dedicated acolytes.

Religious participation in the eugenics movement casts light on the broader question of why eugenics, a movement that in hindsight was so clearly wrong, was for a time so appealing. In letters, speeches, sermons, books, and essays, religious leaders left us their thoughts on eugenics, thoughts that reveal these ministers, priests, and rabbis as having acted overwhelmingly in good faith. They genuinely believed that eugenics would increase human happiness. But their enthusiasm developed in a historical context in which several powerful forces converged to challenge traditional religious ideas, including the rise of science (both professional and popular); the extraordinary social changes brought by industrialization, urbanization, immigration, world war, and economic depression; and major social movements, including the Social Gospel and progressivism. The exploration of this interplay between context and motive in the worldviews of these religious leaders reveals why so few saw the logical conclusion of the eugenics ideas they so eagerly touted.

Within this confluence of historical forces, clergymen had important choices to make about what kinds of reforms to pursue. Looking back, one might expect to find a little more hesitation from religious leaders before they offered their support to a movement that appeared to lack both humility—in that it replaced God with science as the shaper of the human race—and respect for the inviolability of the individual, a hallmark of the Judeo-Christian tradition. How could religious leaders so easily dismiss the sanctity of marriage, an emphasis on the spiritual over the physical, and the acceptance of human imperfections?

The evidence yields a clear pattern about who elected to support eugenic-style reforms and who did not. Religious leaders pursued eugenics precisely when they moved away from traditional religious tenets. The liberals and modernists in their respective faiths—those who challenged their churches to conform to modern circumstances—became the eugenics movement's most enthusiastic supporters. Theologically, these men were creative, deliberately vague, or perhaps even, as their critics contended, deeply confused. In terms of solving social problems, however, their purpose was clear: They were dedicated to facing head-on the challenges posed by modernity. Doing so meant embracing scientific solutions. At the dawn of the twentieth century, Henry Adams's bewilderment at confronting the multiplicity of a mechanical dynamo made him turn back to the Virgin in search of unity, but his anxiety was not widely shared. Most Americans greeted new scientific and technological advances in the spirit of the motto of the 1893 World's Fair: "Science finds, Industry applies. Man conforms. Science discovers, Genius invents, Industry applies, and Man adapts himself to or is molded by new things."[2] A generation after Adams, liberal religious leaders allowed their worldviews to be molded by the promise of the new science of eugenics.

The liberal tenor of religious participation in the eugenics movement also serves as a reminder that eugenics was never exclusively a conservative movement. Eugenic ideas rested comfortably within the mainstream of progressive American reform in the early decades of the twentieth century. It was a movement that the liberals of its day wholeheartedly embraced as an effective form of social engineering, and one that many political leaders viewed as providing justification for a range of state interventions, including immigration restriction and compulsory sterilization.

Religious participation in the eugenics movement yields a story rife with irony and ambiguity, one that requires, at the level of individual engagement with its participants, distinguishing between unintended consequences and unconscious intended consequences.[3] As a story of equivocalities, it is, as historian Robert Nye has suggested about other elements of the history of eugenics, "less emotionally satisfying and more complicated" than a story with unabashed heroes and obvious villains.[4]

Yet these ambiguities reveal a great deal about the relationship between religion and science during the first third of the twentieth century. Groups like the American Eugenics Society's Committee on Cooperation with Clergymen demonstrate that this relationship was often characterized by cooperation; far from the warfare declared by many in that era, religious participation in eugenics shows that secular scientists and clergymen of all faiths were often willing and able to find common ground. More important, they were able to enter a dialogue and influence each other's thinking. When Fr. John Cooper, a Catholic priest, challenged fellow members of the AES to engage the increasingly caustic criticisms of eugenic science made by geneticists, or when dedicated Social Gospel ministers insisted on salvaging the principle of Christian charity by crafting a form of modern "scientific philanthropy," they influenced the general tenor of the eugenics debate. Indeed, though it is impossible to celebrate religious enthusiasm for eugenics, it is plausible to conclude that the eugenics movement, at times, was moderated by the criticisms of some of the ministers, priests, and rabbis who embraced it.

These religious leaders were part of a transitional generation. For their predecessors, the question of theodicy was a constant. Nature's crueler bodily torments were frequent and deadly matters of fact—facts for which their congregations turned to them for explanation. In the first few decades of the twentieth century, religious leaders still had to answer this human need for assurance, of course, but they felt much greater pressure to do so in the language of modern science. In providing answers, they competed with the advice of scientists and social scientists whose knowledge came not from Scripture, but from supposedly impeccable empirical evidence. By the late twentieth century, the results of this struggle for cultural relevance were clear: Americans achieved a stunning secular reversal of the theodicy problem. No longer were we so unsophisticated as to ask how God could allow human suffering; instead, we merely asked how, by harnessing the power of science, we could prevent it. No longer do we approach, with trepidation and a certain degree of awe, the "clumsy, wasteful, blundering, low, and horribly cruel works of nature," as Darwin described them.[5] Instead, we map the human genome and assume that it will serve as a guidepost in our inevitably successful efforts to control nature.

The history of the eugenics movement raises enduring questions about science, religion, morality, and ethics; in some sense, the difficult issues that the preachers and rabbis in this story confronted are with us still, as scientists perfect techniques of genetic manipulation, cloning, and other methods whose implicit aim is to control and "improve" the human race. Echoes of our eugenic past still emerge regularly. In 2002, the *New York Times* featured on its front page the story of the Bogle family of Oregon. The paper described the haplessly named Rooster Bogle, patriarch of the clan, as a man who had tutored his offspring in the fine arts of thievery, violence, drug abuse, and sundry other crimes. To illustrate the pathologies of the Bogles, the *Times* constructed an extended family tree, complete with images of gavels over the names and pictures of those family members who had been or were currently incarcerated.[6] The diagram was eerily similar to those that accompanied the Ishmael, Juke, and Kallikak family studies published earlier in the century by enthusiasts of eugenics. Similarly, where superintendents of state institutions once sterilized scores of the so-called feebleminded to improve the health of the race, today fertility clinics offer parents the option of improving the health of their potential children by making use of a range of eugenic services that go by euphonious phrases such as "family balancing" (for sex selection) and "preimplantation genetic diagnosis" (for the selection of embryos free from inherited disease).

As for our eugenic past, we have come to terms with it in that uniquely American way: by begging forgiveness of the victims and then quickly and conscientiously forgetting it. In May 2002, Gov. Mark Warner of Virginia offered a fulsome apology on behalf of his predecessors to the men and women who had been forcibly sterilized by the state as part of Virginia's eugenics program. "The eugenics movement was a shameful effort in which state government never should have been involved," Warner said, offering "the commonwealth's sincere apology" to the approximately eight thousand citizens sterilized between 1924 and 1979. "We must remember the commonwealth's past mistakes in order to prevent them from recurring.[7] A plaque marking the anniversary of the U.S. Supreme Court's *Buck v. Bell* decision now rests on a roadside in Charlottesville, an act of anticommemoration.

But what we have learned about the history of eugenics earlier in the century has in some sense narrowed the debate about the potential impact of our current genetic technologies. Contemporary condemnations of eugenics invariably focus on the violation of individual rights inherent in such measures as compulsory sterilization. Asked about this "old" form of eugenics, which required coercion enforced by the state, only 8 percent of contemporary Americans approved of making it possible "for nations to produce large numbers of individuals with genetically desirable traits." From this perspective, eugenics would have been unobjectionable (scientific flaws aside) if it had found a way to respect individuals and their reproductive choices. Thus, parents meddling with the genetic composition of their unborn children does not suggest to most people the same assault on free will and individual rights that forcible eugenic sterilization does. As George Annas and others have noted, however, genetic screening, sex selection, and even genetic engineering need not be imposed by the state. People may demand these technologies; it is not unlikely that we will one day insist on them as a right.[8]

Indeed, technologies of genetic improvement are already gaining in popularity, suggesting that recognition of the excesses of our eugenic past has not erased the irrepressible urge to improve the human race. Public opinion surveys over the past decade reveal growing levels of approval for genetic engineering, for the purposes of both therapy and enhancement. A survey conducted by the National Center for Genome Resources in the late 1990s found consistently high approval ratings for allowing scientists to alter genes for the purposes of curing a fatal disease (85 percent); reducing the risk of a usually fatal disease (84 percent); and preventing children from inheriting a usually fatal disease (86 percent). An even higher percentage of physicians and geneticists approved of such use (90 and 96 percent, respectively). As for genetic enhancement, 35 percent of people polled felt it was fine to use genetic engineering to "improve the physical characteristics children would inherit." Another poll found that 25 percent of Americans approved of genetic engineering for the purposes of improving a person's physical appearance and 34 percent to improve a person's intelligence.[9]

The ethical questions that lie at the heart of these new genetic methods are not far removed from those that challenged ministers, priests, and rabbis earlier in the century. What has changed is the influence of religious voices in this debate. Although religious leaders were among some of the most vigorous participants in early debates about the new genetics, today they are largely marginalized, supplanted by a new class of professional bioethicists who work in the halls of academe, not the sanctuaries of churches or synagogues. Contemporary debates over bioethics, with their emphasis on the principles of beneficence, nonmaleficence, justice, and autonomy, reflect this loss; what we have gained in technical precision we have lost in straightforward moral debate. A focus on means has replaced debate over ends.

The human desire for improvement is best understood as a continuum of feeling, one that can rest comfortably alongside the very democratic urges that we assume will prevent the expression of eugenic sentiments in the future. Eugenicists earlier in the century saw nothing unusual in their simultaneous championing of the idea of innate hereditary differences and their participation in a democratic society dedicated to the principle that all men are created equal. They simply believed that the future health of democracy depended on the ability of experts such as themselves to ensure the creation of eugenically ideal children who would, in turn, prove to be better democratic citizens. Many Protestant, Catholic, and Jewish leaders agreed.

Whatever the future holds, we will not be equipped to confront it unless we have an understanding of the ambiguous nature of our eugenic past. When he described "the modern temper" in 1929, critic Joseph Wood Krutch warned his contemporaries that although science was alluring in its promises of improving the human race, ultimately it offered only a "phantom of certitude."[10] Today we are more certain of science, and more comforted by the protections our democracy offers us—protections that we assume will bar the door to eugenics' return. In recalling the honest struggle of these men of faith in the early twentieth century, however, we are reminded that theirs was an attempt to answer some of the same intractable and provocative questions we ask ourselves today: How much can and should we do to improve the human condition, and at what point might our improvements undermine the very things that make us human?

Notes

INTRODUCTION

1. Sermon of Rev. Phillips E. Osgood, 1926, American Eugenics Society Papers, American Philosophical Society Library, Philadelphia, PA.

2. *Newell Dwight Hillis*, pamphlet, Redpath Chautauqua Collection [19–?], University of Iowa Libraries: http://sdrcdata.lib.uiowa.edu/libsdrc/ details.jsp?id=/hillis/3, accessed 3 August 2002; remark about Fosdick in Walter Lippmann, *A Preface to Morals* (New York: Macmillan, 1929), 97.

3. Francis Galton, "Eugenics as a Factor in Religion," in *Essays in Eugenics* (London: Eugenics Education Society, 1909), 69; Francis Galton, "Eugenics: Its Definition, Scope and Aims," *American Journal of Sociology* 10 (July 1904): 5.

4. Galton's zeal is described in Ruth S. Cowan, "Nature and Nurture: The Interplay of Biology and Politics in the Work of Francis Galton," *Studies in the History of Biology* 1 (1977): 139.

5. Galton, "Eugenics: Its Definition, Scope, and Aims," 2–5.

6. Francis Galton, "The Possible Improvement of the Human Breed under Existing Conditions of Law and Sentiment," *Popular Science Monthly* 60 (January 1902): 219. The Parable of the Talents is in Matthew 25:15–30.

7. Missionary quoted in Richard Hofstadter, *Anti-Intellectualism in American Life* (New York: Vintage Books, 1962), 78.

8. More than seventy years later, at an international congress held at the Museum of Natural History in New York City in 1921, the leading figures of the eugenics movement paid tribute to Noyes as a eugenics pioneer, commending the "extraordinary religious devotion" of his Oneida Community and the fact that "no deaf and dumb, blind, crippled, or idiotic children were ever born" to its members. J. H. Noyes quoted in Hilda Herrick Noyes, M.D. and George Wallingform Noyes, A.B., "The Oneida Community Exper-

iment in Stirpiculture," in *Eugenics, Genetics and the Family: Scientific Papers of the Second International Congress of Eugenics* (Baltimore: Williams and Wilkins, 1923), 374. See also Pierrepont B. Noyes, *A Goodly Heritage* (New York: Rinehart and Company, 1958). On utopian communities, see Mark Holloway, *Heavens on Earth: Utopian Communities in America, 1680–1880* (New York: Dover, 1966).

9. H. Noyes and Noyes, "The Oneida Community Experiment in Stirpiculture," 375, 380.

10. Victor L. Hilts, "Obeying the Laws of Hereditary Descent: Phrenological Views on Inheritance and Eugenics," *Journal of the History of the Behavioral Sciences* 18 (1982): 62–77.

11. Robert Fletcher quoted in Carl N. Degler, *In Search of Human Nature: The Decline and Revival of Darwinism in American Social Thought* (New York: Oxford University Press, 1991), 36.

12. Philip R. Reilly, *The Surgical Solution: A History of Involuntary Sterilization in the United States* (Baltimore: Johns Hopkins University Press, 1991). All four of these laws were passed prior to 1910, when the Eugenics Record Office opened.

13. Henry F. May, *The End of American Innocence: A Study of the First Years of Our Own Time, 1912–1917* (New York: Columbia University Press, 1959), 224.

14. Charles E. Rosenberg, *No Other Gods: On Science and American Social Thought* (Baltimore: Johns Hopkins University Press, 1961).

15. Theodore Dwight Bozeman, *Protestants in an Age of Science: The Baconian Ideal and Antebellum American Religious Thought* (Chapel Hill: University of North Carolina Press, 1977), 93–96; Herbert Hovenkamp, *Science and Religion in America, 1800–1860* (Philadelphia: University of Pennsylvania Press, 1978).

16. George Marsden, "Evangelicals and the Scientific Culture: An Overview," in *Religion and Twentieth Century American Intellectual Life*, ed. Michael J. Lacey (Cambridge, UK: Woodrow Wilson International Center for Scholars and Cambridge University Press, 1989), 24; Jon H. Roberts, *Darwinism and the Divine in America: Protestant Intellectuals and Organic Evolution, 1859–1900* (Madison: University of Wisconsin Press, 1988), 233, 166. Discussion of the intersection of organized religion and science in the nineteenth century occurred almost entirely within the context of Protestantism, for Protestants controlled the major religious institutions and publications. By the twentieth century, Catholic and Jewish theologians and intellectuals had reached a critical mass in the country, formed their own institutions, and joined the debate. See Bozeman, *Protestants in an Age of Science*.

17. James Turner, *Without God, without Creed: The Origins of Unbelief in America* (Baltimore: Johns Hopkins University Press, 1985), 187; Roberts, *Darwinism and the Divine*, 241.

18. Turner, *Without God, without Creed*, 39–40.

19. LeConte quoted in Roberts, *Darwinism and the Divine*, 125; see also Hovenkamp, *Science and Religion in America*, 190. John S. Haller Jr., *Outcasts from Evolution: Scientific Attitudes of Racial Inferiority, 1859–1900* (Carbondale: Southern Illinois University Press, 1971), 99, 166.

20. Ronald L. Numbers, "Science and Religion," *Osiris* 1 (1985): 61; John William Draper, *History of the Conflict between Religion and Science* (New York: Appleton, 1874); Andrew Dickson White, *A History of the Warfare of Science with Theology in Christendom*, 2 vols. (New York: Appleton, 1896).

21. "Minutes of the Eugenics Committee of the U.S.A.," 28 March 1925, American Eugenics Society Papers, American Philosophical Society Library.

22. This point is made by Richard Soloway, *Demography and Degeneration: Eugenics and the Declining Birthrate in Twentieth-Century Britain* (Chapel Hill: University of North Carolina Press, 1990), 82–83. Ian Barbour has outlined four models of interaction between science and religion: conflict, independence, dialogue, and integration; all four characterized the relationship of eugenics and religion at some point in its history. See Ian Barbour, *Religion in an Age of Science: The Gifford Lectures* (New York: Harper Collins, 1990), vol. 1.

23. Robert A. Woods, *The City Wilderness* (Boston, 1898).

24. On Roosevelt's understanding of race suicide, see Thomas G. Dyer, *Theodore Roosevelt and the Idea of Race* (Baton Rouge: Louisiana State University Press, 1980). Like the word eugenics, "feebleminded" was a fluid term during the Progressive Era. It was used as a general descriptor for criminals, paupers, alcoholics, epileptics, and people with a wide range of mental deficiencies. Eugenicists crafted grades of feeble-mindedness after the introduction of the Binet-Simon intelligence test in the 1910s; these included (from lowest mental age to highest) idiots, low-grade imbeciles, medium imbeciles, high-grade imbeciles, and morons. In popular works, the term feebleminded continued to be used as a catch-all term. Daniel J. Kevles, *In the Name of Eugenics: Genetics and the Uses of Human Heredity* (Berkeley: University of California Press, 1985), 77–79; "Steps in Mental Development," *Survey* 31 (11 October 1913): 54.

25. Ignatius Donnelly (writing as Edmund Boisgilbert, M.D.), *Caesar's Column: A Story of the Twentieth Century* (Chicago: F.J. Shulte, 1890).

26. On shifting metaphors for nature, see Thomas A. Goudge, "Evolutionism," in *Dictionary of the History of Ideas* (New York: Charles Scribner's Sons, 1973), 2: 179.

27. Image reprinted in *Eugenical News* 17 (November–December 1932).

28. Physician quoted in Kevles, *In the Name of Eugenics*, 58.

29. Voluntary eugenics efforts are more difficult to trace, as some historians of the movement have noted. One historian who has done so is Martin Pernick, *The Black Stork: Eugenics and the Death of "Defective" Babies in American Medicine and Motion Pictures Since 1915* (New York: Oxford University Press, 1996). See also the review of Pernick's book by Edward Larson in *Journal of American History* 84 (September 1997): 698–699.

30. The two major studies of the U.S. eugenics movement are Mark Haller, *Eugenics: Hereditarian Attitudes in American Thought* (New Brunswick, NJ: Rutgers University Press, 1963) and Kevles, *In the Name of Eugenics*. Other studies include Edward Larson, *Sex, Race, and Science: Eugenics in the Deep South* (Baltimore: Johns Hopkins University Press, 1995); Donald Pickens, *Eugenics and the Progressives* (Nashville, TN: Vanderbilt University Press, 1968); Reilly, *The Surgical Solution;* Nicole Rafter, *White Trash: The Eugenic Family Studies* (Chicago: Northeastern University Press, 1988) and *Creating Born Criminals* (Chicago: University of Illinois Press, 1997); Kenneth M. Ludmerer, *Genetics and American Society: A Historical Appraisal* (Baltimore: Johns Hopkins University Press, 1972); Marouf Arif Hasian Jr., *The Rhetoric of Eugenics in Anglo-American Thought* (Athens: University of Georgia Press, 1996); Barry Alan Mehler, "A History of the American Eugenics Society, 1921–1940" (Ph.D. diss., University of Illinois at Urbana-Champaign, 1988). There are also countless article-length studies of the movement, including Garland E. Allan, "The Misuse of

Biological Hierarchies: The American Eugenics Movement, 1900–1940," *History and Philosophy of the Life Sciences* 5 (1983): 105–128; Michael Freeden, "Eugenics and Progressive Thought: A Study in Ideological Affinity," *Historical Journal* 22 (1979): 645–671; Bentley Glass, "Geneticists Embattled: Their Stand against Rampant Eugenics and Racism in America During the 1920s," *Proceedings of the American Philosophical Society Library* 130 (1986): 130–154.

31. Raymond Pearl, for example, wanted eugenics to become "a legitimate field for the Federal Government" and recommended the creation of a bureau to investigate "human breeds," modeled on the existing government bureaus for plant and animal breeding. See Raymond Pearl, "Breeding Better Men," *World's Work* 15 (1908): 9824. The link between eugenics and progressivism is explored in Pickens, *Eugenics and the Progressives*. On progressivism, see Robert H. Wiebe, *The Search for Order, 1877–1920* (New York: Hill and Wang, 1967); Richard Hofstadter, *The Age of Reform: From Bryan to FDR* (New York: Vintage Books, 1955); Robert M. Crunden, *Ministers of Reform: The Progressives' Achievement in American Civilization, 1889–1920* (Chicago: University of Illinois Press, 1984).

32. "Minutes and Discussion," *Proceedings of the National Conference of Charities and Correction, 1888* (Boston: Press of George H. Ellis, 1888), 427, 430 (hereafter cited as *Proceedings, 1888.*

33. A good summary of the impact of urban growth on the churches is in Sydney Ahlstrom, *A Religious History of the American People* (New Haven: Yale University Press, 1972), ch. 44; see also Henry F. May, *Protestant Churches and Industrial America* (New York: Octagon Books, 1963).

34. Porter quoted in Roberts, *Darwinism and the Divine*, 98–99.

35. John Haberton, "Social Science in the Pulpit," *Chautauquan* 14 (1891–1892): 175–176.

36. H. L. Mencken, *A Mencken Chrestomathy* (New York: Vintage Books, 1982), 77, 79.

37. Hofstadter, *The Age of Reform*. Robert Wiebe has challenged Hofstadter's interpretation, arguing that religious leaders were holdouts from an earlier era, "island communities" amid the sea of change that marked the early years of the twentieth century, but Hofstadter's description remains the more compelling. Wiebe, *The Search for Order*.

38. On the idea of "cultural strain," see William R. Hutchison, "Cultural Strain and Protestant Liberalism," *American Historical Review* 76 (April 1971): 386–411. See also Martin E. Marty, *Modern American Religion, vol. 2: The Noise of Conflict* (Chicago: University of Chicago Press, 1991), 32.

39. This description of reformers is from Arthur Schlesinger, *The American as Reformer* (New York: Atheneum, 1968), 67. See also Christopher Lasch, *The New Radicalism in America, 1889–1963: The Intellectual as Social Type* (New York: Norton, 1965), 146. The term "reactionary modernism" has been used to describe the German Right's encounter with the Industrial Revolution; see Jeffery Herf, *Reactionary Modernism: Technology, Culture, and Politics in Weimar and the Third Reich* (Cambridge, UK: Cambridge University Press, 1984).

40. On the growth of the U.S. social sciences, see Dorothy Ross, *The Origins of American Social Science* (Cambridge, UK: Cambridge University Press, 1991).

41. As historian William McGuire King has noted, their efforts also elicited support from secular reformers who believed that the churches and synagogues could "tap social resources not easily motivated by public channels alone." William McGuire King, "The Reform Establishment and the Ambiguities of Influence," in *Between the Times: The Travail of the Protestant Establishment in America, 1900–1960*, ed. William R. Hutchison (Cambridge, UK: Cambridge University Press, 1989), 123.

42. *Survey* 31 (21 March 1914): 764. See also Roy Lubove, *The Professional Altruist: The Emergence of Social Work as a Career, 1880–1930* (Cambridge, MA: Harvard University Press, 1965).

43. Arthur Mann, *Yankee Reformers in the Urban Age: Social Reform in Boston, 1880–1900* (New York: Harper, 1954)., 230. See also Nathan Irvin Huggins, *Protestants against Poverty: Boston's Charities, 1870–1900* (Westport, CT: Greenwood, 1971); Lubove, *The Professional Altruist.*

44. Rev. Wright quoted in Rudolph Vecoli, "Sterilization: A Progressive Measure?" *Wisconsin Magazine of History* 43 (spring 1960): 192.

45. Winthrop S. Hudson, "Discussants on Egal Feldman, 'The Social Gospel and the Jew,'" *American Jewish Historical Quarterly* 58 (1968–1969): 328.

46. "Pastors for Eugenics," *New York Times*, 6 June 1913, 6. Many of the religious leaders who at one time or another publicly supported eugenics—Bishop Cortlandt Whitehead (Protestant Episcopal), Bishop Samuel Fallows (Reform Episcopal), Rabbi Emil G. Hirsch (Reform Jew), Rev. Russell H. Conwell (Baptist), Bishop Charles Williams (Protestant Episcopal), Rev. A. Edwin Kelgwin (Presbyterian), Rev. Newell Dwight Hillis (Congregational), to name but a few—knew each other personally through their secular reform activities. For one example, see John Haynes Holmes's account of the New York City Affairs Committee in his autobiography, *I Speak for Myself: The Autobiography of John Haynes Holmes* (New York: Harper and Brothers, 1959), 215–219.

47. Stow Persons, "Religion and Modernity, 1865–1914," in *The Shaping of American Religion*, ed. James Ward Smith (Princeton: Princeton University Press, 1961), 1: 372.

48. Kenneth Cauthen, *The Impact of American Religious Liberalism* (New York: Harper and Row, 1962), 30. In this passage Cauthen is discussing the Christian tradition, but his description just as easily applies to Reform Jews.

49. Ronald C. White and C. Howard Hopkins, eds. *The Social Gospel: Religion and Reform in Changing America* (Philadelphia: Temple University Press, 1976), 245; Francis L. Broderick, *Right Reverend New Dealer: John A. Ryan* (New York: Macmillan, 1963).

50. Walter Lippmann, *A Preface to Morals* (New York: Macmillan, 1929), 40, 51, 56.

51. Susan Curtis, *A Consuming Faith: The Social Gospel and Modern American Culture* (Baltimore: Johns Hopkins University Press, 1991), 3. See also Paul T. Phillips, *A Kingdom on Earth: Anglo-American Social Christianity, 1880–1940* (University Park: Pennsylvania State University Press, 1996), which reveals the transatlantic character of social Christianity and American Social Gospelers' reliance on the work of leading religious thinkers in Britain.

52. Bryan quoted in Ferenc M. Szasz, "Protestantism and the Search for Stability:

Liberal and Conservative Quests for a Christian America, 1875–1925," in *Building the Organizational Society: Essays on Associational Activities in Modern America*, ed. Jerry Israel (New York: Free Press, 1972), 96.

53. William McGuire King, "An Enthusiasm for Humanity: The Social Emphasis in Religion and Its Accommodation in Protestant Theology," in Lacy, *Religion and Twentieth Century American Intellectual Life*, 64. Rauschenbusch quoted in Glenn C. Altschuler, "Walter Rauschenbusch: Theology, the Church, and the Social Gospel," in *Modern American Protestantism and Its World: Historical Articles on Protestantism in American Religious Life*, ed. Martin E. Marty (New York: K. G. Saur, 1992), 6: 136. See also Donald Meyer, *The Protestant Search for Political Realism, 1919–1941* (Middleton, CT: Wesleyan University Press, 1988), 2–4. For definitions of conservative, liberal, and modernist Protestants, see Paul Conkin, *When All the Gods Trembled: Darwinism, Scopes, and American Intellectuals* (New York: Rowman and Littlefield, 1998); William R. Hutchison, *The Modernist Impulse in American Protestantism* (Durham, NC: Duke University Press, 1992).

54. Curtis, *A Consuming Faith*, 5; Hutchison, *The Modernist Impulse in American Protestantism*, ch. 5.

55. Excerpts from Josiah Strong, *Our Country* (New York: Baker and Taylor for the American Home Missionary Society, 1885), in *American Issues: The Social Record*, 4th ed., ed. Merle Curti (Philadelphia: J.B. Lippincott, 1960), 894–895. On Strong, see also Phillips, *A Kingdom on Earth*, 60–65; John Higham, *Strangers in the Land: Patterns of American Nativism, 1860–1925* (1955; reprint, New Brunswick, NJ: Rutgers University Press, 1994), 39–40.

56. Rauschenbusch quoted in Phillips, *A Kingdom on Earth*, 21. Secular figures prominent in the progressive movement made similar arguments. University of Wisconsin sociologist, economist, and labor historian John R. Commons argued in his *Races and Immigrants in America* (New York: MacMillan, 1907 that the special qualities of the Anglo-Saxon race had produced the unique democratic institutions of the present-day United States.

57. Prayer reprinted in White and Hopkins, *The Social Gospel*, 163.

58. Don S. Kirschner makes a similar argument about the progressives. See "The Ambiguous Legacy: Social Justice and Social Control in the Progressive Era," *Historical Reflections* 2 (1975): 69–88.

59. William McGuire King, "The Biblical Base of the Social Gospel," in *The Bible and Social Reform*, ed. Ernest R. Sandeen (Chico, CA: Scholars Press, 1982), 72–73.

60. Martin E. Marty describes the difference in *Modern American Religion, vol. 1: The Irony of It All, 1893–1919* (Chicago: University of Chicago Press, 1986), 210. On millennialism, see Ferenc Morton Szasz, *The Divided Mind of Protestant America, 1880–1930* (University, Alabama: University of Alabama Press, 1982) and George M. Marsden, *Fundamentalism and American Culture: The Shaping of Twentieth-Century Evangelicalism, 1870–1925* (New York: Oxford University Press, 1980).

61. Bernard I. Bell, "Social Service and the Churches," *Atlantic Monthly* 115 (February 1915): 164.

62. Conkin, *When All the Gods Trembled*, 61–63.

63. On the split in the Protestant churches, see Szasz, *The Divided Mind of Protestant America*; May, *Protestant Churches and Industrial America*; Marsden, *Fundamentalism and American Culture*; and George M. Marsden, "Everyone One's Own Inter-

preter? The Bible, Science, and Authority in Mid-Nineteenth Century America," and Timothy P. Weber, "The Two-Edged Sword: The Fundamentalist Use of the Bible," both in *The Bible in America*, ed. Nathan O. Hatch and Mark A. Noll (New York: Oxford University Press, 1982). Conservative Protestants (the future Fundamentalists) were also active in social reform in the late nineteenth and early twentieth century, primarily through Prohibition campaigns. The difference between conservative and liberal Protestants was the emphasis placed on reform by the latter. See Szasz, "Protestantism and the Search for Stability," 97.

64. Strong's statement is from his book, *The New Era or the Coming Kingdom* (1893) and is quoted in Martin E. Marty, *Modern American Religion, vol. 1: The Irony of It All* (Chicago: University of Chicago Press, 1986), 29.

65. David N. Livingstone makes the point that "many *thought* there was a struggle between science and religion" in the evangelical community. See *Darwin's Forgotten Defenders: The Encounter between Evangelical Theology and Evolutionary Thought* (Grand Rapids, MI: William B. Eerdmans, 1987), 185. See also Roberts, *Darwinism and the Divine in America*.

66. Michael A. Meyer, *Response to Modernity: A History of the Reform Movement in Judaism* (Detroit: Wayne State University Press, 1988), 238, 264.

67. Ibid., 276.

68. Hirsch quoted in Egal Feldman, "The Social Gospel and the Jew," *American Jewish Historical Quarterly* 58 (1968–1969): 313, 316. Feldman argues that a complete reconciliation of the Social Gospel and Reform traditions was never possible, because "imbedded within the Protestant social gospel itself was a deep vein of ambivalence about Judaism which relegated any effort of amalgamation, even under the ideal conditions of progressive minded America, highly improbable."

69. Rabbi Wise quoted in Leonard J. Mervis, "The Social Justice Movement and the American Reform Rabbi," *American Jewish Archives Journal* 7 (June 1955): 203, 205.

70. Rabbi Max Reichler, "Jewish Eugenics," in *Jewish Eugenics and Other Essays* (New York: Block Publishing, 1916).

71. "Jewish Racial Traits," *Eugenical News* 5 (January 1920): 7–8.

72. Hasian, *The Rhetoric of Eugenics*. Hasian devotes a chapter of his book to a discussion of "Catholic Interpretations of Eugenics Rhetoric." Though by far the most detailed treatment of Catholic thought on eugenics, Hasian's relies heavily on the work of British Catholic Thomas Gerrard and does not discuss either Rev. John A. Ryan or Rev. John Cooper, two prominent American Catholics who participated in the organized eugenics movement. He also neglects to discuss the work of Charles Bruehl, the Catholic editor of *Homiletic and Pastoral Review*, who wrote a lengthy book about eugenics and the Catholic Church in the late 1920s.

73. "Hereditary Genius," *Catholic World* 11 (September 1870): 724, 727–728.

74. Jay P. Dolan does note that for Catholics, achievement of the "Kingdom of God on earth" had to take place through the Church. Jay P. Dolan, *The American Catholic Experience: A History from Colonial Times to the Present* (Notre Dame, IN: University of Notre Dame Press, 1992), 304–310. After the release of the encyclical condemning modernism, the Vatican cracked down on American Catholics such as John A. Zahm, a priest and professor at Notre Dame who advanced the idea of theistic evolution in his book, *Evolution and Dogma* (Dolan, 317–319). See also Marty, *Modern*

American Religion, 1: 185; Ahlstrom, *A Religious History of the American People,* 839. On the intellectual "deep freeze" wrought by the encyclicals, see James Hennesey, S.J., *American Catholics: A History of the Roman Catholic Community in the United States* (New York: Oxford University Press, 1981), 202–203.

75. Rev. H. H. Wyman, "Modern Science and Catholic Faith," *Catholic World* 71 (April 1900): 1; Rev. George McDermot, "Mr. Mallock on the Church and Science," *Catholic World* 70 (January 1900): 527.

76. Indeed, Walsh himself belied this prejudice. He had a medical degree, a Ph.D., and an LL.D. and in the years to come would write frequently on hereditary matters. He was also a prolific writer in the field of the history of medicine. See James Walsh, "Father Gregor Mendel: A New Outlook in Heredity," *Ecclesiastical Review* 30 (January 1904): 20 and *Makers of Modern Medicine* (New York: Fordham University Press, 1907).

77. Walsh, "Father Gregor Mendel," 36.

78. William Seton, LL.D., "Heredity in Man," *Catholic World* 75 (October 1901): 67.

79. "Minutes of the American Eugenics Society, 1933–1936," MacArthur Correspondence, American Eugenics Society Papers, American Philosophical Society Library.

80. Like feeblemindedness, "fitness" was an amorphous term that could mean a number of things. It was usually used to describe the sum total of a person's traits, physical and mental, in a general sense. Thus, a feebleminded person was "unfit," whereas a physically and mentally healthy person of good parentage was "fit." Religious leaders urged eugenicists to include moral and spiritual qualities in the fitness equation, and a few eugenicists such as Caleb Saleeby warned that the term was too vague to describe the qualities eugenicists desired in the human race. See ch. 1.

81. John Hedley Brooke, *Science and Religion: Some Historical Perspectives* (Cambridge, UK: Cambridge University Press, 1991), 42–51.

82. Many eugenics supporters did, of course, openly promote coercive strategies against large segments of the American population. My point here is that the religious leaders and other nonscientists who found the movement appealing did not necessarily share these beliefs. I am also keeping in mind historian Thomas Haskell's warning about historians who make "the implicit claim to have successfully reconstructed the historical actor's unconscious intention." Thomas Haskell, "Capitalism and the Origins of the Humanitarian Sensibility," *American Historical Review* 90 (1985): 339–361, 547–566.

I. FERVENT CHARITY

1. Charles Sheldon, *In His Steps* (1896; reprint, Chicago: John C. Winston, 1937); Washington Gladden, *Social Salvation* (Boston: Houghton Mifflin, 1902), 1902), 30; see also Lasch, *The New Radicalism in America,* 163–164.

2. Sheldon, *In His Steps;* Timothy Miller, *Following in His Steps: A Biography of Charles M. Sheldon* (Nashville: University of Tennessee Press, 1988); Paul Boyer, "In His Steps: A Reappraisal," *American Quarterly* 23 (spring 1971).

3. David J. Pivar, *Purity Crusade: Sexual Morality and Social Control, 1868–1900* (Westport, CT: Greenwood Press, 1973), 266; for a representative statement on social

purity, see John Harvey Kellogg, *Social Purity: An Address Delivered at Battle Creek, Michigan, November 28, 1886* (Battle Creek, MI: Health Publishing, 1886).

4. Spencer quoted in Degler, *In Search of Human Nature*, 11.

5. James A. Field, "The Progress of Eugenics," *Quarterly Journal of Economics* 26 (November 1911): 45. The National Conference of Charities and Correction (NCCC) grew out of the American Social Science Association. Its annual conferences brought together leaders in social reform and its *Proceedings* were a widely circulated explication of current ideas. Social and economic issues dominated the conferences after 1910, and in 1917 the NCCC was reorganized as the National Conference of Social Work. See John D. Buenker and Edward R. Kantowicz, eds., *Historical Dictionary of the Progressive Era, 1890–1920* (New York: Greenwood Press, 1988).

6. See Huggins, *Protestants against Poverty*.

7. W. D. P. Bliss, "The Church and Social Reform Workers," *Outlook* 82 (1906): 122–125.

8. "Discussion on Provision for the Feebleminded"; Rev. M. Dana, "The Care and Disposal of Dependent Children," *Proceedings, 1888*, 401, 238.

9. Paul Phillips notes that the institutional church "was based upon the idea of expanded social services, from soup kitchens to banks to gymnasium classes, operated by churches in an effort to reestablish their central social role in the cities." See Phillips, *A Kingdom on Earth*, 70. Biographical information on McCulloch from Allen Johnson and Dumas Malone, eds., *Dictionary of American Biography* (New York: Charles Scribner's Sons, 1960), 6: 8; Genevieve C. Weeks, *Oscar Carleton McCulloch, 1843–1891: Preacher and Practitioner of Applied Christianity* (Indianapolis: Indianapolis Historical Society, 1976). Weeks downplays McCulloch's eugenic studies, devoting only a few pages to it in her biography. This is a remarkable omission given the importance McCulloch himself attached to his eugenics work.

10. Johnson and Malone, *Dictionary of American Biography*, 8.

11. Oscar C. McCulloch, "The Tribe of Ishmael: A Study in Social Degradation," *Proceedings, 1888*, 155. McCulloch revealed his theological training when he named this family the "Ishmaelites." This was not their real surname, but referred instead to the biblical story of Ishmael. See Genesis 16:11–12: "And the angel of the Lord said unto her, Behold, thou art with child, and shalt bear a son, and shalt call his name Ishmael, because the Lord hath heard thy affliction. And he will be a wild man; his hand will be against every man, and every man's hand against him; and he shall dwell in the presence of all his brethren."

12. Richard Lewis Dugdale, *The Jukes: A Study in Crime, Pauperism, Disease, and Heredity* (1877; reprint, New York: G.P. Putnam and Sons, 1895), 70. Kevles mentions Dugdale in *In the Name of Eugenics*, 71. Degler, *In Search of Human Nature*, also discusses Dugdale, although he incorrectly calls him "Robert Dugdale," 37–38. See also Rosenberg, *No Other Gods*, 45–46.

13. Dugdale, *The Jukes*, 26.

14. McCulloch, "The Tribe of Ishmael," 154.

15. Ibid., 155–156.

16. Ibid., 157.

17. Ibid., 158–159.

18. Weeks, *Oscar C. McCulloch*, 211–212.

19. Ibid., 175.

20. Rev. William Frederic Slocum, "Drunkards' Families," *Proceedings, 1888,* 131, 133.

21. Weeks, *Oscar C. McCulloch,* 211–212, 217.

22. See, for example, Casper Redfield, *Control of Heredity: A Study of the Genesis of Evolution and Degeneracy* (Chicago: Monarch Book, 1903), 208–211, which reprinted large passages from McCulloch's work (though Redfield misspells McCulloch's name as "McCullock"); Arthur H. Estabrook, "National Conference of Charities and Correction," *Eugenical News* 1 (June 1916): 42–43. Interest in McCulloch's and Dugdale's work remained strong enough that in 1911, one of the country's largest eugenics organizations reopened and reevaluated both family studies; see "The Jukes," *Eugenical News* 1 (October 1916): 72–73. There is even evidence that McCulloch might have had a direct personal influence on a man who would later become prominent in the eugenics movement. One of McCulloch's parishioners in the 1870s and 1880s was David Starr Jordan, then a professor at Butler University. Jordan went on to become a well-known spokesman for eugenics and president of Stanford University. He quoted extensively from McCulloch's work in his 1913 book, *Footnotes to Evolution: A Series of Popular Addresses on the Evolution of Life* (New York: D. Appleton, 1913), ch. 12; see also Weeks, *Oscar C. McCulloch,* xv.

23. See Weeks, *Oscar C. McCulloch,* 148; Robert Moats Miller, "Review of *Oscar C. McCulloch,*" *Journal of American History* 64 (1977): 815.

24. Weeks, *Oscar C. McCulloch.*

25. "Discussion on Provision for the Feeble-Minded," *Proceedings, 1888,* 402.

26. This example is discussed by Rosenberg, *No Other Gods,* 46.

27. The term "regeneration" appeared frequently in Social Gospel writings, for example. Walter Rauschenbusch claimed that a Christianity informed by the Social Gospel would have a "conscious regenerating influence on the common life of the race," making it "fitter for its social mission than ever before." Shailer Mathews argued that Social Christianity was dedicated to the "replacing of bad men by good men" and described the good ones as those "regenerated" by their awareness of the social teachings of Jesus. See Walter Rauschenbusch, *Christianity and the Social Crisis* (1907; reprint, New York: Harper and Row, 1964), 209–210; on Mathews, see W. King, "The Biblical Base of the Social Gospel," 73. Regeneration's opposite was "degeneration." See the essays in J. Edward Chamberlin and Sander L. Gilman, eds., *Degeneration: The Dark Side of Progress* (New York: Columbia University Press, 1985).

28. Samuel Z. Batten, "The Redemption of the Unfit," *American Journal of Sociology* 14 (September 1908): 246, 242, 233, 260. Ordained in 1886, Batten traveled in the mainstream currents of Social Gospel and progressive thought and was well-known among his coreligionists for his participation in organizations such as Walter Rauschenbusch's Brotherhood of the Kingdom for his writings on social issues; see Curtis, *A Consuming Faith,* 141–142.

29. Degler states that most social scientists had finally rejected Lamarckianism by about 1913. Degler, *In Search of Human Nature,* 20–23; see also Peter J. Bowler, *The Mendelian Revolution: The Emergence of Hereditarian Concepts in Modern Science and Society* (Baltimore: Johns Hopkins University Press, 1989), 47, 156. George Stocking finds a similar stance among American social scientists. They were "occupationally predisposed to resist" non-Lamarckian doctrines because the inheritance of acquired characteristics was so much more compatible with their "general

environmental orientation" than was strict hereditarianism. George W. Stocking Jr.,
"Lamarckianism in American Social Science, 1890–1915," *Journal of the History of Ideas* 23 (1962): 252.

30. Batten, "The Redemption of the Unfit," 258. Throughout the Old Testament, for example, God is referred to as the "Redeemer," and in the New Testament believers are reminded that redemption from sin is possible only through the blood of Christ. See, e.g., Isaiah 41:14 ("thy Redeemer, the Holy One of Israel"); Isaiah 49:26 ("I the Lord am thy Savior and thy Redeemer, the mighty one of Jacob"); and in the New Testament, Romans 3:24 ("the redemption that is in Christ"); Ephesians 1:7 ("In whom we have redemption through his blood, the forgiveness of sins"); Hebrews 9: 12 ("but by his own blood he entered in once into the holy place, having obtained eternal redemption for us").

31. Concern over the declining birthrate reached its peak in Britain at this time, and Meyer's book focused almost exclusively on this problem. Frederick B. Meyer, *Religion and Race-Regeneration* (London: Cassell, 1912), 7–8, 10. For background on British eugenics and the declining birthrate problem, see Soloway, *Demography and Degeneration;* Donald MacKenzie, "Eugenics in Britain," *Social Studies of Science* 6 (1976): 499–532. J. D. Douglas, ed., *Twentieth-Century Dictionary of Christian Biography* (Grand Rapids, MI: Baker Books, 1995), 254.

32. Meyer, *Religion and Race-Regeneration,* 20.

33. Amory Bradford, *Heredity and Christian Problems* (New York: Macmillan, 1895), 239. In the book, Bradford, a Congregational minister from New Jersey, also argued that Jesus had not been subject to the laws of human heredity due to his status as an "exception among men."

34. Meyer, *Religion and Race-Regeneration,* 24, 22.

35. Ibid., 53.

36. J. H. F. Peile, "Eugenics and the Church," *Eugenics Review* 1 (1909): 163. Soloway also describes Peile's contribution to the eugenics debate; see *Demography and Degeneration,* 82.

37. Peile, "Eugenics and the Church," 163–164, 166–170.

38. Ibid., 160.

39. "Heredity at Church Congress," *Nature* 84 (6 October 1910): 431.

40. Kevles, *In the Name of Eugenics,* 45–46.

41. This is the impression given by someone who knew Davenport; see M. Demerec, "Charles Benedict Davenport, June 1, 1866–February 18, 1944," Charles Davenport Papers, American Philosophical Society Library (hereafter cited as Davenport Papers, APS).

42. "Experimental Evolution on Long Island," *New York Times,* 3 June 1906, sec. 3, 1.

43. See Kevles, *In the Name of Eugenics,* ch. 3; Rosenberg, *No Other Gods,* 91–97.

44. Kevles, *In the Name of Eugenics,* 54–55.

45. Like the terms "feebleminded" and "fit," "degenerate" was an ambiguous but often used descriptor of people whom eugenicists believed carried bad hereditary material. The fear of "degeneration" of the race existed long before the eugenics movement and was a common metaphor in the biological sciences. See the essays in Chamberlin and Gilman, *Degeneration,* especially Nancy Stepan, "Biological Degeneration: Races and Proper Places."

46. Charles Davenport, *Eugenics* (New York: Henry Holt, 1910), 35.

47. Charles Davenport, *Heredity in Relation to Eugenics* (New York: Henry Holt, 1911), 254–255, 260.

48. "The Heredity Commission," *New York Times*, 20 May 1906, 8. The *Times* misprinted Hays's name as "William Hayes" in this article.

49. Barbara A. Kimmelman, "The American Breeders' Association: Genetics and Eugenics in an Agricultural Context, 1903–1913," *Social Studies of Science* 13 (1983): 163.

50. "The Heredity Commission," 8.

51. "Report of the Committee on Eugenics," *American Breeders' Magazine* 1 (1910): 128.

52. "Narrow Limits for Breeding Men," *American Breeders' Magazine* 1 (1910): 143–145; "The Field of Eugenics," *American Breeders' Magazine* 2 (1911): 140.

53. The Charities and Corrections crowd had proven receptive to hereditary explanations for social problems since the 1880s, and by this time included discussions of eugenics in their conferences as a matter of course. H. E. Jordan, "Heredity as a Factor in the Improvement of Social Conditions," *American Breeders' Magazine* 2 (1911): 249–250.

54. Ibid., 250.

55. Galton, "Eugenics as a Factor in Religion," 70.

56. H. Jordan, "Heredity as a Factor in the Improvement of Social Conditions," 250.

57. Caleb W. Saleeby, *Parenthood and Race Culture* (1909; reprint, New York: Moffat, Yard, 1911), 17–18, 351–352.

58. Saleeby was one of the more outspoken members of a group of eugenicists who believed that alcohol was a racial poison. In their view, alcoholism was a vice that led to the dissolution of the drinker and the degeneration of his or her offspring through hereditary transmission of this tendency (ibid., 315–318); Bartlett C. Jones, "Prohibition and Eugenics," *Journal of the History of Medicine and Allied Science* 18 (1963): 158–172.

59. Saleeby, *Parenthood and Race Culture*, 352.

60. G. Stanley Hall, "Eugenics: Its Ideals and What It Is Going to Do," *Religious Education* 6 (June 1911): 157.

61. One of his students was eugenicist Henry H. Goddard, the man responsible for bringing the Binet-Simon intelligence tests to the United States in 1908, and later for publishing one of the most enduring eugenic family studies of the twentieth century, *The Kallikak Family*. It is likely that Goddard and other students gained from Hall not only a respect for eugenics but an understanding of its links to religion. Biographical information from Johnson and Malone, *Dictionary of American Biography*, 127–130.

62. For example, speaking before the American Social Hygiene Association in 1914, he said that from "a prophylactic point of view . . . the chief need of youth is religion, define it as you will, for any is better than none, and the need of all our work would be far less if religion had not lapsed to a subordinate place in the life of the average youth." G. Stanley Hall, "Education and the Social Hygiene Movement," *Social Hygiene* 1 (December 1914): 35.

63. G. Stanley Hall, *Jesus, the Christ, in the Light of Psychology*, 2 vols. (New York:

Doubleday, Page, 1917), vol. 1, 36–37, 260. Historian R. Laurence Moore has noted
that the presumed audience for much of Hall's work in the *American Journal of Religious Psychology and Education* (which he edited from 1904 to 1915) was seminary professors and theology students, ministers, missionaries, and Sunday School teachers.
See R. Laurence Moore, "Secularization: Religion and the Social Sciences," in W.
Hutchison, *Between the Times*, 234.

64. G. Hall, "Eugenics," 154.

65. Ibid., 153–155.

66. Ibid., 157.

67. Charles Davenport, "Eugenics: A Subject for Investigation Rather Than Instruction," n.d.; Davenport Papers, APS. Kenneth Ludmerer argues that Davenport
was inconsistent in his condemnations of eugenics popularizers and propagandists,
but I found no evidence of inconsistencies during these early years of the eugenics
movement. He was very suspicious of their work and complained about them often.
See Ludmerer, *Genetics and American Society*, 53.

68. Rosenberg, *No Other Gods*, 10.

69. John Williams Gibson, *Golden Thoughts on Chastity and Procreation* (Naperville, IL: J.L. Nichols, 1903).

70. Mr. and Mrs. John Williams Gibson, *Social Purity; Or the Life of the Home
and the Nation Including Heredity, Prenatal Influences, etc. etc.* (New York: J.L. Nichols,
1903), ix, 33.

71. Ibid., 19–20. The biblical passage cited is Exodus 20:5.

72. Gibson and Gibson, *Social Purity*, 19–20, 26. The Gibsons did not provide
direct citations for the biblical passages they quoted, presumably because they assumed their readers were familiar with the stories. The above passage is from Exodus
34:7. References to the decline of France and other European countries were not uncommon in Progressive Era literature. With a belief in man's ability to progress came
a sense (among Americans) that the United States was a nation on the rise, whereas
Europe was a continent in decline. See Wiebe, *The Search for Order*, 226. France was a
favorite target in such discussions. During the late nineteenth century, social purity
reformers expressed particular dread about French immorality, calling it "a contagious
disease." Reformers such as Anthony Comstock lobbied to keep French novels and
French art, deemed immoral, out of the United States. Pivar, *Purity Crusade*, 161.

73. Gibson and Gibson, *Social Purity*, ix; the Bible verse is John 8:32.

74. Redfield held more than fifty patents, mainly for improvements to machinery. His designs for machinery won him praise at the 1893 World's Fair in Chicago,
and he applied the principles of mechanics to his studies of heredity in later books,
such as *Dynamic Evolution* (1913) and *Human Heredity* (Chicago: Heredity Publishing,
1921). Biographical information from *National Cyclopedia of American Biography* (New
York: James T. White, 1930), 100: 425. Redfield, *Control of Heredity*, 17.

75. Redfield, *Control of Heredity*, 122–123. Redfield labeled Moses one of history's
"One Hundred Greatest Men," a list that also included Mohammed, Confucius, and
Buddha.

76. Redfield, for example, had an interesting view of the laws of heredity—a variation on Lamarckianism—which he labeled "use-inheritance theory." Counter to the
scientific claims of eugenicists, Redfield believed that traits could be passed from parent to child *only* after the parent had himself made use of the trait. Hence, he con-

cluded that children born to older parents were more likely to have stronger mental capacities, the wisdom of the parents' older age and experience having accumulated to a more concentrated degree in the child. His evidence for this was the biblical figure of Solomon, who, he claimed, had been a "late reproduction" who had inherited his wisdom from his father, David (ibid., 190).

77. See, for example, Hester Pendleton, *The Parent's Guide: Or, Human Development through Inherited Tendencies* (1871; reprint, New York: Garland, 1984). On child-rearing advice campaigns, see Richard A. Meckel, *Save the Babies: American Public Health Reform and the Prevention of Infant Mortality, 1850–1929* (Baltimore: Johns Hopkins University Press, 1990).

78. A. L. McCrimmon, *The Child in the Normal Home* (Chicago: American Baptist Publication Society, 1910), 3–4.

79. Ibid., 10.

80. W. J. Truitt, M.D., *Eugenics* (1904; reprint, Marietta, OH: S.A. Mullikan, 1917), 3. Fallows would participate in future discussions of eugenics. His interest in the subject likely was sparked by his experience as president of the Board of Managers of the Illinois State Reformatory and as a social reformer; he served as rector of St. Paul's Church in Chicago from 1879 until his death in 1922. See Alice Katherine Fallows, *Everybody's Bishop* (New York: J.H. Sears, 1927).

81. Pivar, *Purity Crusade*, 170.

82. Christopher Lasch, *Haven in a Heartless World: The Family Besieged* (New York: Basic Books, 1977), 8–10, 13–16.

83. Ibid., 15.

84. "Unrelenting Opponent of Sexual Slavery," *Lucifer the Light Bearer*, 24 May 1906, 1; "Greatest of All Reforms," *Lucifer the Light Bearer*, 3d series, 30 July 1903, 2. See also *American Journal of Eugenics* 2 (August 1908): 202–203.

85. *Lucifer the Light-Bearer*, 26 April 1906, 1. A federal obscenity statute known as the Comstock Act (after reformer Anthony Comstock) became part of the Federal Criminal Code in 1873. It prohibited the use of the public mails for sending "obscene, lewd, or lascivious" books, pamphlets, pictures, or other publications of "an indecent character." Twenty-four states passed legislation conforming to these guidelines. See Pivar, *Purity Crusade*.

86. *American Journal of Eugenics* 2 (September–October 1908): 237–238; Moses Harman, "Yesterday, Today, Tomorrow," *American Journal of Eugenics* 1 (July 1907): 30.

87. *American Journal of Eugenics* 1(September 1907): 166–171; (August 1907): 97.

88. Martin Pernick makes this point about eugenics films made in the early twentieth century. See *The Black Stork*, 14.

89. Field, "The Progress of Eugenics," 39.

90. Francis Galton, "Why a Man with a Long Pedigree Is Inclined to Ferocity," *Current Literature* 42 (January 1907): 102–103.

91. David Starr Jordan, "The Blood of the Nation: A Study of the Decay of Races through the Survival of the Unfit," *Popular Science Monthly* 59 (May 1901): 97–98.

92. Thomas J. Gerrard, "The Catholic Church and Race Culture," *Dublin Review* 149 (July 1911): 67.

93. Webb, a strong supporter of eugenics, is quoted in Hasian, *The Rhetoric of Eugenics*, 90.

94. On the history of institutionalization, see David J. Rothman, *The Discovery of*

the Asylum (Boston: Little, Brown, 1971) and *Conscience and Convenience: The Asylum and Its Alternatives in Progressive America* (Boston: Little, Brown, 1980).

95. Text of the Indiana law quoted in Reilly, *The Surgical Solution*, 46–47, 30–33. See also Donald K. Pickens, "The Sterilization Movement: The Search for Purity in Mind and State," *Phylon* 28 (spring 1967): 78–94. A typical statement of support for sterilization at this time can be found in Walter N. Thayer, "What May We Do with Our Criminals?" *Survey* 24 (9 July 1910): 587–589. I discuss sterilization in more detail in ch. 5.

96. Reilly, *The Surgical Solution*, 30–31.

97. Theo. Laboure, "A Backward Glimpse over the Articles on Vasectomy," *Ecclesiastical Review* 48 (May 1913): 555. Over twenty-four articles were written for this debate, with the vast majority opposing sterilization; nevertheless, Donovan's and Laboure's support is noteworthy as it demonstrates the diversity of Catholic opinion on this issue.

98. "The Morality and Lawfulness of Vasectomy," *Ecclesiastical Review* 44 (May 1911): 564.

99. Ibid., 569.

100. Laboure, "A Backward Glimpse," 556–557; "The Morality and Lawfulness of Vasectomy," 563.

101. "The Morality and Lawfulness of Vasectomy," 570.

102. Austin O'Malley, "Vasectomy in Defectives," *Ecclesiastical Review* 44 (June 1911): 704–705.

103. "The Morality and Lawfulness of Vasectomy," 567.

104. It is worth noting, however, that these Catholic writers focused on *criminal degeneracy* as a justification for sterilization (and they all presumed that a criminal forfeited some of his freedom by breaking the law). They did not yet directly discuss sterilization of *noncriminal* degenerates.

105. Gerrard, "The Catholic Church and Race Culture," 58.

106. Thomas J. Gerrard, *The Church and Eugenics* (St. Louis: B. Herder, 1912), 9.

107. Ibid., 23–24. The passage is Matthew 6:33: "But seek ye first the kingdom of God and his righteousness; and all these things shall be added unto you."

108. Ibid., 37–38.

109. Ibid., 37.

110. Catholics would make a similar argument about the Church and hygiene in the 1920s. "The Catholic Church had always taught hygiene . . . she went considerably farther than the hygienists by constituting herself an enforcement agency . . . she had a definite program of enforcement . . . She had thus anticipated the modern hygienic movement by many centuries!" The author of this statement, R. A. Muttkowski, Ph.D., then outlined the hygienic benefits of Advent, Lent, and Holy Week. "The Practical Hygiene of the Church," *Thought* 1 (June 1926): 139.

111. Gerrard, *The Church and Eugenics*, 41, 44, 46.

112. Thomas Gerrard, "Sanctity and Racial Betterment," *Catholic World* 95 (1912): 726–728.

113. Gerrard's construction of a Catholic eugenics did not signal an uncritical embrace of the eugenics movement. Like most Catholic leaders, he opposed eugenic sterilization because he considered it unnecessarily severe, preferring eugenic segregation of the unfit as a preventive measure. Gerrard, *The Church and Eugenics*, 33–35.

114. W. Hope Jones, "Review of *The Church and Eugenics*," *Eugenics Review* 4 (January 1913): 412.

115. J. W. Slaughter, "Selection in Marriage," *Eugenics Review* (October 1909): 158–159.

116. Galton, "Eugenics: Its Definition, Scope, and Aims," 1.

117. William E. Kellicott, *The Social Direction of Human Evolution: Outline of the Science of Eugenics* (New York: D. Appleton, 1911), 230–231; John M. Coulter, "The Religious and Character Value of the Curriculum: Biology," *Religious Education* 6 (December 1911): 365–368. Coulter also praised the Mosaic code for upholding certain "biological laws," noting that "some of the most important precepts of religion are statements of biological truth"; likewise, he reminded scientists that Jesus was an appealing example because he had "the most scientific attitude towards religion that any religious leader has ever shown."

118. Field, "The Progress of Eugenics," 1.

119. Gerrard, *The Church and Eugenics*, 26.

2. CERTIFYING EUGENIC PURITY

1. "Two 'Health Marriages': Chicago Idea for a Perfect Union Meets Quick Response," *New York Times*, 11 April 1912, 1. Dean Sumner's statement read in full: "Persons desiring to be married at the cathedral will be expected to conform with the following regulations: (1) Both must have been baptized; (2) neither may have a divorced husband or wife living; (3) someone known to the cathedral clergy must vouch for the identity of each; (4) they must bring at least two persons who know them to act as witnesses of the ceremony; (5) each must present a certificate properly signed by a reputable physician to the effect that he or she has neither an incurable nor communicable disease and is mentally normal; (6) arrangements must be made at least three days before the day appointed for the ceremony, in order that the banns may be published at three public services of the cathedral." See *The Churchman* 107 (25 January 1913): 116.

2. "The Restriction of Marriage," *The Outlook* 100 (6 April 1912): 760. Sumner's activities have been virtually ignored by historians. One exception (although Sumner is mentioned only in passing) is Diane B. Paul, *Controlling Human Heredity: 1865 to the Present* (Amherst, NY: Humanity Books, 1995), 10.

3. Sumner later earned a D.D. from Northwestern University. Biographical information from Johnson and Malone, *Dictionary of American Biography* (New York: Charles Scribner's Sons, 1943), vol. 21, supplement 1, 678–679; *Who's Who in America* (Chicago: Marquis Publications, 1966), 1: 1206; *The Churchman* 149 (15 September 1935): 25.

4. John Henry Hopkins, D.D., S.T.D., *The Great Forty Years in the Diocese of Chicago, 1893–1934* (Chicago: Centenary Fund, 1936), 125. Sumner was also involved with the Chicago Board of Education's efforts to teach sex hygiene in the public schools, a campaign spearheaded by superintendent Ella Flagg Young; on this campaign, see Jeffrey P. Moran, "Modernism Gone Mad: Sex Education Comes to Chicago, 1913," *Journal of American History* 83 (September 1996): 481–513.

5. "Dean Sumner," pamphlet, Redpath Chautauqua Collection, University of

Iowa Libraries [19-?]: http://sdrcdata.lib.uiowa.edu/libsdrc/details.jsp?id=/sumner/1, accessed 3 August 2002.

6. Chicago Vice Commission, *The Social Evil in Chicago: A Study of Existing Conditions* (Chicago: Gunthorp-Warren, 1911); Graham Taylor, "Police Efficiency the First Effect of Vice Inquiries," *Survey* 28 (1912): 136, 139. See also Louis Filler, *The Muckrakers* (1939; reprint, Stanford: Stanford University Press, 1976), 286–287, 242; Allan Brandt, *No Magic Bullet: A Social History of Venereal Disease in the United States Since 1880* (New York: Oxford University Press, 1985), 50.

7. Winston Churchill, *The Inside of the Cup*: ftp://ftp.ibiblio.org/pub/docs/books/gutenberg/etext04/wc27w10.txt, accessed 9 September 2002. See also May, *The End of American Innocence*, 49.

8. Brandt, *No Magic Bullet*, 8, 19, 50–51. Antivice crusades must also be understood in the context of society's concern over the sexuality of young unmarried women in the cities, as Mary Odem has shown in *Delinquent Daughters: Protecting and Policing Adolescent Female Sexuality in the United States, 1885–1920* (Chapel Hill: University of North Carolina Press, 1995), especially ch. 4, "The 'Delinquent Girl' and Progressive Reform."

9. Brandt, *No Magic Bullet*, 47–48. Walter Lippmann, *A Preface to Politics* (New York: Mitchell Kennerley, 1913), 135–136.

10. "Must be Normal and Well to Wed," *New York Times*, 25 March 1912, 3. Information on Anderson from Hopkins, *The Great Forty Years in the Diocese of Chicago*, 62, 69.

11. "Must be Normal and Well to Wed," 3.

12. Evangelical (conservative) Protestants had different concerns about Sumner's plan and related liberal proposals for social reform, which I discuss later.

13. "The Restriction of Marriage," 760. Fallows was enthusiastic about eugenics. In 1904 he wrote the introduction to a hefty book about eugenics that went through five printings. In it he declared eugenics a "profound and far-reaching question" of human nature. Truitt, *Eugenics*, ch. 1.

14. "Bishop Whitehead Approves," *New York Times*, 26 March 1912, 11.

15. "Should Ministers Marry the Physically Unfit?" *New York Times*, 2 June 1912, 10; "Pastors for Eugenics," *New York Times*, 6 June 1913, 10.

16. "Should Ministers Marry the Physically Unfit?" 10; "Eugenics Supported by the Church," *Current Literature* 52 (May 1912): 565; biographical information on Hirsch in Bernard Martin, "The Social Philosophy of Emil G. Hirsch," *American Jewish Archives Journal* 6 (1954): 151–165.

17. Rudolph I. Coffee, "Pittsburgh Clergy and the Social Evil," *Survey* 29 (1912–1913): 815; *Survey* 35 (1913): 97; biographical information from *National Cyclopedia of American Biography*, vol 42.

18. "Will Marry Healthy Only: 200 Chicago Pastors Indorse Plan to Have Doctor's Certificate," *New York Times*, 28 May 1912, 1.

19. "Eugenics Supported by the Church," 565.

20. "Should Ministers Marry the Physically Unfit?" 4.

21. "Will Wed Only the Sound: Montclair Pastor Will Insist on a Certificate of Good Health," *New York Times*, 5 May 1913, 1; "Only Healthy Can Marry: Montclair Pastor Told to Perform Ceremony for None Other," *New York Times*, 15 May 1913, 1.

Rev. Weirs later became head of the New York Liberal Ministers' Association Committee on Eugenics, mentioned earlier.

22. "Pastor Favors Eugenics: The Rev. R. C. Hull Will Ask Congregation to Adopt His Views," *New York Times,* 14 July 1913, 7. Rev. Charles L. Walworth of the Morrow Memorial Methodist Church in Maplewood, New Jersey, publicly advocated eugenic marriage, and in New York, two ministers who, according to the *New York Times,* performed the "largest number of fashionable marriages" in the city (Rev. Charles Slattery of Grace Church and Rev. William P. Merrill of Brick Presbyterian Church) endorsed Sumner's proposal. See *Eugenical News* 1 (March 1916): 18; "Pastors for Eugenics," 10.

23. "Pastor Adopts Eugenics: Won't Perform Marriages for the Physically Unfit," *New York Times,* 26 May 1913, 1.

24. "Must Prove Health: No More Weddings at Fort Washington Church without Certificates," *New York Times,* 3 June 1913, 9; " 'Health Marriages' More Frequent," *Literary Digest* (21 February 1914): 384.

25. "Eugenists Taking Courage," *New York Times,* 22 May 1913, 10.

26. "Bishops Approve Plan to Apply Eugenics to Marriage," *New York Times,* 31 March 1912, 1.

27. The *Literary Digest* reported that "churches all over the country are discussing and voting on the question"; see "Health Marriages More Frequent," 384; "Apparently the Plan Works Well," *New York Times,* 11 April 1913, 8.

28. Judging by the number of special sermons he preached in various churches and the many requests for his presence at religious conferences and meetings, Sumner's standing and prestige in the Protestant Episcopal Church were not diminished by his eugenic reform activities. During the Lent and Easter seasons that immediately followed his March 1912 decree, he spoke on subjects ranging from poverty, the social evil, and childhood education to the development of industry and "Dependent, Defective, and Delinquent Children" at several venues in Chicago; Albany, New York; Concord, New Hampshire; and Charleston, South Carolina. His support for eugenic marriage also led to his appointment in 1915 to the Eugenics Committee on Education and Extension of the American Genetic Association (formerly the American Breeders' Association). Sumner's many activities are chronicled in the pages of *The Churchman* 107 (1 February 1913): 147; (15 February 1913): 212; (8 March 1913): 312, 314; (15 March 1913): 343; (29 March 1913): 420; (3 May 1913): 586; see also *Journal of Heredity* 5 (August 1914): 340.

29. Walter T. Sumner, "The Church and Moral Progress," in *Social Service at the General Convention of 1913* (New York: Joint Commission on Social Service of the Protestant Episcopal Church, Church Missions House, 1913), 23, 25–26.

30. "A Bishop's Indictment of Present-Day Christianity," *Current Literature* 51 (July 1911): 65–66; biographical information on Williams from obituary in *New York Times,* 15 February 1923, 19.

31. *The Outlook* 105 (1913): 466, 520–521.

32. William McGuire King, "The Emergence of Social Gospel Radicalism: The Methodist Case," in Marty, *Modern American Protestantism,* 6: 223.

33. *The Churchman* 108 (November 1913): 690.

34. Joint Commission on Social Service of the Protestant Episcopal Church, *So-*

cial Service at the Episcopal Church (New York: Church Missions House, 1914); *The Churchman* 108 (November 1913): 736.

35. *Social Service at the General Convention of 1913*, appendix D.

36. *The Churchman* 107 (5 April 1913): 454.

37. *Survey* 31 (1913–1914): 95; Huggins, *Protestants against Poverty*. The New York Federation of Churches, for example, sponsored an extensive data collection project in Manhattan. Federation workers and volunteers gathered statistics on the character of Manhattan's population, including the number of foreign-born whites and the extent of the problem of "defective children" in the area. By 1913, Congregationalists had created a supervisory Commission on Social Service that included as part of its draft objectives "to study the social waste caused by vice, crime, and bad economic conditions." See "Telling the Churches Where They Are," *Survey* 29 (1912–1913): 689–692; Congregationalist information reprinted in White and Hopkins, *The Social Gospel*, 191–192.

38. "A Methodist Call for Social Service," *Survey* 28 (1912–1913): 261; Thomas F. Gailor, "The Power of Religion in the Home," *The Churchman* 107 (29 November 1913): 731.

39. John M. Glenn, "The Church and Social Work," *The Churchman* 108 (23 August 1913): 247. This is a reprint of an address Glenn delivered at the National Conference of Charities and Corrections held in Seattle that year.

40. Survey results reported in Szasz, *The Divided Mind of Protestant America*, 43.

41. *The Churchman* 107 (24 May 1913): 681; (7 June 1913): 1278; (14 June 1913): 777; (21 June 1913): 800, 809; (28 June 1913): 842; (30 August 1913): 280.

42. *The Churchman* 107 (21 June 1913): 809; (14 June 1913): 777.

43. "Petitions, Resolutions, and Memorials," *The Churchman* 108 (18 October 1913): 520.

44. "Health Certificates for Matrimony," *Literary Digest* 46 (7 June 1913): 1278.

45. Reform Jewish support also rested on a similar embrace of the secular social reform impulse, despite the fact that their theology was distinct in many ways from the Protestant Social Gospel.

46. "Gibbons on Health Test: Against Requiring Doctor's Certificate from Couples before Marrying," *New York Times*, 29 March 1912, 10.

47. "Wildcat Eugenism," *America* 9 (30 August 1913): 495. For a more detailed exposition of Catholic views on marriage at this time, see H. A. Brann, "The Catholic Doctrine of Marriage," *American Catholic Quarterly Review* 8 (July 1883): 385–404: "As marriage is a sacrament, though having the nature of a contract, the Catholic Church claims exclusive control over it, and permits the State to legislate only with regard to its civil effects. If the State does more than this, the Church considers it an intrusion."

48. "Eugenics Supported by the Church," 566; Pernick, *The Black Stork*, 101.

49. "Health Certificates for Matrimony," 1278–1279.

50. For expressing his opposition, Campbell was pilloried as an antiscientific reactionary by the *New York Times*. In a June 1913 editorial, the paper said that by "refusing to lead their flocks" and rejecting the "newer light" science had shed on marriage, ministers such as Rev. Campbell endangered the health of the race. See "Has No Use for Eugenics: Methodist Says Churches Are Running Riot on Marriage," *New*

York Times, 10 June 1913, 8; "His Question Needs Amendment," *New York Times*, 11 June 1913, 8.

51. Bell was a well-known leader in the Protestant Episcopal Church, a prolific writer, and president of St. Stephen's College from 1920 to 1933. In 1946 he became canon of the Cathedral where Dean Sumner had made his mark, SS. Peter and Paul in Chicago. For biographical information, see *National Cyclopedia of American Biography*, 43: 202–203. B. Bell, "Social Service and the Churches," 164; Marsden, *Fundamentalism and American Culture*, 92.

52. Sunday quoted in Lyle W. Dorsett, *Billy Sunday and the Redemption of Urban America* (Grand Rapids, MI: William B. Eerdmans, 1991), 48–49; Marty, *Modern American Religion*, 1: 217.

53. The years 1910–1915 also witnessed the publication of twelve volumes called *The Fundamentals*, meant to stand as evangelical Protestants' "Testimony to the Truth." Szasz, "Protestantism and the Search for Stability," 98; Marsden, *Fundamentalism and American Culture*, 86, 118–119.

54. "Marriage and Physical Examinations," *The Presbyterian* 83 (2 July 1913): 8. "The Brotherhood Convention," *The Churchman* 108 (11 October 1913): 481–485; Rt. Rev. David Greer, "The Redemption of Social Service," *The Churchman* 108 (12 November 1913): 69; Rev. G. A. Carstensen, "The Church Congress," *The Churchman* 108 (12 April 1913): 476.

55. "A Warning Safely Disregarded," *New York Times*, 29 May 1913, 10.

56. *Survey* 28 (1912): 766; eight states prohibited marriage by imbeciles and the feebleminded; fifteen states barred the idiotic; nine prohibited epileptics from marrying; and four states prohibited those with venereal diseases from contracting marriage. Kansas and Connecticut allowed marriage if the afflicted woman was over 45 years of age. Jesse Spaulding Smith, "Marriage, Sterilization and Commitment Laws Aimed at Decreasing Mental Deficiency," *Journal of the American Institute of Criminal Law and Criminology* 5 (September 1914): 364–370; Stevenson Smith et al., *A Summary of the Laws of the Several States . . .* , Bulletin of the University of Washington, No. 82, Bailey and Babette Gatzert Foundation for Child Welfare, May 1914.

57. Dr. A. Mjoen, "Legal Certification of Health before Marriage," *Eugenics Review* 4 (January 1913): 356–362.

58. Fred S. Hall, *Medical Certification for Marriage: An Account of the Administration of the Wisconsin Marriage Law as It Relates to the Venereal Diseases* (New York: Russell Sage Foundation, 1925), 13, 81.

59. Ibid., 17.

60. "Wisconsin Ousts Cupid!" *New York Times*, 2 January 1914, 1; *Wisconsin Medical Journal* article referred to in William F. Snow, "The Swing of the Pendulum on Sex Hygiene," *Survey* 32 (1914): 6.

61. "Wisconsin Ousts Cupid!" *Peterson v. Widule* (Wisconsin, 17 June 1914, 147 N.W. 966), in "Decisions of State Courts on Points of Public Law," *American Political Science Review* 8 (November 1914): 680. The original 1913 law was replaced by a revised law in 1915, which provided free laboratory services by the state and gave the examining physician more discretion in determining whether laboratory tests were needed.

62. *New York Times*, 23 March 1915, 1; 27 March 1912, 8; "The Cost of Eugenics," *The Nation* 97 (14 August 1913): 137. Rhode Island also passed a resolution, but

it linked eugenic marriage and miscegenation; the resolution "prohibited the marriage of Caucasians with Negroes" and required health certificates for marriage for all
potential brides and grooms. In 1917, New York passed a eugenic marriage law that
required sworn statements to the effect that the contracting parties did not have communicable diseases. Falsification of such statements was considered perjury under
the law. See "Only Healthy May Wed," *New York Times*, 18 May 1917, 12.

63. "Eugenic Marriage Plan for Paterson," *New York Times*, 5 November 1915, 9;
The Survey 29 (1912): 348; "Eugenic Marriage Law for Virginia," *New York Times*, 17
January 1914, 18.

64. Judge Sabath's evidence for the incompetence of one of these women was
the fact that she appeared confused in the courtroom and "made no objection when
the physician summoned by the City Psychopathic Laboratory stuck a pin in her forehead." See "Need for Eugenics Law," *Survey* 34 (1915): 532. As early as 1912, the Illinois State Conference of Charities and Correction had a Eugenics Committee that
passed resolutions in favor of marriage restrictions for the feebleminded. Judge Goodnow quoted in Michael Willrich, "The Two Percent Solution: Eugenic Jurisprudence
and the Socialization of American Law, 1900–1930," *Law and History Review* 16
(spring 1998): 101. On the issue of delinquent girls and feeblemindedness, see Odem,
Delinquent Daughters and Rafter, *Creating Born Criminals*.

65. Dr. Oscar Dowling, "The Marriage Health Certificate: A Deeply Rooted Social Problem," *American Journal of Public Health* 5 (November 1915): 1140.

66. "Resume of Legislation on Matters Relating to Social Hygiene Considered
by the Various States During 1914," *Social Hygiene* 1 (December 1914): 93–107.

67. "Wildcat Eugenism," editorial, *America* 9 (30 August 1913): 494; Thomas J.
Gerrard, "Eugenics and Catholic Teaching," *Catholic World* 95 (June 1912): 297, 300.

68. *New York Times*, 26 March 1912, 12; emphasis added.

69. "Doctor Ridicules Laws for Eugenics," *New York Times*, 21 June 1914, 14.

70. Charles Davenport, "Marriage Laws and Customs," in *Problems in Eugenics:
First International Eugenics Congress, 1912* (London: Eugenics Education Society, 1912),
154. Charles Davenport, *State Laws Limiting Marriage Selection Examined in the Light of
Eugenics*, Eugenics Record Office Bulletin No.9, Eugenics Record Office, New York,
1913.

71. Samuel G. Smith, "Eugenics and the New Social Consciousness," in *Problems
in Eugenics*, 482; Alice Hamilton assessed Conklin's *Science* essay in "Heredity and
Responsibility," *Survey* 29 (1912–1913): 866; Caleb Saleeby's thoughts on health certificates were discussed in a book review in *Survey* 28 (1912): 106. One eugenicist, Roswell Johnson of the University of Pittsburgh, seized on the "selectional aspect" of venereal disease to argue that efforts like Dean Sumner's prevented nature from taking
its course among the immoral. By engaging in immoral behavior and contracting disease, Johnson reasoned, these individuals proved their inferior quality and often
brought sterility upon themselves; hence, "the decrease of their racial contribution is
directly a gain rather than a loss." Roswell Johnson, "Eugenic Aspect of Sexual Immorality," *Journal of Heredity* 8 (March 1917): 121.

72. "The Breeding of Men," *American Breeders' Magazine* 2 (1911): 298.

73. "The Marriage License Clerk," *American Breeders' Magazine* 4 (1913): 59, 77.

74. Kimmelman, "The American Breeders' Association," 190.

75. Editorial in the *Medical Record*, reprinted in *Journal of Heredity* 5 (February

1914): 91; condemnation issued by State Charities Commission of Illinois in its Fourth Annual Report, reprinted in *Journal of Heredity* 5 (October 1914): 430.

76. W. C. Rucker, "More 'Eugenic' Laws," *Journal of Heredity* 6 (May 1915); *Journal of Social Hygiene* 1 (June 1915): 490–491.

77. C. Davenport, *Heredity in Relation to Eugenics*, 258.

78. In one of his speeches on health certificates, Sumner quoted part of a poem written by Ella Wheeler Wilcox which placed the blame for feeble children squarely on the shoulders of men:

> Folks talk too much of a soul
> From heavenly joys debarred
> And not enough of the babes unborn
> By the sins of their fathers scarred.

Walter T. Sumner, "The Health Certificate: A Safeguard against Vicious Selection in Marriage," in *Proceedings of the First National Conference on Race Betterment* (Battle Creek, MI: Race Betterment Foundation, 1914), 509, 513. Dowling, "The Marriage Health Certificate," 1141; Edward L. Keyes, "Can the Law Protect Matrimony from Disease?" *Social Hygiene* 1 (December 1914): 10, 13.

79. Bernard C. Roloff, "The 'Eugenic' Marriage Laws of Wisconsin, Michigan, and Indiana," *Social Hygiene* 6 (April 1920): 233–234. The Wisconsin Supreme Court clarified provisions of Wisconsin's Uniform Evasion Act, as this part of the law was called, in a 1920 case, *Lyannes v. Lyannes*, 177 N.W. 683. See "Eugenic Marriage Law Has No Extraterritorial Effect," *Social Hygiene* 6 (October 1920): 619–620.

80. Roloff, "The 'Eugenic' Marriage Laws," 230–231.

81. Blumer quoted in Ian Robert Dowbiggin, *Keeping America Sane: Psychiatry and Eugenics in the United States and Canada, 1880–1940* (Ithaca, NY: Cornell University Press, 1997), 94.

82. Larson, *Sex, Race, and Science*, 100; Larson notes that along with segregation, sterilization, and immigration restriction, the public considered marriage restrictions a major element of the eugenics movement.

83. Pernick, *The Black Stork*, 51, 53.

84. Aaron Hoffman, "Does Anybody Want a Comedian: A Monologue," part 3, 1915, Library of Congress Rare Book and Special Collections Division: http://memory .loc.gov, digital ID (h)varseps38313, accessed 3 August 2002.

85. "Banns Law Proposed in Georgia," *Journal of Heredity* 7 (September 1916): 415.

86. "The Great Unmarried," *Journal of Heredity* 7 (December 1916): 559.

87. A. E. Hamilton, "What to Say about Marriage?" *Journal of Heredity* 7 (February 1916): 78–79.

88. A. E. Hamilton, "Eugenics," *Pedagogical Seminary* 21 (March 1914): 35–36; *American Breeders' Magazine* 4 (1913): 63. By 1916 the list of colleges and universities offering courses in eugenics included Agnes Scott, Antioch, Barnard, Bryn Mawr, Columbia, Colgate, Cornell, Dartmouth, Harvard, Johns Hopkins, Indiana State, Louisiana State, MIT, Missouri Wesleyan, Monmouth, Northwestern, Oberlin, Ohio State, Penn State, Princeton, Radcliffe, Rutgers, Smith, Swarthmore, Tulane, the Universities of California, Chicago, Denver, Kansas, Kentucky, Maine, Michigan, Minnesota,

Pennsylvania, Texas, Virginia, Wisconsin, and Wyoming, Vassar College, Wellesley, and Yale. *Eugenical News* 1 (1916): 18.

89. Morton A. Aldrich et al., *Eugenics: Twelve University Lectures* (New York: Dodd, Mead, 1914), xiii.

90. Ibid., 73–74, 135–136, 228, 314–315.

91. Allan F. Davis, *Spearheads for Reform: The Social Settlements and the Progressive Movement, 1890–1914* (New York: Oxford University Press, 1967), 12, xii. Ray Ginger, *Age of Excess: The United States from 1877 to 1914* (New York: Macmillan, 1965), 90.

92. Correspondence in Davenport Papers, APS. The Davenport brothers came from a devout family. Their father was a temperance advocate and an ardent abolitionist, as well as a founder and elder in Henry Ward Beecher's Plymouth Congregational Church in Brooklyn. The family began each day with prayer. See Kevles, *In the Name of Eugenics*, 49–50, 52. Kevles mentions William Davenport but neglects to discuss the eagerness with which he applied himself to compiling eugenic family studies.

93. Higham, *Strangers in the Land*, 119. Higham also notes, "The Italians were often thought to be the most degraded of the European newcomers. They were swarthy, more than half of them were illiterate, and almost all were victims of a standard of living lower than that of any of the other prominent nationalities. They were the ragpickers and the poorest of the common laborers" (66).

94. William Davenport to Charles Davenport, 8 March 1919; 24 March 1911; Charles Davenport to William Davenport, 7 June 1911, Davenport Papers, APS.

95. Charles B. Davenport, *The Family History Book*, Eugenics Record Office Bulletin No. 7 (Cold Spring Harbor, NY: Eugenics Record Office, September 1912), 46, 48–49, 50–51. Charles also used data gathered by William in his study *Inheritance of Stature* (Cold Spring Harbor, NY: Eugenics Record Office Bulletin No. 18, 1917), originally published in *Genetics* 2 (July 1917): 313–389.

96. William Davenport to Charles Davenport, 22 October 1921; 18 February 1922, Davenport Papers, APS.

97. The definitive guide for these studies was Charles Davenport and Harry H. Laughlin, *How to Make a Eugenical Family Study* (Cold Spring Harbor, NY: Eugenics Record Office Bulletin No. 13, 1915). ERO fieldworker Wilhelmine E. Key, for example, wrote a series of articles for the *Journal of Heredity* on "Better American Families" which mapped out a plan for building eugenic families. See "Better American Families, 1–3," *Journal of Heredity* 10 (January 1919): 11–13; (February 1919): 80–83; (March 1919): 107–110. On the eugenic family studies, see Rafter, *White Trash*.

98. A. H. Estabrook, "The Two-Family Apartment," *Survey* 29 (1912–1913): 853–854. On Dugdale, see ch. 1. Eugenicist Arnold L. Gesell offered a similar family study called "The Village of a Thousand Souls" in *American Magazine* that same year. Gesell constructed a "eugenic map" of the unnamed town, marking houses with symbols for feeblemindedness, insanity, alcoholism, epilepsy, suicides, criminal tendencies, eccentricities, and tuberculosis. One of the eccentricities he gave particular attention to was religious fanaticism. See Arnold L. Gesell, "The Village of a Thousand Souls," *American Magazine* 76 (October 1913): 11–15.

99. H. H. Goddard, *The Kallikak Family: A Study in the Heredity of Feeble Mind-*

edness (New York: Macmillan, 1913), 12, 18, 81–85. On Goddard, see Kevles, *In the Name of Eugenics*, 77–79; Degler, *In Search of Human Nature*, 36–40. Degler incorrectly lists Goddard's name as "Herbert H. Goddard" rather than Henry Herbert Goddard; he also challenges Stephen Jay Gould's interpretation of Goddard's hereditarianism. See Stephen Jay Gould, *The Mismeasure of Man* (New York: Norton, 1981). Also see Leila Zenderland, *Measuring Minds: Henry Herbert Goddard and the Origins of American Intelligence Testing* (Cambridge, UK: Cambridge University Press, 1998), 15.

100. On Elizabeth Kite's conversion and eugenics activities, see Patrick Allitt, *Catholic Converts: British and American Intellectuals Turn to Rome* (Ithaca, NY: Cornell University Press, 1997), 134–141.

101. Elizabeth S. Kite, "The 'Pineys,'" *Survey* 31 (1913–1914): 7–13, 38–40.

102. John McPhee, *The Pine Barrens* (New York: Farrar, Straus and Giroux, 1967), 48.

103. Kite, "The 'Pineys,'" 38–40.

104. Kite quoted in Zenderland, *Measuring Minds*, 160.

105. Kite, "The 'Pineys,'" 40.

106. "The Week: New Jersey," *The Churchman* 107 (13 September 1913): 349; McPhee, *The Pine Barrens*, 52. On Kite's Piney study, see also Rafter, *White Trash*, 164–165.

107. Elizabeth S. Kite, "Unto the Third Generation," *Survey* 28 (1912): 791; Alexander Johnson, "Wards of the State" *Survey* 31 (1913–1914): 355. Johnson was another convert to eugenics. In 1913, he resigned from his position as general secretary of the National Conference of Charities and Correction to become head of the new Extension Department of the Vineland Training School. The Extension Department was a "publicity and propagandist agency." Johnson had gained experience working with the feebleminded when he was an administrator at the Indiana School for Feebleminded Youth at Ft. Wayne in the 1890s. He named his lakefront Indiana home "Yggdrasil," the term for a huge ash tree in Norse mythology that overspreads the world and binds earth, hell, and heaven together. See "A New Force in the War on Feeblemindedness," *Survey* 29 (January 1913): 487–491; see also E. M. East, "Hidden Feeblemindedness," *Journal of Heredity* 8 (May 1917): 215–217.

108. Edwin Grant Conklin, *Heredity and Environment in the Development of Men* (Princeton: Princeton University Press, 1917), 426.

109. *Problems in Eugenics*, xi–xiv.

110. "Preachers and Eugenics," *American Breeders' Magazine* 4 (1913): 62, 63.

111. Ibid., 64, 66–67.

112. Ibid., 63, 64.

113. E. Lyttelton, "Eugenics, Ethics and Religion," *The Nineteenth Century* 74 (July 1913): 157.

114. "Eugenic Marriage Topic of Pulpits," *New York Times*, 9 June 1913, 9; "Pastors for Eugenics," 10. Both Kelgwin and Laidlaw were representative of the Protestant social service reform impulse. Laidlaw, as executive secretary of the New York Federation of Social Service, oversaw an extensive compilation of statistics on New York neighborhoods whose purpose was to foster more efficient church social service. See "Telling the Churches Where They Are," 692.

115. The play (also known by its French title, *Les Avaries*) was a commercial suc-

cess in its stagings in New York, Washington, D.C., and Chicago. See John C. Burnham, "The Progressive Era Revolution in American Attitudes toward Sex," *Journal of American History* 59 (March 1973): 892–893, 905–906.

116. *Survey* 29 (1912–1913): 338; "The Crusade for Purity," *Literary Digest* 47 (2 August 1913): 176–177. Rev. Gunn's denominational and church affiliations were not given in the article.

117. *Survey* 31 (1913–1914): 170.

118. Information on Wise and the Free Synagogue from *National Cyclopedia of American Biography*; obituary in *New York Times*, 20 April 1949, 28. See also Carl Hermann Voss, ed., *Stephen S. Wise: Servant of the People* (Philadelphia: Jewish Publication Society of America, 1970).

119. Dodge quoted in Ronald Steel, *Walter Lippmann and the American Century* (Boston: Little, Brown, 1980), 50.

120. *Survey* 33 (1914–1915): 348; "In Praise of Eugenics," *Eugenics* 2 (February 1929): 36. Scientific eugenicists eventually embraced marriage health certificates, at least in part. In 1928, the American Eugenics Society, in a joint meeting with the Eugenics Research Association, resolved to support legislation that would require written statements that "neither of the contracting parties have a father, mother, sister, brother, or cousin who was born blind." In the absence of such written assurance, couples would have to post a $1,000 bond as insurance against future children who became burdens on the state. Though this proposal initially targeted hereditary blindness, it was later extended to include other traits. "Dr. Howe's Resolution; Minutes of the Joint Session of the AES and ERA," 2 June 1928, American Eugenics Society Papers, American Philosophical Society Library. See also Mehler, "A History of the American Eugenics Society, 1921–1940," 95.

121. Editorial quoted in "Dean Sumner," Redpath Chautauqua Collection.

3. PROTESTANT PROMOTERS AND JEWISH EUGENICS

1. John Harvey Kellogg, "Address of Welcome to the Conference," in *Proceedings of the First National Conference on Race Betterment, January 8–12, 1914* (Battle Creek, MI: Race Betterment Foundation, 1914), 1 (hereafter cited as *Proceedings, 1914*).

2. Advertisement in *Survey* 31 (1913–1914). Kellogg is perhaps better known for two foods he developed and promoted: peanut butter and corn flakes (his brother founded the Kellogg's cereal company). Biographical information on Kellogg from Alden Whitman, ed., *American Reformers* (New York: H. W. Wilson, 1985), 494–496. On Seventh-Day Adventists, see W. W. Spaulding, *A History of Seventh-Day Adventists*, 2 vols. (Washington, D.C.: Review and Herald Publishing Association, 1949).

3. Newell Dwight Hillis, *The Influence of Christ in Modern Life, Being a Study of the New Problems of the Church in American Society* (New York: Macmillan, 1900), 32.

4. Biographical information from obituary, *New York Times*, 26 February 1929, 27; Dumas Malone, ed., *Dictionary of American Biography* (New York: Charles Scribner's Sons, 1932), 9: 56; "Plymouth Church's New Educational Building," *The Outlook* 108 (2 December 1914): 745.

5. *Newell Dwight Hillis*, pamphlet, Redpath Chautauqua Collection, University of Iowa Libraries [19-?]: http://sdrcdata.lib.uiowa.edu/libsdrc/details.jsp?id=/hillis/3, accessed 3 August 2002.

6. "Eugenic Marriage Topic of Pulpits," *New York Times,* 9 June 1913, 9.

7. H. H. Laughlin, *The Scope of the Committee's Work; Report of the Committee to Study and to Report on the Best Practical Means of Cutting Off the Defective Germ-Plasm in the American Population* (Cold Spring Harbor, NY: ERO Bulletin No. 10A, 1914), 7. The summary of Hillis's Committee duties was as follows: "*Morals and Ethics*: Eugenics and democracy. The attitude of the various churches toward the proposal to sterilize persons known to possess defective germ-plasms. The ethical, moral, and ontological aspects of sterilization. Eugenical limitations of marriages by the ministry." Other ministers on the General Committee included Rev. Caroline Bartlett Crane, an ordained Unitarian minister who by 1914 was a full-time social reformer, and Rev. Charles C. Creegan, president of Fargo College in Fargo, North Dakota.

8. Newell Dwight Hillis, "Factory Degeneration," in *Proceedings, 1914,* 353, 351, 355; the first biblical passage quoted is Hosea 8:7, "For they have sown the wind, and they shall reap the whirlwind: it hath no stalk: the bud shall yield no meal: if so be it yield, the strangers shall swallow it up." The second passage is Galatians 6:8, "For he that soweth to his flesh shall of the flesh reap corruption; but he that soweth to the Spirit shall of the Spirit reap life everlasting."

9. Ibid., 355.

10. *Newell Dwight Hillis,* Redpath Chautauqua Collection.

11. "Dr. Hillis on the Social Diseases," *The Presbyterian* 83 (10 September 1913): 3–5.

12. Ibid.; quotation from *Current Opinion* cited in May, *The End of American Innocence,* 344.

13. "Race Betterment," *The Churchman* 109 (31 January 1914): 135.

14. *Proceedings, 1914,* 2, 509–513. Other participants included eugenicists Charles Davenport, H. H. Laughlin, and Roswell Johnson, and reformers Booker T. Washington and Hastings Hart. J. H. Kellogg, "First Race Betterment Conference at Battle Creek," *Survey* 31 (1913–1914): 652.

15. "Constructive Suggestions for Race Betterment—Summarized," in *Proceedings, 1914,* 554–589.
"Report of the Secretary," in *Proceedings, 1914,* 594–595.

16. John Harvey Kellogg to Charles Davenport, 24 September 1913, Davenport Papers, APS.

17. This was an argument that several Catholics and Protestants made with regard to eugenics in the early twentieth century; see ch. 1. Kellogg, *Social Purity,* 29–30, 34. The "Social Purity Pledge Card" that Kellogg evidently passed out at this lecture had in bold letters "Thou God Seest Me" and "Blessed are the Pure in Heart" printed on the top and bottom of each card.

18. "Report of the Secretary," 594–596; Stephen Smith, "President's Address: The Principles of Race Betterment," in *Proceedings, 1914,* 19.

19. *Redemption: A Masque of Race Betterment,* in *Proceedings of the Second National Conference on Race Betterment, August 4–8, 1915* (Battle Creek, MI: Race Betterment Foundation, 1915), 138–143 (hereafter cited as *Proceedings, 1915*). The cast of over two hundred were students from the University of California, Berkeley; see Robert Rydell, *World of Fairs: The Century of Progress Expositions* (Chicago: University of Chicago Press, 1993), 42.

20. *Proceedings, 1915,* vi. See also John Harvey Kellogg to Charles Davenport, 29

August 1915, Davenport Papers, APS. Religious participants at the 1915 Conference included Revs. Hillis, Sumner, Caroline Bartlett Crane, and A. F. Cunningham (of Texas) and Bishop John W. Hamilton (Methodist Episcopal Church, San Francisco).

21. *Proceedings, 1915,* xi. Bishop Hamilton came from a family that contributed several leaders to American Methodism. His father was a circuit-riding Methodist preacher, and of the five children born to the elder Hamilton, two became Methodist bishops and another a Methodist preacher. See *Dictionary of American Biography,* 21: 371–373.

22. *Proceedings of the Third Race Betterment Conference, January 2–6, 1928* (Battle Creek, MI: Race Betterment Foundation, 1928).

23. Davenport to Kellogg, 14 May 1914; 15 January 1916; 16 March 1916, Davenport Papers, APS.

24. Charles Davenport, "Eugenics as a Religion," 1916, Lectures, Davenport Papers, APS.

25. Ibid.

26. See, for example, Conklin, *Heredity and Environment in the Development of Men,* 424.

27. "Empty Cradles Worst War Horror: Professor Irving Fisher Says They Will Overshadow Every Other Tragedy of the Conflict," *New York Times,* 25 July 1915, sec.4, 6; see also Paul Popenoe, "Is War Necessary?" *Journal of Heredity* 9 (October 1918): 257–262. Of course, not everyone agreed with this diagnosis. One writer cautioned the public against automatically accepting the "wild statements of the overenthusiastic eugenicists" with regard to war. This writer claimed that a natural readjustment occurred in a population after a conflict. See "Mistakes of the Eugenists about War," *New York Times,* 3 December 1915, 10.

28. The book was written under the auspices of the World Peace Foundation. See *"War's Aftermath* Review," *Journal of Heredity* 6 (September 1915): 404, 406.

29. The CTCA was established in April 1917 to organize and centralize training camp activities. The YMCA was another key player in the training camps, setting up "Hostess Houses" where girlfriends and wives could enjoy chaperoned visits with the enlisted men and organizing a wide range of athletic activities to provide, as Raymond Fosdick noted, "a legitimate expression for the healthy animal spirit which, when pent up, will invariably assert itself in some form of lawlessness." See Brandt, *No Magic Bullet,* 60–61.

30. Ibid., 53, 59.

31. Daniel Kevles, "Testing the Army's Intelligence: Psychologists and the Military in World War I," *Journal of American History* 55 (1968–1969): 580. On intelligence testing in World War I, see also Gould, *The Mismeasure of Man,* 192–233; John Carson, "Army Alpha, Army Brass, and the Search for Army Intelligence," *Isis* 84 (1993): 278–309; JoAnne Brown, *The Definition of a Profession: The Authority of Metaphor in the History of Intelligence Testing, 1890–1930* (Princeton: Princeton University Press, 1992), 109–125.

32. Ahlstrom, *A Religious History of the American People,* 884.

33. Myers and Sunday quoted in Ray H.Abrams, *Preachers Present Arms* (New York: Round Table Press, 1933), 104, 106.

34. John Haynes Holmes, along with other pacifist religious leaders such as William P. Merrill, Robert E. Speer, Charles E. Jefferson, and Frederick Lynch, were ac-

tive in antiwar organizations such as the American Union Against Militarism and the Fellowship of Reconciliation. Holmes in particular was uncompromising in his stand, and wrote *New Wars for Old* in 1916, outlining his views. His pacifist stance clashed with the pro-war beliefs of the American Unitarian Association and was a major impetus for his severing ties with the Unitarians in 1919. His church became the non-denominational Community Church. On Holmes, see *I Speak for Myself.* Rev. George Reid Andrews of St. Paul's Congregational Church in Brooklyn called pacifists "passivists" in a sermon preached in 1918. See George Reid Andrews, *When Love Fights,* sermon, St. Paul's Congregational Church, Brooklyn, 10 March 1918, 6.

35. Abrams, *Preachers Present Arms,* 79, 112.

36. Ibid., 96–97, 98–100, 108–198; *Dictionary of American Biography,* 9: 56–57. There is no evidence that such a conference was ever planned or ever took place.

37. S. J. Holmes and C. M. Doud, "The Approaching Extinction of the *Mayflower* Descendants," *Journal of Heredity* 9 (November 1918): 299, 296. See also J. Gardner Bartlett, "The Increase, Diffusion, and Decline of the *Mayflower* and other New England Stock," *Journal of Heredity* 10 (March 1919): 141–142.

38. Conklin, *Heredity and Environment,* 450.

39. Higham, *Strangers in the Land,* 243.

40. Bourne quoted in Christopher Lasch, *The True and Only Heaven: Progress and Its Critics* (New York: Norton, 1991), 334–335.

41. Andre Siegfried's observations are from his 1927 book *America Comes of Age.* Siegfried is quoted in Marty, *Modern American Religion,* 2: 64.

42. Madison Grant, "Discussion of Article on Democracy and Heredity," *Journal of Heredity* 10 (1919): 165.

43. This argument was outlined in full in Prescott F. Hall, "Immigration Restriction and World Eugenics," *Journal of Heredity* 10 (March 1919): 125–127: "Just as we isolate bacterial invasions, and starve out the bacteria by limiting the area and amount of their food supply, so we can compel an inferior race to remain in its native habitat, where its own multiplication in a limited area will, as with all organisms, eventually limit its numbers and therefore its influence." See also Robert DeCourcy Ward, "Immigration after the War," *Journal of Heredity* 8 (April 1917): 147–152.

44. It is worth noting that Ross focused on political exploitation and not on the exploitation immigrants were far more likely to suffer as workers. "What Is Americanism?" symposium, *American Journal of Sociology* 20 (January 1915): 471. On Ross, see also May, *The End of American Innocence,* 348–349; Dorothy Ross, *The Origins of American Social Science,* 233–235. Ross outlined his theories on immigration in full in his 1914 book *The Old World in the New* (New York: Century, 1914).

45. Madison Grant, *The Passing of the Great Race* (New York: Charles Scribner's Sons, 1916), 46–47. See also Charles C. Alexander, "Prophet of American Racism: Madison Grant and the Nordic Myth," *Phylon* 23 (spring 1962): 77.

46. M. Grant, *The Passing of the Great Race,* 81, 14, 44–45. Yet, if Grant directed his animus at Jews in particular, he also repudiated organized religion in general, an element of his work often overlooked by historians. Like other eugenicists' indictments, Grant's assault on Christianity emphasized that the misplaced altruism of churches had led to the perpetuation of the feebleminded. He called regard for "what are believed to be divine laws" utterly "mistaken," and deemed the idea of the sanctity of human life "a sentimental belief." The laws of nature "require the obliteration of

the unfit," he said, "and human life is valuable only when it is of use to the community or race." Although Grant did not mention Catholicism specifically, he did repeat Galton's criticism of Catholic clerical celibacy, noting that "it is now impossible to say to what extent the Roman Church by these methods has impaired the brain capacity of Europe," leaving the perpetuation of the race "to be carried on by the brutal, the servile, and the stupid." For Galton's criticism, see ch. 1. Higham mentions in passing Grant's assault on Christian humanitarianism; see Higham, *Strangers in the Land*, 157.

47. Frederick Lynch, *The New Opportunities of the Ministry* (New York: Fleming H. Revell, 1912), 82–84.

48. F. Meyer, *Religion and Race-Regeneration*. On Meyer, see ch. 1.

49. Rev. Percy Stickney Grant, "American Ideals and Race Mixture," *North American Review* 195 (April 1912): 514, 522.

50. W. Jett Lauck, "The Real Significance of Recent Immigration," *North American Review* 195 (February 1912): 201.

51. Higham, *Strangers in the Land*, 189–193. Efforts to exclude the Chinese succeeded in 1902, and the Immigration Act of 1917 instituted further limits on Asian immigrants.

52. Horace M. Kallen, "Democracy versus the Melting Pot: A Study of American Nationality," reprinted in *Readings in Social Problems*, ed. Albert B. Wolfe (Boston: Ginn, 1916), 370–371.

53. Israel Zangwill, *The Melting-Pot* (1908; reprint, New York: Arno Press, 1975), 34. Biographical information from Daniel Walden, "Israel Zangwill," in *Dictionary of Literary Biography*, ed. Stanley Weintraub (Michigan: Gale Research Company, 1982), 10: 238–242. On the question of intermarriage and Jewish racial identity, see Eric Louis Goldstein, "Race and the Construction of Jewish Identity in America, 1875–1945" (Ph.D. diss., University of Michigan, 2000).

54. Zangwill, *The Melting Pot*, 95, 184–185.

55. Ibid., appendix, 210–211. See also Israel Zangwill, *Chosen Peoples: The Hebraic Ideal versus the Teutonic* (New York: Macmillan, 1919).

56. "Race Genetics Problems," editorial, *American Breeders' Magazine* 2 (1911): 231.

57. M. Grant, *The Passing of the Great Race*, 197–198.

58. Leonard Dinnerstein, *Anti-Semitism in America* (New York: Oxford University Press, 1994), 58–59; Alan M. Kraut, *Silent Travelers: Germs, Genes, and the "Immigrant Menace"* (Baltimore: Johns Hopkins University Press, 1994), 143. See also Higham, *Strangers in the Land*, 66–67, 277–279; Nathan Glazer, *American Judaism* (1957; reprint, Chicago: University of Chicago Press, 1989); M. Meyer, *Response to Modernity*; Irving Howe, *World of Our Fathers* (New York: Harcourt Brace Jovanovich, 1976).

59. Abraham Cahan, *The Rise of David Levinsky* (1917; reprint, New York: Harper and Row, 1960), 526, 529. For background on Cahan, see John Higham's introductory essay to the 1960 edition of *The Rise of David Levinsky*.

60. Dinnerstein, *Anti-Semitism in America*, 73–74, 181–185.

61. Robert Singerman, "The Jew as Racial Alien: The Genetic Component of American Anti-Semitism," in *Anti-Semitism in American History*, ed. David A. Gerber (Chicago: University of Illinois Press, 1986), 104–105.

62. On Saleeby, see ch. 1.

63. Kevles, *In the Name of Eugenics*, 46. See, for example, Charles Davenport, "Comparative Social Traits of Various Races," Lectures, Davenport Papers, APS, a study of fifty-one students from the Washington Irving High School for Girls in New York City, 1921. In Davenport's rendering, Germans ranked highest for leadership, pertinacity, humor, frankness, loyalty, and generosity; Jews ranked highest in obtrusiveness.

64. Charles Davenport, "Immigration in Relation to the Physical, Mental and Moral Condition of the Population," n.d., Lectures, Davenport Papers, APS.

65. H. B. Hayden to Frederick Osborn (later referred to Davenport), 8 April 1924; Charles Davenport to H. B. Hayden, 21 April 1924, Davenport Papers, APS.

66. R. N. Salaman, "Heredity and the Jew," *Eugenics Review* 3 (October 1911): 197, 190, 192–193, 199.

67. Louis D. Covitt, "The Anthropology of the Jews," *The Monist* 26 (July 1916): 395–396. Covitt's article was also summarized briefly in *Eugenical News* 2 (September 1917): 75.

68. Eugenicist quoted in Singerman, "The Jew as Racial Alien," 109.

69. Covitt, "The Anthropology of the Jews," 394.

70. Pearl quoted in Elazar Barkan, *The Retreat of Scientific Racism: Changing Concepts of Race in Britain and the United States between the World Wars* (Cambridge, UK: Cambridge University Press, 1992), 215–217.

71. Charles Davenport to Madison Grant, 7 April 1923, Davenport Papers, APS.

72. Dr. Edward T. Devine, for example, reported much lower infant mortality rates for Jewish immigrants in New York than for other immigrant groups. See "The Increase of Ignorance," *Journal of Heredity* 8 (April 1917): 181.

73. Levyn's findings were reprinted in Laughlin, *The Scope of the Committee's Work*, 32–33.

74. Ibid., 34.

75. Henry H. Goddard, "Mental Tests and the Immigrant," *Journal of Delinquency* 2 (September 1917): 243–278, reprinted in *Journal of Heredity* 8 (December 1917): 554–556.

76. Maynard M. Metcalf, "Evolution and Man," *Journal of Heredity* 7 (August 1916): 357.

77. A. A. Brill, "The Adjustment of the Jew to the American Environment," *Mental Hygiene* 2 (April 1918): 220, 225, 231.

78. Maurice Fishberg, *The Jews: A Study in Race and Environment* (New York: Walter Scott, 1911), 516, 549–550. On Fishberg's career, see Kraut, *Silent Travelers*, 138–139, 147–157; Howard Markel, "Di Goldine Medina (The Golden Land): Historical Perspectives of Eugenics and the East European (Ashkenazi) Jewish-American Community, 1880–1925," *Health Matrix: Journal of Law-Medicine* (winter 1997): 61.

79. Fishberg, *The Jews*, 553. In 1911, Boas, a German Jewish immigrant, measured the skulls of immigrants and their children and, after documenting changes in head shape, concluded that environmental factors such as nutrition played a far greater role in determining these so-called racial characteristics. See Kraut, *Silent Travelers*, 146.

80. Extracts from these articles appeared in the *Journal of Heredity*; see Maurice Fishberg, "Eugenics in Jewish Life," *Journal of Heredity* 8 (December 1917): 544–547.

81. "Jewish Racial Traits," *Eugenical News* 5 (January 1920): 7–8. As historian Elazar Barkan has noted, Jewish scientists such as Fishberg faced another hurdle: They were "discredited on the question of race for having a subjective, minority, agenda." See Barkan, *The Retreat of Scientific Racism,* 9.

82. William Trant, "Jew and Chinaman," *North American Review* 195 (February 1912): 249–251. Another writer challenged Trant's portrait of Jews as inferior by noting the many leading intellectuals who were Jewish, concluding that "in the face of all these shining lights the argument that the Jews are an inferior race bursts like a soap-bubble." Nahum Wolf, "Are the Jews an Inferior Race?" *North American Review* 195 (April 1912): 495.

83. Periodicals such as *Current Opinion* and *Harper's Weekly* condemned the publication of the *Protocols.* See, for example, "Is There a World-Wide Jewish Peril?" *Current Opinion* 69 (1920): 840–843. On Henry Ford's anti-Semitism, see Dinnerstein, *Anti-Semitism in America,* 80–83.

84. Quoted in Feldman, "The Social Gospel and the Jews," 308–322.

85. *American Hebrew* (4 April 1890): 165, quoted in ibid., 308–322.

86. "Rabbi Sees Peril in Intermarriage," *New York Times,* 10 May 1909, 4.

87. "Dr. Wise against Intermarriage," *New York Times,* 4 October 1909, 20.

88. "Rabbis Cut Short Marriage Debate," *New York Times,* 12 November 1909, 5; "Rabbis' Conference Split on Marriage," *New York Times,* 17 November 1909, 7.

89. Cahan, *The Rise of David Levinsky,* 527–528.

90. Zueblin took his positive view of race mixture only so far. As to "the Negro question," he said that "the black race is immature" and was therefore "not now near enough to the white race for mixture." See "Says the Race Should Mix," *New York Times,* 17 May 1909, 18.

91. Fishberg, *The Jews,* 554–555. Fishberg later presented a paper, "Intermarriage between Jews and Christians," at the Second International Congress of Eugenics in 1921. See *Eugenics in Race and State: Scientific Papers of the Second International Congress of Eugenics* (Baltimore: Williams and Wilkins, 1923). Intermarriage remained a point of tendentious debate among Jewish leaders despite the fact that, prior to 1960, intermarriage rates between Jews and non-Jews remained below 10 percent. See Dinnerstein, *Anti-Semitism in America,* 241; Glazer, *American Judaism,* 160–161.

92. Rabbi Max Reichler, *Jewish Eugenics and Other Essays* (New York: Bloch, 1916), 10–11. The other two essays in the book are Rabbi Joel Blau, "The Defective in Jewish Law and Literature," and Rev. Dr. David de Sola Pool, "Capital Punishment among the Jews." Pool later became a member of the American Eugenics Society; see ch. 4.

93. Biographical information from Reichler's obituary, *New York Times,* 24 August 1957, 15.

94. Reichler, *Jewish Eugenics,* 10–11, 12. The parenthetical definitions are Reichler's. The Talmudic passages he cited are Sifra, Mezora ch. 3; Pesachim 112b; and Nedarim 20a. On general prohibitions against marriage of "defectives," see Tur Eben Haezer, Piryah Veribyah, ch. 4.

95. Walter J. Hadden, Charles H. Robinson, Mary Ries Melendy, et al. *The Science of Eugenics and Sex Life, the Regeneration of the Human Race* (Philadelphia, PA: National Publishing Co., ca. 1914), 73.

96. Reichler, *Jewish Eugenics*, 14–15, 17–18.

97. W. E. Kellicott, *The Social Direction of Human Evolution: Outline of the Science of Eugenics* (New York: D. Appleton, 1911), 238; Reichler, *Jewish Eugenics.*, 18.

98. Fishberg, "Eugenics in Jewish Life," 545.
Fisherg quoted in Kraut, *Silent Travelers*, 148.

99. *Survey* 31 (1913–1914): 170.

4. EUGENICISTS DISCOVER JESUS

1. The first meeting involved only four eugenicists: Fisher, Charles Davenport, Henry Fairfield Osborn of the Museum of Natural History in New York, and Clarence Cook Little. The new organization experienced several name changes before settling on the American Eugenics Society. After Ad Interim Committee it became the Eugenics Committee of the United States of America, the Eugenics Society of the United States, and finally, on 30 January 1926, the American Eugenics Society. For the sake of clarity, I refer to the group as the American Eugenics Society (AES) throughout; see "Minutes of the Executive Committee of the Second International Congress of Eugenics," American Eugenics Society papers, American Philosophical Society Library (hereafter cited as AES papers, APS); see also Mehler, "A History of the American Eugenics Society, 1921–1940." Sinclair Lewis, *Arrowsmith* (New York: Signet, 1998), 194.

2. Adolf Meyer, "Organization of Eugenics Investigation," *Eugenical News* 2 (September 1917): 67–68, emphasis in original; A. E. Hamilton, "Let's Positivize Our Negative Eugenics," *Journal of Heredity* 7 (July 1916): 309–310.

3. Ad writer quoted in Jackson Lears, *Fables of Abundance: A Cultural History of Advertising in America* (New York: Basic Books, 1994), 226.

4. "Number Devoted to the Eugenics Society of the United States," *Eugenical News* 8 (August 1923): 78, 80.

5. Leon F. Whitney to Charles Davenport, 1 December 1926, Davenport Papers, APS.

6. American Eugenics Society, *A Eugenics Catechism*, 1926, AES Papers, APS.

7. *Catechism* requests, AES Papers, APS.

8. Mehler, "A History of the American Eugenics Society," 67.

9. "Eugenics Exhibit at the Sesqui-Centennial," *Eugenical News* 11 (November 1926): 172. Exhibit material reprinted in Rydell, *World of Fairs*, 54. See ch. 2 of Rydell's book, " 'Fitter Families for Future Firesides': Eugenics Exhibitions between the Wars," in *World of Fairs*. See also Kevles, *In the Name of Eugenics*, 62. One of the most colorful descriptions of these eugenics exhibits can be found in Albert Edward Wiggam, "New Styles in Ancestors," *World's Work* 55 (December 1927): 142–150.

10. "Human Stock at the Kansas Free Fair," *Eugenical News* 7 (October 1922): 111.

11. *Eugenical News* 10 (1925): 27.

12. "Fitter Family Contests at State Fairs," *Eugenical News* 9 (June 1924): 50.

13. Rydell, *World of Fairs*, 49–50.

14. Florence Brown Sherbon, "Popular Education," *Eugenics* 2 (November 1929): 36–37.

15. Rev. MacArthur later became secretary of the AES and edited a monthly col-

umn, *Eugenics and the Church*, in *Eugenics* magazine. He was also a prize-winner in the first eugenics sermon contest. See "News and Notes," *Eugenics* 3 (April 1930): 149.

16. Kevles, *In the Name of Eugenics*, 62; see also promotional pamphlet for *Eugenics* in Correspondence, Davenport Papers, APS. Fisher's assigning the task of finding the motto to Grant is mentioned in "Minutes of the American Eugenics Society," 31 October 1925, AES Papers, APS; on Wiggam's use of the picture of the medal, see Albert E. Wiggam, *The Next Age of Man* (Indianapolis: Bobbs-Merrill, 1927). The full verse is Psalms 16:6, "The lines are fallen unto me in pleasant places; yea, I have a goodly heritage."

17. See Paul, *Controlling Human Heredity*, 11; see also Charles Rosenberg, "Martin Arrowsmith: The Scientist as Hero," in *No Other Gods*, 123–131.

18. Paul Popenoe and Roswell Hill Johnson, *Applied Eugenics* (reprint, 1927; New York: Macmillan, 1918), 400.

19. "Minutes of the Ad Interim Committee, International Commission on Eugenics," 9 June 1922; "Minutes of the Eugenics Committee of the U.S.A.," 9 August 1922, AES papers, APS.

20. "Minutes of the Ad Interim Committee," 9 June 1922, AES papers, APS. By 1925, the Advisory Council did include Rabbi Louis Mann of Sinai Temple Congregation, Chicago, but there is no record in the minutes as to why they lifted their temporary ban on Jewish members.

21. Letter in "Minutes of the Eugenics Committee of the U.S.A.," 1922, AES Papers, APS.

22. Advisory Council letterhead, 1927, AES Papers, APS.

23. On Fosdick's confrontation with the fundamentalists, see Marsden, *Fundamentalism and American Culture*, 171–173. Fosdick soon found another pulpit, the Park Avenue Baptist Church, which later became the Riverside Church (in the Morningside Heights section of New York) in 1931.

24. Fosdick quoted in pamphlet *Eugenics at Work*, 1931, AES Papers, APS. Rev. Fosdick's papers, which are deposited in the library at Union Theological Seminary in New York, yield no trace of his participation in the eugenics movement. Fosdick himself prepared the papers for the archives, and as he lived long enough to see eugenics thoroughly discredited, it is possible that he withheld those documents that revealed his participation in the movement. AES papers reveal his participation, however.

25. Harry Emerson Fosdick, *Christianity and Progress* (New York: Fleming H. Revell, 1922), 87, 94; Cauthen, *The Impact of American Religious Liberalism*, 62, 67; Lippmann, *A Preface to Morals*, 97. See also Ahlstrom, *A Religious History of the American People*, 911; Robert Moats Miller, *Harry Emerson Fosdick: Preacher, Pastor, Prophet* (New York: Oxford University Press, 1985). Funded by John D. Rockefeller Jr.'s fortune, Riverside Church under Fosdick's leadership became a landmark of liberal Protestantism; the main entrance of the Gothic cathedral featured statues of "forty-two leading personalities of science, philosophy, and religion," including Charles Darwin and Albert Einstein. See the description in *The WPA Guide to New York City* (1939; reprint, New York: New Press, 1992), 388–389. See also Szasz, "Protestantism and the Search for Stability," 96.

26. This number is from Charles H. Lippy, ed., *Twentieth-Century Shapers of American Popular Religion* (New York: Greenwood Press, 1989), 144.

27. Biographical information from *Dictionary of American Biography*, 1944, supplement 3, 446–448; *National Cyclopedia of American Biography*, 479. Two of Bishop Lawrence's sons became leaders in the Protestant Episcopal Church, one as bishop of Western Massachusetts and the other as suffragan bishop of Massachusetts. His daughter Sarah married Rev. Charles L. Slattery, who, on Bishop Lawrence's retirement, succeeded his father-in-law as bishop of Massachusetts.

28. Bishop William Lawrence, "The Convention Sermon," reprinted in *The Churchman* 108 (11 October 1913): 486.

29. "Minutes of the Eugenics Committee of the U.S.A.," 6 September 1922, AES papers, APS.

30. "Minutes of the Eugenics Committee of the U.S.A.," 26 October 1923, AES Papers, APS.

31. Ellsworth Huntington Papers, Series II, letter from Henry Strong Huntington to family, 22 March 1930; 24 June 1930, Yale University Library.

32. "Committee on Cooperation with Clergymen," *Eugenical News* 13 (April 1928): 53.

33. Henry Strong Huntington to Charles Davenport, 13 April 1916; Davenport to Huntington, 2 July 1918; Huntington to Davenport, 23 February 1922, Correspondence, Davenport Papers, APS.

34. Irving Fisher (then chairman of AES) writing on behalf of Huntington, to Rev. John A. Ryan, 7 April 1925, John A. Ryan Papers, Mullen Library, Catholic University of America (hereafter cited as Ryan Papers, CUA).

35. The members of the committee were Rev. George Reid Andrews, Miss Jane Bellows, Dr. S. Parkes Cadman, Rev. John M. Cooper, Dr. William C. Covert, Dr. Robert N. Donaldson, Rev. John W. Elliott, Rev. Elmer S. Forbes, Rev. Harry Emerson Fosdick, Dr. F. K. Fretz, Rev. Charles W. Gilkey, Mr. A. J. Gregg, Prof. Rolvix Harlan, Dr. Rufus M. Jones, Rev. Alva M. Kerr, Rev. Charles N. Lathrop, Rabbi Louis L. Mann, Dr. Harold Marshall, Bishop Francis J. McConnell, Bishop John M. Moore, Dr. Charles Clayton Morrison, Dr. Frank M. Padelford, Bishop Edward L. Parsons, Dr. A. Ray Petty, Dr. E. P. Pfatteicher, Dr. Daniel A. Poling, Rabbi David de Sola Pool, Dr. Merton S. Rice, Dr. John A. Ryan, Dr. Frederick Shannon, Rev. Guy Emery Shipler, Dr. Ralph Sockman, Dr. George Stewart, Rev. John W. Suter, Rev. Alva M. Taylor, Dr. Worth M. Tippy, Dr. James I. Vance, and Rev. Benjamin S. Winchester. See Committee on Cooperation with Clergymen letterhead, 1927, AES Papers, APS.

36. Biographical information on Lynch from *Who Was Who in America* (Chicago: Marquis, 1966), vol. 1; information on Morrison from Douglas, *Twentieth-Century Dictionary of Christian Biography*, 263. After the demise of the eugenics movement, Shipler offered his support for birth control, voluntary euthanasia, and more liberal divorce laws; see obituary in *New York Times*, 20 April 1968, 33. Shipler was also accused of being a communist in the 1940s and 1950s.

37. Francis J. McConnell, "The Next Great Step for the Church," *Christian Century* 45 (21 June 1928): 790. Biographical information on McConnell from Gordon Melton, *Religious Leaders of America* (Detroit: Gale Research, 1991); obituary, *New York Times*, 19 August 1953, 29.

38. I discuss Rabbi Mann's eugenics activities in full in ch. 5. Biographical infor-

mation on Pool from obituary, *New York Times*, 2 December 1970, 50; on Reichler, see ch. 3.

39. I discuss the participation of Revs. Ryan and Cooper in detail in ch. 5, placing it in the context of the birth control movement and growing Catholic opposition to eugenics. Biographical information on Jones from *Dictionary of American Biography*, supplement 4, 441.

40. Batten, "Redemption of the Unfit"; also see ch. 1.

41. The seven were Rev. S. Parkes Cadman (Congregationalist), Rev. Harry Emerson Fosdick (Baptist), Rev. Charles W. Gilkey (Baptist), Rev. Francis J. McConnell (Protestant Episcopal), Rev. Merton S. Rice (Methodist Episcopal), Rev. Frederick F. Shannon (Independent), and James I. Vance (Presbyterian). See "21,843 Choose 25," *Christian Century* 41 (25 December 1924): 1673; Charles Franklin Thwing, "American Pulpit Leaders," *American Review of Reviews* 71 (March 1925): 261–267.

42. The details of this meeting were outlined in a letter from Henry Strong Huntington to John A. Ryan, 21 December 1926, Ryan Papers, CUA.

43. See, for example, Charles Davenport to John Harvey Kellogg, 14 May 1914; 15 January 1916; 16 March 1916; correspondence, Davenport Papers, APS.

44. "Committee on Cooperation with Clergymen," *Eugenical News* 13 (April 1928): 53; and see Henry S. Huntington, "Where Do Ministers Come From?" *Eugenics* 1 (December 1928): 22–28. The topic was popular: Rev. Huntington's brother Ellsworth spoke at a Committee luncheon on the eugenic lessons one could learn from a study of ministers' and missionaries' children.

45. "Committee on Cooperation with Clergymen," 53.

46. "Minutes of the American Eugenics Society," 3 January 1927, AES Papers, APS.

47. It is impossible not to wonder how different these sermon contests would have been had they not included the lure of a cash prize. "Prizes for Sermons on Eugenics," *Eugenical News* 11 (March 1926): 48; Committee on Cooperation with Clergymen pamphlet, *Conditions of the Awards for the Best Sermons on Eugenics*, 1926, AES Papers, APS.

48. "Prizes for Sermons on Eugenics," 48. It also provided an opportunity for information gathering. The 1930 contest included a requirement that the participating minister submit a "parish questionnaire" detailing the size and health of church members' families; see "Questionnaire for the Study of Local Parish as the Basis for a Eugenics Sermon for the 1930 Prize Contest of the American Eugenics Society," AES Papers, APS.

49. "Sermons on Eugenics," *Eugenical News* 11 (April 1926): 56. The archives yielded no Catholic entries.

50. Sermon by Rev. A. Nelson Willis, Union Baptist Church, Poindexter, Kentucky, 1928, AES Papers, APS; sermon by Rev. Kenneth R. Close of Miami Beach Congregational Church, Miami Beach, Florida, 1926; sermon by Rev. R. Homer Gleason of First Universalist Church, Rochester, Minnesota, 1928, AES Papers, APS.

51. Sermon by Rev. D. W. Charlton, First Baptist Church, Altavista, Virginia, 1928; sermon by Rev. Duncan P. Cameron, First Presbyterian Church at Cottage Grove, Oregon, 1926, AES Papers, APS.

52. Sermon by Rev. H. P. Marley of Elm Street Christian Church, Greensboro, North Carolina, AES Papers, APS.

53. Sermon marked no. 3, 1926 contest (many of the sermons in the AES Archives, which were numbered for the purposes of judging the contests, were at some point archived without their author information, making it impossible to determine who wrote them); Rev. R. Homer Gleason (second-prize winner in 1928 contest), "Wanted: A Better Humanity," *Eugenics* 2 (August 1929): 13.

54. Sermon by Rev. H. Arndt of Montgomery Presbyterian Church, Montgomery, Ohio, 1926; sermon by Rev. James L. Smiley of St. Luke's Protestant Episcopal Chapel, Eastport, Maryland, 1926, AES Papers, APS. The story of Noah is told in Genesis 6–9; the destruction of Sodom and Gomorrah in Genesis 19.

55. Sermon by Rev. Charles Parker Connolly of the Church of the Christian Union in Rockford, Illinois, 1926, AES Papers, APS. The parable of the Good Samaritan is told in Luke 10: 30–37.

56. Sermon by Rev. George C. Fetter of First Baptist Church, Ottawa, Illinois, 1926, AES Papers, APS.

57. "Eugenic Sermon Contest, 1926, correspondence of judges," AES Papers, APS; "News and Notes," *Eugenics* 2 (April 1929): 34; *Conditions of the Awards for the Best Sermons on Eugenics*, 1926; Dallas L. Short to Henry Strong Huntington, 14 September 1928, AES Papers, APS.

58. On Dight, see Gary Phelps, "The Eugenics Crusade of Charles Fremont Dight," *Minnesota History* 49 (1984): 99–109. Dight kept in touch with national eugenics organizations as well, and the *Eugenical News* reviewed his 1922 booklet, *Human Thoroughbreds—Why Not?*; see *Eugenical News* 7 (May 1922): 63. Sermon by Rev. Phillips E. Osgood of St. Mark's Church, Minneapolis, Minnesota, 1926, AES Papers, APS; Osgood's sermon was also published in his parish newspaper, *St. Mark's Outlook* 16 (15 May 1926).

59. Sermon by Rev. Phillips E. Osgood, 1926. Biographical information from *National Cyclopedia of American Biography*, vol. 45; obituary, *New York Times*, 7 November 1956, 29. Osgood was also a member of the National Department of Religious Education of the Protestant Episcopal Church, and on his win, the AES noted that it was "gratifying to find that the winner of the first prize is particularly interested in religious education." See "Prize Winners in the First Sermon Contest," *Eugenical News* 12 (September 1927): 125.

60. Sermon by Rev. Kenneth C. MacArthur, Federated Church (Congregational-Baptist), Sterling, Massachusetts, 1926, AES Papers, APS. On MacArthur's fitter family win, see "News and Notes," *Eugenics* 3 (April 1930): 149.

61. William A. Matson, "A Chosen Seed for a Chosen People," *Eugenics* 2 (August 1929): 3. The AES published the prize-winning sermons for 1928 in this issue of *Eugenics*.

62. Sermon by Rev. Kenneth C. MacArthur, 1926.

63. Metcalf, "Evolution and Man," 364.

64. Popenoe and Johnson, *Applied Eugenics*, 399–400. Eugenicist Irving Fisher spoke on a similar theme at St. Mark's in-the-Bouwerie Church in New York; "Eugenics Talk in Church," *New York Times*, 4 May 1925, 19.

65. "Recommends Scientific Morality, Not Free Love," *Christian Century* 44 (7 July 1927): 837–838.

66. Rt. Rev. E. W. Barnes, "Some Reflections on Eugenics and Religion," *Eugenics Review* 18 (April 1926–January 1927): 10, 14. Biographical information from Doug-

las, *Twentieth-Century Dictionary of Christian Biography*, 43; see also "British Bishop Urges Repression of the Unfit," *New York Times*, 18 February 1926, 12.

67. Dr. Albert Edward Wiggam, pamphlet, Redpath Chautauqua Collection, University of Iowa Libraries [1940]: http://sdrcdata.lib.uiowa.edu/libsdrc/details.jsp?id= wiggam/2, accessed 3 August 2002. "News and Notes," *Eugenics* 2 (November 1928): 27–28.

68. Dr. Albert Edward Wiggam, pamphlet, Redpath Chautauqua Collection, University of Iowa Libraries [1911]: http://sdrcdata.lib.uiowa.edu/libsdrc/details.jsp?id= wiggam/4, accessed 3 August 2002.

69. Albert Edward Wiggam, *The New Decalogue of Science* (Indianapolis: Bobbs-Merrill, 1922), 22, table of contents, 104. Excerpts from the book also appeared in *Current Opinion* 73 (1922): 512–514.

70. Wiggam, *The New Decalogue of Science*, 104, 110–111, emphasis in the original.

71. Mark Haller quotes part of this last statement and attributes it to an unnamed professor at the Hartford School. I found the same quotation in one of the unmarked sermons for the 1926 contest. See Haller, *Eugenics: Hereditarian Attitudes in American Thought*, 83; and see sermon marked no. 2, AES Papers, APS.

72. On Barton, see Donald R. McCoy, *Coming of Age: The United States during the 1920s and 1930s* (New York: Penguin, 1973), 118–119. For other examples of the uses of Jesus, see Patrick Allitt, "The American Christ," *American Heritage* (November 1988): 129–141. Lippmann, *Preface to Morals*, 318.

73. Wiggam, *The New Decalogue of Science*, 239.

74. See also Wiggam's other publications, including *The Fruit of the Family Tree* (New York: Garden City Publishing, 1924); "The Religion of the Scientist," *World's Work* 50 (August 1925); "The Rising Tide of Degeneracy: What Everybody Ought to Know about Eugenics," *World's Work* 53 (November 1926): 25–33; "Shall I Marry This Man?" *Good Housekeeping* 84 (June 1927): 28–29, 253; *The Next Age of Man*.

75. Wiggam, *The New Decalogue of Science*, 134.

76. Full-page promotional advertisement for *The New Decalogue of Science*, published in *The Outlook* 141 (30 September 1925).

77. Walter B. Pitkin, "The New Testament of Science," *The Century* 114 (June 1927): 170–171.

78. Copy of Fosdick sermon in George Reid Andrews Papers, Southern Historical Collection, University of North Carolina, Chapel Hill; see also Fosdick, *Christianity and Progress*, 115.

79. Charles Davenport to Henry Strong Huntington, 15 March 1922, correspondence, Charles Davenport Papers, APS.

80. Kathy J. Cooke, "A Gospel of Social Evolution: Religion, Biology, and Education in the Thought of Edwin Grant Conklin" (Ph.D. diss., University of Chicago, 1994), 28–29, 6.

81. Conklin, *Heredity and Environment in the Development of Men*, 464–465, 489, 502. Conklin also frequently cited Scripture in articles he wrote about eugenics; see "Value of Negative Eugenics," *Journal of Heredity* 6 (December 1915): 538–540; "The Value of Zoology to Humanity: The Cultural Value of Zoology," *Science* (15 March 1915): 337. The story of the handwriting on the wall is in Daniel 5; the verse Conklin quoted verbatim is Daniel 5:27.

82. *The American Eugenics Society*, pamphlet, 1927, AES papers, APS, emphasis in original.

83. The Galton Society included eugenicists such as Charles Davenport, H. H. Laughlin, Madison Grant, Frederick Adams Woods, and Henry F. Osborn. Biographical information on Inge from Douglas, *Twentieth-Century Dictionary of Christian Biography*, 186–187; see also R. M. Helm, *The Gloomy Dean: The Thought of William Ralph Inge* (Winston-Salem, NC: J. F. Blair, 1962). Inge frequently singled out Catholic leaders for criticism, and in a response to one such lashing, the *Catholic World* wrote, "They still call him the 'gloomy dean.' But it would seem that he gets a good deal of fun out of life—the satanic fun of scandalizing innocent, conservative people." *Catholic World* 132 (October 1930): 105.

84. W. R. Inge, "Eugenics and Religion," *Eugenics Review* 12 (1920): 262. Inge's first essay, along with an essay by Rev. James H. F. Peile, appeared in the first volume of *Eugenics Review*; Peile's essay is discussed in ch. 1; see also W. R. Inge, *Lay Thoughts of a Dean* (Garden City, NJ: Garden City Publishing, 1926), ch. 10, "Eugenics."

85. W. R. Inge, "Some Moral Aspects of Eugenics," *Birth Control Review* 4 (June 1920): 9. Inge outlined these arguments in more detail in *Assessments and Anticipations* (London: Cassell, 1929), 209–216.

86. Henry Fairfield Osborn to Charles Davenport, 3 February 1921, Correspondence, Davenport papers, APS.

87. "Galton Society," *Eugenical News* 10 (June 1925): 69.

88. Shailer Mathews, ed., *Contributions of Science to Religion* (New York: D. Appleton, 1927), 410, 412–413; Mathews's essay was titled "Science Gives Content to Religious Thought." Charles Davenport contributed an essay, "Eugenics," to the volume as well.

89. Grossman's paper and the discussion following it were summarized in *Eugenical News* 14 (July 1929): 104–106.

90. "Proceedings of the Second Field Workers Conference," 20–21 June 1913, Davenport Papers, APS; "Brigham Young: An Illustration of Prepotency," *Journal of Heredity* 7 (February 1916): 51–54.

91. Roswell H. Johnson, "Eugenics and Mormonism," *Eugenics* 1 (November 1928): 5–8. The results of Johnson's study were also noted in "Lauds Mormon Marriage," *New York Times*, 12 November 1928, 13.

92. Johnson, "Eugenics and Mormonism," 5–8. Johnson originally presented his findings at a Joint Session of the Eugenics Research Association and the American Eugenics Society, 2 June 1928; see *Eugenical News* 13 (July 1928): 93, 95.

93. "The Birth Rate of Methodist Clergymen," *Journal of Heredity* 8 (October 1917): 455–459.

94. Clarence Campbell, "Presidential Address of the Eugenics Research Association: Positive Eugenics," *Eugenical News* 14 (July 1929): 96–97.

95. "The Religious Number," editorial, *Eugenics* 1 (December 1928): 33.

96. Florence Brown Sherbon, "The Preacher's Part," *Eugenics* 1 (December 1928): 3.

97. Kenneth C. MacArthur, "Eugenics and the Church," *Eugenics* 1 (December 1928): 9.

98. "Is Christian Morality Harmful, Over-Charitable to the Unfit?" *Eugenics* 1 (December 1928): 20.

99. Ibid., 21.

100. "The Religious Number," 33.

101. Ellen Welles Page, "A Flapper's Appeal to Parents," *Outlook* (6 December 1922); "Newspapers Best the Churches, says Broun," *The Churchman* 139 (12 January 1929): 25.

102. Lippmann, *A Preface to Morals*, 120. Joseph Wood Krutch, *The Modern Temper: A Study and a Confession* (1929; reprint, New York: Harcourt Brace, 1984), 13. James quoted in Alfred North Whitehead, *Science and the Modern World* (1925; reprint, New York: Free Press, 1997), 3.

103. A. Whitehead, *Science and the Modern World*, 192.

5. STERILIZATION, BIRTH CONTROL

1. See, for example, Kevles, *In the Name of Eugenics*, 118–119. See also Hasian's chapter on "Catholic Interpretations of Eugenics Rhetoric" in his book, *The Rhetoric of Eugenics in Anglo-American Thought*, 89–111.

2. Aquinas's natural law doctrine was the synthesis of biblical faith and Aristotelian philosophy, and was outlined in his two great summaries of human knowledge, *Summa contra Gentiles* and *Summa Theologica*. See Alister McGrath, *Christian Theology* (Oxford: Blackwell, 1994), 43–44, 48–50; Paul Sigmund, *Natural Law and Political Thought* (Cambridge, MA: Winthrop, 1971).

3. Dolan, *The American Catholic Experience*, 352.

4. On the Bishop's Program, see Aaron I. Abell, "The Bishops' 1919 Program," *Social Order* (March 1962): 109–118; David J. O'Brien, "The American Priest and Social Action," in *The Catholic Priest in the United States: Historical Investigations*, ed. John T. Ellis (Collegeville, MN: St. John's University Press, 1971), 442; David J. O'Brien, *American Catholics and Social Reform: The New Deal Years* (New York: Oxford University Press, 1968).

5. Dolan, *The American Catholic Experience*, 349–356; Aaron I. Abell, *American Catholicism and Social Action: A Search for Social Justice, 1865–1950* (Garden City, NY: Hanover House, 1960), 189–233.

6. On Ryan, see Broderick, *Right Reverend New Dealer*; Patrick W. Gearty, *The Economic Thought of Monsignor John A. Ryan* (Washington, DC: Catholic University of America Press, 1953).

7. Irving Fisher to John A. Ryan, 7 April 1925; Ryan to Fisher, 17 April 1925, Box 48, Ryan Papers, CUA.

8. Broderick, *Right Reverend New Dealer*, 138–139.

9. John A. Ryan, "The Small Family and National Decadence," *Ecclesiastical Review* 30 (1 February 1904): 150–151.

10. Bowler, *The Mendelian Revolution*, 168; see also Kenneth M. Ludmerer, "American Geneticists and the Eugenics Movement, 1905–1935," *Journal of the History of Biology* 2 (fall 1969): 337–362; Barkan, *The Retreat of Scientific Racism*. Two examples of the geneticists' critique are Herbert Spencer Jennings, *Prometheus, or Biology*

and the Advancement of Man (New York: E.P. Dutton, 1925); Raymond Pearl, "The Biology of Superiority," *American Mercury* 12 (November 1927): 257–266.

11. John M. Cooper to Irving Fisher, 8 September 1922; Cooper to Fisher, 17 June 1923; Fisher to Cooper, 3 July 1923; Robert L. Dickinson to John M. Cooper, 21 May 1925, John M. Cooper Papers, Catholic University of America (hereafter cited as Cooper Papers, CUA). Biographical information from biographical summary in guide to the collection of the Cooper Papers.

12. In his understanding of Scripture Cooper sounded remarkably like a Protestant modernist, arguing that "the Bible is not a scientific textbook. It is a book of religion and morals." *Religion and Science*, radio addresses, 18 February 1926; 4 February 1926, Cooper Papers, CUA.

13. "Religion Course, 1917–1922," Cooper Papers, CUA.

14. In the sermon, Cooper also endorsed the noncompulsory segregation of the feebleminded "in permanent farming colonies." He did not note where this Mass was given, but it was presumably at St. Matthew's, where he was assistant pastor from 1905 to 1918. "Church and Eugenics," High Mass, 14 January 1917, Cooper Papers, CUA.

15. John M. Cooper to Leon F. Whitney, 19 September 1930; Cooper to Whitney, 8 April 1930; Cooper to Joseph C. Flynn, 19 March 1928, Cooper Papers, CUA.

16. "Is Eugenics Racial Snobbery? Does it Condemn Whole Peoples?" *Eugenics* 2 (February 1929): 20.

17. Jennings quoted in Barkan, *The Retreat of Scientific Racism*, 202–203.

18. Information on Cooper's anthropological fieldwork from the biographical summary in the guide to the collection, Cooper Papers, CUA.

19. John M. Cooper to Leon F. Whitney, 8 April 1930, Cooper Papers, CUA.

20. Leon F. Whitney to John M. Cooper, 16 January 1925; Cooper to Whitney, 20 January 1925, Cooper Papers, CUA. The two correspondents also frequently discussed clerical celibacy, with Whitney confessing, "I feel sad, for I think to myself as any eugenist would 'There ain't a-goin to be no more John Coopers.' In a case like that it is too bad there has to be such a thing as heredity." High praise indeed from a eugenicist. See Whitney to Cooper, 23 March 1925.

21. Joseph C. Flynn to John M. Cooper, 13 March 1928, Cooper Papers, CUA.

22. Letter of Ellsworth Huntington to Henry Strong Huntington, 26 April 1927, Ellsworth Huntington Papers, Yale University Library.

23. The student was Rev. Leo Francis Lamb of the Society of the Atonement; his 1926 doctoral dissertation, "The Catholic Church and Eugenics," is included among Rev. Ryan's papers; Ryan Papers, CUA.

24. W. S. Anderson to Leon F. Whitney, 20 March 1928, AES Papers, APS. Two sisters from a prosperous New Orleans family, Jean and Kate Gordon, had actively promoted eugenic sterilization legislation and answered this religious opposition by invoking their Unitarian God as their defender: "The voice of God is directing us today just as much as He ever did, and far from interfering with the will of God, on sex questions, we are doing his work when through the knowledge he has sent us, we try to stamp out of His world the unfit." Gordons quoted in Kathryn M. Kemp, "Jean and Kate Gordon: New Orleans Social Reformers, 1898–1933," *Louisiana History* 24 (1983): 398.

25. Flick received one of the highest awards given to Catholic laymen: the Lae-

tare Medal from Notre Dame University. He was also one of the founders of the American Catholic Historical Society (1884). Biographical information from R. C. Schuyler, ed., *Dictionary of American Biography* (New York: Charles Scribner's Sons, 1958), 22: 196–197; see also Ella M. E. Flick, *Beloved Crusader: Lawrence F. Flick, Physician* (Philadelphia: Dorrance, 1944). Flick's statistics gathering on tuberculosis was not an idle calculus. Tuberculosis was the leading cause of death in the United States during most of Flick's lifetime, and he himself suffered from the affliction; he also founded the first antituberculosis society in the United States, the Pennsylvania Society for the Prevention of Tuberculosis, in 1892. On tuberculosis, see Nancy Tomes, "Moralizing the Microbe: The Germ Theory and the Moral Construction of Behavior in the Late-Nineteenth-Century Antituberculosis Movement," in *Morality and Health*, ed. Allan M. Brandt and Paul Rozin (New York: Routledge, 1997), 271–294; Mark Caldwell, *The Last Crusade: the War on Consumption, 1862–1954* (New York: Atheneum, 1988); Sheila M. Rothman, *Living in the Shadow of Death: Tuberculosis and the Social Experience of Illness in American History* (Baltimore: Johns Hopkins University Press, 1994).

26. Lawrence F. Flick, *Eugenics* (Philadelphia: John Joseph McVey, 1913), 17–18, 27; see also Lawrence F. Flick, "Eugenics and Mental Diseases," *Ecclesiastical Review*, 6th series 1 (August 1914): 151–158.

27. Sir Betram C. Windle, "A Rule of Life," *Catholic World* 103 (August 1916): 586. On Windle, see Allitt, *Catholic Converts*, 168–169.

28. Henry Somerville, "Eugenics and the Feeble-Minded," *Catholic World* 105 (May 1917): 216. In 1922, in a series of articles in the *New Republic*, Lippmann attacked the conclusions eugenicists had drawn from the IQ tests administered to Army recruits during World War I. "Intelligence is not an abstraction like length and weight; it is an exceedingly complicated notion which nobody has as yet succeeded in defining," he said. Lippmann quoted in Kevles, *In the Name of Eugenics*, 129; see Walter Lippmann, "The Mental Age of Americans," *New Republic* (25 October 1922): 213–215; Walter Lippmann, "Tests of Hereditary Intelligence," *New Republic* (22 November 1922): 328–330.

29. G. K. Chesterton, *Eugenics and Other Evils* (New York: Dodd and Mead, 1927), 4, 104. Chesterton wrote most of the essays in the book just before the First World War, when eugenics first began to garner significant public attention. On Chesterton, see his *Autobiography* (London: Hutchinson, 1930) and Michael Finch, *G. K. Chesterton: A Biography* (London: Weidenfeld and Nicolson, 1986).

30. Chesterton, *Eugenics and Other Evils*, 22–23, 10, 104.

31. Rev. Thomas Slater, S.J., *Questions of Moral Theology* (New York: Benziger Brothers, 1915), 259–260; on Gerrard, see ch. 1 above.

32. Slater, *Questions of Moral Theology*, 260, 264.

33. Ibid., 266, 269.

34. Charles Bruehl, "The State and Eugenical Sterilization," *Homiletic and Pastoral Review* 27 (October 1926): 6–7; Charles Bruehl, "The Church and Race Improvement," *Homiletic and Pastoral Review* 26 (June 1926): 905.

35. Charles Bruehl, "Sterilization and Heredity," *Homiletic and Pastoral Review* 27 (December 1926): 225–226, 230.

36. Charles Bruehl, *Birth Control and Eugenics in the Light of Fundamental Ethical Principles* (New York: Joseph F. Wagner, 1928), 218. Rev. Cooper wrote to Bruehl con-

gratulating him on this book and calling it "the best thing we now have in our English Catholic literature on the subject." John M. Cooper to Charles P. Bruehl, 28 September 1928, Cooper Papers, CUA. See also review in *Fortnightly Review* 35 (15 July 1928): 282, and "The Catholic View," *Eugenics* 1 (November 1928): 38.

37. The phrase "true eugenics" was used by Rev. James J. Walsh, "The Place of Religion in Eugenics," in *What about Sterilization*, a series of articles published by the National Catholic Welfare Conference News Service, 22 October 1934; the idea is similar to Rev. Thomas Gerrard's efforts to craft a "Catholic eugenics." For a general discussion of this, see Hasian, *The Rhetoric of Eugenics*, ch. 5.

38. All data on sterilization legislation are drawn from Reilly, *The Surgical Solution*.

39. It is worth noting that the archbishop did concede that the state needed "to protect itself against defective procreation." He argued that sterilization was simply too extreme a measure. Archbishop quoted in Vecoli, "Sterilization: A Progressive Measure?", 200. Sterilization legislation had secular critics as well. Writing in the *Journal of the American Institute of Criminal Law and Criminology* in 1913, lawyer Charles A. Boston compared the tactics of sterilization supporters to King Herod's attempt to eliminate a potential rival by ordering the slaughter of all infants under the age of 2. Both Herod and sterilization supporters acted on half-formed assumptions and enacted "unnecessarily harsh" penalties to achieve their goals. The story of Herod is told in Matthew 2:16; Charles A. Boston, "A Protest against Laws Authorizing the Sterilization of Criminals and Imbeciles," *Journal of the American Institute of Criminal Law and Criminology* 4 (September 1913): 337, 326–327, 331. On the *Ecclesiastical Review* debate, see ch. 1 above.

40. Reilly, *The Surgical Solution*, 51, 54–55; Kevles, *In the Name of Eugenics*, 110–111.

41. Harry H. Laughlin, *Eugenical Sterilization in the United States* (Chicago: Psychopathic Laboratory of the Municipal Court of Chicago, 1922); see also Harry H. Laughlin, *The Legal, Legislative, and Administrative Aspects of Sterilization* (Cold Spring Harbor, NY: Eugenics Record Office Bulletin No. 10B, 1914). Laughlin was also active in promoting the 1924 Johnson Immigration Act, and his testimony before the House Committee on Immigration and Naturalization was instrumental in getting the measure passed; see Reilly, *The Surgical Solution*, ch. 5; Randall D. Bird and Garland Allen, "The J.H.B. Archive Report: The Papers of Harry Hamilton Laughlin, Eugenicist," *Journal of the History of Biology* 14 (fall 1981): 339–354.

42. Reilly, *The Surgical Solution*, 67–68.

43. Laughlin quoted in Kevles, *In the Name of Eugenics*, 110; see also Stephen Jay Gould, "Carrie Buck's Daughter," *Natural History* (July 1984): 14–18.

44. U.S. 200 (1927). *Buck v. Bell* has been called Holmes's most notorious opinion, but it should be noted that every justice considered a "progressive" on the Supreme Court bench joined him in upholding the sterilization law; the only dissenter was Justice Pierce Butler, a conservative and a Catholic who left no written record explaining his dissent. See G. Edward White, *Justice Oliver Wendell Holmes: Law and the Inner Self* (New York: Oxford University Press, 1993), 404–408; Robert J. Cynkar, "*Buck v. Bell*: 'Felt Necessities' vs. Fundamental Values?" *Columbia Law Review* 81 (November 1981): 1418–1461.

45. See Table 4, "Sterilizations of Institutionalized Persons in the United States,

1907–1941" in Reilly, *The Surgical Solution*, 97, 88. Reilly also notes that after 1930, a much higher percentage of the inmates sterilized were women; see 94–95.

46. Bruehl, *Birth Control and Eugenics*, 78.

47. Francis S. Betten, S.J., "Sterilization, Morality, and Our Supreme Court," *Catholic Daily Tribune*, 21 September 1929; "Legal Status of Sterilization Laws in the United States," *Ecclesiastical Review* (October 1934): 403.

48. Roswell Johnson, "Legislation," *Eugenics* 2 (April 1929): 35.

49. John F. Doherty to John A. Ryan, 15 March 1928; Ryan to Doherty, 23 March 1928, Ryan Papers, CUA. Ironically, the law Rev. Doherty was concerned about was passed after the considerable lobbying efforts of physician and eugenics enthusiast Charles F. Dight; Dight was aided in his lobbying by his friend Rev. Phillips Osgood, rector of St. Mark's Church in Minneapolis, who won one of the AES's eugenic sermon contests (in which, not surprisingly, he endorsed eugenic sterilization laws). See ch. 4.

50. Mr. J. G. Hearty to John A. Ryan, 5 May 1927; Ryan to Hearty, 9 May 1927, Ryan Papers, CUA. Ryan's biographer Francis Broderick says that Holmes was "one of Ryan's enduring heroes." See Broderick, *Right Reverend New Dealer*, 98.

51. This summary of Mayer's application of natural law to the question of sterilization appeared in *Archiv fur soziale Hygiene und Demographie* 4 (1929). Paul Popenoe translated it for eugenicists as "Eugenics in Roman Catholic Literature," *Eugenics* 3 (February 1930): 6. Joseph Mayer, *Gesetzlicke Unfruchtbarmachung Geisteskranker* (Freiburg im Breisgau: Herder, 1927); see Paul Popenoe's review of Mayer's book, "A Roman Catholic View of Sterilization," *Journal of Social Hygiene* 14 (March 1928), which was also reprinted in *Collected Papers on Eugenic Sterilization in California*, ed. E. S. Gosney (Pasadena: Human Betterment Foundation, 1930), 186–189.

52. Mayer, *Gesetzlicke Unfruchtbarmachung Geisteskranker*, translated as "Eugenics in Roman Catholic Literature," 6.

53. It is worth emphasizing that Mayer's claims applied to criminals and psychopaths, and not to the more general category of people called "feebleminded." On Aquinas's political philosophy, see Ernest L. Fortin, "St. Thomas Aquinas," in *History of Political Philosophy*, 3d ed., ed. Leo Strauss and Joseph Cropsey (Chicago: University of Chicago Press, 1987), 253–259.

54. Of course, the physicians writing in 1936 were challenging many of the eugenics movement's key contentions about sterilization, and so in that sense they, too, had an agenda and could have manipulated Mayer's work. Nevertheless, their interpretation provides a necessary corrective to Popenoe's. Mayer quoted in Committee of the American Neurological Association for the Investigation of Eugenical Sterilization, *Eugenical Sterilization: A Reorientation of the Problem* (New York: Macmillan, 1936), 61–63.

55. Charles Bruehl, "Eugenics and Marriage," *Homiletic and Pastoral Review* 27 (February 1927): 458.

56. John A. Ryan, "The Catholic Church and Birth Restriction," *Survey* 35 (4 March 1916): 671; John A. Ryan, "The Fallacy of 'Bettering One's Position,'" *Catholic World* 86 (November 1907): 150–151; see also John A. Ryan, *The Church and Socialism and Other Essays* (Washington, DC: University Press, 1919), 217–235; John A. Ryan, "Is Birth Control Right? A Debate. Part II: The Wrong of It," *Forum* 78 (July 1927): 15–19; Broderick, *Right Reverend New Dealer*, 148–149.

57. John M. Cooper, *Birth Control* (Washington, DC: National Catholic Welfare Council, 1923), 8; see also John M. Cooper, "The Catholic Case against Birth Control," *Columbia* 9 (July 1930): 8–9, 30.

58. David Kennedy, *Birth Control in America: The Career of Margaret Sanger* (New Haven: Yale University Press, 1970); see also Carole R. McCann, *Birth Control Politics in the United States, 1916–1945* (Ithaca, NY: Cornell University Press, 1994); Linda Gordon, *Woman's Body, Woman's Right. A Social History of Birth Control in America* (New York: Penguin Books, 1977); James Reed, *From Private Vice to Public Virtue: The Birth Control Movement and American Society Since 1830* (New York: Basic Books, 1978).

59. This is according to S. Adolphus Knopf in his book, *The Medical, Social, Economic, Moral, and Religious Aspects of Birth Control* (New York: Knopf, 1926), 37. It seems likely that the meeting Knopf refers to was of the National Council of the Episcopal Church; see "Episcopalians Join Birth Control Foes," *New York Times*, 22 January 1926, 19.

60. Comstock law quoted in Ellen Chesler, *Woman of Valor: Margaret Sanger and the Birth Control Movement in America* (New York: Doubleday, 1992), 68; see also 70.

61. Lippmann, *A Preface to Morals*, 291.

62. Henry Fairfield Osborn, "Birth Selection vs. Birth Control," *Forum* 88 (August 1932): 79. The article was given as a speech at the Third International Congress of Eugenics; see *A Decade of Progress in Eugenics: Scientific Papers of the Third International Congress of Eugenics* (Baltimore: Williams and Wilkins, 1934), 29–41; "Birth Control Peril to Race, Says Osborn," *New York Times*, 23 August 1932, 1, 16; Charles Davenport to John J. Burke, 21 January 1926, Correspondence, Davenport Papers, APS; *New York Times*, 23 October 1927, sec. 3, 5; Conklin, *Heredity and Environment in the Development of Men*, 454.

63. "Minutes of the American Eugenics Society Meeting," 6 September 1922, AES Papers, APS. Eugenicists in the AES were not the only ones wary of linking their activities to the birth control movement. When a separate Southern California branch of the AES was formed in 1928, they voted to have no formal cooperation with the birth control movement. See "Minutes of Directors Meeting," 6 January 1930, Southern California Branch Records, AES Papers, APS; "Seventh Meeting of the Board of Directors of the American Eugenics Society," 14 February, 1929, AES Papers, APS.

64. On the recruitment of biologists, see Merriley Borell, "Biologists and the Promotion of Birth Control Research, 1918–1938," *Journal of the History of Biology* 20 (spring 1987): 51–87; Margaret Sanger, "The Eugenic Value of Birth Control Propaganda," *Birth Control Review* 5 (October 1921): 5. On Sanger's eugenic beliefs, see Linda Gordon, "The Politics of Population: Birth Control and the Eugenics Movement," *Radical America* 8 (July–August 1974): 61–97.

65. *Birth Control Review* 5 (December 1921): 1.

66. Borrell, "Biologists and the Promotion of Birth Control Research," 58–59. Other birth control activists dissuaded Whitney from provoking an arrest by telling him it would be better for the movement if a physician was arrested. Whitney later complained that one of the doctors who had volunteered "is still out of jail and has done nothing whatever as far as I can find out toward bringing the matter to a head." Leon F. Whitney to H. A. Crossland, 25 March 1927, AES Papers, APS.

67. Biographical information from *National Cyclopedia of American Biography*,

vol. 51; "The Luncheon," *Birth Control Review* 7 (December 1923): 319. Rabbi Goldstein established the Free Synagogue's Social Service Division and was regarded as one of the earliest authorities on marriage counseling; see obituary, *New York Times*, 21 March 1955, 25; Kerry M. Olitzky, Lance J. Sussman, and Malcolm H. Stern, eds. *Reform Judaism in America: A Biographical Dictionary and Sourcebook* (Westport, CT: Greenwood, 1993), 75–76; Sidney E. Goldstein, "Control of Parenthood as a Moral Problem: The Case for and against Birth Control," *Birth Control Review* 6 (October 1922): 195. In 1929, the Central Conference of American Rabbis became the first national religious body in the United States to approve of birth control; they justified their support by arguing that "there is a growing and justified widespread opinion that the citizenship material ought to be more carefully and eugenically selected." See M. Meyer, *Response to Modernity*, 312–313.

67. In a 1930 letter, Fosdick wrote, "As you know I am an ardent advocate of what is ordinarily called Birth Control, that is to say I feel that our present laws are thoroughly unwise, and that physicians ought to be trusted with authority to give contraceptive information to those to whom they think it ought to go." Harry Emerson Fosdick to John Elwood, 8 January 1930, Harry Emerson Fosdick Papers, Union Theological Seminary Library; see also *Birth Control Review* (January 1928).

68. Matthew 13:25: "But while men slept, his enemy came and sowed tares among the wheat, and went his way." "Unnatural?" *Birth Control Review* 4 (November 1920): 1; 7 (July 1923): 179.

69. Lippmann, *Preface to Morals*, 89. Liberal Protestant support for birth control reached a high point in 1930, when the Lambeth Conference of Bishops of the Anglican Church announced its support for artificial contraception, reversing its earlier opposition to the practice. One year later, a committee of the Federal Council of the Churches of Christ in America also formally approved of contraception (though the full Federal Council never formally adopted the committee's report). See *The Lambeth Conferences (1867–1948)* (London: SPCK, 1948); and see criticism of the Conference in *Catholic World* 132 (December 1930): 349–351.

70. "Legislative Program of the American Eugenics Society," *Eugenical News* 3 (March 1928): 40; "American Eugenics Society," 1927, AES papers, APS.

71. *Eugenics at Work*, pamphlet, 1931, AES Papers, APS; Frederick Osborn, "History of the American Eugenics Society," 1971, AES Papers, APS. Historian Garland Allen has argued that this shift toward the birth control movement was so significant that the eugenics movement in fact became a population control movement by 1940. Barry Mehler contends that this shift was part of the movement's larger migration toward an examination of sociological and environmental questions. See Garland Allen, "From Eugenics to Population Control," *Science for the People* (July–August 1980): 22; Mehler, "A History of the American Eugenics Society, 1921–1940," 137–139.

72. "The Birth Rate of Genius: Does Contraception Curb It?" *Eugenics* 2 (May 1929): 18–20.

73. Rev. McClorey had argued that if eugenicists had had their way in the nineteenth century, Charles Darwin, a "neurasthenic" man, would not have been allowed to be born. Edward East responded that McClorey was all wrong. Darwin was not neurasthenic; he merely suffered from occasional bouts of indigestion (ibid., 18–20). Of the link between genius and contraception, John Cooper wrote to *Eugenics* managing editor C. P. Ives, "My very own strong opinion is that we really do not know any-

thing about it." John M. Cooper to C. P. Ives, 1 April 1929, Cooper Papers, CUA. The back-and-forth between Catholics and birth control supporters also raged in the pages of their respective journals and magazines. After New York Archbishop Patrick J. Hayes asked police to prevent a meeting of the ABCL in New York in 1921, the *Birth Control Review* called the Church a "dictatorship of celibates" who practiced "sinister and unscrupulous methods." Margaret Sanger accused the Church of trying to "force their opinions and code of morals upon the Protestant members of this country," an act she considered "an interference with the principles of democracy." "Hayes Denounces Birth Control Aim," *New York Times*, 21 November 1921, 1, 6; "Church Control?" *Birth Control Review* 5 (December 1921): 3; "Reply by Margaret Sanger to Archbishop Hayes," *Birth Control Review* 6 (January 1922): 16.

74. This measure was part of the AES's 1928 legislative program.

75. Guy Irving Burch to John M. Cooper, 3 June 1930; Cooper to Burch, 4 June 1930; Burch to Cooper, 13 June 1930; Cooper to Burch, 18 November 1930, Cooper Papers, CUA.

76. "Sterilization: Its Legality, Need. A Catholic, Some Eugenicists Speak," *Eugenics* 3 (May 1930): 181. In the symposium, the magazine lists Fr. Donovan's name as "Samuel," but in the *Ecclesiastical Review* series he is named "Stephen"; see ch 1.

77. *Encyclical on Marriage*, authorized English text of the Encyclical Letter of His Holiness Pope Pius XI (Washington, DC: National Catholic Welfare Conference, 1931), 26–27, 22.

78. Ibid., 25, 26–27.

79. *America* 44 (7 March 1931): 517; (31 January 1931): 398.

80. *Commonweal* 13 (21 January 1931): 309. The *Homiletic and Pastoral Review* clarified that this condemnation applied both to positive and negative eugenic measures. See "Decree on Sexual Education and Eugenics," Roman Documents, *Homiletic and Pastoral Review* 31 (June 1931): 993.

81. "The Sterilization Craze," *America* 44 (14 March 1931): 541–542.

82. Leon F. Whitney to John M. Cooper, 15 January 1931; Cooper to Whitney, 23 January 1931, Cooper Papers, CUA.

83. John A. Ryan, "The Moral Teaching of the Encyclical," *Ecclesiastical Review* (March 1931): 268.

84. *New York Times* editorial quoted in William I. Lonergan, S.J., "The Christian Ideal of Marriage," *America* 44 (24 January 1931): 379.

85. "Pope Pius XI's Encyclical on Marriage," *Eugenical News* 16 (February 1931): 21.

86. "Encyclical Stirs Wide Comment Here," *New York Times*, 10 January 1931, 3.

87. John M. Cooper to Leon F. Whitney, 9 April 1931, Cooper Papers, CUA.

88. John M. Cooper to Joseph C. Flynn, 19 March 1928, Cooper Papers, CUA.

89. Cooper to Whitney, 9 April 1931.

90. Ibid.

91. See, for example, the lengthy explanation of Church ethics Cooper gave to Whitney during one of their debates over birth control; John M. Cooper to Leon F. Whitney, 12 June 1930, Cooper Papers, CUA.

92. It is also clear that Rev. Cooper's interest in religion and science did not wane in the aftermath of his resignation. He organized a Round Table of Catholic

Scientists for the 1933 meeting of the American Association for the Advancement of Science, during which he stressed "the millennium-old cooperation between science and religion," for example. In 1939, he received the Mendel Medal from Villanova College (Pennsylvania), an award given annually to "outstanding scientists who are members in good standing in the Catholic faith" and who have given "practical demonstration of the fact that between true science and true religion there is no real conflict." See "Catholic Scientists' Round Table," *America* 48 (14 January 1933): 353; notice from *Extension Magazine* (June 1939); Mendel Medal ceremony program, Cooper Papers, CUA.

93. John M. Cooper to Leon F. Whitney, 9 April 1931; "Ryan Statement," Cooper Papers, CUA. Area newspapers subsequently picked up and reprinted Ryan's statement.

94. "Ryan Statement," Cooper Papers, CUA.

95. Ryan's public resignation generated friction with the AES's Leon Whitney. Whitney told Cooper, "Ryan wrote me what I consider a really nasty letter." Whitney's correspondence with Cooper ended on a more conciliatory note, with Whitney telling him that he hoped Cooper would "continue your friendly interest in the movement." Leon F. Whitney to John M. Cooper, 21 April 1931, Cooper Papers, CUA. On Ryan, see Broderick, *Right Reverend New Dealer*, 154.

96. "In the Name of Eugenics," *America* 54 (8 February 1936): 415; article by Rev. M. P. Hill, "The Catholic's Ready Answer," cited in Leo Francis Lamb, "The Catholic Church and Eugenics," dissertation submitted to Catholic University, 1926, Ryan Papers, Catholic University of America, 20–21; Jerome Blake, "Hysterilization," *America* 51 (9 June 1934): 206.

97. Mariann S. Olden, *History of the Development of the First National Organization for Sterilization* (N.p., 1976), 28–31. Olden's 1935 pamphlet, *Sterilization and the Organized Opposition*, was used by Nazi leaders in Germany to counter Catholic opposition to the country's sterilization laws. See Stefan Kuhl, *The Nazi Connection: Eugenics, American Racism, and German National Socialism* (New York: Oxford University Press, 1994), 58–59.

98. In one editorial, for example, *America* said of Olden, "She finds sterilization the cure for so many ills of defectives, that the thought occurs: might it not be helpful for her to experiment with it? Her IQ may be gathered from her own statements." "Comment," *America* 56 (6 February 1937): 411; Hasian, *The Rhetoric of Eugenics*, 103.

99. Charles Bruehl, "Moral Aspects of Eugenics," *Homiletic and Pastoral Review* 26 (July 1926): 1011.

6. TWILIGHT CONVERTS

1. Rydell, *World of Fairs*, 8–9; Aldous Huxley, *Brave New World* (New York: Harper and Row, 1932).

2. Rydell notes that although the number of delegates to the Third International Congress was low, eugenicists claimed that more than fifteen thousand people viewed the exhibit (which covered 10,000 square feet and included 267 displays) at the American Museum of Natural History; Rydell, *World of Fairs*, 55. Robert Cook, "Is Eugenics Half-Baked?" in *A Decade of Progress in Eugenics*, 441–446.

3. Richard H. Pells, *Radical Visions and American Dreams: Culture and Social Thought in the Depression Years* (Middletown, CT: Wesleyan University Press, 1973), 78.

4. See ch. 5. It is worth noting that the eugenics movement in the United States did not take on a more racist tone in the wake of Catholic departure, as William Schneider argues it did in France; see *Quality and Quantity: The Quest for Biological Regeneration in Twentieth-Century France* (Cambridge, UK: Cambridge University Press, 1990). Mehler, "A History of the American Eugenics Society, 1921–1940," 108–111.

5. "Genes and Eugenics," *New York Times*, 24 August 1932, 16; "Against Sterilization," *New York Times*, 26 January 1936, 8. Other anecdotal evidence of changing attitudes about the eugenics movement could be found in Harvard University's decision in 1927 to turn down a $60,000 bequest made for the establishment of a eugenics course at the university. Harvard "did not deem it right to pledge itself to teach that the treatment of defective and criminal classes by surgical procedures was a sound doctrine." See "Harvard Declines a Legacy to Found Eugenics Course," *New York Times*, 8 May 1927, 1.

6. "Minutes of the joint session of the AES and Eugenics Research Association," 4 June 1932, AES Papers, APS. In their survey of sterilization, Paul Popenoe and E. S. Gosney of the Human Betterment Foundation estimated the cost of caring for inmates in segregation as $500 a piece per year. E. S. Gosney and Paul Popenoe, *Sterilization for Human Betterment* (New York: Macmillan, 1929), 113.

7. Degler, *In Search of Human Nature*, 202; Wilfrid Parsons, "The Mass Mind in 1932," *America* 48 (7 January 1933): 329.

8. Frederick Osborn, "Memorandum on the Eugenics Situation in the United States," 24 May 1933, AES Papers, APS.

9. "Eugenics and Democracy," *New York Times*, 16 May 1937, 8.

10. "Eugenics for Democracy," *Time* 36 (9 September 1940): 34. See also Kevles, *In the Name of Eugenics*, 173; Mehler, "A History of the American Eugenics Society," 112–113.

11. Osborn quoted in Mehler, "A History of the American Eugenics Society," 277. Mehler does not agree with Kevles about the degree to which the eugenics movement shifted to what Kevles deemed a "reform eugenics." He sees more continuity than change between hard-line hereditarians such as Laughlin and socially oriented "reform" eugenicists such as Osborn. For an example of Osborn's new approach, see "Tentative Proposals for Field Research in the Social Aspects of Eugenics," wherein Osborn outlines a eugenic research plan modeled partly on Robert and Helen Lynd's 1929 study of Muncie, Indiana, *Middletown*; Lorimer File, Charles Davenport Papers, American Philosophical Society Library.

12. The biggest obstacle to Osborn's plans, Charles Davenport, retired in 1934; he had kept a tight hold on the reins of the Carnegie Institution's Cold Spring Harbor Station right up to his retirement. In the late 1920s, for example, he singlehandedly blocked a popular effort to combine the Eugenics Research Association and the AES and to discontinue the publication of *Eugenical News*. This led Leon Whitney to write to eugenicist Paul Popenoe, complaining about how they all had "to toady to Davenport." Leon F. Whitney to Paul Popenoe, 21 February 1929, AES Papers, APS; see also Mehler, "A History of the American Eugenics Society," 108.

13. Mehler also argues that Osborn was "without doubt the most important figure in American eugenics in the post–World War II period" ("A History of the American Eugenics Society," iii, 271). One of Osborn's contemporaries offered a brief history of this shift; see Clairette P. Armstrong, "Toward a Democratic Eugenics," *Journal of Heredity* 30 (April 1939): 163–165.

14. For example, between 1937 and 1939, the AES organized eight conferences on eugenics in relation to recreation, nursing, education, medicine, publicity, birth control, housing, and the church; see Mehler, "A History of the American Eugenics Society," 271; Frederick Osborn, "The American Concept of Eugenics," *Journal of Heredity* 30 (March 1939): 110.

15. Reinhold Niebuhr, *Moral Man and Immoral Society: A Study in Ethics and Politics* (New York: Charles Scribner's Sons, 1932). Ironically, Niebuhr pointed to the very same weakness of science that Francis Galton had understood: its inability to inspire men to action. "They may be very scientific in projecting their social goal and in choosing the most effective instruments for its attainment," Niebuhr wrote, "but a motive force will be required to nerve them for their task which is not easily derived from the cool objectivity of science" (xv). On Niebuhr, see Richard Wightman Fox, *Reinhold Niebuhr: A Biography* (New York: Pantheon, 1985). Horton quoted in Martin E. Marty, *Modern American Religion*, 1: 304, 306. Lippmann, *A Preface to Morals*, 8–9.

16. Frederick Osborn, "Social Morality in a Diminishing Population," prepared for *Scribner's* magazine, 1935, AES Papers, APS.

17. Description of 1930 meeting in "News and Notes," *Eugenics* 3 (January 1930): 27. In his history of the AES, Frederick Osborn says that most of the Society's committees "shrank into complete desuetude" by decade's end. See Frederick Osborn, "History of the American Eugenics Society," 1971, AES Papers, APS. In 1938, the AES agreed to settle the sermon contest prize money by paying winners 50 cents on the dollar; see "Minutes of the Board of Directors of the AES," 9 March 1938, AES Papers, APS.

18. Biographical information on Speer from Douglas, *Twentieth-Century Dictionary of Christian Biography*, 360; see also Robert E. Speer, "The Next Great Step for the Church," *Christian Century* 45 (12 April 1928): 469–470.

19. "Eugenics in a Planned Society," American Eugenics Society meeting, May 1934, Anita Newcomb McGee Papers, Manuscript Division, Library of Congress (hereafter cited as McGee Papers, LOC).

20. On McConnell, see ch. 4. Unfortunately, neither McConnell's nor Goldstein's papers are extant, and the conference program explicitly stated that "the conference will not be open to reporters," so no news accounts exist either. "The AES Round Table Conference and Annual Meeting," program, 7 May 1936, AES Papers, APS.

21. "Preliminary Notes on the Conference on Eugenic Education," 20 March 1937, AES Papers, APS.

22. "Calls for Caution in Family Guidance," *New York Times*, 14 April 1938, 21. On Catholics' use of eugenic rhetoric, see Hasian, *The Rhetoric of Eugenics in Anglo-American Thought*, 89–111.

23. "News and Notes," *Eugenics* 3 (April 1930): 149.

24. Clarence Cook Little to Kenneth C. MacArthur, 30 July 1928; MacArthur to Little, 4 August 1928, AES Papers, APS.

25. This biographical sketch is pieced together from information MacArthur provided to the AES; see especially *Eugenics* 3 (April 1930): 149. MacArthur does not appear in any of the standard biographical reference works such as the *Dictionary of American Biography, National Cyclopedia of American Biography,* or *Who's Who,* or in any of the major religious directories; I was unable to locate his obituary.

26. Sermon by Kenneth C. MacArthur, Federated Church, Sterling, Massachusetts, 1928, AES Papers, APS. MacArthur expressed similar sentiments in his 1926 sermon contest entry; see ch. 4.

27. In listing the contributors to the special "preachers' issue," the editors noted that the paper MacArthur wrote "will later be used in a book treating the interrelationship of eugenics and the church which Dr. MacArthur is planning" (but which, evidently, he never wrote). Kenneth C. MacArthur, "Eugenics and the Church," *Eugenics* 1 (December 1928): 6, 7.

28. Edwin A. Kirkpatrick (chairman of the Massachusetts State Eugenics Committee) to Lillian Armstrong (corresponding secretary of the AES), 27 July 1928; Armstrong to Kirkpatrick, 30 July 1928, AES Papers, APS.

29. On MacArthur's activities, see "Minutes of the Joint Session of the AES and the Eugenics Research Association," 17 May 1930, AES Papers, APS; "News and Notes," *Eugenical News* 3 (June 1930): 231.

30. Kenneth C. MacArthur, "The Church and Courtin'," *Eugenics* 3 (July 1930): 278.

31. Kenneth C. MacArthur, "Eugenics and Unity," *Eugenics* 3 (November 1930): 439.

32. Kenneth C. MacArthur, "Church Combination," *Eugenics* 3 (August 1930): 318. MacArthur's figures likely came from Leon F. Whitney and Ellsworth Huntington's book, *The Builders of America,* which devoted an entire chapter to the issue of "Religion and the Birth Rate." Whitney and Huntington produced charts comparing each denomination's and religion's production of men for *Who's Who.* Unitarians trumped everyone, producing 1,185 entries for every 100,000 Unitarians; they were followed by Universalists, Episcopalians, Congregationalists, and Presbyterians (all the denominations from which the eugenics movement drew its largest number of religious supporters). At the bottom of this list were the United Brethren, Evangelicals, Lutherans, and Catholics, with between 3 and 8 men per 100,000. Mormons, Disciples of Christ, and Adventists did not fare much better. Those at the lower end of the scale were deemed the "less intellectual" religions. Whitney and Huntington also criticized Catholic clerical celibacy in the book. See Leon F. Whitney and Ellsworth Huntington, *The Builders of America* (New York: William Morrow, 1927), 186–204.

33. Sermon of Kenneth C. MacArthur, 1928, AES Papers, APS; *New York Times* accounts of Kenneth MacArthur's eugenics activities in the 1930s nearly all mentioned that he was the son of Rev. Robert MacArthur; see, for example, "Get Eugenics Drive Post," *New York Times,* 17 March 1930, 31.

34. Kenneth C. MacArthur, "Answering Some Critics," *Eugenics* 3 (December 1930): 469.

35. MacArthur mentioned "the murderer Hickman" in this example; MacArthur, "Eugenics and the Church," 7.

36. "Seeks Drastic Curb on Entry of Aliens," *New York Times,* 18 May 1930,

16; MacArthur, "Eugenics and the Church," 7; MacArthur, "Eugenics and Unity," 439.

37. The timing of these changes is drawn from Osborn, "History of the American Eugenics Society."

38. MacArthur's name appeared in the minutes of an AES Executive Committee meeting in 1937 as a possible participant for a conference of eugenics lecturers; that same year, he is mentioned in a list of AES members who attended the thirteenth annual meeting of the Society. "Minutes of the AES Executive Committee," 8 September 1937, AES Papers, APS. A mass mailing from AES secretary Rudolf C. Bertheau in 1939 suggested that though he was not an officer of the Society, MacArthur "represent[ed] the Society for this purpose in the New England District," giving lectures to interested groups. The last notation in the AES records of MacArthur's participation in the movement came in 1939 and was in keeping with his more than decade-long interest in religion and eugenics: he is listed as a conferee at the 1939 AES Conference on the Relation of Eugenics and the Church. Mass mailing from Rudolf C. Bertheau, March 1939, AES Papers, APS. "List of Conferees," Conference on the Relation of Eugenics and the Church, New York City, 8 May 1939, AES Papers, APS.

39. Biographical information from "Who's Who: George Reid Andrews," *Chautauquan Daily*, August 16, 1927, Box 3; entry in J. D. Schwarz, ed., *Religious Leaders of America*, vol. 2, George Reid Andrews Papers, Southern Historical Collection, University of North Carolina, Chapel Hill, Archives (hereafter cited as Andrews Papers, UNC Chapel Hill).

40. "Divorce, from the Racial View: What Is the Eugenical Ideal?" *Eugenics* 3 (October 1930): 384–385.

41. George Reid Andrews to Leon F. Whitney, 9 January 1931; Whitney to Andrews, 12 January 1931; Andrews to Whitney, 14 January 1931, AES Papers, APS.

42. "Meeting of the Board of Directors of the AES," 3 November 1933, AES Papers, APS; "Meeting of the Board of Directors of the AES," 15 February 1934, AES Papers, APS.

43. "Eugenics in a Planned Society," May 1934 meeting of the American Eugenics Society, McGee Papers, LOC. There is, of course, the possibility that Rev. Andrews did not enjoy his full-time ministerial duties in Bridgeport and so joined the AES to return to the kind of administrative work he had done for the Church and Drama League. However, the enthusiasm he had for eugenics suggests that even if this were the case, he was also motivated by a genuine belief in the efforts of the AES.

44. C. P. Paul, "Minister Says Clean Movies Will Prevail," *Charlotte News*, 4 February 1934; "Ninth Annual Meeting of the AES," 15 May 1934, AES Papers, APS; "Meeting of the Board of Directors of the AES," 15 February 1934; 4 October 1934; 9 January 1935, AES Papers, APS.

45. George Reid Andrews, "Tomorrow's Children," n.d. (likely ca. 1935–1936, as Andrews mentions statistics from 1935 and lists his affiliation as secretary of the AES), Andrews Papers, UNC Chapel Hill. Ellsworth Huntington, *Tomorrow's Children: The Goal of Eugenics* (New York: J. Wiley and Sons, 1935).

46. Program and menu in Andrews Papers, UNC Chapel Hill; "Minutes of the Executive Committee Meeting," 27 May 1936; "Board of Directors Meeting," 28 May 1936, AES Papers, APS; George Reid Andrews to Board of Directors of the AES, 5 October 1936, AES Papers, APS.

47. Guy Irving Burch, "Report of the Secretary of the AES," 15 May 1934, AES Papers, APS.

48. George Reid Andrews to Board of Directors of the AES, 5 October 1936, AES Papers, APS. The AES Board of Directors at the time of Andrews's removal was Ellsworth Huntington, president; Willystine Goodsell, vice president; Frederick Osborn, secretary-treasurer; Chauncey Belknap, Guy Irving Burch, Watson Davis, Henry P. Fairchild, Irving Fisher, Mrs. Shepard Krech, Clarence C. Little, Henry F. Perkins, Paul Popenoe, Mrs. Frank A. Vanderlip, Albert E. Wiggam, and Milton C. Winternitz. See list on program for annual dinner, 7 May 1936, Andrews Papers, UNC Chapel Hill.

49. "Meeting of the Board of Directors of the AES," 8 October 1936, AES Papers, APS.

50. "New Jersey Renews Sterilization Plan," *New York Times*, 3 January 1937, 6. In the article, Andrews is described as the former executive secretary of the American Eugenics Society, suggesting that this credential remained a viable one for him; no copy of the speech survives in his papers.

51. Andrews also reached new heights of rhetorical bombast when he responded to the Catholic argument that sterilization was an unnatural practice, asking, "Because wearing clothes is unnatural are our opponents ready to lead a Nudist movement?" George Reid Andrews, "Sterilization," an address before the New Jersey Health and Sanitary Association, Princeton, New Jersey, 10 December 1937, Andrews Papers, UNC Chapel Hill.

52. The exception was the California-based Human Betterment Foundation, which gathered an eclectic mix of members.

53. All information on the Conference is contained in "Conference on the Relation of Eugenics and the Church," 8 May 1939, AES Papers, APS (hereafter cited as "Eugenics and the Church Conference").

54. The invitation did assure recipients, however, that the conference was "invitational and closed" to facilitate free discussion of "controversial subjects." "Eugenics and the Church Conference."

55. Mass mailing, "Conference on the Relation of Eugenics to the Church"; Program, 1939, AES Papers, APS.

56. "Eugenics and the Church Conference."

57. The authors and titles of the four papers were Dr. Leland Foster Wood (secretary of the Committee on Marriage and the Home, Federal Council of Churches of Christ in America, New York City), "Religious Significance of Eugenics"; Rabbi Louis I. Newman (Congregation Rodeph Sholom, New York City), "The Modern Jew Looks at Programs of Human Betterment"; Father Francis J. Connell (Seminary at Mt. Saint Alphonsus, Esopus, New York), "The Catholic Church and Eugenics"; Rev. Charles Stanley Jones (Congregational Church, Burlington, Vermont), "The Pastor and Practical Eugenics" (ibid.). The record of the discussion following the presentation of the four papers is relatively brief and only one of the papers survives in the AES records.

58. Kuhl, *The Nazi Connection*, 82.

59. Francis J. Connell, "The Catholic Church and Eugenics," paper read before the American Eugenics Society, 8 May 1939, AES Papers, APS. The phrase "true eugenics" made frequent appearances in Catholic discussions of the subject in the 1930s. In 1934, Fordham University Medical School professor Rev. James J. Walsh

noted the Church's historical position as eugenic arbiter: "The Catholic Church did much for eugenics in the older days, long before the invention of the scientific term." In contemporary times, he said, the Church "is ready to be as helpful for the improvement of the race—true eugenics—now as ever before, provided the proper means are employed." James J. Walsh, "The Place of Religion in Eugenics," in *What about Sterilization?*, a series of articles published by the National Catholic Welfare Conference News Service, 22 October 1934. On Bruehl and others, see ch. 5. Rev. Connell moved to Catholic University in 1940 as a professor of moral theology and published *Father Connell Answers Moral Questions* in 1960. He also served as a theologian to the Second Vatican Council, 1962–1965. Biographical information from *Who Was Who in America* (Chicago: Marquis Publications, 1968), vol. 4.

60. Discussion following papers, "Eugenics and the Church Conference." One year later, Osborn wrote that the clergy "have a heavy responsibility and a great opportunity to educate public opinion" about eugenics. Frederick Osborn, *Preface to Eugenics* (New York: Harper and Brothers, 1940), 258–259.

61. "Eugenics and the Church Conference."

62. Niebuhr quoted in Cauthen, *The Impact of American Religious Liberalism*, 232; see also R. Laurence Moore, "Secularization: Religion and the Social Sciences," in W. Hutchison, *Between the Times*, 246, where he notes that Niebuhrian neo-orthodoxy "held that the liberal effort to preserve religion as an ally of science represented a costly and largely futile investment."

63. Degler, *In Search of Human Nature*.

64. Rydell, *World of Fairs*, 3.

65. Kevles says that "the revelations of the Holocaust all but buried the eugenic ideal," and eugenics was "virtually a dirty word in the United States" after that point. In a somewhat delayed recognition of this fact, in 1972 the AES formally changed its name to the Society for the Study of Social Biology. See Kevles, *In the Name of Eugenics*, 251–252.

CONCLUSION

1. A. Whitehead, *Science and the Modern World*, 181, 188.

2. Henry Adams, *The Education of Henry Adams* (1907; reprint, New York: Library of America, Vintage Books, 1990); statement from Guide to the Columbian Exposition, 1893, in Jacques Barzun, *From Dawn to Decadence: 500 Years of Western Cultural Life* (New York: Harper Collins Publishers, 2000), 600.

3. As Thomas Haskell has shown, sorting out these kinds of motives is often impossible. Haskell, "Capitalism and the Origins of the Humanitarian Sensibility," 339–361, 547–566.

4. Robert A. Nye, "The Rise and Fall of the Eugenics Empire," *Historical Journal* 36 (1993): 688.

5. This is from a letter Darwin wrote to J. D. Hooker in 1856, quoted in Roberts, *Darwinism and the Divine in America*, 130–131.

6. Fox Butterfield, "Father Steals Best: Crime in an American Family," *New York Times*, 21 August 2002, 1.

7. Peter Hardin, "Apology for Eugenics Set: Warner Action Makes Virginia First State to Denounce Movement," *Richmond Times-Dispatch*, 2 May 2002, 1; see also

"Eugenics," *Richmond Times-Dispatch*, 8 May 2002, 12; William Branigin, "Warner Apologizes to Victims of Eugenics," *Washington Post*, 3 May 2002, B1.

8. George J. Annas, *Some Choice: Law, Medicine, and the Market* (New York: Oxford University Press, 1998); see also John H. Evans, *Playing God? Human Genetic Engineering and the Rationalization of Public Bioethical Debate* (Chicago: University of Chicago Press, 2002), 150.

9. National Center for Genome Resources, *National Survey of Public and Stakeholders Attitudes and Awareness of Genetic Issues* (Washington, DC: National Center for Genome Resources, 1996); Yankelovich Partners conducted the survey for Time/CNN; Philip Elmer-Dewitt, "The Genetic Revolution: New Technology Enables us to Improve on Nature. How Far Should We Go?" *Time* 143 (17 January 1994). Still another poll conducted one year earlier by Harris Research for the March of Dimes found similar attitudes: 43 percent approved of using genetic engineering to "improve the physical characteristics children would inherit," and 42 percent approved of the same for improving 'the intelligence level children will inherit." March of Dimes Birth Defects Foundation, *Genetic Testing and Gene Therapy: National Survey Findings* (White Plains, NY: March of Dimes, September 1992).

10. Joseph Wood Krutch, *The Modern Temper: A Study and a Confession* (New York, Harcourt Brace & Company, 1929; reprint 1984), 126–157.

Selected Bibliography

MANUSCRIPT SOURCES

American Philosophical Society Library, Philadelphia, PA
  Archives of the American Eugenics Society
  Eugenics Record Office Papers
  Charles B. Davenport Papers
  American Philosophical Society Papers on Science, 1720–1958
  Papers Relating to Leon F. Whitney
Catholic University of America, Mullen Library, Washington, D.C.
  John Montgomery Cooper Papers
  John Augustine Ryan Papers
Library of Congress, Manuscript Division, Washington, D.C.
  John Haynes Holmes Papers
  Anita Newcomb McGee Papers
New York Public Library, Rare Books and Special Collections, New York, NY
  William Henry Matthews Papers
Union Theological Seminary, Burke Library, New York, NY
  Harry Emerson Fosdick Papers
University of North Carolina at Chapel Hill, Southern Historical Collection
  George Reid Andrews Papers
Yale University, Sterling Library, New Haven, CT
  Ellsworth Huntington Papers

PUBLISHED PRIMARY SOURCES

Books

Aldrich, Morton A., et al. *Eugenics: Twelve University Lectures.* New York: Dodd, Mead, 1914.

Allen, G. *The Families Whence High Intelligence Springs.* New York: Eugenics Record Office, 1926.

American Eugenics Society. *A Eugenics Catechism.* New Haven, CT: American Eugenics Society, 1926, 1929.

———. *Organized Eugenics.* New Haven, CT: American Eugenics Society, 1931.

———. *Practical Eugenics: Aims and Methods of the American Eugenics Society.* New York: N.p., 1938.

American Neurological Association, Committee for the Investigation of Eugenical Sterilization. *Eugenical Sterilization: A Reorientation of the Problem.* New York: Macmillan, 1936.

Atkins, G. G. *Religion in Our Times.* New York: Round Table Press, 1932.

Baker, LaReine Helen McKenzie. *Race Improvement or Eugenics: A Little Book on a Great Subject.* New York: Dodd, Mead, 1912.

Barr, Martin W. *Mental Defectives: Their History, Treatment, and Training.* Philadelphia: Blakiston, 1904.

Bauer, Erwin, Eugen Fischer, and Fritz Lenz. *Human Heredity.* Trans. Eden and Cedar Paul. New York: Macmillan, 1931.

Bell, Alexander Graham. *A Few Thoughts Concerning Eugenics.* Washington, DC: Press of Judd and Detweiler, 1908.

Bellamy, Edward. *Looking Backward.* New York: New American Library, 1888.

Berstein, C. *Social Care of the Mentally Deficient.* Washington, DC: National Catholic Welfare Conference, 1930.

Boas, Franz. *Anthropology and Modern Life.* New York: Norton, 1928.

———. *Materials for the Study of Inheritance in Man.* New York: Columbia University Press, 1928.

Bradford, Amory. *Heredity and Christian Problems.* New York: Macmillan, 1895.

Brigham, Carl C. *A Study of American Intelligence.* 1923. Reprint, with a foreword by R. M. Yerkes. New York: Kraus, 1975.

Brown, Mary Jane. *An Introduction to Eugenics.* Boston: Chapman and Grimes, ca. 1935.

Brown, William Adams. *The Life of Prayer in a World of Science.* New York: Charles Scribner's Sons, 1927.

Bruehl, Charles P. *Birth Control and Eugenics in Light of Fundamental Ethical Principles.* New York: Joseph F. Wagner, 1928.

Bryan, William Jennings, and Mary Baird Bryan. *The Memoirs of William Jennings Bryan.* Philadelphia: John C. Winston, 1925.

Buckham, John Wright. *Progressive Religious Thought in America.* New York: Houghton Mifflin, 1919.

Buckton, Alice Mary. *A Catechism of Life.* London: Methuen, 1912.

Burbank Society. *Choosing Our Children.* Santa Rosa, CA: Luther Burbank Society, ca. 1914.

Burtt, E. A. *Religion in an Age of Science.* London: Williams and Norgate, 1930.

Cahan, Abraham. *The Rise of David Levinsky.* 1916. Reprint, New York: Harper and Row, 1960.

Carr-Saunders, A. M. *Eugenics.* New York: Henry Holt, 1926.

Castle, William E. *Genetics and Eugenics.* Cambridge, MA: Harvard University Press, 1927.

Cavert, Samuel McCrea. *The Church through Half a Century.* New York: Charles Scribner's Sons, 1936.

Chamberlin, Ralph Vary. *The Kingdom of Man.* Salt Lake City: Extension Division, University of Utah, 1938.

Charles, Enid. *The Twilight of Parenthood.* New York: Norton, 1934.

Chesterton, G. K. *Eugenics and Other Evils.* New York: Dodd and Mead, 1927.

Chicago Vice Commission. *The Social Evil in Chicago; A Study of Existing Conditions.* Chicago: Gunthorp-Warren, 1911.

Cole, Stewart Grant. *The History of Fundamentalism.* New York: R.R. Smith, 1931.

Coleridge, Samuel Taylor. *Biographia Literaria.* 1817; reprint, New York: E. P. Dutton, 1934.

Conklin, Edwin Grant. *Heredity and Environment in the Development of Men.* Princeton: Princeton University Press, 1917.

———. *The Direction of Human Evolution.* New York: Charles Scribner's Sons, 1922.

———. *Evolution and the Bible.* Chicago: American Institute of Sacred Literature, 1922.

Conway, Bertrand L. *The Church and Eugenics.* New York: Paulist Press, 1900.

Cooper, John M. *Birth Control.* Washington, DC: National Catholic Welfare Council, 1923.

Cotton, E. H. *Has Science Discovered God?* New York: Thomas Y. Crowell, ca. 1931.

Cowdry, E. V. *Human Biology and Racial Welfare.* New York: P.B. Hoeber, 1930.

Cross, F. L. *Religion and the Reign of Science.* New York: Longmans, Green, 1930.

Darwin, Leonard. *The Need for Eugenic Reform.* London: J. Murray, 1926.

Davenport, Charles B. *Eugenics.* New York: Henry Holt, 1910.

———. *Heredity in Relation to Eugenics.* New York: Henry Holt, 1911.

———. *State Laws Limiting Marriage Selection Examined in the Light of Eugenics.* Cold Spring Harbor, NY: Eugenics Record Office Bulletin No. 9, 1913.

Davenport, Charles B., and Harry H. Laughlin. *How to Make a Eugenical Family Study.* Cold Spring Harbor, NY: Eugenics Record Office Bulletin No. 13, 1915.

Davies, Stanley P. *Social Control of the Mentally Deficient.* New York: Thomas Y. Crowell, 1930.

A Decade of Progress in Eugenics: Scientific Papers of the Third International Congress of Eugenics. Baltimore: Williams and Wilkins, 1934.

Dechman, Louis. *Within the Bud: Procreation of a Healthy, Happy and Beautiful Child of the Desired Sex, a Biological Teaching of Eugenics.* Seattle: Washington Printing, 1916.

Downing, E. R. *Elementary Eugenics.* Chicago: University of Chicago Press, 1928.

Draper, John William. *History of the Conflict between Religion and Science.* New York: Appleton, 1874.

Drawbridge, C. L. *The Religion of Scientists: Being Recent Opinions Expressed by 200 Fellows of the Royal Society on the Subject of Religion and Theology.* New York: Macmillan, 1932.

Dugdale, Richard. *The Jukes: A Study in Crime, Pauperism, Disease, and Heredity.* 1877; reprint, New York: G.P. Putnam and Sons, 1895.

Eames, Blanche. *Principles of Eugenics: A Practical Treatise.* New York: Moffat, Yard, 1914.

East, Edward M. *Mankind at the Crossroads.* New York: Charles Scribner's Sons, 1923.

———. *Heredity and Human Affairs.* New York: Scribner's Sons, 1927.

Ellis, Havelock. *The Task of Social Hygiene.* New York: Houghton Mifflin, 1912.

———. *Essays in War-Time: Further Studies in the Task of Social Hygiene.* Boston: Houghton Mifflin, 1917.

Estabrook, Arthur H. *Mongrel Virginians: The Win Tribe.* Baltimore: Williams and Wilkins, 1926.

Eugenics in Race and State: Scientific Papers of the Second International Congress of Eugenics, 22–28 September 1921. Baltimore: Williams and Wilkins, 1923.

Fischer, Irving, and Eugene Lyman Fisk. *How to Live: Rules for Healthful Living Based on Modern Science.* New York: Funk and Wagnalls, 1916.

Fishberg, Maurice. *The Jews: A Study in Race and Environment.* New York: Walter Scott, 1911.

Flick, Lawrence Francis. *Eugenics.* Philadelphia: J.J. McVey, 1913.

Fosdick, Harry Emerson. *Christianity and Progress.* New York: Fleming H. Revell, 1922.

———. *The New Knowledge and the Christian Faith.* Sermon preached at the First Presbyterian Church, New York City, 21 May 1922. Pitts Theology Library, Emory University.

———. *The Living of These Days: An Autobiography.* New York: Harper, 1956.

Frank, Marc Henry. *Eugenics and Sex Relations for Men and Women.* New York: Preferred Publications, 1932.

Galton, Francis. *Hereditary Genius: An Inquiry into Its Laws and Consequences.* London: Macmillan, 1869.

———. *English Men of Science: Their Nature and Nurture.* 1874. Reprint, with an introduction by Ruth Cowan, London: Cass, 1970.

———. *Inquiries into Human Faculty and Its Development.* London: J.M. Dent and Sons, 1883.

———. *Memories of My Life.* London: Methuen, 1908.

———. *Essays in Eugenics.* London: Eugenics Education Society, 1909.

Gates, Reginald R. *Heredity and Eugenics.* New York: Macmillan, 1923.

Gerrard, Thomas John. *The Church and Eugenics.* St. Louis: B. Herder, 1912.

———. *Marriage and Parenthood: The Catholic Ideal.* New York: J.F. Wagner, 1937.

Gibson, Mr. and Mrs. John Williams. *Social Purity: Or, the Life of the Home and the Nation Including Heredity, Prenatal Influences, etc., etc.* New York: J.L. Nichols, 1903.

Goddard, Henry H. *The Kallikak Family: A Study in the Heredity of Feeblemindedness.* New York: Macmillan, 1913.

———. *Feeblemindedness: Its Causes and Consequences.* New York: Macmillan, 1914.

———. *Human Efficiency and Levels of Intelligence.* Princeton: Princeton University Press, 1920.

Goldsmith, W. M. *The Laws of Life: Principles of Evolution, Heredity and Eugenics.* Boston: N.p., 1922.

Gosney, E. S., ed. *Collected Papers on Eugenic Sterilization in California*. Pasadena: Human Betterment Foundation, 1930.

Gosney, E. S., and Paul Popenoe. *Sterilization for Human Betterment*. New York: Macmillan, 1929.

Grant, Madison. *The Passing of the Great Race*. New York: Charles Scribner's Sons, 1916.

———. *The Conquest of a Continent*. New York: Charles Scribner's Sons, 1933.

Grant, Madison, and Charles Stewart Davison, eds. *The Alien in Our Midst*. New York: Galton, 1930.

Graubard, M. A. *Genetics and the Social Order*. New York: Tomorrow, 1935.

Greenwood, William O. *Biology and Christian Belief*. New York: Macmillan, 1939.

Guyer, M. F. *Being Well-Born: Introduction to Eugenics*. Indianapolis: Bobbs-Merrill, 1916.

Hadden, Walter J., Charles H. Robinson, Mary Ries Melendy, et al. *The Science of Eugenics and Sex Life, The Regeneration of the Human Race*. Philadelphia, PA: National Publishing Company, ca. 1914.

Haldane, J.B.S. *Heredity and Politics*. New York: Norton, 1938.

Hall, Fred S. *Medical Certification for Marriage: An Account of the Administration of the Wisconsin Marriage Law as It Relates to the Venereal Diseases*. New York: Russell Sage Foundation, 1925.

Hall, G. Stanley. *Jesus, the Christ, in the Light of Psychology*. 2 vols. New York: Doubleday, Page, 1917.

Hatch, Willis Marion. *The Ideal Family: A Private Manual on the Science of Procreation, with a Chapter on Sex at Will*. Edinboro, PA: Eudora Book, 1908.

Hauber, U. A. *Inheritance of Mental Defect*. Washington, DC: National Catholic Welfare Conference, 1930.

Hillis, Newell Dwight. *The Influence of Christ in Modern Life, Being a Study of the New Problems of the Church in American Society*. New York: Macmillan, 1900.

Hogben, Lancelot. *Genetic Principles in Medicine and Social Science*. London: Williams and Norgate, 1931.

———. *Nature and Nurture*. New York: Norton, 1933.

Holmes, John Haynes. *The Revolutionary Function of the Modern Church*. New York: G.P. Putnam's Sons, 1912.

———. *I Speak for Myself: The Autobiography of John Haynes Holmes*. New York: Harper and Brothers, 1959.

Holmes, Samuel J. *Studies in Evolution and Eugenics*. New York: Harcourt, Brace, 1923.

———. *The Eugenic Predicament*. New York: Harcourt, Brace, 1933.

———. *Human Genetics and Its Social Import*. New York: McGraw-Hill, 1936.

Hooton, E. A. *Apes, Men, and Morons*. New York: G.P. Putnam's Sons, 1937.

Hopkins, John Henry, S.T.D. *The Great Forty Years of the Diocese of Chicago, 1893–1934*. Chicago: Centenary Fund, 1936.

Hoyt, Arthur S. *The Pulpit and American Life*. New York: Macmillan, 1921.

Hunter, George William. *A Civic Biology: Presented in Problems*. New York: American Book, 1914.

Huntington, Ellsworth. *Tomorrow's Children: The Goal of Eugenics*. New York: J. Wiley and Sons, 1935.

Huxley, J. S. *Science, Religion, and Human Nature*. London: Watts & Co., 1930.

Inge, William Ralph. *Outspoken Essays*. New York: Longmans, Green, 1922.

———. *Lay Thoughts of a Dean*. Garden City, NJ: Garden City Publishing, 1926.

———. *Science and Ultimate Truth*. New York: Longmans, Green, 1926.

———. *Assessments and Anticipations*. London: Cassell and Co., 1929.

Jefferis, Benjamin Grant. *Searchlights on Health: The Science of Eugenics, a Guide to Purity and Physical Manhood, Advice to Maiden, Wife and Mother*. Naperville, IL: J.L. Nichols, 1919.

———. *Safe Counsel, or Practical Eugenics*. Naperville, IL: J.L. Nichols, ca. 1925.

Jennings, Herbert S. *Prometheus, or Biology and the Advancement of Man*. New York: E.P. Dutton, 1925.

———. *The Biological Basis of Human Nature*. London: Faber and Faber, 1930.

Jennings, Herbert S., et al. *Scientific Aspects of the Race Problem*. Washington, DC: Catholic University of America Press, 1941.

Jordan, David Starr. *Footnotes to Evolution: A Series of Popular Addresses on the Evolution of Life*. New York: D. Appleton, 1913.

Jordan, Harvey E. *The Eugenical Aspect of Venereal Disease*. Baltimore: Franklin Printing Co., ca. 1912.

Kellicott, W. E. *The Social Direction of Human Evolution: Outline of the Science of Eugenics*. New York: D. Appleton, 1911.

Kellogg, John Harvey. *Social Purity: An Address Delivered at Battle Creek, Michigan, November 28, 1886*. Battle Creek, MI: Health Publishing, 1886.

———. *Harmony of Science and the Bible on the Nature of the Soul*. Battle Creek, MI: Review and Herald Publishing, 1879.

Kirsch, Felix M. *Training in Chastity: A Problem in Catholic Character Education*. New York: Benziger Brothers, 1930.

Knopf, Sigard Adolphus. *The Medical, Social, Economic, Moral, and Religious Aspects of Birth Control*. New York: Knopf, 1926.

Krutch, Joseph Wood. *The Modern Temper: A Study and a Confession*. 1929. Reprint, New York: Harcourt Brace & Company, 1984.

Landman, J. H. *Human Sterilization*. New York: Macmillan, 1932.

Laughlin, H. H. *The Scope of the Committee's Work*: Report of the Committee to Study and to Report on the Best Practical Means of Cutting Off the Defective Germ-Plasm in the American Population. Cold Spring Harbor, NY: Eugenics Record Office Bulletin No. 10A, 1914.

———. *The Legislative, Legal, and Administrative Aspects of Sterilization*. Cold Spring Harbor, NY: Eugenics Record Office Bulletin No. 10B, 1914.

———. "Analysis of America's Modern Melting Pot." *Hearings before the House Committee on Immigration and Naturalization, 67th Congress, 3rd Session*. Washington, DC: Government Printing Office, 1922.

———. *Eugenical Sterilization in the United States*. Chicago: Psychopathic Laboratory of the Municipal Court of Chicago, 1922.

Lippmann, Walter. *Drift and Mastery: An Attempt to Diagnose the Current Unrest*. New York: Mitchell Kennerly, 1914.

———. *American Inquisitors: A Commentary on Dayton and Chicago*. New York: Macmillan, 1928.

———. *A Preface to Morals*. New York: Macmillan, 1929.

Luther Burbank Society. *Choosing Our Children*. Santa Rosa, CA: Luther Burbank Society, ca. 1914.

Lynch, Frederick. *The New Opportunities of the Ministry*. New York: Revell, 1912.

Lyttelton, Edward. *The Christian and Birth Control*. New York: Macmillan, 1929.

Marsh, Frank L. *Evolution, Creation and Science*. Washington, DC: Review and Herald, 1947.

Mathews, Shailer. *The Faith of Modernism*. New York: Macmillan, 1924.

Mathews, Shailer, et al. *Contributions of Science to Religion*. New York: Appleton, 1927.

Mayer, Joseph. *Gesetlziche Unfruchtbarmachung Geisteskranker* (The legal sterilization of the mentally diseased). Freiburg im Breisgau: Herder, 1927.

McCrimmon, A. L. *The Child in the Normal Home*. Chicago: American Baptist Publication Society, 1910.

Melendy, Mary Ries. *Perfect Health and Beauty for Parents and Children*. N.p., 1906.

Melendy, Mary Ries, and M. H. Frank. *Modern Eugenics for Men and Women: A Complete Medical Guide to Thorough Understanding of the Principles of Health and Sex Relations*. New York: Preferred Publications, 1928.

Meyer, Frederick Brotherton. *Religion and Race-Regeneration*. London: Cassell, 1912.

Moeller, Henry. *Pastoral of the Most Reverend Archbishop of Cincinnati: On Choosing a Consort, Qualifications of a Consort, Qualities of a Parent, Eugenics, Sex-hygiene, etc.* Cincinnati: n.p., 1915.

Montavan, William F. *Eugenic Sterilization in the Laws of the State*. Washington, DC: National Catholic Welfare Conference, n.d.

Moore, Edward R. *The Case against Birth Control*. New York: Century, 1931.

Morrow, Prince A. *Social Diseases and Marriage: Social Prophylaxis*. New York: Lea Brothers, 1909.

Muller, H. J. *Out of the Night: A Biologist's View of the Future*. 1935. Reprint, New York: Garland, 1984.

Myerson, Abraham. *The Inheritance of Mental Diseases*. Baltimore: Williams and Wilkins, 1925.

National Council on Public Morals, National Birthrate Commission. *Youth and the Race: The Development and Education of Young Citizens for Worthy Parenthood*. London: E.P. Dutton, 1923.

Nearing, Scott. *The Super-Race: An American Problem*. New York: B.W. Huebsch, 1912.

———. *Social Religion: An Interpretation of Christianity in Terms of Modern Life*. New York: Macmillan, 1913.

Needham, Joseph. *Science, Religion, and Reality*. 1925. Reprint, New York: George Braziller, 1955.

Newman, Horatio H. *Readings in Evolution, Genetics, and Eugenics*. Chicago: University of Chicago Press, 1925.

Newsholme, Henry Pratt. *Christian Ethics and Social Health*. London: J. Heritage, 1937.

New York State Board of Charities, Bureau of Analysis and Investigation. *Bibliography of Eugenics and Related Subjects*. Compiled by Gertrude E. Hall, Ph.D. Albany: New York State Board of Charities, 1913.

Niebuhr, Reinhold. *Moral Man and Immoral Society: A Study in Ethics and Politics*. New York: Charles Scribner's Sons, 1932.

———. *The Irony of American History*. New York: Scribner, 1952.

Olden, Marian S. *Human Betterment Was Our Goal*. Princeton: M.S. Norton, ca. 1963–1971.

Osborn, Frederick. *Preface to Eugenics*. New York: Harper and Brothers, 1940.

Osborn, Henry Fairfield. *From the Greeks to Darwin*. New York: Macmillan, 1908.

Patten, Simon N. *The Social Basis of Religion*. New York: Macmillan, 1911.

Pearson, Karl. *The Problem of Practical Eugenics*. London: Dulau, 1909.

———. *The Scope and Importance to the State of the Science of National Eugenics*. London: Dulau, 1909.

———, ed. *The Life, Letters, and Labours of Francis Galton*. 4 vols. Cambridge, UK: Cambridge University Press, 1914–1930.

Pendleton, Hester. *The Parent's Guide: Or, Human Development through Inherited Tendencies*. 1871. Reprint, New York: Garland, 1984.

Pitt-Rivers, George H. *Weeds in the Garden of Marriage*. London: N. Douglas, 1931.

Pope Pius XI. *Casti Connubi: On Christian Marriage*. Authorized English text of the encyclical letter of His Holiness Pope Pius XI. Washington, DC: National Catholic Welfare Conference, 1931.

Popenoe, Paul. *The Conservation of the Family*. 1926. Reprint, New York: Garland, 1984.

Popenoe, Paul, and R. H. Johnson. *Applied Eugenics*. New York: Macmillan, 1918.

Price, James Russell. *The Call for Fathers*. Chicago: Vive Publishing, ca. 1915.

Problems in Eugenics: Proceedings of the First International Eugenics Congress, 1912. London: Eugenics Education Society, 1912.

Proceedings of the First National Conference on Race Betterment. Battle Creek, MI: Race Betterment Foundation, 1914.

Proceedings of the National Conference of Charities and Correction, 1888. Boston: Press of George H. Ellis, 1888.

Proceedings of the Second National Conference on Race Betterment. Battle Creek, MI: Race Betterment Foundation, 1915.

Proceedings of the Third National Conference on Race Betterment. Battle Creek, MI: Race Betterment Foundation, 1928.

Rauschenbusch, Walter. *Christianity and the Social Crisis*. 1907. Reprint, New York: Harper and Row, 1964.

Redfield, Casper Lavater. *Control of Heredity: A Study of the Genesis of Evolution and Degeneracy, Illustrated by Diagrams and Types of Character*. Chicago: Monarch, 1903.

———. *Human Heredity*. Chicago: Heredity Publishing, 1921.

Reed, Charles Alfred Lee. *Marriage and Genetics: Laws of Human Breeding and Applied Eugenics*. Cincinnati: Galton Press, 1913.

Reichler, Max. *Jewish Eugenics and Other Essays*. New York: Bloch Publishing, 1916.

Rice, Thurman Brooks. *Racial Hygiene: A Practical Discussion of Eugenics and Race Culture*. New York: Macmillan, 1929.

Robinson, William J. *Practical Eugenics: Four Means of Improving the Human Race*. New York: Critic and Guide, 1912.

———. *Eugenics, Marriage and Birth Control*. New York: Critic and Guide, 1917.

———. *Fewer and Better Babies: Birth Control*. New York: Critic and Guide, 1928.

Ross, Edward A. *The Old World in the New*. New York: Century, 1914.

———. *Seventy Years of It: An Autobiography*. New York: D. Appleton, 1936.

Ryan, John Augustine. *Family Limitation and the Church and Birth Control*. New York: Paulist Press, ca. 1916.

———. *The Church and Socialism and Other Essays*. Washington, DC: Catholic University Press, 1919.

———. *A Catechism of the Social Question*. New York: Paulist Press, 1921.

———. *The Catholic Church and the Citizen*. New York: Macmillan, 1928.

———. *Moral Aspects of Sterilization*. Washington, DC: N.p., 1930.

———. *Questions of the Day*. Boston: Stratford, 1931.

———. *Human Sterilization*. Washington, DC: National Catholic Welfare Conference, 1936.

———. *Social Doctrine in Action: A Personal History*. New York: Harper and Brothers, 1941.

Saleeby, Caleb W. *Parenthood and Race Culture*. 1909; reprint New York: Moffat, Yard, 1911.

———. *Progress of Eugenics*. New York: Funk and Wagnalls, 1914.

———. *The Eugenic Prospect: National and Racial*. London: T.F. Unwin, 1921.

Sanger, Margaret. *The Case for Birth Control*. New York: Modern Art Printing, 1917.

———. *The Pivot of Civilization*. New York: Brentano's, 1922.

———. *Motherhood in Bondage*. New York: Brentano's, 1928.

———. *Margaret Sanger: An Autobiography*. New York: Norton, 1938.

Savage, Minot J. *The Passing and the Permanent in Religion*. New York: Putnam's Sons, 1901.

Schiller, Ferdinand C. S. *Eugenics and Politics: Essays*. London: Constable, 1926.

———. *Social Decay and Eugenical Reform*. New York: R. Long and R.R. Smith, 1932.

Schmiedeler, Edgar. *Sterilization in the United States*. Washington, DC: National Catholic Welfare Conference, 1943.

Shannon, T. W. *Nature's Secrets Revealed: Scientific Knowledge of Laws of Sex, Life, and Heredity; Or, Eugenics*. Marietta, OH: S.A. Mullikan, 1916.

Siegel, Morris. *Constructive Eugenics and Rational Marriage*. Toronto: McClelland and Stewart, 1934.

Slater, Thomas, S.J. *Questions of Moral Theology*. New York: Benziger Brothers, 1915.

Smith, Stevenson, et al. *A Summary of the Laws of the Several States*. Bulletin of the University of Washington, No. 82. Bailey and Babette Gatzert Foundation for Child Welfare, 1914.

Stoddard, Lothrop. *The Rising Tide of Color against White World Supremacy*. New York: Scribner, 1920.

———. *The Revolt against Civilization: The Menace of the Underman*. New York: Charles Scribner's Sons, 1922.

———. *Scientific Humanism*. New York: Charles Scribner's Sons, 1926.

Strahan, Samuel A. K. *Marriage and Disease: A Study of Heredity and the More Important Family Degenerations*. New York: D. Appleton, 1892.

Strong, Josiah. *Our Country*. New York: Baker and Taylor for the American Home Missionary Society, 1885.

Surbled, Georges. *Catholic Moral Teaching and Its Relation to Medicine and Hygiene*. St. Louis: B. Herder, 1930.

The Synagogue: Its Relation to Modern Thought and Life; Papers Delivered at the 32nd Council, Union of American Hebrew Congregations. Philadelphia: N.p., 1931.

Todd, Arthur J. *Theories of Social Progress: A Critical Study of the Attempts to Formulate the Conditions of Human Advance.* New York: Macmillan, 1918.

Truitt, W. J. *Eugenics.* Marietta, OH: S.A. Mullikan, 1917.

Underwood, Weeden B. *A Textbook of Sterilization.* Erie, PA: American Sterilization Co., 1934.

United States, Bureau of the Census. *Feeble-minded and Epileptics in Institutions: 1923.* Washington, DC: Government Printing Office, 1926.

United States, House of Representatives. *Hearings before the Committee on Immigration and Naturalization.* Seventy-First Congress. Washington, DC: Government Printing Office, 1930.

Walston, C. *Eugenics, Civics, and Ethics.* Cambridge, UK: Cambridge University Press, 1920.

Whetham, William C. D., and Catherine D. Whetham. *The Family and the Nation: A Study in Natural Inheritance and Social Responsibility.* New York: Longmans, Green, 1909.

White, Andrew Dickson. *A History of the Warfare of Science with Theology in Christendom.* 2 vols. New York: Appleton, 1896.

Whitehead, Alfred North. *Science and the Modern World.* 1925. Reprint, New York: Free Press, 1997.

Whitehead, Clayton S. *Ethical Sex Relations; Or, The New Eugenics.* Chicago: John A. Hertel, 1928.

Whiting, Phineas Westcott. *A Series of Eight Radio Talks on Heredity and Human Problems.* Pittsburgh, 1929. Broadcast from the University of Pittsburgh studio of KDKA, Westinghouse Electric and Manufacturing Company, Pittsburgh, PA.

Whitney, Leon F. *A Charity to Lessen Charity.* New Haven, CT: American Eugenics Society, 1926.

———. *The Case for Sterilization.* New York: Frederick A. Stokes, 1934.

Whitney, Leon F., and Ellsworth Huntington. *The Builders of America.* New York: Morrow, 1927.

Wickham, Harvey. *The Misbehaviorists: Pseudo-Science and the Modern Temper.* New York: Dial Press, 1928.

Wiggam, Albert E. *The New Decalogue of Science.* Indianapolis: Bobbs-Merrill, 1922.

———. *The Fruit of the Family Tree.* Indianapolis: Bobbs-Merrill, 1924.

———. *The Next Age of Man.* New York: Blue Ribbon Books, 1927.

Wilbur, Earl M. *The First Century of the Liberal Movement in American Religion.* Boston: N.p., 1916.

Williams, Charles D. *A Valid Christianity for To-Day.* New York: Macmillan, 1909.

Wise, Stephen S. *Changing Years: The Autobiography of Stephen Wise.* New York: G.P. Putnam's Sons, 1949.

———. *Stephen S. Wise Papers, 1874–1949.* Waltham, MA: American Jewish Historical Society, 1978.

Woods, Robert A. *The City Wilderness.* Boston, 1898.

Zangwill, Israel. *The Melting-Pot.* 1908. Reprint, New York: Arno Press, 1975.

———. *Chosen Peoples: The Hebraic Ideal versus the Teutonic.* New York: Macmillan, 1919.

Articles

Adami, G. "Unto Third and Fourth Generation: Study in Eugenics." *Canadian Medical Association Journal* 2 (1912): 963–983.
———. "The True Aristocracy." *Scientific Monthly* 13 (1921): 420–434.
Babbott, F. L. "Eugenical Research and National Welfare." *Eugenical News* 12 (1927): 93–102.
Bamfield, K. B. "Eugenics and the Sunday School Teacher." *Eugenics Review* 5 (1913–1914): 262.
Barker, L. F. "The Amelioration of the Conditions of the Handicapped and the Possibilities of Reduction of Their Numbers by Modifications of Heredity and of Environment." *Journal of the Michigan Medical Society* 34 (1935): 268–280.
Barnes, Reverend E. W. "Some Reflections on Eugenics and Religion." *Eugenics Review* 18 (1926–1927): 7–14.
———. "Science, Religion, and Moral Judgments." *Nature* 166 (1950): 455–457.
Batten, Samuel Zane. "The Redemption of the Unfit." *American Journal of Sociology* 14 (September 1908): 233–260.
Belford, John L. "Eugenics: The Religious Standpoint." *Long Island Medical Journal* 8 (1914): 292–295.
Bell, Alexander Graham. "A Few Thoughts Concerning Eugenics." *National Geographic* 11 (February 1908): 122.
Bell, Bernard Iddings. "Social Service and the Churches." *Atlantic Monthly* 115 (February 1915): 164.
Bell, J. H. "Eugenic Control and Its Relationship to the Science of Life and Reproduction." *Virginia Monthly Magazine* 58 (1931): 590–595.
Blacker, Charles P. "The Premarital Health Schedule and the Press." *Eugenics Review* 28 (1936–1937): 129–142.
Bluemel, C. S. "Binet Tests on Two Hundred Juvenile Delinquents." *Training School Bulletin* 12 (December 1915).
Boas, Franz. "Eugenics." *Scientific Monthly* 3 (1916): 471–478.
Booth, Meyrick. "Religious Belief as Affecting the Growth of Population." *Hibbert Journal* 13 (1914): 138–154.
Boston, Charles A. "A Protest against Laws Authorizing the Sterilization of Criminals and Imbeciles." *Journal of the American Institute of Criminal Law and Criminology* (1913): 326–358.
Brann, H. A. "The Catholic Doctrine of Marriage." *American Catholic Quarterly Review* 8 (July 1883): 385–404.
Brill, A. A. "The Adjustment of the Jew to the American Environment." *Mental Hygiene* 2 (April 1918): 220–231.
Brown, William Adams. "Changes in Theological Thought During the Last Generation." *Methodist Quarterly Review* 60 (1911): 38–47.
Bruehl, Charles. "The Church and Race Improvement." *Homiletic and Pastoral Review* 26 (June 1926): 903–913.
———. "Moral Aspects of Eugenics." *Homiletic and Pastoral Review* 26 (July 1926): 1011–1020.
———. "Eugenical Sterilization." *Homiletic and Pastoral Review* 26 (August 1926): 1123–1131.

———. "Moral Aspects of Sterilization." *Homiletic and Pastoral Review* (September 1926): 1235–1243.

———. "The State and Eugenical Sterilization." *Homiletic and Pastoral Review* 27 (October 1926): 1–9.

———. "The Morality of Sterilization." *Homiletic and Pastoral Review* 27 (November 1926): 113–119.

———. "Sterilization and Heredity." *Homiletic and Pastoral Review* 27 (December 1926): 225–231.

———. "Practical Objections against Legalized Sterilization." *Homiletic and Pastoral Review* 27 (January 1927): 341–48.

———. "Eugenics and Marriage." *Homiletic and Pastoral Review* 27 (February 1927): 457–465.

———. "Eugenical Education." *Homiletic and Pastoral Review* 27 (March 1927): 569–576.

———. "The Church and True Eugenics." *Homiletic and Pastoral Review* 27 (April 1927): 689–697.

———. "Eugenics in the Christian Sense." *Homiletic and Pastoral Review* 27 (May 1927): 801–809.

Buck v. Bell, Superintendent. 274 U.S. 200 (1927). *United States Reports 274*, United States Supreme Court (October Term, 1926): 200–208.

Burrell, David J. "How a More Kindly Relation between Jews and Christians May Be Furthered." *American Citizen* 1 (December 1912); 2 (February 1913); 4 (June 1913); 7 (December 1913).

Campbell, C. G. "The Eugenics Research Association: Human Evolution and Eugenics." *Eugenical News* 15 (1930): 89–97.

———. "The American Racial Outlook." *Eugenical News* 18 (1933): 45.

Cance, A. E., Irving Fisher, et al. "War, Immigration, and Eugenics." *Journal of Heredity* 7 (1916): 243–248.

Cofer, L. E. "Eugenics and Immigration." *Journal of Heredity* 6 (1915): 170–174.

Cole, Leon J. "Biological Eugenics." *Journal of Heredity* 5 (July 1914): 308.

Coleman, Lawrence J. "Is the Eugenist Scientific?" *Modern Schoolman* 12 (1934): 3–6.

Collins, Percy. "The Progress of Eugenics." *Scientific American* 109 (13 December 1913): 459.

Conklin, Edwin G. "Biology and Democracy." *Scribner's Magazine* 65 (1919): 408.

———. "Some Recent Criticism of Eugenics." *Eugenical News* 13 (1928): 61–65.

Conway, Bertrand L. "The Church and Eugenics." *Catholic World* 128 (November 1928): 151.

Coolidge, Calvin. "Whose Country Is This?" *Good Housekeeping* 72 (February 1921): 13–14, 106, 109.

Cooper, John M. "The Catholic Case against Birth Control." *Columbia* 9 (July 1930): 8–9.

Coulter, John M. "The Religious and Character Value of the Curriculum: Biology." *Religious Education* 6 (December 1911): 365–368.

Covitt, Louis D. "The Anthropology of the Jews." *The Monist* 26 (July 1916): 366–396.

Cox, Ignatius W. "The Folly of Human Sterilization." *Scientific American* 151 (October 1934): 189.

Crane, R. Newton. "Marriage Laws and Statutory Experiments in Eugenics in the United States." *Eugenics Review* 2 (April 1910): 73.

Crapsey, Algernon. "The Shame of the Churches." *Nation* 118 (16 January 1924): 53.

Darrow, Clarence. "The Edwardses and the Jukeses." *American Mercury* 6 (1925): 147–157.

———. "The Eugenics Cult." *American Mercury* 8 (June 1926): 137.

Davenport, Charles B. "Report of Committee on Eugenics." *American Breeders' Magazine* 1 (1910): 129.

———. "Eugenics and Euthenics." *Popular Science Monthly* (December 1910): 20.

———. "Eugenics and Charity." *Proceedings of the National Conference of Charities and Corrections* (1912): 280–282.

———. "Some Social Applications of Modern Principles of Heredity." *Transactions of the Fifteenth International Congress on Hygiene and Demography* 4 (1912): 658.

———. "Heredity, Culpability, Praiseworthiness, Punishment, and Reward." *Popular Science Monthly* 72 (July 1913): 35.

———. "The Importance to the State of Eugenic Investigation." *Proceedings of the First National Conference of Race Betterment, Jan. 8–12, 1914* (1914): 450–456.

———. "The Effects of Race Intermingling." *Proceedings of the American Philosophical Society* 46 (1917): 364–368.

———. "The Mechanism of Organic Evolution." *Annual Report of the Smithsonian Institution, 1930* (Washington, DC: Government Printing Office, 1931), 417–429.

Davenport, Gertrude. "The Eugenics Movement." *The Independent* (18 January 1912): 146–148.

———. "Society and the Feebleminded." *The Independent* (27 April 1914): 170.

David, Paul R. "The 'Sterilization Spectre.'" *Journal of Heredity* 44 (1933): 120–121.

Davis, W. E. "The Divine Plan of Racial Integrity." *Virginia Monthly Magazine* 52 (1925–1926): 288–290.

Dawson, George E. "100 Superfine Babies: What the Science of Eugenics Found in the Babies of Our Contest." *Good Housekeeping* (February 1912): 238–241.

Dickenson, Charles H. "The Social Purpose of Liberal Christianity." *Christian Century* 42 (12 March 1925): 344.

Dight, C. F. "Eugenics and Our Social Nature." *Medical World* 54 (1936): 177.

Donovan, Stephen M. "The Morality of the Operation of Vasectomy." *Ecclesiastical Review* 44 (1911): 562–574.

Dowling, Oscar. "The Marriage Health Certificate: A Deeply Rooted Social Problem." *American Journal of Public Health* 5 (November 1915): 1140.

Drake, Dr. Durant. "The Acceleration of Moral Progress." *Scientific Monthly* 2 (1916): 601–606.

Duvall, J. C. "The Purpose of Eugenics." *Birth Control Review* 8 (1924–1925): 344–366.

East, Edward M. "Hidden Feeblemindedness." *Journal of Heredity* 8 (1917): 215–217.

Editorial. "Catholic and Protestant Relations." *Christian Century* (14 April 1927): 456–457.

Ellis, Havelock. "Birth Control and Eugenics." *Eugenics Review* 9 (April 1917): 35.

"Eugenics and Happiness." *The Nation* 95 (1912): 75–76.

"Eugenics and Religion: Summary of a Debate Arranged by the Eugenics Society, April 25, 1933." *Eugenics Review* 25 (1933–1934): 101–103.

"Eugenics and Sex Hygiene." *Ecclesiastical Review* 8 (May 1913): 627–630.

"Eugenics for Democracy." *Time* 36 (9 September 1940): 34.

Evans, Hiram W. "The Klan's Fight for Americanism." *North American Review* 223 (1926): 33–63.

Federal Council of the Churches of Christ. "Moral Aspects of Birth Control." *Current History* 34 (1931): 97–100.

Feldman, W. M. "Eugenics from Jewish Standpoint." *Child* 4 (1913–1914): 785–791.

Field, James A. "The Progress of Eugenics." *Quarterly Journal of Economics* 26 (November 1911): 39–45.

Fielding, William J. "The Morality of Birth Control." *Birth Control Review* 4 (November 1920): 12–13.

Fisher, Irving. "Impending Problems of Eugenics." *Scientific Monthly* 13 (1921): 214–231.

Flick, Lawrence. "Eugenics and Mental Diseases." *Ecclesiastical Review*, 6th series, 1 (1914): 151–158.

Fosdick, Harry Emerson. "Shall the Fundamentalists Win?" *Christian Work* 102 (10 June 1922): 716.

———. "Evolution and Religion." *Ladies Home Journal* (September 1925): 12, 180, 183–185.

———. "Religion and Birth Control." *Outlook and Independent* (19 June 1929): 301.

Gailor, Thomas F. "The Power of Religion in the Home." *The Churchman* 107 (29 November 1913): 731.

Galton, Francis. "Hereditary Talent and Character." *Macmillan's Magazine* 12 (June 1865): 157–166.

———. "Statistical Inquiries into the Efficacy of Prayer." *Fortnightly Review* 12 (August 1872): 125–135.

———. "The Possible Improvement of the Human Breed under Existing Conditions of Law and Sentiment." *Popular Science Monthly* 60 (January 1902): 219.

———. "Eugenics: Its Definition, Scope, and Aims." *American Journal of Sociology* 10 (July 1904): 5.

———. "Eugenics as a Factor in Religion," in *Essays in Eugenics*. London: Eugenics Education Society, 1909.

———. "Why a Man with a Long Pedigree Is Inclined to Ferocity." *Current Literature* 42 (January 1907): 102–103.

Gartley, A. "Study in Eugenic Genealogy." *American Breeders' Magazine* 3 (1912): 241–249.

Gerrard, Thomas J. "The Catholic Church and Race Culture." *Dublin Review* 149 (July 1911): 55.

———. "Eugenics and Catholic Teaching." *Catholic World* 95 (June 1912): 289–304.

———. "Sanctity and Racial Betterment." *Catholic World* 95 (1912): 726–728.

Gessell, Arnold L. "The Village of a Thousand Souls." *American Magazine* 76 (1913): 11–15.

Glenn, John M. "The Church and Social Work." *The Churchman* 108 (23 August 1913): 247.

Goddard, Henry Herbert. "Mental Tests and the Immigrant." *Journal of Delinquency* 2 (1917): 243–277.

Gough, John Jay. "A Program of Treatment for the Feebleminded." *Catholic Charities Review* (May 1926).

Grant, Madison. "Discussion of Article on Democracy and Heredity." *Journal of Heredity* 10 (1919): 164–165.

Grant, Reverend Percy Stickney. "American Ideals and Race Mixture." *North American Review* 195 (April 1912): 514–522.

Haberton, John. "Social Science in the Pulpit." *Chautauquan* 14 (1891–1892): 175–179.

Haldane, J. B. S. "Heredity: Some Fallacies." In *Science and Everyday Life*. London: Lawrence and Wishart, 1939.

Hall, G. Stanley. "Eugenics: Its Ideals and What It Is Going to Do." *Religious Education* 6 (June 1911): 152–159.

———. "Education and the Social Hygiene Movement." *Social Hygiene* 1 December 1914): 35.

Hall, Prescott F. "Immigration Restriction and World Eugenics." *Journal of Heredity* 10 (March 1919): 125–127.

Hamilton, A. E. "Eugenics." *Pedagogical Seminary* 21 (March 1914): 28–61.

———. "What to Say about Marriage?" *Journal of Heredity* 7 (February 1916): 78–79.

Hankins, Frank. "The Interdependence of Eugenics and Birth Control." *Birth Control Review* 15 (June 1931): 170–171.

Hard, William. "The Catholic Church Accepts the Challenge." *Metropolitan* (January 1920): 27.

Harding, T. S. "Are We Breeding Weaklings?" *American Journal of Sociology* 42 (1936–1937): 672–681.

Hawkinson, O. "Eugenics and Its Relation to the Community." *Illinois Medical Journal* 70 (1936): 376–379.

"Hereditary Genius." *Catholic World* 11 (September 1870): 721–732.

Hodson, Cora B. S. "International Federation of Eugenic Organizations: Report of the 1936 Conference." *Eugenics Review* 28 (1936–1937): 217–219.

Holmes, John Haynes. "The Catholic Issue." *Nation* (3 May 1943): 596.

Holmes, S. J. "The Opposition to Eugenics." *Science* 89 (1939): 351–357.

Holt, W. L. "Economic Factors in Eugenics." *Popular Science Monthly* 83 (1913): 471–483.

Horder, Lord. "Eugenics and the Doctor." *British Medical Journal* 1 (1933): 1057–1060.

———. "The Case for Eugenics." *British Medical Journal* 2 (1935): 694.

Hough, Ellis J. "Terrors of the Protestant Ministry." *Presbyterian Advance* 40 (30 January 1930): 18.

Huntington, Ellsworth. "The Eugenic Point of View." *Contraception* 1 (1935): 109.

———. "The Puritan as a Racial Stock." *Eugenical News* (1935): 49.

Inge, William Ralph. "Some Moral Aspects of Eugenics." *Birth Control Review* 4 (June 1920): 9.

———. "Eugenics and Religion." *Eugenics Review* 12 (1920): 257–265.

Ireland, Alleyne. "Democracy and the Accepted Facts of Heredity: A Biological View of Government." *Journal of Heredity* 9 (December 1918): 341.

Israel, Edward L. "The Catholic Problem." *Reconstructionist* (May 1941): 6.

Jennings, Herbert S. "Undesirable Aliens." *Survey* 51 (15 December 1923): 309–312, 364.

———. "Heredity and Environment." *Scientific Monthly* 19 (September 1924): 234–238.

———. "Health Progress and Race Progress: Are They Incompatible?" *Journal of Heredity* 18 (1927): 271–276.

Johnson, Roswell H. "Eugenic Aspects of Sexual Immorality." *Journal of Heredity* 8 (March 1917): 121.

———. "Eugenic Aspects of Birth Control." *Birth Control Review* 6 (1922): 16.

———. "Eugenics and Mormonism." *Eugenics* 1 (1928): 5–8.

Jordan, David Starr. "The Blood of the Nation: A Study in the Decay of Races through the Survival of the Unfit." *Popular Science Monthly* 59 (May 1901): 97–98.

———. "The Eugenics of War." *American Breeders' Magazine* 4 (1913): 140.

Jordan, Harvey E. "Heredity as a Factor in the Improvement of Social Conditions." *American Breeders' Magazine* 2 (1911): 246–254.

Kenkel, F. P. "Eugenics under Catholic Custom and Laws." *Central-Blatt and Social Justice* 19 (February 1927): 368.

Kennedy, Walter B. "The Supreme Court and Social Legislation." *Catholic Charities Review* 7 (1923): 208–212.

Key, W. E. "Better American Families." *Journal of Heredity* 10 (1919): 107–110.

Kite, Elizabeth. "Unto the Third Generation." *Survey* 28 (1912): 789–791.

———. "The 'Pineys.'" *Survey* 31 (1913–1914): 7–13, 38–40.

Kohs, Samuel C.. "New Light on Eugenics." *Journal of Heredity* 6 (October 1915): 447–450.

Kroeber, Alfred L. "Inheritance by Magic." *American Anthropology* 18 (January 1916): 19–40.

———. "The Superorganic." *American Anthropologist*, new series 19 (April–June 1917): 163–213.

Laboure, Theo. "A Backward Glimpse over the Articles on Vasectomy." *Ecclesiastical Review* 48 (May 1913): 553–563.

Landman, J. H. "Race Betterment by Human Sterilization." *Scientific American* 150 (June 1934): 293.

Lapp, John A. "Justice First." *Catholic Charities Review* 11 (1927): 201–209.

Laughlin, H. H. "Eugenics." *Nature Study Review* (March 1912): 111.

———. "The Relation of Eugenics to Other Sciences." *Eugenics Review* 11 (June 1919): 53–64.

———. "The Eugenics Exhibit at Chicago: A Description of the Wall-panel Survey of Eugenics Exhibited in the Hall of Science, Century of Progress Exhibition, Chicago, 1933–1934." *Journal of Heredity* 26 (1935): 155–162.

Lewis, A. "German Eugenic Legislation: An Examination of Fact and Theory." *Eugenics Review* 26 (1934): 183–191.

Lonergan, Father William I., S.J. "The Morality of Sterilization Laws." *America* (13 March 1926).

Lyttelton, Edward. "Eugenics, Ethics, and Religion." *The Nineteenth Century* 7 (July 1913): 157.

Mangold, George B. "Unlawful Motherhood." *Forum* 53 (1915): 335–343.

McCulloch, Reverend Oscar C. "The Tribe of Ishmael: A Study in Social Degradation." In *Proceedings of the National Conference of Charities and Corrections* (1888): 154–159.

Mencken, H. L. "Utopia by Sterilization." *American Mercury* 41 (August 1937): 406.

Metcalf, Maynard M. "Evolution and Man." *Journal of Heredity* 7 (August 1916): 364.

"The Morality and Lawfulness of Vasectomy." *Ecclesiastical Review* 44 (May 1911): 564.

More, Louis Trenchard. "The Scientific Claims of Eugenics." *Hibbert Journal* 13 (1915): 355–66.

Muller, Hermann J. "The Dominance of Economics over Eugenics." *Scientific Monthly* 37 (July 1933): 40.

Muttkowski, Dr. R. A. "The Practical Hygiene of the Church." *Thought* (June 1926).

Myerson, Abraham. "A Critique of Proposed 'Ideal' Sterilization Legislation." *Archives of Neurology and Psychiatry* 33 (1935): 453–466.

Nabours, R. K. "Limitations and Promises of Eugenics." *Journal of Heredity* 14 (1923): 277–288.

Nearing, Nellie M. L., and Scott Nearing. "When a Girl Is Asked to Marry." *Ladies Home Journal* (March 1912): 7, 69–70.

Niebuhr, Reinhold. "Shall We Proclaim the Truth or Search for It?" *Christian Century* 42 (12 March 1925): 334.

———. "How Adventurous Is Dr. Fosdick?" *Christian Century* 44 (6 January 1927): 17–18.

Ochsner, A. J. "Surgical Treatment of Habitual Criminals." *Journal of the American Medical Association* 32 (April 1899): 867–868.

O'Hara, Edwin V. "The Works of Dr. John A. Ryan." *America* (24 February 1923): 448–449.

O'Malley, Austin. "Vasectomy in Defectives." *Ecclesiastical Review* 44 (June 1911): 684–705.

Osborn, Frederick. "Implications of the New Studies in Population and Psychology for the Development of Eugenics Philosophy." *Eugenical News* 22 (1937): 104–107.

———. "Development of a Eugenic Philosophy." *American Sociological Review* 2 (June 1937): 391–394.

———. "The American Concept of Eugenics." *Journal of Heredity* 30 (1939): 110.

———. "History of the American Eugenics Society." *Social Biology* 21 (1974): 115–126.

Osborn, Henry Fairfield. "Birth Selection vs. Birth Control." *Forum* 88 (August 1932): 79.

Pearl, Raymond. "The Biology of Superiority." *American Mercury* 12 (November 1927): 260.

———. "Breeding Better Men." *World's Work* 15 (1908): 9818–9824.

Peile, Reverend J. H. F. "Eugenics and the Church." *Eugenics Review* 1 (1909): 163–173.

Pitkin, Walter B. "The New Testament of Science." *The Century* 114 (June 1927): 170–171.

Popenoe, Paul. "Nature or Nurture?" *Journal of Heredity* 6 (May 1915): 227.

———. "Will Morality Disappear?" *Journal of Heredity* 9 (October 1918): 270.

"Popular Appreciation of Scientists." *Nation* 74 (16 January 1902): 47.

Roloff, Bernard C. "The 'Eugenic' Marriage Laws of Wisconsin, Michigan, and Indiana." *Social Hygiene* 6 (April 1920): 233–234.

Ross, Edward A. "The Causes of Race Superiority." *Annals of the American Academy of Political and Social Science* 18 (1 July 1901): 67–89.

Rucker, W. C. "More 'Eugenic' Laws." *Journal of Social Hygiene* 1 (June 1915): 490–491.

Ryan, John Augustine. "The Small Family and National Decadence." *Ecclesiastical Review* (February 1904): 140–155.

———. "Is the Modern Spirit Anti-Religious?" *Catholic World* (May 1907): 185, 188.

———. "The Fallacy of 'Bettering One's Position.'" *Catholic World* (November 1907): 145–156.

———. "Catholic Social Principles and Practical Social Remedies." *Fortnightly Review* (March 1912): 143–145.

———. "The Church and Social Work." *Proceedings of the National Conference of Charities and Corrections* (1913): 156–158.

———. "The Social Side of Charity" *Proceedings of the Third Biennial Meeting of the National Conference of Catholic Charities* (1914): 269–273.

———. "Family Limitation." *Ecclesiastical Review* 54 (1916): 684–696.

———. "Unprotected Natural Rights." *Commonweal* (15 June 1927): 151–152.

———. "Is Birth Control Right? A Debate. Part II: The Wrong of it." *Forum* (July 1927): 18–19.

———. "The 'Perverted Faculty' Argument against Birth Prevention." *Ecclesiastical Review* (August 1928): 133–145.

———. "Sterilization." *Ecclesiastical Review* 84 (1931): 267–271.

———. "The Moral Teaching of the Encyclical." *Ecclesiastical Review* (March 1931): 267–268.

———. "Economic and Social Objections to Birth Control." *National Catholic Welfare Council press release*, 19 May 1932.

———. "The Attitude of the Roman Catholic Church towards Radical Social Reforms." *Community Forum* (n.d.): 15.

Salaman, Redcliffe N. "Heredity and the Jew." *Journal of Genetics* 1 (1911): 273–292.

Schiller, F. C. S. "Eugenics as a Moral Ideal: The Beginning of a Progressive Reform." *Eugenics Review* 22 (1930–1931): 103–109.

Schufeldt, R. W. "The Man of the Future." *Science* 18 (16 October 1891): 218–219.

Seton, William. "Heredity in Man." *Catholic World* 75 (October 1901): 67.

Smith, Jesse Spaulding. "Marriage, Sterilization, and Commitment Laws Aimed at Decreasing Mental Deficiency." *Journal of the American Institute of Criminal Law and Criminology* 5 (September 1914): 364–370.

Snow, William F. "The Swing of the Pendulum on Sex Hygiene." *Survey* 32 (1914): 6.

Somerville, Henry. "Eugenics and the Feeble-Minded." *Catholic World* 105 (1917): 209–218.

"Sterilization Conflicts." *Commonweal* (12 April 1935): 680–681.

Stoller, James H. "Human Heredity." *Popular Science Monthly* 37 (July 1890): 359–365.

Strunsky, Simeon. "Race Culture." *Atlantic Monthly* 110 (December 1912): 851.

Talbert, Dr. Ernest L. "On Francis Galton's Scientific Contribution to the Psychology of Religion." *Scientific Monthly* 37 (1933): 53–54.

Thayer, Walter N. "What May We Do with Our Criminals?" *Survey* 24 (9 July 1910): 587–589.

Thomson, J. A. "Eugenics and War." *Popular Science Monthly* 86 (1915): 417–427.

Thorndike, Edward L. "The Decrease in Size of American Families." *Popular Science Monthly* 63 (May 1903): 64–70.

———. "Eugenics: Intellect and Character." *Popular Science Monthly* 83 (1913): 125–138.

Wallace, Alfred Russell. "Human Selection." *Popular Science Monthly* 38 (November 1890): 106.

Walsh, James J. "The Story of Organized Care of the Insane and Defectives." *Catholic World* 104 (November 1916): 226–228.

———. "Race Betterment." *Commonweal* 19 (1934): 371–372.

Ward, Lester F. "Eugenics, Euthenics, and Eudemics." *American Journal of Sociology* 181 (May 1913): 751.

Whetham, W. C. D. and C. D. Whetham. "Decadence and Civilisation." *Hibbert Journal* 10 (October 1911): 193.

Wiggam, Albert E. "The Religion of the Scientist." *World's Work* 50 (August 1925).

———. "The Rising Tide of Degeneracy: What Everybody Ought to Know about Eugenics." *World's Work* 53 (1926): 25–33.

———. "Shall I Marry This Man?" *Good Housekeeping* 84 (June 1927): 28–29.

———. "New Styles in Ancestors." *World's Work* 55 (December 1927): 142–150.

———. "Are Dummies Born or Made?" *Ladies Home Journal* 57 (March 1940): 123.

Wilcox, Ella Wheeler. "The Forecast." *Good Housekeeping* (July 1912): 130.

Windle, Bertram C. A. "A Rule of Life." *Catholic World* 103 (August 1916): 577–587.

Wolfe, A. B. "Literature of Eugenics." *American Economic Review* 3 (March 1913): 165.

Woods, Frederick Adams. "Will Not Morality Necessarily Improve?" *Journal of Heredity* 9 (November 1918): 332.

Yerkes, Robert M. "Testing the Human Mind." *Atlantic Monthly* 131 (March 1923): 367.

Published Secondary Sources: Books and Articles

Abell, Aaron I. *American Catholicism and Social Action: A Search for Social Justice, 1865–1950.* Garden City, NY: Hanover House, 1960.

———. "The Bishops' 1919 Program." *Social Order* (March 1962): 109–118.

Abrams, Ray H. *Preachers Present Arms.* New York: Round Table Press, 1933.

Adams, Mark B., ed. *The Wellborn Science: Eugenics in Germany, France, Brazil and Russia.* New York: Oxford University Press 1990.

Ahlstrom, Sydney. "Continental Influence on American Christian Thought Since World War I." *Church History* 27 (September 1958): 256–272.

———. *A Religious History of the American People.* New Haven: Yale University Press, 1972.

Alchon, Guy. *The Invisible Hand of Planning: Capitalism, Social Science, and the State in the 1920s.* Princeton: Princeton University Press, 1985.

Alexander, Charles C. "Prophet of American Racism: Madison Grant and the Nordic Myth." *Phylon* 23 (spring 1962): 73–90.

Allen, Frederick Lewis. *Only Yesterday: An Informal History of the 1920s.* New York: Harper and Brothers, 1931.

Allen, Garland E. "Genetics, Eugenics, and Class Struggle." *Genetics* 79 (June 1975): 29–45.

———. "Genetics, Eugenics, and Society: Internalists and Externalists in Contemporary History of Science." *Social Studies of Science* 6 (1976): 105–122.

———. "The Misuse of Biological Hierarchies: The American Eugenics Movement, 1900–1940." *History and Philosophy of the Life Sciences* (Italy) 5 (1983): 105–128.

———. "The Eugenics Record Office at Cold Spring Harbor, 1910–1940: An Essay in Institutional History." *Osiris* 2 (1986): 225–264.

———. "Old Wine in New Bottles: From Eugenics to Population Control in the Work of Raymond Pearl." In *The Expansion of American Biology*, ed. Keith R. Benson, Jane Maienschein, and Ronald Rainger. New Brunswick, NJ: Rutgers University Press, 1991.

Allitt, Patrick. "The American Christ." *American Heritage* (November 1988): 129–141.

———. *Catholic Converts: British and American Intellectuals Turn to Rome.* Ithaca, NY: Cornell University Press, 1997.

Anderson, Eric. "Prostitution and Social Justice: Chicago, 1910–1915." *Social Service Review* 48 (1974): 203–228.

Appleby, Scott. *Church and Age Unite! The Modernist Impulse in American Catholicism.* Notre Dame, IN: University of Notre Dame Press, 1992.

Bailey, Beth L. "Scientific Truth . . . and Love: The Marriage Education Movement in the United States." *Journal of Social History* 20 (1987): 711–732.

Bajema, Carl J., ed. *Eugenics: Then and Now.* Stroudsburg, PA: Dowden, Hutchinson and Ross, 1976.

Baltzell, E. Digby. *The Protestant Establishment: Aristocracy and Caste in America.* New Haven: Yale University Press, 1964.

Bannister, Robert. *Social Darwinism: Science and Myth in Anglo-American Thought.* Philadelphia: Temple University Press, 1979.

Barbour, Ian G. *Issues in Science and Religion.* Englewood Cliffs, NJ: Prentice-Hall, 1966.

———. *Religion in an Age of Science: The Gifford Lectures.* Vol. 1. New York: Harper Collins, 1990.

Baritz, Loren, ed. *The Culture of the Twenties.* Indianapolis: Bobbs-Merrill, 1970.

Barkan, Elazar. "Mobilizing Scientists against Nazi Racism, 1933–1939." In *Bones, Bodies, Behavior: Essays on Biological Anthropology*, ed. George W. Stocking. Madison: University of Wisconsin Press, 1988.

———. "Reevaluating Progressive Eugenics: Herbert S. Jennings and the 1924 Immigration Legislation." *Journal of the History of Biology* 24 (1991): 91–112.

———. *The Retreat of Scientific Racism: Changing Concepts of Race in Britain and the United States between the World Wars.* Cambridge, UK: Cambridge University Press, 1992.

Barker, David. "The Biology of Stupidity: Genetics, Eugenics and Mental Deficiency in the Inter-War Years." *British Journal of the History of Science* 22 (1989): 347–375.

Barnes, Barry. *Scientific Knowledge and Sociological Theory.* London: Routledge and Kegan Paul, 1974.

Beardsley, E. H. "The American Scientist as Social Activist." *Isis* 64 (1973): 50–66.

Beckley, Harlan. *Passion for Justice: Retrieving the Legacies of Walter Rauschenbusch, John A. Ryan, and Reinhold Niebuhr.* Louisville, KY: John Knox Press, 1992.

Bellomy, Donald C. "Two Generations: Modernists and Progressives, 1870–1920." *Perspectives in American History*, new series 3 (1987): 269–306.

Betts, John Rickards. "Darwinism, Evolution and American Catholic Thought, 1860–1900." *Catholic Historical Review* 45 June 1959): 161–185.

Bird, Randall D., and Garland Allen. "The J.H.B. Archive Report: The Papers of H. H. Laughlin." *Journal of the History of Biology* 14 (1981): 339–353.

Borell, Merriley. "Biologists and the Promotion of Birth Control Research, 1918–1938." *Journal of the History of Biology* 20 (spring 1987): 51–87.

Bowler, Peter J. *The Mendelian Revolution: The Emergence of Hereditarian Concepts in Modern Science and Society.* Baltimore: Johns Hopkins University Press, 1989.

———. "The Role of the History of Science in the Understanding of Social Darwinism and Eugenics." *Impact of Science on Society* 40 (1990): 273–278.

———. *Biology and Social Thought, 1850–1914.* Berkeley: Office for History of Science and Technology, University of California at Berkeley, 1993.

Bozeman, Theodore Dwight. *Protestants in an Age of Science: The Baconian Ideal and Antebellum American Religious Thought.* Chapel Hill: University of North Carolina Press, 1977.

Brandt, Allan M. *No Magic Bullet: A Social History of Venereal Disease in the United States Since 1880.* New York: Oxford University Press, 1985.

Broderick, Francis L. *Right Reverend New Dealer: John A. Ryan.* New York: Macmillan, 1963.

Brooke, John Hedley. *Science and Religion: Some Historical Perspectives.* Cambridge, UK: Cambridge University Press, 1991.

Burnham, John C. "The Progressive Era Revolution in American Attitudes toward Sex." *Journal of American History* 59 March 1973): 885–908.

Bush, Lester E. "Ethical Issues in Reproductive Medicine: A Mormon Perspective." *Dialogue* 18 (1985): 40–66.

Buss, Allan R. "Galton and the Birth of Differential Psychology and Eugenics: Social, Political, and Economic Forces." *Journal of the History of the Behavioral Sciences* 12 (1976): 47–58.

Canovan, Margaret. *G. K. Chesterton: Radical Populist.* New York: Harcourt, Brace, Jovanovich, 1977.

Carden, Maren Lockwood. *Oneida: Utopian Community to Modern Corporation.* Baltimore: Johns Hopkins University Press, 1969.

Carey, Allison C. "Gender and Compulsory Sterilization Programs in America, 1907–1950." *Journal of Historical Sociology* 11 (March 1998): 74–105.

Carlen, Claudia, ed. *The Papal Encyclicals, 1903–1939.* New York: New American Library, 1981.

Carson, John. "Army Alpha, Army Brass, and the Search for Army Intelligence." *Isis* 84 (1993): 278–309.

Carter, Paul A. *The Decline and Revival of the Social Gospel: Social and Political Liberalism in American Protestant Churches, 1920–1940.* New York: Archon, 1954.

———. "The Fundamentalist Defense of the Faith." In *Change and Continuity in Twentieth-Century America: The 1920s,* ed. John Braemen, Robert H. Bremner, and David Brody. Columbus: Ohio State University Press, 1968.

Cauthen, Kenneth. *The Impact of American Religious Liberalism.* New York: Harper and Row, 1962.

Chamberlin, J. Edward, and Sander L. Gilman, eds. *Degeneration: The Dark Side of Progress.* New York: Columbia University Press, 1985.

Chambers, Clarke A. *Seedtime of Reform: American Social Service and Social Action, 1918–1933.* Ann Arbor: University of Michigan Press, 1967.

Chase, Allan. *The Legacy of Malthus: The Social Cost of the New Scientific Racism.* New York: Knopf, 1977.

Cherry, Conrad, ed. *God's New Israel: Religious Interpretations of American Destiny*. Englewood Cliffs, NJ: Prentice-Hall, 1971.

———. *Hurrying toward Zion: Universities, Divinity Schools, and American Protestantism*. Indianapolis: Indiana University Press, 1995.

Clampett, Frederick W. *Luther Burbank, "Our Beloved Infidel": His Religion of Humanity*. Westport, CT: Greenwood Press, 1970.

Cohen, Naomi W. "The Challenges of Darwinism and Biblical Criticism to American Judaism." *Modern Judaism* 4 (May 1984): 121–157.

Commager, Henry Steele. *The American Mind: An Interpretation of American Thought and Character Since the 1880s*. New Haven: Yale University Press, 1950.

Conkin, Paul. *When All the Gods Trembled: Darwinism, Scopes, and American Intellectuals*. New York: Rowman and Littlefield, 1998.

Cooke, Kathy J. "Human Fertility and Differential Birthrates in American Eugenics and Genetics: A Brief History." *Mount Sinai Journal of Medicine* 65 (May 1998): 161–166.

Cowan, Ruth S. "Nature and Nurture: The Interplay of Biology and Politics in the Work of Francis Galton." *Studies in the History of Biology* 1 (1977): 135–207.

———. *Sir Francis Galton and the Study of Heredity in the Nineteenth Century*. New York: Garland, 1985.

Cravens, Hamilton. *Triumph of Evolution: American Scientists and the Heredity-Environment Controversy, 1900–1914*. Philadelphia: University of Pennsylvania Press, 1978.

Croce, Paul Jerome. *Science and Religion in the Era of William James. Vol. 1: Eclipse of Certainty, 1820–1880*. Chapel Hill: University of North Carolina Press, 1995.

Crook, Paul. "W. R. Inge and the Cultural Crisis, 1899–1920." *Journal of Religious History* 16 (1991): 410–432.

Cross, Robert D. *The Emergence of Liberal Catholicism in America*. Cambridge, MA: Harvard University Press, 1958.

Crow, James F. "Eugenics: Must It Be a Dirty Word?" *Contemporary Psychology* 33 (1988): 10–12.

Crunden, Robert M. *Ministers of Reform: The Progressives' Achievement in American Civilization, 1889–1920*. Chicago: University of Chicago Press, 1984.

Curran, Charles E. *Directions in Catholic Social Ethics*. Notre Dame, IN: University of Notre Dame Press, 1985.

Curti, Merle. *Human Nature in American Thought: A History*. Madison: University of Wisconsin Press, 1980.

Curtis, Susan. *A Consuming Faith: The Social Gospel and Modern American Culture*. Baltimore: Johns Hopkins University Press, 1991.

Cynkar, R. J. "*Buck v. Bell*: Felt Necessities v. Fundamental Values?" *Columbia Law Review* 81 (1981): 1418–1461.

Dann, Kevin. "From Degeneration to Regeneration: The Eugenics Survey of Vermont, 1925–1936." *Vermont History* 59 (winter 1991): 5–29.

Davis, Allen F. *Spearheads for Reform: The Social Settlements and the Progressive Movement, 1890–1914*. New York: Oxford University Press, 1967.

Degler, Carl. *In Search of Human Nature: The Decline and Revival of Darwinism in American Social Thought*. New York: Oxford University Press, 1991.

Devlin, Dennis S. "Better Living through Heredity: Michael F. Guyer and the American Eugenics Movement." *Michigan Academician* 16 (1984): 199–208.

Dietrich, Donald J. "Catholic Eugenics in Germany 1920–1945: Hermann Muckermann, S.J. and Joseph Mayer." *Journal of Church and State* 34 (1992): 575–600.

Dikotter, Frank. "Race Culture: Recent Perspectives on the History of Eugenics." *American Historical Review* 103 (April 1998): 467–478.

Dinnerstein, Leonard. *Anti-Semitism in America.* New York: Oxford University Press, 1994.

Divine, Robert. *American Immigration Policy, 1924–1952.* New Haven: Yale University Press, 1951.

Dolan, Jay P. *The American Catholic Experience: A History from Colonial Times to the Present.* Notre Dame, IN: University of Notre Dame Press, 1992.

Dorsett, Lyle. *Billy Sunday and the Redemption of Urban America.* Grand Rapids, MI: William B. Eerdmans, 1991.

Dowbiggin, Ian Robert. "An Exodus of Enthusiasm: G. Alder Blumer, Eugenics, and U.S. Psychiatry, 1890–1920." *Medical History* 36 (1992): 379–402.

———. *Keeping America Sane: Psychiatry and Eugenics in the United States and Canada, 1880–1940.* Ithaca, NY: Cornell University Press, 1997.

Dyer, Thomas G. *Theodore Roosevelt and the Idea of Race.* Baton Rouge: Louisiana State University Press, 1980.

Ellis, John Tracy. *Perspectives in American Catholicism.* Baltimore: Helicon, 1963.

Fallows, Alice Katherine. *Everybody's Bishop.* New York: J.H. Sears, 1927.

Farrall, Lyndsay A. "The History of Eugenics: A Bibliographical Review." *Annals of Science* 36 (1979): 111–123.

———. *The Origins and Growth of the English Eugenics Movement, 1865–1912.* New York: Garland, 1985.

Fass, Paula S. *The Damned and the Beautiful: American Youth in the 1920s.* New York: Oxford University Press, 1977.

Feldman, Egal. "The Social Gospel and the Jew." *American Jewish Historical Quarterly* 58 (1968–1969): 308–322.

Filler, Louis. *The Muckrakers.* 1939. Reprint, Stanford: Stanford University Press, 1968.

Fong, Melanie, and Larry O. Johnson. "The Eugenics Movement: Some Insight into the Institutionalization of Racism." *Issues in Criminology* 9 (1974): 89–115.

Fortin, Ernest L. "St. Thomas Aquinas." In *History of Political Philosophy*, ed. Leo Strauss and Joseph Cropsey, 253–259. Chicago: University of Chicago Press, 1987.

Fox, Richard Wightman. "The Culture of Liberal Protestant Progressivism, 1875–1925." *Journal of Interdisciplinary History* 23 (winter 1993): 639–660.

———. *Reinhold Niebuhr: A Biography.* New York: Pantheon, 1985.

Freeden, Michael. "Eugenics and Progressive Thought: A Study in Ideological Affinity." *Historical Journal* 22 (1979): 645–671.

———. "Eugenics and Ideology." *Historical Journal* 26 (1983): 959–962.

Garside, P. L. "Unhealthy Areas: Town Planning, Eugenics, and the Slums, 1890–1974." *Planning Perspectives* 3 (1988): 24–46.

Gasking, Elizabeth. "Why Was Mendel's Work Ignored?" *Journal of the History of Ideas* 20 (1959): 60–84.

Gavin, Donald P. *The National Conference of Catholic Charities, 1910–1960.* Milwaukee: Catholic Life Publications, 1962.

Gearty, Patrick William. *The Economic Thought of Monsignor John A. Ryan.* Washington, DC: Catholic University of America Press, 1953.

Gelb, Steven A. "Myths, Morons, Psychologists: The Kallikak Family Revisited." *Review of Education* 11 (1985): 255–259.

———. "Henry H. Goddard and the Immigrants, 1910–1917: The Studies and Their Social Context." *Journal of the History of the Behavioral Sciences* 22 (October 1986): 324–332.

———. "Social Deviance and the 'Discovery' of the Moron." *Disability, Handicap, and Society* 2 (1987): 247–258.

———. "Degeneracy Theory, Eugenics, and Family Studies." *Journal of the History of the Behavioral Sciences* 26 (July 1990): 242–245.

Gilbert, James. *Redeeming Culture: American Religion in an Age of Science.* Chicago: University of Chicago Press, 1997.

Glass, Bentley. "Geneticists Embattled: Their Stand against Rampant Eugenics and Racism in America During the 1920s." *Proceedings of the American Philosophical Society Library* 130 (1986): 130–154.

Glass, Bentley, Owsei Temkin, and William J. Strauss Jr., eds. *Forerunners of Darwin: 1754–1859.* Baltimore: Johns Hopkins University Press, 1959.

Glazer, Nathan. *American Judaism.* 1957. Reprint, Chicago: University of Chicago Press, 1989.

Goldman, Eric F. *Rendezvous with Destiny: A History of Modern American Reform.* 1952. Reprint, New York: Vintage, 1977.

Gordon, Linda. "The Politics of Population: Birth Control and the Eugenics Movement." *Radical America* 8 (1974): 61–97.

———. "Birth Control and the Eugenists." *Science for the People* 9 (March–April 1977): 8–15.

———. *Woman's Body, Woman's Right: A Social History of Birth Control in America.* New York: Penguin Books, 1977.

Gorrell, Donald K. *The Age of Social Responsibility: The Social Gospel in the Progressive Era, 1900–1920.* Macon, GA: Mercer University Press, 1988.

Gould, Stephen Jay. *The Mismeasure of Man.* New York: Norton, 1981.

———. "Science and Jewish Immigration." In *Hen's Teeth and Horse's Toes.* New York: Norton, 1983.

Graham, Loren R. "Science and Values: The Eugenics Movement in Germany and Russia in the 1920s." *American Historical Review* 82 (1977): 1133–1164.

———. *Between Science and Values.* New York: Columbia University Press, 1981.

Green, Harvey. *The Uncertainty of Everyday Life, 1915–1945.* New York: Harper Collins, 1992.

Greene, John C. *The Death of Adam: Evolution and Its Impact on Western Thought.* 1959. Reprint, Ames: Iowa State University Press, 1996.

Griffin, Clifford S. "Religious Benevolence as Social Control, 1815–1860." *Mississippi Valley Historical Review* 44 (December 1957): 423–444.

Haller, John S., Jr. *Outcasts from Evolution: Scientific Attitudes of Racial Inferiority, 1859–1900.* Carbondale: Southern Illinois University Press, 1971.

————. "The Role of Physicians in America's Sterilization Movement, 1894–1925." *New York State Journal of Medicine* 89 (1989): 169–179.

Haller, Mark. *Eugenics: Hereditarian Attitudes in American Thought.* New Brunswick, NJ: Rutgers University Press, 1963.

————. "Social Science and Genetics: A Historical Perspective." In *Genetics*, ed. D. C. Glass. New York: Rockefeller University Press, 1968.

Halsey, William M. *The Survival of American Innocence: Catholicism in an Era of Disillusionment, 1920–1940.* Notre Dame, IN: University of Notre Dame Press, 1980.

Handlin, Oscar. *Adventure in Freedom: 300 Years of Jewish Life in America.* New York: McGraw-Hill, 1954.

Handy, Robert T. "The American Religious Depression." *Church History* 29 (1960): 3–16.

————. *A Christian America: Protestant Hopes and Historical Realities.* New York: Oxford University Press, 1971.

————. *A History of Union Theological Seminary in New York.* New York: Columbia University Press, 1987.

Harwood, Jonathan. "Nature, Nurture, and Politics: A Critique of the Conventional Wisdom." In *The Meritocratic Intellect*, ed. James V. Smith and David Hamilton. Aberdeen, Scotland: Aberdeen University Press, 1980.

————. *Styles of Scientific Thought: The German Genetics Community, 1900–1930.* Chicago: University of Chicago Press, 1993.

Hasian, Marouf Arif, Jr. *The Rhetoric of Eugenics in Anglo-American Thought.* Athens: University of Georgia Press, 1996.

Haskell, Thomas L., ed. *The Authority of Experts: Studies in History and Theory.* Bloomington: Indiana University Press, 1984.

————. "Capitalism and the Origins of the Humanitarian Sensibility." *American Historical Review* 90 (1985): 339–361, 547–566.

Hatch, Nathan O., and Mark Noll, eds. *The Bible in America.* New York: Oxford University Press, 1982.

Hawkins, Mike. *Social Darwinism in European and American Thought, 1860–1945: Nature as Model and Nature as Threat.* Cambridge, UK: Cambridge University Press, 1997.

Hawley, Ellis W. *The Great War and the Search for a Modern Order: A History of the American People and Their Institutions, 1917–1933.* New York: St. Martin's Press, 1979.

Helm, R. M. *The Gloomy Dean: The Thought of William Ralph Inge.* Winston-Salem, NC: J.F. Blair, 1962.

Hennesey, James, S.J. *American Catholics: A History of the Roman Catholic Community in the United States.* New York: Oxford University Press, 1981.

Herf, Jeffrey. *Reactionary Modernism: Technology, Culture, and Politics in Weimar and the Third Reich.* Cambridge, UK: Cambridge University Press, 1984.

Herrnstein, R. J., and Mark Snyderman. "Intelligence Tests and the Immigration Act of 1924." *American Psychologist* 38 (September 1983): 986–995.

Higham, John. *Strangers in the Land: Patterns of American Nativism, 1860–1925.* 1955. Reprint, New Brunswick, NJ: Rutgers University Press, 1994.

Hilts, Victor L. "Obeying the Laws of Hereditary Descent: Phrenological Views on Inheritance and Eugenics." *Journal of the History of the Behavioral Sciences* 18 (1982): 62–77.

Hirsch, David Einhorn. *Rabbi Emil G. Hirsch: The Reform Advocate*. Chicago: Whitehall, 1968.

Hofstadter, Richard. *Social Darwinism in American Thought, 1860–1915*. Philadelphia: University of Pennsylvania Press, 1944.

———. *The Age of Reform: From Bryan to FDR*. New York: Vintage, 1955.

———. *Anti-Intellectualism in American Life*. New York: Vintage, 1962.

Hollinger, David. *Science, Jews, and Secular Culture: Studies in Mid-Twentieth Century American Intellectual History*. Princeton: Princeton University Press, 1996.

Holloway, Mark. *Heavens on Earth: Utopian Communities in America, 1680–1880*. New York: Dover, 1966.

Hopkins, Charles H. "Rauschenbusch and the Brotherhood of the Kingdom." *Church History* 7 (1938): 138–156.

———. *The Rise of the Social Gospel in American Protestantism, 1865–1915*. New Haven: Yale University Press, 1940.

Horsman, Reginald. *Race and Manifest Destiny: The Origins of American Racial Anglo-Saxonism*. Cambridge, MA: Harvard University Press, 1981.

Hovenkamp, Herbert. *Science and Religion in America, 1800–1860*. Philadelphia: University of Pennsylvania Press, 1978.

Hudson, Winthrop S. "Discussants on Egal Feldman, 'The Social Gospel and the Jew.'" *American Jewish Historical Quarterly* 58 (1968–1969): 328.

Huggins, Nathan Irvin. *Protestants against Poverty: Boston's Charities, 1870–1900*. Westport, CT: Greenwood, 1971.

Hughley, J. Neal. *Trends in Protestant Social Idealism*. New York: Kings Crown Press, 1948.

Hutchison, J. A. *We Are Not Divided: A Critical and Historical Study of the Federal Council of the Churches of Christ in America*. New York: Round Table Press, 1941.

Hutchison, William R. "Cultural Strain and Protestant Liberalism." *American Historical Review* 76 (April 1971): 386–411.

———. "The Americanness of the Social Gospel: An Inquiry in Comparative History." *Church History* 44 (1975): 367–381.

———. *The Modernist Impulse in American Protestantism*. Durham, NC: Duke University Press, 1992.

———, ed. *Between the Times: The Travail of the Protestant Establishment in America, 1900–1960*. Cambridge, MA: Cambridge University Press, 1989.

Jacobsen, Douglas, and William Vance Trollinger Jr., eds. *Reforming the Center: American Protestantism, 1900 to the Present*. Grand Rapids, MI: William B. Eerdmans, 1998.

Jelen, Ted G. *The Political World of the Clergy*. Westport, CT: Praeger, 1993.

Jones, Bartlett C. "Prohibition and Eugenics." *Journal of the History of Medicine and Allied Sciences* 18 (1963): 158–172.

Jones, Greta. "Eugenics and Social Policy between the Wars." *Historical Journal* 25 (1982): 717–728.

———. *Social Hygiene in Twentieth-Century Britain*. London: Croom Helm, 1986.

Kamrat-Lang, Deborah. "Healing Society: Medical Language and American Eugenics." *Science in Context* 1 (1995): 175–196.

Kemp, Kathryn W. "Jean and Kate Gordon: New Orleans Social Reformers, 1893–1933." *Louisiana History* 24 (1983): 389–401.

Kennedy, David M. *Birth Control in America*. New Haven: Yale University Press, 1970.

Kevles, Daniel. "Testing the Army's Intelligence: Psychologists and the Military in World War I." *Journal of American History* 55 (1968–1969): 565–581.

———. *In the Name of Eugenics: Genetics and the Uses of Human Heredity*. Berkeley: University of California Press, 1985.

———. "Unholy Alliance." *The Sciences* 26 (September–October 1986): 24–30.

Kimmelman, Barbara A. "The American Breeders' Association: Genetics and Eugenics in an Agricultural Context, 1903–1913." *Social Studies of Science* 13 (1983): 163–204.

King, Miriam, and Steven Ruggles. "American Immigration, Fertility, and Race Suicide at the Turn of the Century." *Journal of Interdisciplinary History* 20 (1990): 347–369.

King, William McGuire. "The Biblical Base of the Social Gospel." In *The Bible and Social Reform*, ed. Ernest R. Sandeen. Chico, CA: Scholars Press, 1982.

Kirschner, Don S. "The Ambiguous Legacy: Social Justice and Social Control in the Progressive Era." *Historical Reflections* 2 (1975): 69–88.

Kline, Wendy. *Building a Better Race: Gender, Sexuality, and Eugenics from the Turn of the Century to the Baby Boom*. Berkeley: University of California Press, 2001.

Kraut, Alan M. *Silent Travelers: Germs, Genes, and the "Immigrant Menace."* Baltimore: Johns Hopkins University Press, 1994.

Kuhl, Stefan. *The Nazi Connection: Eugenics, American Racism, and German National Socialism*. New York: Oxford University Press, 1994.

Lacey, Michael J., ed. *Religion and Twentieth Century American Intellectual Life*. Cambridge, UK: Woodrow Wilson International Center for Scholars and Cambridge University Press, 1989.

Larson, Edward J. *Trial and Error: The American Controversy over Creation and Evolution*. New York: Oxford University Press, 1985.

———. *Sex, Race and Science: Eugenics in the Deep South*. Baltimore: Johns Hopkins University Press, 1995.

———. *Summer for the Gods: The Scopes Trial and America's Continuing Debate over Science and Religion*. New York: Basic Books, 1997.

Lasch, Christopher. *Haven in a Heartless World: The Family Besieged*. New York: Basic Books, 1977.

Latta, M. C. "The Background for the Social Gospel in American Protestantism." *Church History* 5 (1936): 256–270.

Lears, T. J. Jackson. *No Place of Grace: Antimodernism and the Transformation of American Culture, 1880–1920*. New York: Pantheon, 1981.

Leuchtenberg, William E. *The Perils of Prosperity, 1914–1932*. Chicago: University of Chicago Press, 1958.

Lindberg, David C., and Ronald L. Numbers, eds. *God and Nature: Historical Essays on the Encounter between Christianity and Science*. Berkeley: University of California Press, 1986.

Lippy, Charles H., ed. *Twentieth-Century Shapers of American Popular Religion*. New York: Greenwood Press, 1989.

Livingstone, David L. *Darwin's Forgotten Defenders: The Encounter between Evangelical*

Theology and Evolutionary Thought. Grand Rapids, MI: William B. Eerdmans, 1987.

Lubove, Roy. *The Professional Altruist: The Emergence of Social Work as a Career, 1880–1930.* Cambridge, MA: Harvard University Press, 1965.

Ludmerer, Kenneth. "American Geneticists and the Eugenics Movement, 1905–1935." *Journal of the History of Biology* 2 (1969): 337–362.

———. *Genetics and American Society: An Historical Appraisal.* Baltimore: Johns Hopkins University Press, 1972.

MacDowell, E. Carleton. "Charles B. Davenport, 1866–1944: A Study of Conflicting Influences." *Bios* 17 (1946): 3–50.

MacKenzie, Donald. *Statistics in Britain, 1865–1930: The Social Construction of Scientific Knowledge.* Edinburgh: Edinburgh University Press, 1981.

Macnicol, John. "The Voluntary Sterilization Campaign in Britain, 1918–1939." *Journal of the History of Sexuality* 2 (1992): 422–438.

Mann, Arthur. *Yankee Reformers in an Urban Age: Social Reform in Boston, 1880–1900.* New York: Harper, 1954.

Markel, Howard. "Di Goldine Medina (The Golden Land): Historical Perspectives of Eugenics and the Eastern European (Ashkenazi) Jewish-American Community." *Health Matrix: Journal of Law-Medicine* (winter 1997): 49–64.

Marks, Jonathan. "Historiography of Eugenics." *American Journal of Human Genetics* 52 (1993): 650–652.

Marsden, George. *Fundamentalism and American Culture: The Shaping of Twentieth Century Evangelicalism, 1870–1925.* New York: Oxford University Press, 1980.

———. "Everyone One's Own Interpreter? The Bible, Science, and Authority in Mid-Nineteenth Century America." In *The Bible in America,* ed. Nathan O. Hatch and Mark A. Noll. New York: Oxford University Press, 1982.

———. *The Soul of the American University: From Protestant Establishment to Established Nonbelief.* New York: Oxford University Press, 1994.

Martin, Bernard. "The Social Philosophy of Emil G. Hirsch." *American Jewish Archives Journal* 6 (1954): 151–165.

Marty, Martin E. *Modern American Religion. Vol. 1: The Irony of It All.* Chicago: University of Chicago Press, 1986.

———. *Modern American Religion. Vol. 2: The Noise of Conflict.* Chicago: University of Chicago Press, 1991.

———, ed. *Modern American Protestantism and Its World: Historical Articles on Protestantism in American Religious Life.* Vol. 6. New York: K.G. Saur, 1992.

May, Henry F. *The End of American Innocence: A Study of the First Years of Our Own Time, 1912–1917.* New York: Columbia University Press, 1959.

———. *Protestant Churches and Industrial America.* New York: Octagon Books, 1963.

Mazumdar, Pauline. *Eugenics, Human Genetics, and Human Failings: The Eugenics Society, Its Sources and Its Critics in Britain.* London: Routledge, 1992.

McCann, Carole R. *Birth Control Politics in the United States, 1916–1945.* Ithaca, NY: Cornell University Press, 1994.

McGrath, Alister E. *Science and Religion: An Introduction.* London: Blackwell, 1999.

McKeown, Elizabeth. *War and Welfare: American Catholics and World War I.* New York: Garland, 1988.

McLaren, Angus. *Our Own Master Race: Eugenics in Canada, 1885–1945*. Toronto: McClelland and Stewart, 1990.

McPhee, John. *The Pine Barrens*. New York: Farrar, Straus and Giroux, 1967.

Mead, Sidney E. *The Lively Experiment: The Shaping of Christianity in America*. New York: Harper and Row, 1963.

Meckel, Richard A. *Save the Babies: American Public Health Reform and the Prevention of Infant Mortality, 1850–1929*. Baltimore: Johns Hopkins University Press, 1990.

Mervis, Leonard J. "The Social Justice Movement and the American Reform Rabbi." *American Jewish Archives Journal* 7 (June 1955): 171–230.

Meyer, Donald B. *The Protestant Search for Political Realism, 1919–1941*. Middletown, CT: Wesleyan University Press, 1988.

Meyer, Michael A. *Response to Modernity: A History of the Reform Movement in Judaism*. Detroit: Wayne State University Press, 1988.

Miller, Robert Moats. *American Protestantism and Social Issues, 1919–1939*. Chapel Hill: University of North Carolina Press, 1958.

———. *Harry Emerson Fosdick: Preacher, Pastor, Prophet*. New York: Oxford University Press, 1985.

Moore, R. Lawrence. *Religious Outsiders and the Making of America*. New York: Oxford University Press, 1986.

Moran, Jeffrey P. "Modernism Gone Mad: Sex Education Comes to Chicago, 1913." *Journal of American History* 83 (September 1996): 481–513.

Noll, Steven. *Feebleminded in Our Midst: Institutions for the Mentally Retarded in the South, 1900–1940*. Chapel Hill: University of North Carolina Press, 1995.

Numbers, Ronald L. "Science and Religion." *Osiris* 1 (1985): 59–80.

Numbers, Ronald L., and Darrel W. Amundsen, eds. *Caring and Curing: Health and Medicine in the Western Religious Tradition*. New York: Macmillan, 1986.

Nye, Robert. "The Rise and Fall of the Eugenics Empire." *Historical Journal* 36 (1993): 687–700.

O'Brien, David J. *American Catholics and Social Reform: The New Deal Years*. New York: Oxford University Press, 1968.

———. "The American Priest and Social Action." In *The Catholic Priest in the United States: Historical Investigations*, ed. John T. Ellis. Collegeville, MN: St. John's University Press, 1971.

Odem, Mary. *Delinquent Daughters: Protecting and Policing Adolescent Female Sexuality in the United States, 1885–1920*. Chapel Hill: University of North Carolina Press, 1995.

Paul, Diane. "Eugenics and the Left." *Journal of the History of Ideas* 45 (1984): 567–590.

———. *Controlling Human Heredity: 1865 to the Present*. Amherst, NY: Humanity Books, 1995.

Pauly, Philip J. "The Eugenics Industry: Growth or Restructuring?" *Journal of the History of Biology* 26 (spring 1993): 131–145.

Pells, Richard. *Radical Visions and American Dreams: Culture and Social Thought in the Depression Years*. Middletown, CT: Wesleyan University Press, 1973.

Pernick, Martin. *The Black Stork: Eugenics and the Death of "Defective" Babies in American Medicine and Motion Pictures Since 1915*. New York: Oxford University Press, 1996.

Perrett, Geoffrey. *Days of Sadness, Years of Triumph: The American People, 1939–1945.* Baltimore: Penguin, 1973.

Persons, Stow. "Religion and Modernity, 1865–1914." In *The Shaping of American Religion,* vol. 1, ed. James Ward Smith and A. Leland Jamison. Princeton: Princeton University Press, 1961.

Phelps, Gary. "The Eugenics Crusade of Charles Fremont Dight." *Minnesota History* 49 (1984): 99–109.

Phillips, Paul T. *A Kingdom on Earth: Anglo-American Social Christianity, 1880–1840.* University Park: Pennsylvania State University Press, 1996.

Pick, Daniel. *Faces of Degeneration: A European Disorder, c. 1848–c. 1918.* Cambridge, UK: Cambridge University Press, 1989.

Pickens, Donald. "The Sterilization Movement: The Search for Purity in Mind and State." *Phylon* 28 (spring 1967): 78–94.

———. *Eugenics and the Progressives.* Nashville, TN: Vanderbilt University Press, 1968.

Piper, John F. *The American Churches in World War I.* Columbus: Ohio State University Press, 1985.

Pivar, David J. *Purity Crusade: Sexual Morality and Social Control, 1868–1900.* Westport, CT: Greenwood Press, 1973.

Porter, Charlotte M. "The Rise of Parnassus: Henry Fairfield Osborn and the Hall of the Age of Man." *Museum Studies Journal* 1 (spring 1983): 26–34.

Proctor, Robert N. *Racial Hygiene: Medicine under the Nazis.* Cambridge, MA: Harvard University Press, 1988.

———. "Eugenics among the Social Sciences: Hereditarian Thought in Germany and the United States." In *The Estate of Social Knowledge,* ed. JoAnne Brown and David K. vanKeuren. Baltimore: Johns Hopkins University Press, 1991.

Provine, William B. "Geneticists and the Biology of Race-Crossing." *Science* 182 (23 November 1973): 795.

———. "Geneticists and Race." *American Zoologist* 26 (1986): 857–887.

Radford, John P. "Sterilization versus Segregation: Control of the 'Feebleminded'. 1900–1938." *Social Science and Medicine* 33 (1991): 449–458.

Rafter, Nicole Hahn. *White Trash: The Eugenic Family Studies.* Boston: Northeastern University Press, 1988.

———. "White Trash: Eugenics as Social Ideology." *Society* 26 (November/December 1988): 43–49.

———. "Claims-Making and Socio-Cultural Context in the First U.S. Eugenics Campaign." *Social Problems* 39 (1992): 17–34.

———. *Creating Born Criminals.* Chicago: University of Illinois Press, 1997.

Ravetz, Jerome K. *Scientific Knowledge and Its Social Problems.* Oxford: Oxford University Press, 1971.

Reed, James. *From Private Practice to Public Virtue: The Birth Control Movement and American Society Since 1830.* New York: Basic Books, 1978.

Regner, Sidney L. "The Rise and Decline of the Sunday Service." *Journal of Reform Judaism* (fall 1980): 30–38.

Reilly, Philip R. *The Surgical Solution: A History of Involuntary Sterilization in the United States.* Baltimore: Johns Hopkins University Press, 1991.

Richards, Robert. *Darwin and the Emergence of Evolutionary Theories of Mind and Behavior*. Chicago: University of Chicago Press, 1987.

Roberts, Jon H. *Darwinism and the Divine in America: Protestant Intellectuals and Organic Evolution, 1859–1900*. Madison: University of Wisconsin Press, 1988.

Roohan, James E. *American Catholics and the Social Question, 1865–1900*. New York: Arno, 1976.

Rosenberg, Charles E. *No Other Gods: On Science and American Social Thought*. Baltimore: Johns Hopkins University Press, 1961.

———. "Woods or Trees? Ideas and Actors in the History of Science." *Isis* 79 (1988): 556–570.

Ross, Dorothy. *The Origins of American Social Science*. Cambridge, UK: Cambridge University Press, 1991.

———, ed. *Modernist Impulses in the Human Sciences, 1870–1930*. Baltimore: Johns Hopkins University Press, 1994.

Rothman, David J. *The Discovery of the Asylum*. Boston: Little, Brown, 1971.

———. *Conscience and Convenience: The Asylum and Its Alternatives in Progressive America*. Boston: Little, Brown, 1980.

Rudwick, Martin. "Senses of the Natural World and Senses of God: Another Look at the Historical Relation of Science and Religion." In *The Sciences and Theology in the Twentieth Century*, ed. A. R. Peacocke. Notre Dame, IN: University of Notre Dame Press, 1981.

Rushton, Alan R. *Genetics and Medicine in the United States, 1800–1922*. Baltimore: Johns Hopkins University Press, 1994.

Ryan, Halford L. *Harry Emerson Fosdick: Persuasive Preacher*. New York: Greenwood Press, 1989.

Rydell, Robert W. *World of Fairs: The Century of Progress Expositions*. Chicago: University of Chicago Press, 1993.

Sandeen, Ernest R. *The Roots of Fundamentalism: British and American Millennarianism, 1800–1930*. Chicago: University of Chicago Press, 1970.

Schapiro, Robert. *The Reform Rabbi in the Progressive Era*. New York: Garland, 1988.

Schlesinger, Arthur M. "A Critical Period in American Religion, 1875–1900." *Proceedings of the Massachusetts Historical Society* 64 (June 1932): 523–547.

Schneider, William. "Toward the Improvement of the Human Race: The History of Eugenics in France." *Journal of Modern History* 54 (1982): 268–291.

———. *Quality and Quantity: The Quest for Biological Regeneration in Twentieth-Century France*. Cambridge, UK: Cambridge University Press, 1990.

Schwarz, Richard W. *John Harvey Kellogg, M.D.* Nashville: Southern Publishing Association, 1970.

Sealander, Judith. *Private Wealth and Public Life: Foundation Philanthropy and the Reshaping of American Social Policy from the Progressive Era to the New Deal*. Baltimore: Johns Hopkins University Press, 1997.

Searle, Geoffrey R. "Eugenics and Politics in the 1930s." *Annals of Science* 36 (1979): 159–179.

Singerman, Robert. "The Jew as Racial Alien: The Genetic Component of American Anti-Semitism." In *Anti-Semitism in American History*, ed. David A. Gerber. Chicago: University of Illinois Press, 1986.

Slawson, Douglas J. *The Foundation and First Decade of the National Catholic Welfare Council.* Washington, DC: Catholic University of America Press, 1992.

Smith, J. David, and Edward A. Polloway. "Institutionalization, Involuntary Sterilization, and Mental Retardation: Profiles from the History of the Practice." *Mental Retardation* 31 (August 1993): 208–214.

Smith, Gary Scott. *The Search for Social Salvation: Social Christianity and America, 1880–1925.* Lanham, MD: Lexington Books, 2000.

Smith, J. David. *Minds Made Feeble: The Myth and Legacy of the Kallikaks.* Rockville, MD: Aspen Systems, 1985.

Soloway, Richard A. *Demography and Degeneration: Eugenics and the Declining Birthrate in Twentieth-Century Britain.* Chapel Hill: University of North Carolina Press, 1990.

Sorin, Gerald. *Tradition Transformed: The Jewish Experience in America.* Baltimore: Johns Hopkins University Press, 1997.

Spaulding, W. W. *A History of Seventh-Day Adventists.* 2 vols. Washington, DC: Review and Herald, 1949.

Stocking, George W. "Lamarckianism in American Social Science, 1890–1915." *Journal of the History of Ideas* 23 (1962): 239–256.

Szasz, Ferenc Morton. "Protestantism and the Search for Stability: Liberal and Conservative Quests for a Christian America, 1875–1925." In *Building the Organizational Society: Essays on Associational Activities in Modern America,* ed. Jerry Israel. New York: Free Press, 1972.

———. "The Progressive Clergy and the Kingdom of God." *Mid-America* 55 (1973): 3–20.

———. *The Divided Mind of Protestant America, 1880–1930.* University, Alabama: University of Alabama Press, 1982.

Teller, Michael E. *The Tuberculosis Movement: A Public Health Campaign in the Progressive Era.* New York: Greenwood Press, 1988.

Timberlake, James H. *Prohibition and the Progressive Movement, 1900–1920.* Cambridge, MA: Harvard University Press, 1963.

Tobey, Ronald C. *The American Ideology of National Science, 1919–1930.* Pittsburgh: University of Pittsburgh Press, 1971.

Trent, James W., Jr. *Inventing the Feeble Mind: A History of Mental Retardation in the United States.* Berkeley: University of California Press, 1994.

Trombley, Stephen. *The Right to Reproduce: A History of Coercive Sterilization.* London: Weidenfeld and Nicolson, 1988.

Tucker, William H. *The Science and Politics of Racial Research.* Urbana: University of Illinois Press, 1994.

Urofsky, Melvin I. *A Voice That Spoke for Justice: The Life and Times of Stephen S. Wise.* Albany: State University of New York Press, 1982.

Vecoli, Rudolph. "Sterilization: A Progressive Measure?" *Wisconsin Magazine of History* 43 (spring 1960): 190–202.

Vigue, Charles L. "Eugenics and the Education of Women in the U.S." *Journal of Educational Administration and History* 19 (1987): 51–55.

Voss, Carl Herman, ed. *Stephen S. Wise: Servant of the People.* Philadelphia: Jewish Publication Society of America, 1969.

————. *Rabbi and Minister: The Friendship of Stephen S. Wise and John Haynes Holmes.* Buffalo: Prometheus Books, 1980.

Warner, Michael. *Changing Witness: Catholic Bishops and Public Policy, 1917–1994.* Grand Rapids, MI: Eerdmans, 1995.

Weber, Timothy P. *Living in the Shadow of the Second Coming: Premillennialism, 1875–1925.* New York: Oxford University Press, 1979.

————. "The Two-Edged Sword: The Fundamentalist Use of the Bible." In *The Bible in America,* ed. Nathan O. Hatch and Mark Noll. New York: Oxford University Press, 1982.

Weeks, Genevieve C. *Oscar Carleton McCulloch, 1843–1891: Preacher and Practitioner of Applied Christianity.* Indianapolis: Indianapolis Historical Society, 1976.

Weeks, Jeffrey. *Sex, Politics, and Society: The Regulation of Sexuality Since 1800.* New York: Longman, 1981.

Weingart, Peter. "Eugenics: Medical or Social Science?" *Science in Context* 8 (1995): 197–207.

Weiss, Sheila. *Race Hygiene and National Efficiency: The Eugenics of William Schallmayer.* Berkeley: University of California Press, 1987.

Wheeler, Reginald W. *A Man Sent from God: A Biography of Robert E. Speer.* New York: Fleming H. Revell, 1956.

White, Ronald C., and C. Howard Hopkins, eds. *The Social Gospel: Religion and Reform in Changing America.* Philadelphia: Temple University Press, 1976.

Wiebe, Robert. *The Search for Order, 1877–1920.* New York: Hill and Wang, 1967.

Willrich, Michael. "The Two Percent Solution: Eugenic Jurisprudence and the Socialization of American Law, 1900–1930." *Law and History Review* 16 (spring 1998): 63–111.

Wyatt, Philip R. "John Humphrey Noyes and the Stirpiculture Experiment." *Journal of the History of Medicine and Allied Sciences* 31 (1976): 55–66.

Zeitlin, Joseph. *Disciples of the Wise: The Religious and Social Opinions of American Rabbis.* New York: Teacher's College, Columbia University, 1945.

Zenderland, Leila. *Measuring Minds: Henry Herbert Goddard and the Origins of American Intelligence Testing.* New York: Cambridge University Press, 1998.

Unpublished Dissertations

Cooke, Kathy. "An American Gospel of Social Evolution: Religion, Education, and Biology in the Thought of Edwin Grant Conklin." Ph.D. diss., University of Chicago, 1994.

Goldstein, Eric L. "Race and the Construction of Jewish Identity in America, 1875–1945." Ph.D. diss., University of Michigan, 2000.

Mehler, Barry. "A History of the American Eugenics Society, 1921–1940." Ph.D. diss., University of Illinois at Urbana-Champaign, 1988.

Index

LaVergne, TN USA
15 September 2009
158005LV00002B/2/P

9 780195 156799